Voice and Grammatical Relations
in Austronesian Languages

Studies in Constraint-Based Lexicalism

A series edited by
Miriam Butt, *University of Konstanz*
Tracy Holloway King, *Xerox Palo Alto Research Center*
Jean-Pierre Koenig, *State University of New York at Buffalo*

The aim of this series is to make work in various nonderivational, lexicalist approaches to grammar available to a wide audience of linguists. In approaches of this kind, grammar is seen as the interaction of constraints from multiple dimensions of linguistic substance, including information about syntactic category, grammatical relations, and semantic and pragmatic interpretation.

Studies in
Constraint-Based Lexicalism

Voice and Grammatical Relations in Austronesian Languages

edited by
Peter K. Austin and Simon Musgrave

CSLI
PUBLICATIONS
Center for the Study of
Language and Information
Stanford, California

Copyright © 2008
CSLI Publications
Center for the Study of Language and Information
Leland Stanford Junior University
Printed in the United States
12 11 10 09 08   1 2 3 4 5

Library of Congress Cataloging-in-Publication Data

Voice and grammatical relations in Austronesian languages /
edited by Peter K. Austin and Simon Musgrave.

p. cm. – (Studies in constraint-based lexicalism)

Includes bibliographical references and index.

ISBN-13: 978-1-57586-500-3 (pbk. : alk. paper)
ISBN-10:   1-57586-500-9 (pbk. : alk. paper)
ISBN-13: 978-1-57586-499-0 (cloth : alk. paper)
ISBN-10:   1-57586-499-1 (cloth : alk. paper)
1. Austronesian languages—Voice.
2. Austronesian languages—Verb.
3. Austronesian languages—Syntax.
I. Austin, Peter K. II. Musgrave, Simon, 1959–

PL5034.V65 2008
499′.2–dc22   2007051284
CIP

CSLI was founded in 1983 by researchers from Stanford University, SRI
International, and Xerox PARC to further the research and development of
integrated theories of language, information, and computation. CSLI headquarters
and CSLI Publications are located on the campus of Stanford University.

CSLI Publications reports new developments in the study of language,
information, and computation. Please visit our web site at
http://cslipublications.stanford.edu/
for comments on this and other titles, as well as for changes
and corrections by the authors, editors, and publisher.

Contents

Contributors   vii

Preface and Acknowledgments   ix

Abbreviations   x

1   **Introduction   1**
      SIMON MUSGRAVE

2   **The Place Of Philippine Languages In A Typology Of Voice Systems   22**
      WILLIAM A. FOLEY

3   **Voice And Grammatical Relations In Indonesian: A New Perspective   45**
      I WAYAN ARKA AND CHRISTOPHER MANNING

4   **Voice And The Syntax Of ==A/-A Verbs In Balinese   70**
      I WAYAN ARKA

5   **Objective Voice And Control Into Subject Clauses In Balinese   90**
      I WAYAN ARKA AND JANE SIMPSON

6   The Grammatical Function OBJ In Indonesian   128
SIMON MUSGRAVE

7   Grammatical Properties Of The Ergative Noun Phrase In Tongan
157
MICHAEL DUKES

8   Voice And Being Core: Evidence From (Eastern) Indonesian Languages   183
I WAYAN ARKA

9   Hierarchies In Argument Structure Increasing Processes: Ranking
Causative And Applicative   228
MARK DONOHUE

10 Lexical Categories And Voice In Tagalog   247
NIKOLAUS P. HIMMELMANN

Language Index   294

Name Index   296

Subject Index   300

Contributors

I WAYAN ARKA: Department of Linguistics RSPAS, Australian National University, Canberra ACT 0200, Australia.
Wayan.Arka@anu.edu.au

PETER K. AUSTIN: Department of Linguistics, SOAS, University of London, Thornhaugh Street, Russell Square, London WC1H 0XG, UK.
pa2@soas.ac.uk

MARK DONOHUE: Linguistics Program, Monash University, Victoria 3800, Australia.
mark@donohue.cc

MICHAEL DUKES: InQuira Inc, 851 Traeger Avenue, Suite 125, San Bruno CA 94066, USA.
mdukes@inquira.com

WILLIAM A. FOLEY: Department of Linguistics, University of Sydney, NSW 2006, Australia.
wilfoley@arts.usyd.edu.au

NIKOLAUS HIMMELMANN: Sprachwissenschaftliches Institut, Ruhr Universität Bochum, D44780 Bochum, Germany.
himmelma@linguistics.ruhr-uni-bochum.de

CHRISTOPHER D. MANNING: Department of Computer Science, Gates Building 4A, 353 Serra Mall, Stanford CA 94305-9040, USA.
manning@cs.stanford.edu

SIMON MUSGRAVE: Linguistics Program, School of Languages, Cultures and Linguistics, Monash University, Victoria 3800, Australia.
Simon.Musgrave@arts.monash.edu.au

JANE SIMPSON: Department of Linguistics, University of Sydney, NSW 2006, Australia.
jhs@mail.usyd.edu.au

Preface and Acknowledgements

This volume grew out of a workshop organised by the editors during the 1998 Lexical Functional Grammar annual conference held in conjunction with the Australian Linguistic Institute at Queensland University. We are grateful to the conference's local organisers Chris Manning and Jane Simpson for their help with the workshop, and also to Mary Laughren, the Institute convenor, for enabling us to take part. Following the workshop, we invited participants to submit revised versions of their papers for publication. We also approached I Wayan Arka, Mark Donohue, and Nikolaus Himmelmann, who we knew were all working on relevant areas of Austronesian morphosyntax, and invited them to contribute to our planned volume. We received the full set of contributions at the end of 2001, however due to several intercontinental moves on both our parts, the editing process has taken rather longer than we had hoped.

The syntax of Austronesian languages has been the subject of quite a deal of new research over the past 20 years and has revealed that these languages have many fascinating characteristics which are rather different to those that cross-linguistic researchers have investigated in detail in other languages to date. The topic of grammatical functions and verbal valence is of particular importance for Austronesian, given that there are complexities in this area that are not apparent in other language groups, such as multiple voice categories and conflicting evidence about the nature of grammatical functions such as 'subject' and 'object'. We hope that the papers presented here stimulate further research on this important and so far under-researched language group.

Melbourne and London

February 2006

Abbreviations

1,2,3	1st, 2nd, 3rd person	N	nasal
ABS	absolutive	NEG	negation
ACC	accusative	NOM	nominative
ACT	active	NR	nominalizer
ADV	adverb	OBJ	object
AG	agent	OBL	oblique
ALL	allative	OV	objective voice
ANTI	antipassive	P	patient
APPL	applicative	PASS	passive
ART	article	PERF	perfective aspect
AV	agentive voice	PIV	pivot
CAUS	causative	PL	plural
CONJ	conjunction	PM	predicate marker
CORE	term	PN	proper name
CV	conveyance voice	POSS	possessive
DAT	dative	PRES	present
DEF	definite	PROG	progressive aspect
DET	determiner	PRON	pronoun
DIM	diminutive	PROX	proximal
DIR	directional	PST	past
DIST	distal	PV	patient voice
EMPH	emphatic	QW	question word
ERG	ergative	RCP	reciprocal
EX	exclusive	RED	reduplication
EXIST	existential	REFL	reflexive
FINV	final vowel	REL	relative clause marker
FOC	focus	RL	realis
FUT	future	RP	recent perfective
GEN	genitive	SG	singular
GER	gerund	SI	subject infix
H.R.	high register	SPEC	specific article
IN	inclusive	STAT	stative
INGR	ingressive	SUBJ	subject
INSTR	instrumental	TNS	tense
INT	intensifier	TOP	topic
INV	inverse	TR	transitive
IRR	irrealis	TRNS	transitivizer
LNK	linker	UNDR	undergoer
LOC	locative	VC	voice
LV	locative voice	VR	verbaliser
MED	medial		

1

Introduction*

Simon Musgrave

1 The Austronesian Language Family

The Austronesian family consists of approximately 1200 languages which
are spoken from Madagascar in the west to Easter Island in the east, from
Taiwan in the north to New Zealand in the south. The point of dispersal of
the original population was certainly Taiwan. Whether any of the 14 surviving Formosan languages form groups together is in dispute, but it is agreed
by all scholars that all the non-Formosan languages form a single group
(Malayo-Polynesian) at the same level as any Formosan groups. The grouping of these remaining languages broadly follows the migration pattern of a
seafaring people, south and east from Taiwan with occasional aberrations
which seem to be the result of groups backtracking. The first-order groupings within Malayo-Polynesian (henceforth M-P) are Western M-P and
Central-Eastern M-P. The majority of the languages discussed in this volume are Western M-P languages, with the exception of Tongan (Dukes'

* Thanks to Peter Austin for discussion of the issues treated here and for comments on previous drafts. Thanks also to Diane Massam and John Bowden for assistance, and to the audience of the workshop at LFG98 which formed the basis for this book. This introduction was
written while the author was part of the research project "Lexicon and Syntax" directed by
Pieter Muysken.

Voice and Grammatical Relations in Austronesian Languages.
Simon Musgrave and Peter Austin

paper) which belongs to the Oceanic branch of Eastern M-P within Central-Eastern M-P, and some of the languages discussed in Arka's second paper, which are from the Central M-P branch. General surveys of the whole family are provided by Clark (1990) and Tryon (1995), while Adelaar and Himmelmann (2005) covers all the languages outside of the Oceanic branch. Recent surveys of linguistic research on the Austronesian family are Klamer (2002) and Massam (1998), the latter concentrating on work in the generative tradition.

The surveys cited above discuss specific features as typical of Austronesian languages, or of some subgroup of them. Such an enterprise is inevitably risky and is of limited value. Nevertheless, one aspect of the structure of some Austronesian languages has been the subject of great interest in the wider linguistic community since Bloomfield's classic study (1917) of the Tagalog language (Western M-P, the Philippines): the distinctive way in which verbal diathesis can be varied. Such phenomena are the subject of many of the papers in this collection. Some of the basic data, and an approach to them in a constraint-based lexicalist framework, are set out in the following section. The concluding section of this introduction gives an overview of the papers to follow.

2 The Problem of Voice and Grammatical Relations in Western Austronesian

It is a characteristic of the Austronesian languages of Formosa, the Philippines, Madagascar, and (at least) western Indonesia (henceforth Western Austronesian or WAn.) that many verbs can head more than one type of transitive clause. The form of the verb will be different for each possibility, and there may be corresponding changes in the marking or position of the noun phrases in the clause, but the verb root will be identifiably the same. Examples from Tagalog, Bahasa Indonesia and Balinese follow:

(1)   Tagalog
     a.   *Kumain   ng   isda   ang   bata   (k-um-ain)*
         eat   CORE   fish   SUBJ   child
         'The child ate (*the) fish.'

     b.   *Kinain   ng   bata   ang   isda   (k-in-ain)*
         eat   CORE   child   SUBJ   fish
         'A child ate the fish.'

(2)　　　Indonesian

 a. *Ali membaca buku itu*
   Ali *meN*-read book the
   'Ali read the book.'

 b. *Buku itu dibaca (oleh) Ali*
   book the *di*-read (by) Ali
   'The book was read by Ali.'

 c. *Buku itu saya baca*
   book the 1SG read
   'I read the book.' or 'The book, I read.'

(3)　　　Balinese

 a. *Nyoman lempag tiang*
   Nyoman hit 1SG
   'I hit Nyoman.'

 b. *Tiang ng-lempag Nyoman*
   1SG N-hit Nyoman
   'I hit Nyoman.'

   In each of these languages, the function of distinguishing the two arguments of the transitive verb is divided between verbal morphology and noun phrase coding properties. In Tagalog, for instance, the infix in the verb stem in example (1a) indicates that the noun marked by *ang* is the higher thematic argument of the verb, while the infix in example (1b) indicates that the noun marked by *ang* is the lower thematic argument of the verb.[1] The verb prefixes of Indonesian and Balinese operate in a similar fashion, indicating the thematic status of the leftmost argument of the clause. Where the clauses are directly comparable (i.e. excluding example (2c)), propositional meaning is not altered by the different codings (modulo constraints on the referentiality of the NPs associated with various functions to be discussed later). Various syntactic tests establish that the Tagalog nominal marked with *ang*, the leftmost nominal in Indonesian and the preverbal nominal in Balinese have (at least some) subject properties, and that the other nominal has similar syntactic privileges in both clause types (Schachter 1976, Kroeger 1993, Artawa and Blake 1997). In many languages of the Philippines and in the Formosan languages, there are further

---

[1] This description of example (1b) is a simplification. The infix *-in-* is actually an aspect marker which cannot co-occur with the suffix *-in* which is the true marker for the thematic status of the subject in this clause.

possibilities in which non-terms can be treated as subject, and there is a consensus that Proto M-P should be reconstructed with a four-way system (Ross 2004, Wolff 1973). In the following discussion, these additional possibilities are not dealt with in detail, as their occurrence is more restricted and any analysis which can deal with the central problem, that one verb can have two transitive forms selecting different subjects, can easily be extended to these other cases.

We will assume that the semantic relations associated with basic lexical entries of verbs in WAn languages are not different in kind to those assumed for other languages. Thus, the Balinese verb exemplified above will have at least the following information associated with it in the lexicon:

lempag < Agent, Patient >

We will also assume that it is possible to identify some notion of syntactic subject in WAn languages. Many scholars from Schachter (1976) onwards have noted that not all of the properties taken as typical of subjects in European languages are always associated with the subject so identified in WAn languages. For example, while the subject in these languages is the only argument accessible to relativization, it may only be the antecedent for reflexives when it is also the highest thematic argument. When the subject and the highest thematic argument are not identical, antecedence of reflexives is a property which remains associated with the highest thematic argument:

(4)   Balinese

   a.   *Awakne   tingalin=a*
         self   see=3
         '(S)he saw her/himself.'

   b.   *Ia   ningalin   awakne*
         3   N-see   self
         '(S)he saw her/himself.'

   c.   **Wayan   tingalin   awakne*
         Wayan   OV.see   self

We suggest that this division of properties can be explained by assuming a division between properties which are universally semantically based, as argued by Dixon (1979, 1994) and properties which are associated with a syntactic notion of subject identified on a language- and construction-specific basis. The correct identification of this subject on the basis of syntactic properties has been investigated in detail by Schachter (1976) and Kroeger (1993) for Tagalog (see also Cena 1995 and Schachter 1996), Artawa and Blake (1997) for Balinese, and by various scholars for other languages (e.g. Chung 1976 for Indonesian and Schachter 1984 for Toba Batak).

The discussion above makes it clear that surface syntactic properties are not consistent across the group of WAn languages we are considering. Balinese is clearly a configurational language with a VP constituent. In the Balinese examples above, the post-verbal NP must be adjacent to the verb while the NP which appears pre-verbally in examples (3a) and (3b) can appear following the VP. Similar patterns have been described for, among others, Toba Batak (Schachter 1984) and Pendao (Quick 1997); Indonesian shows a similar, if less strict, pattern. Tagalog, on the other hand, is non-configurational according to Kroeger (1993), and certainly has more word order possibilities than the other languages mentioned above. Here, a model such as Lexical Functional Grammar (LFG) offers clear advantages for analysis. The interesting comparisons to be made between these languages are those at the level of predicate-argument relations and grammatical relations, and the discussion is greatly simplified when theory internal considerations do not require the varied surface coding of grammatical relations to be accounted for by configurations which are identical at some level (see also Austin & Bresnan 1996).

We have established that WAn languages allow two codings for many transitive clauses and that a different nominal can be identified as syntactic subject in each of these clause types. Having understood this much, a problem arises immediately: can the second argument in clauses such as those above be treated as an object? The theory-neutral descriptive statement in the first paragraph of this section would imply that there should be no doubt on this point; the clauses are transitive and have two arguments. Nevertheless, there has been a reluctance on the part of previous investigators to take a clear position on this issue, at least with regard to the clause type with the less agentive argument as subject. In part, this can be attributed to the wish to analyze the pattern seen in the examples as a voice alternation of a familiar type and therefore to treat one clause type as having an object, and the other as intransitive.[2] We believe that the evidence provides no basis for

---

[2] The reluctance to call a non-subject agent an object is also partly due to the default pairing of agent and subject in a nominative-accusative alignment system; similar problems arise in the discussion of ergative-absolutive systems.

any analysis which treats such pairs as differing in transitivity; it is not possible to analyze these pairs of clauses as active and passive (or active and antipassive). However, there is one view of ergative/absolutive systems which claims that there are no true transitive clauses in them (Bresnan and Kanerva 1989 n.32, cf. Manning 1996a:39 and references cited there. See also Dukes, this volume, for arguments that Tongan should be analyzed in this way.). Therefore, on this view both clause types might be intransitive, no difference in transitivity would be assumed but there would also be no objects.

The morphological evidence suggests that the form with the thematically lower argument as subject (hereafter OV)) is basic. This is immediately evident in Balinese and Indonesian, where the unaffixed verb appears in OV clauses[3] and is also suggested by more complex considerations for Tagalog (De Guzman 1992). It is also the case that in all the languages which we will consider here, except Indonesian, the OV form is more common in discourse than the form in which the highest thematic argument is subject (hereafter AV).[4] This has led many scholars to take the OV forms as basic and to analyze these languages as having ergative/absolutive systems (e.g. Artawa & Blake 1997, Blake 1988, Gerdts 1988, De Guzman 1988). However, in each of the languages considered here, non-term arguments are clearly distinguished by the presence of prepositions, or in Tagalog, the oblique marker *sa*, and by syntactic tests (see for example Kroeger 1993: 40-48). The non-subject agent need not be coded as a non-term, although the possibility exists in Indonesian at least, and this forces us to conclude that both OV and AV clauses are true transitive clauses, and to reject the intransitive ergative analysis.

Some doubt about the syntactic status of the non-subject argument of transitive clauses nevertheless remains, particularly for the Philippine languages where subject choice is not restricted to the term arguments of the verb. To take examples from Tagalog, the verb *bigay* 'give' takes only two term arguments in AV and OV forms:

---

[3] Arka and Simpson, this volume, treat the Balinese form as containing a zero prefix.

[4] The exact figures vary—see previously cited sources and also Cooreman, Fox and Givón 1984 and Shibatani 1988. In general, the text counts offer little support to either possible analysis in terms of traditional voice alternations. OV forms predominate in most studies, which certainly eliminates the nominative/accusative analysis, but AV forms are far more common than would be warranted if such clauses are analysed as antipassives. See also our remarks below on the referentiality constraints which influence the form chosen in all the languages under consideration.

(5) | *Nagbigay* | *ng* | *korbata* | *sa* | *lalake* | *ang* |
|---|---|---|---|---|---|
| *-in-mag-bigay* | | | | | |
| AV-give | CORE | tie | OBL | man | SUBJ |
| *babae* | | | | | |
| woman | | | | | |

'The woman gave a/the man a tie.'

Cross-linguistically, if second objects are possible, we would expect them to be possible with this verb. Therefore, Tagalog appears not to allow second objects. But when the same verb appears in a form which identifies the Beneficiary as subject, it has two arguments (the term arguments) marked in the same way as the non-subject argument of a transitive clause (cf. examples (1a) and (1b)):

(6) | *Binigyan* | *ng* | *babae* | *ng* | *korbata* | *ang* |
|---|---|---|---|---|---|
| *b-in-igay-an* | | | | | |
| VC-give | CORE | woman | CORE | tie | SUBJ |
| *lalake* | | | | | |
| man | | | | | |

'A woman gave the man a tie.'

This example might be taken to show that Tagalog **does** allow double object constructions.[5] Double objects also seem to be possible in clauses in recent perfective aspect, where no nominal appears with the marker *ang*, but two NPs can be marked as non-subject terms:[6]

(7) | *Kakakain* | *ng* | *leon* | *ng* | *tigre* |
|---|---|---|---|---|
| *k-ka-RD-ain* | | | | |
| RP-eat | CORE | lion | CORE | tiger |

'The lion ate the tiger.' (*The tiger ate the lion.)

---

[5] This issue is clouded by the fact that *ng* is also used to mark the possessive relation within noun phrases. Many previous treatments have therefore claimed that the two *ng*s in examples such as 6 are homophonous but functionally distinct. We see no reason to adopt this view. The marker may have distinct functions in marking predicate-argument relations and adnominal relations, but this does not mean that both functions can appear in the same level of constituency.

[6] Gerundive nominalizations have a similar pattern.

This clause is not ambiguous, and it might therefore be argued that there is a dissociation of grammatical functions and surface marking in such clauses, with the subject being exceptionally marked by *ng* (this is essentially the position taken by Guilfoyle, Hung and Travis 1992). Kroeger (1993:53-54) shows that extraction, otherwise a property of syntactic subjects in Tagalog, is always possible for the agent in these constructions, and sometimes also for the Patient, suggesting that there may not be a unique subject in such constructions. The interpretation of such clauses appears to be determined by linear order. Both the constructions discussed in this paragraph suggest that the status of the putative grammatical function *object* in Tagalog (the *ng* marked nominal in a transitive clause) is in some doubt,[7] and that it is best treated as a marker of termhood, not as a marker of a specific grammatical function.

The typical situation which prevails in WAn languages, then, is that transitive verbs have two alternative lexical forms with the same semantic relations and with both arguments available to be linked to grammatical functions (GFs). The linking of semantic roles to GFs is **inverse** (to borrow a term from Manning 1996a) for the more common form, and **direct** for the other form. No theory of linking which is based on hierarchies of semantic roles and hierarchies of GFs can account for these patterns without stipulating the linking in one case. Treating a(rgument)-structure as an independent level which is the locus of valence-changing operations, as argued for by Manning (1996a), does not seem to be any help with this problem. Manning argues that the information represented at a-structure is firstly, the division between terms and obliques, and secondly, thematic obliqueness within each of these subdivisions. Thematic obliqueness is lexical information in this scheme and therefore cannot be manipulated. Consequently, any changes in linking patterns must be attributed to changes in which arguments have term status and which do not, as in the classical analysis of passive. We have argued above that the inverse and direct transitive clauses of WAn do not have different valencies, and therefore the existence of a separate level of a-structure does not solve this problem. Note that genuine valence-changing operations are available in these languages: Balinese has passive constructions (Arka and Simpson, this volume), Indonesian has causatives and applicatives (and also passive on the analysis of Arka and Manning, this volume, see also Donohue, this volume, on causatives and applicatives in Tukang Besi), and Tagalog has causatives (Carrier-Duncan 1985). Perhaps most strikingly, Toba Batak (Schachter 1984) has two pos-

---

[7] See also Arka and Simpson's paper in this volume for discussion of the Balinese facts. Arka and Simpson use the expression *term complement* for non-subject agents.

sibilities for the coding of verbs with three logical arguments, such as 'give', essentially the same as dative shift in English. The beneficiary can either be introduced by a preposition, or with the same surface form as the other two arguments of the verb. Note that this valence-changing operation is independent of the marking of the verb for AV or OV clause type; both prefixes allow either expression of the recipient:[8]

(8) a. *Mangalean biang si Torus tu si Ria*
           AV-give dog ART Torus to ART Ria
           'Torus is giving a dog to Ria.'

      b. *Mangalean si Ria si Torus biang*
           AV-give ART Ria ART Torus dog
           'Torus is giving Ria a dog.'

      c. *Dilean si Torus biang i tu si*
           OV-give ART Torus dog the to ART
           Ria
           Ria
           'Torus gave the dog to Ria.'

      d. *Dilean si Torus si Ria biang i*
           OV-give ART Torus ART Ria dog the
           'Torus gave the dog to Ria.'

Such evidence thus suggests that a-structure and subject choice are independent factors in WAn languages.

This possibility is further supported by evidence from Tagalog regarding clauses with two arguments marked by *ng*. Even when no subject seems to be selected (example (6)), the a-structure status of arguments is still apparent. The same is true where a non-term subject is selected, as is possible in Tagalog, Malagasy and the Formosan languages. In all such cases in Tagalog, terms are marked by *ng* and their syntactic status is confirmed by the impossibility of fronting them (Kroeger 1993:43-46). For example, a circumstantial oblique such as the location in the following clause can become a subject in these languages:

---

[8] The difference in tense in the translations of these examples is not significant. Schachter (1984 n.6) reports that his consultant translated AV clauses as present tense, and OV clauses as past tense *in the absence of any temporal context*. But either clause type can be translated with either tense, given an appropriate context.

(9) a. *Binili*   *ng*   *lalake*   *ang*   *isda*   *sa*
         OV-buy   CORE   man   SUBJ   fish   OBL
         tindahan
         store
         'The man bought the fish at the store.'

    b. *Binilhan*   *ng*   *lalake*   *ng*   *isda*   *ang*
         VC-buy   CORE   man   CORE   fish   SUBJ
         tindahan
         store
         'The man bought fish at the store.'

As before, agent and theme both remain terms when another subject is selected. Assuming, as would seem plausible, that semantic relations such as location are not part of the argument list in a verb's lexical entry, these considerations lead to a view of Philippine languages in which the a-structure projected by the lexical entries of verb roots is not the level at which subject selection is accomplished. It is the affixes which attach to the verb roots which complete the specification of syntactic relations. Further support for such a view comes from constraints on subject choice in WAn languages. Across these languages, such constraints operate and always depend on the referential nature of the NPs filling argument roles. Thus, Artawa and Blake note that the Balinese nasal (AV) construction is used regularly where the patient is non-specific or indefinite, and in imperatives the choice is obligatory (1997:488-9); Schachter cites work showing that in Toba Batak the primary determinant of verb type is the individuation of the patient (1984:124); and where the patient is definite in Tagalog, OV forms are effectively obligatory in free clauses.[9] The situation as regards Indonesian is less clear-cut, but similar effects are reported (see Cartier 1983 for discussion). Clearly such factors correlate with topicality, which is certainly relevant to subject selection, but, at least for Tagalog, there are data available which show that topicality is not the crucial factor (Kroeger 1993:ch.3). Valence-changing operations, which is to say a-structure operations, are not normally sensitive to such semantic factors, and this suggests that subject selection in these languages is rather different from the process in more familiar languages.

The view that verb affixes are the locus of grammatical relations in WAn has also been advocated by Sells (1998) in a LFG framework, and we

---

[9] See Cena 1995 for some exceptions, and Adams and Manaster-Ramer 1988 for discussion of exactly what sort of definiteness is involved.

would suggest that Principles and Parameters work such as that of Guil-foyle *et al* (1992) and Voskuil (1993) can be seen as similar in spirit (see discussion below). However, the assignment of grammatical relations in WAn languages does share some characteristics with more familiar systems. Several languages restrict subject choices to terms (Balinese, Toba Batak, Indonesian), and the languages which allow other possibilities are still sensitive to the a-structure status of arguments. In Tagalog, the infix *-um-* indicates that the highest thematic argument is subject, but it is semantically unrestricted. The discussion of Carrier-Duncan (1985) makes this clear, giving examples of verbs such as *b-um-uti* 'get better', where the subject is certainly not an agent. Similarly, the suffixes *-in* and *-an* indicate that the lower thematic term is subject. In this case, there is greater semantic specificity, but there is still some flexibility. But when non-terms are selected as subject, the verbal morphology is more semantically specific; for example the prefix *i-* normally indicates that a beneficiary is subject, and the suffix *-an* is generally used for locational subjects. Another example of effects of this type can be seen in the Toba Batak dative shift construction (example (8)). For the AV verb form, the agent is subject in both cases (example (8a) and (8b)), but the next highest non-oblique is included in the VP. So in example (8a), the theme is adjacent to the verb, but in example (8b) it is the non-oblique recipient. With the OV verb form, the second highest available thematic argument becomes subject; thus the theme is subject in example (8c), and the recipient in example (8d). The next available syntactic position within the VP is then occupied by the highest available argument, the agent, in each case. The descriptive generalization which Schachter makes on the basis of these examples is:

(10)   Interchange the Dative and the patient (1984:ex.38)

and this indeed captures the a-structure effect of the change. When the recipient is non-oblique, it is available for linking before the theme. Toba Batak and Tagalog have alternative strategies for meeting functional needs here. Although Toba Batak allows only two verb forms, note that in the examples above it is possible for each of the three arguments to be subject, thus making it possible to relativize on each of the arguments.[10]

The evidence discussed here leads to the view that subject selection in WAn languages is at least partially independent of the normal process of

---

[10] Given that Schachter reports that OV verbs are about twice as common as AV verbs, the arguments in favour of treating Toba Batak as ergatively aligned are as valid as those for other WAn languages. There is, however, a well-known generalization to the effect that no syntactically ergative language has ditransitive verbs. We would therefore take this construction as further evidence against treating WAn languages as syntactically ergative.

linking arguments to grammatical functions. When the effects of that independent process are discounted, however, it would seem that the linking principles used in these languages are very similar to those investigated in other languages. The two principles may even interact at times, as in the Toba Batak dative shift construction. Another interaction can be seen in the case of the Balinese passive. Passive is only compatible with the unaffixed (or zero-affixed) verb form and this is a predictable result of the account presented here. Passivization is an a-structure operation which makes the highest thematic argument unavailable for linking to a grammatical function. With only one term available for subject selection, only one verb form should be possible, and as the higher thematic argument has been made unavailable, the verb form which selects the lower thematic argument as subject (unaffixed / zero-affixed) is the only possibility.

3   Parallel Structures Versus Derivations

The discussion above has, we hope, demonstrated that the issues to be faced in analyzing WAn languages can be seen very clearly in a framework such as LFG. The correct answers do not fall out from the framework automatically, but it becomes clear that the solutions must be sought in the linkage between arguments in lexical entries and GF assignments in f-structure and the role that verb affixes play in mediating this linkage. Surface coding features of GFs are not relevant to this problem. The division of properties between two nominals in the clause is handled naturally in a model allowing parallel representations, such as LFG. The *semantic* properties are associated with the most prominent argument in a(rgument)-structure, and the *syntactic* properties are associated with the most prominent argument in f-structure, the grammatical function SUBJECT. Such a division of labour has been argued for by Manning (1996a,b) and profitably employed in other analyses (e.g. Wechsler and Arka 1998, Arka and Manning this volume).

In this section, we briefly compare such an approach to the problems presented in section 2 with a derivational approach such as the Principles and Parameters (P&P) framework. The discussion of the derivational approach will be based on that of Guilfoyle *et al* (1992), as the most detailed proposal made in that tradition about the basic syntax of WAn languages. However, the arguments made will not depend on the specifics of that analysis, as we assume that any P&P treatment of these problems will preserve its essential features.[11]

3.1 Subject Selection

The data presented above seem to require an analysis in which the linking of an argument to the subject function is directly specified rather than following from general principles. This is particularly clear in the case of languages such as Tagalog and Malagasy, which allow non-core arguments to be subjects. But it is also true for languages like Balinese and Toba Batak, where the less prominent thematic argument can be subject while the more prominent thematic argument remains a core argument. The classical account of valence-changing phenomena such as passive requires the pairing of elements from two separate hierarchies, a thematic hierarchy and a hierarchy of grammatical relations. The crucial move in this type of account is that the most prominent thematic argument must link to the most prominent grammatical relation, unless it is eliminated from consideration by having its status changed ('demotion' in the metaphor of Relational Grammar). Such a system predicts that the pattern seen in these languages should not be possible. If one posits a nominative-accusative alignment or an ergative-absolutive alignment, the linking of the putative passive or antipassive will have to be stipulated. However, the more extensive possibilities of the Philippine-type systems, and the independence of subject selection from other alternations seen in Toba Batak, suggest that the simplest analysis is to stipulate the linking of one thematic role to subject for every case, even those in which general linking principles might seem to apply.

This solution poses an immediate problem for a P&P analysis: *subject* is a configurational notion in that framework, therefore some mechanism is necessary to ensure that the argument that is to be subject ends up in the correct position. The canonical answer to such a problem is the Case Filter (NPs move to positions in which they can acquire case), and this is the answer adopted by Guilfoyle, Hung and Travis. They suggest that, in a system such as that of Tagalog, the morphology which identifies the thematic role of the subject case marks some other argument, forcing the movement of the "correct" argument to the specifier of IP position, where it can receive case. There are several problems with such an account. Firstly, it seems to assume that verbs in these languages have no inherent case-assigning property. This claim is contrary to standard assumptions and is also empirically

---

[11] For criticism of specific aspects of Guilfoyle, Hung and Travis's analysis, see Schachter (1996) for Tagalog and Musgrave (2001) for Indonesian.

challenged by examples such as the Tagalog recent perfective construction exemplified in (7) and the Indonesian unaffixed construction discussed in Musgrave (this volume). Secondly, this analysis is counter-intuitive in that the verbal morphology is clearly tied to one argument semantically, but it is precisely that argument with which it must lack a syntactic tie. This is particularly clear in the case of non-core arguments which become subject in Tagalog or Malagasy. In such cases, the core arguments of the verb are case-marked in situ, and therefore some other NP must move to occupy Spec of IP (assuming the Extended Projection Principle). This implies that obliques are, in general, not case-marked at the relevant stage of the derivation. But then consider the case where there are two obliques: which one will move? Such a scenario forces the conclusion that there is some relation between the verbal morphology and the argument selected as subject beyond the lack of case-marking.[12] It can also be noted that this type of account tacitly acknowledges that such systems stand outside of the traditional typology of voice systems (as argued in detail by Foley, this volume). Although Guilfoyle *et al* (1992) speak of 'passive' in these languages, this is very different from widely-accepted analyses of passive (e.g. Jaeggli 1986). The standard accounts treat the verbal morphology associated with passive (and presumably also antipassive) as *absorbing* case, but the case-marking account of WAn languages crucially assumes that the verbal morphology associated with so-called passive voice *assigns* case (in a particular fashion).

The type of analysis which is most natural in a framework with parallel representations avoids these complications. The relation between verbal morphology and subject selection is direct, and is handled in the lexicon. Morphemes which attach to verbs have as part of their lexical information the semantic role of the argument that they select as subject. The full verb forms which are the output of the lexicon inherit this specification. Some stipulation is required, but as a feature in the lexicon which is the appropriate place for such idiosyncrasy, and in a natural fashion: the stipulation reflects our intuitive understanding of the role of the verbal morphology.[13]

---

[12] We assume that in the case of a clause with a core argument as subject and also an oblique some economy principle can be invoked to ensure that it is the core argument which moves to subject position.

[13] The title of an early study of Tagalog morphosyntax (Blake 1906) is "Expression of case by the verb in Tagalog".

3.2 Binding

When it comes to accounting for the binding facts, we would suggest that the two frameworks actually offer identical accounts, although this is not immediately obvious. The parallel representations account of these facts assumes that the relevant representation for the checking of binding relations is argument structure (Manning 1996a, b, Wechsler and Arka 1998, Manning and Sag 1999, Arka and Manning, this volume). This representation combines information about the term status of arguments with information about thematic prominence, with terms out-ranking non-terms and thematic prominence determining ranking within each category. Where the arguments in question are both terms, as in the crucial examples given above (examples (1) to (3)), argument structure prominence is identical to thematic prominence. The derivational framework assumes that binding relations are checked in some syntactic representation which forms a step in the derivation. In order to account for the crucial examples, the relevant step in the derivation must be prior to the movement of a non-agent NP to the subject position, that is, at a point where the agent generated in Spec of VP still c-commands any other NP inside VP. In fact, it must be stipulated for these languages that binding relations are checked *only* at some such stage in the derivation. But if the initial stage of a syntactic derivation is taken to directly reflect lexical properties, which include a list of verbal arguments ranked by thematic prominence, then this must include exactly the same information as the argument structure representation discussed above. The two accounts make identical predictions and should have identical empirical coverage and a choice between them can only be made on theoretical grounds. On that basis, we suggest that an account which does not require a language-specific (or language-group-specific) stipulation is to be preferred.

We can also mention here that subsequent P&P work has raised the issue of whether only two subject positions should be recognized, as in Guilfoyle *et al* (1992). It is not clear to us whether such considerations would substantially change the type of analysis which is possible or desirable. Arka (this volume, "Voice and Being Core: Evidence from (Eastern) Indonesian Languages") discusses in some detail the implications of allowing each one of the parallel representations to have its own scale of prominence and therefore its own most prominent argument, and presents data which display the range of effects which he predicts should be possible.

4   The Papers

The papers in this volume fall into three groups. One group contains papers dealing with the problems discussed in the preceding sections and a second group deals with other problems of transitivity in Austronesian languages. Two papers deal with both of these areas. Finally, there is a single paper which deals with problems of lexical categorization, specifically in Tagalog. The relevance of this issue to the general themes of the collection is discussed below.

The first group contains four papers:

FOLEY's paper presents a number of arguments as to why Philippine-type languages do not fit into the traditional typology of voice systems. He argues that there are good reasons not to treat these languages as having active and passive voice, that is they do not have nominative-accusative alignment. But the same type of arguments also rule out treating them as having ergative and antipassive voices. The conclusion is that the typology must be expanded to include the type *symmetrical voice system*.

ARKA AND MANNING's paper examines clauses with inverse linking patterns in Indonesian. The binding possibilities in the various subtypes of such clauses show a more complex system than might be assumed on the basis of data such as that in example (2). Arka and Manning's analysis shows that Indonesian has clause types with reverse linking and two term arguments, ergative clauses following the terminology of Manning (1996a), and also clauses types with reverse linking and only a single core argument, passive clauses in other words. The dividing line between the various types does not fall in the place that might be expected on the basis of the gross morpho-syntactic differences between the various possibilities.

ARKA's paper on Balinese draws similar conclusions about Balinese clauses with non-subject agents: both ergative and passive structures are possible, with one morpheme (or two homophonous morphemes) having an ambiguous role. A common feature of these last two papers is that pronouns are treated differently to other nominals, and that ergative structures are associated with a realization of pronouns which is closer to morphology than to syntax.

ARKA AND SIMPSON's paper examines the consequences for the theory of control of the ergative type of structure. They discuss Balinese data which show that, in an ergative construction, a clausal argument in subject position can have its own subject controlled by the non-subject agent argument. Such a possibility is ruled out by theories of control such as that of Bresnan (1982) or that of Zaenen and Engdahl (1994). Arka and Simpson propose a modified theory which predicts the Balinese facts also.

There are three papers in the second group, dealing with problems of transitivity:

MUSGRAVE's paper examines the status of the grammatical relation OB-JECT in Indonesian. Most accounts of the syntax of this language take the class of transitive verbs to be co-extensive with the class of verbs which participate in the morphological opposition seen in example (2). But all such verbs can also appear without morphological marking, and in this case their non-subject argument shares syntactic properties with the non-subject argument of a class of emotion and cognition predicates, properties which differ from those of the non-subject argument of the traditional transitive verbs. Therefore, it is not obvious which properties can be taken as criterial for the object relation. The solution proposed is that two types of clause structure occur in this language: subject-predicate structures and subject-verb phrase structures.

DUKES's paper deals with the Oceanic language Tongan, and considers whether it should be analyzed as being ergative. His examination of the data shows that, although agents are not the usual choice for subject with apparently transitive verbs, the evidence that any clauses in the language have two term arguments is weak. This conclusion agrees with the argument of Margetts (1999), who analyses another Oceanic language (Saliba) as being fundamentally intransitive and suggests that the characterization may extend to the whole Oceanic group. Dukes proposes to analyze Tongan quasi-transitive verbs as selecting for an agentive adjunct, and provides an implementation of this analysis in a Head-Driven Phrase Structure Grammar formalism.

DONOHUE's paper examines the mechanisms available for increasing the valence of verbs in the Tukang Besi language. He shows that although the language has both applicative and causative morphology, the applicative can be ambiguous between the two functions in some cases. This ambiguity is related to the fact that some intransitive verbs behave both as unergatives and as unaccusatives. The ambiguity in the applicative process is dependent on this prior ambiguity; as noted by e.g. Austin 1997, the same morpheme can have different effects on intransitive bases depending on their classification.

ARKA's paper on languages of Eastern Indonesia includes material which overlaps both the subject areas of the two groups discussed above.

This paper argues for a typology of voice systems deduced from the possible configurations of linkings of prominent arguments across parallel representations. A crucial role is attributed to pragmatic prominence in this linking, and the predicted patterns are shown to occur in the languages examined. This material extends the analysis of Austronesian voice systems both by presenting new data, and by fitting the data into a typology which follows from basic principles. This paper also touches on the problem of transitivity, with data showing languages which allow passives of verbs which lack a corresponding two-argument active form. Matches and mismatches between transitivity changes and voice alternations are predicted by Arka's analysis through the interaction of pragmatic prominence and available morphosyntactic resources.

Finally, HIMMELMANN's paper addresses the question of the nature of lexical categorization in Tagalog. Foley's paper which appears here was originally the preface to a proposal which linked the voice system of Tagalog and other Philippine-type languages to the fuzziness (or lack) of boundaries between lexical classes in those languages (see Himmelmann 1991, Gil 1993). Foley argues that the Tagalog lexicon distinguishes function words and content words, but that content words are not further categorized. Himmelmann responds to this position with arguments to show that it is necessary to separate an ontological level, a lexical level and a syntactic level in discussing questions of word class membership. Mismatches between the ontological and lexical levels are well-known, but less attention has been paid to mismatches between the lexical and syntactic level. Himmelmann provides evidence that at the syntactic level Tagalog makes very little distinction between classes of content words. He also demonstrates that there are formal distinctions of morphology and stress between word classes at the lexical level.

5 References

Adams, Karen & Alexis Manaster-Ramer. 1988. Some questions of topic/focus choice in Tagalog. *Oceanic Linguistics* 27:79–101.

Adelaar, K. Alexander & Nikolaus Himmelmann (ed.). 2005. *The Austronesian languages of Asia and Madagascar*. London: Curzon Press.

Artawa, Ketut & Barry J. Blake. 1997. Patient primacy in Balinese. *Studies in Language* 21:483–508.

Austin, Peter K. 1997. Causatives and applicatives in Australian Aboriginal Languages. In *Dative and related phenomena* ed. Kazuto Matsumura and Tooru Hayasi. 165–225. Tokyo: Hitsuji Shobo.

Austin, Peter & Joan Bresnan. 1996. Non-configurationality in Australian languages. *Natural Language and Linguistic Theory* 14:215–268.

Blake, Barry J. 1988. Tagalog and the Manila—Mt Isa Axis. *LaTrobe Working Papers in Linguistics* 1:77–90.

Blake, Frank R. 1906. Expression of case by the verb in Tagalog. *Journal of the American Oriental Society* 27:183–189.

Bloomfield, Leonard. 1917. *Tagalog Texts with Grammatical Analysis*. University of Illinois Studies in Language and Literature Vol. III, part 2–4. Urbana: The University of Illinois.

Bresnan, Joan. 1982. Control and complementation. *Linguistic Inquiry* 13.3:343–434.

Bresnan, Joan & Jonni Kanerva. 1989. Locative inversion in Chichewa: a case study of factorization in grammar. *Linguistic Inquiry* 20:1–50.

Carrier-Duncan, Jill. 1985. Linking of thematic roles in derivational word formation. *Linguistic Inquiry* 16:1–34.

Cartier, Alice. 1983. Strategies of the definite/indefinite patient in passive sentences. In *Papers from the Third International Conference on Austronesian Linguistics* ed. Amran Halim, Lois Carrington & S. A. Wurm. 251–267. Canberra: Pacific Linguistics (C-77).

Cena, Resty M. 1995. Surviving without relations. Unpublished MS.

Chung, Sandra. 1976. On the subject of two passives in Indonesian. In *Subject and Topic* ed. Charles Li. 57–98. New York: Academic Press.

Clark, Ross. 1990. The Austronesian languages. In *The Major Languages of East and South East Asia* ed. Bernard Comrie. 173–184. London: Routledge.

Cooreman, Anne, Barbara Fox & Talmy Givón. 1984. The Discourse definition of ergativity. *Studies in Language* 8:1–34.

De Guzman, Videa P. 1988. Ergative analysis for Tagalog: an analysis. In *Studies in Austronesian Linguistics* ed. Richard McGinn. 323–345. Athens, Ohio: Ohio University Center for Southeast Asia Studies.

De Guzman, Videa P. 1992. Morphological evidence for the primacy of patient as subject in Tagalog. In *Papers in Austronesian Linguistics No.2* ed. Malcolm D. Ross. Canberra: Pacific Linguistics (A-82).

Dixon, R. M. W. 1979. Ergativity. *Language* 55:59–138.

Dixon, R. M. W. 1994. *Ergativity*. Cambridge, UK: Cambridge University Press.

Gerdts, Donna. 1988. Antipassives and Causatives in Ilokano: Evidence for an ergative analysis. In *Studies in Austronesian Linguistics* ed. Richard McGinn. 295–321. Athens, Ohio: Ohio University Center for Southeast Asia Studies.

Gil, David. 1993. Tagalog semantics. In *Proceedings of the 19th Annual Meeting of the Berkeley Linguistics Society* ed. J.S. Guenter, B. S. Kaiser & C. C. Zoll. 390–403.

Guilfoyle, Eithne, Henrietta Hung & Lisa Travis. 1992. SPEC of IP and SPEC of VP: Two subjects in Austronesian languages. *Natural Language and Linguistic Theory* 10:375–414.

Himmelmann, Nikolaus P. 1991. *The Philippine Challenge to Universal Grammar*. Arbeitspapier No.15, Neue Folge. Köln: Institut für Sprachwissenschaft.

Jaeggli, Osvaldo A. 1986. Passive. *Linguistic Inquiry* 17:587–622.

Klamer, Marian. 2002. Ten years of synchronic Austronesian linguistics. *Lingua* 112:933–965.

Kroeger, Paul. 1993. *Phrase Structure and Grammatical Relations in Tagalog*. Stanford: CSLI.

Li, Charles N. (ed.). 1976. *Subject and Topic*. New York: Academic Press.

Manning, Christopher D. 1996a. *Ergativity: Argument structure and grammatical relations*. Stanford: CSLI.

Manning, Christopher D. 1996b. Argument Structure as a Locus for Binding Theory. Paper presented at the Lexical-Functional Grammar workshop, Grenoble, France, August 1996.

Manning, Christopher D. & Ivan A. Sag. 1999. Dissociations between Argument Structure and Grammatical Relations. In *Lexical And Constructional Aspects of Linguistic Explanation* ed. Gert Webelhuth, Jean-Pierre Koenig & Andreas Kathol. 63–78. Stanford: CSLI.

Margetts, Anna. 1999. *Valence and Transitivity in Saliba an Oceanic Language of Papua New Guinea*. MPI Series in Psycholinguistics No. 12. Nijmegen: Max Planck Institute for Psycholinguistics.

Massam, Diane. 1998. Introduction (to special issue on Austronesian languages). *Canadian Journal of Linguistics/Revue canadienne de linguistique* 43:275–281.

McGinn, Richard (ed.). 1988. *Studies in Austronesian Linguistics*. Athens, Ohio: Ohio University Center for Southeast Asia Studies.

Musgrave, Simon. 2001. Pronouns and morphology: undergoer subject clauses in Indonesian. In *Yearbook of Morphology 2000* ed. Gert Booij & Jaap van Marle. 155–186. Dordrecht/Boston/London: Kluwer Academic Publishers.

Quick, Phillip. 1997. Primary verbs in Pendao. Paper presented at the 8th International Conference on Austronesian Linguistics, Taipei.

Ross, Malcolm D. 2004. Notes on the prehistory and internal subgrouping of Malayic. In *Papers in Austronesian subgrouping and dialectology* ed. John Bowden & Nikolaus Himmelmann. 97–109. Canberra: Pacific Linguistics (PL 563).

Schachter, Paul. 1976. The Subject in Philippine languages: Topic, Actor, Actor-Topic, or None of the Above. In *Subject and Topic* ed. Charles Li. 491–518. New York: Academic Press.

Schachter, Paul. 1984. Semantic-role-based syntax in Toba Batak. In *Studies in the Structure of Toba Batak*. ed. Paul Schachter. 122–149. UCLA Occasional Papers in Linguistics, No. 5. Stanford: Department of Linguistics, UCLA.

Schachter, Paul. 1996. *The Subject in Tagalog: Still none of the above*. UCLA Occasional Papers in Linguistics No.15. Stanford: UCLA.

Sells, Peter. 1998. The function of voice markers in the Philippine languages. In *Morphology and its Relation to Phonology and Syntax* ed. G. Lapointe, D. K. Brentari & P. M. Farrell. 111–137. Stanford: CSLI.

Shibatani, Masyoshi. 1988. Voice in Philippine languages. In *Passive and Voice* ed. M. Shibatani. Amsterdam: John Benjamins.

Tryon, Darrell T. 1995. The Austronesian languages. In *Comparative Austronesian Dictionary: an Introduction to Austronesian studies* ed. Darrell T. Tryon. Berlin/New York: Mouton de Gruyter.

Voskuil, Jan E. 1993. Verbal inflection in Indonesian. In *Topics in Descriptive Austronesian Linguistics (Semaian 1)* ed. Ger P. Reesink. 159–180. Leiden: Vakgroep Talen en Culturen van Zuidoost-Azië en Oceanië.

Wechsler, Stephen & I Wayan Arka. 1998. Syntactic ergativity in Balinese: an argument structure based theory. *Natural Language and Linguistic Theory* 16:387–441.

Wolff, John U. 1973. Verbal inflection in Proto-Austronesian. In *Parangal kay Cecilio Lopez* ed. Andrew Gonzalez. 71–91. Quezon City: Linguistic Society of the Philippines.

Zaenen, Annie, and Elisabet Engdahl. 1994. Descriptive and theoretical syntax in the lexicon. In *Computational approaches to the lexicon* ed. B. T. S. Atkins & A. Zampolli. 181–212. Oxford: Oxford University Press.

2

The Place of Philippine Languages in a Typology of Voice Systems

WILLIAM A. FOLEY

1 The Philippine Voice System

The analysis of voice in Philippine languages, typically called the 'focus system' (e.g. Ramos 1974; Ramos and Bautista 1986), has been a source of contention for nearly a hundred years (Blake 1906), and this shows no sign of letting up (Schachter 1976; McGinn 1988; Gerdts 1988; Shibatani 1988; Guilfoyle, Hung and Travis 1992; Kroeger 1993). The present paper attempts to set a framework for this debate by arguing that neither of the usually available voice types, passive or antipassive, is an adequate analysis of the Philippine voice system and that a new type, the symmetrical voice system, needs to be recognized. The presentation will be largely negative, arguing at length against both a passive and particularly an antipassive analysis of Philippine voice systems, leading us to the claim that Philippine languages exhibit a third voice type distinct from both of these.

The nature of the basic facts which underlie all this debate can be seen in the following sentences from Tagalog (the sentences are slightly unnatu-

Voice and Grammatical Relations in Austronesian Languages.
Simon Musgrave and Peter Austin
Copyright © 2007, CSLI Publications.

ral in that Philippine languages, like most languages, do have a strong preference for no more than one full noun phrase per clause, but they are grammatical and do illustrate the nature of the voice system well):

(1)   a.   *b-**um**-ili*   *ng*   *isda*   *sa*   *tindahan*   ***ang***
               VC-buy   CORE   fish   OBL   store
               lalake
               man
               'The man bought fish in the store.'

      b.   *bi-bilh-**in***   *ng*   *lalake*   *sa*   *tindahan*
               IRR-buy-VC   CORE   man   OBL   store
               isda
               fish
               'The man will buy the fish in the store.'

      c.   *bi-bilh-**an***   *ng*   *lalake*   *ng*   *isda*   ***ang***
               IRR-buy-VC   CORE   man   CORE   fish
               tindahan
               store
               'The man will buy fish in the store.'

      d.   ***ipam**-bi-bili*   *ng*   *lalake*   *ng*   *isda*   ***ang***
               VC-IRR-buy   CORE   man   CORE   fish
               salapi
               money
               'The man will buy fish with the money.'

      e.   ***i**-bi-bili*   *ng*   *lalake*   *ng*   *isda*   ***ang***
               VC-IRR-buy   CORE   man   CORE   fish
               bata
               child
               'The man will buy fish for the child.'

    Note that the root of the verb *bili* 'buy' (reduplicated in (1b)-(e) to *bibili* to indicate irrealis modality, i.e. '*will* buy') takes a range of different affixes: *-um-*, *-in*, *-an*, *ipaN-* and *i-*. The choice of each affix is determined by the semantic properties of whichever NP is preceded by *ang*. If the *ang* NP is causer, performer or initiator of the event (let's abbreviate this as the actor), in this case the buyer, the verb takes the infix *-um-* (1a). On the other hand, if the *ang* NP is the participant affected or undergoing a change in location or ownership as a result of the event (what I will call the undergoer (Foley and Van Valin (1984)), in these examples the thing bought, the verb takes the suffix -*in* (1b). Other possibilities are also available: the *ang* NP can denote the place where the event is accomplished (the suffix -*an*; (1c)), the instrument used to accomplish the event (the prefix *ipaN*-; (1d)) or the person who benefits from the event (the prefix *i*-; (1e)). In each case it is the affix on the verb which marks the semantic role of the *ang* NP: hence the description by Blake nearly a hundred years ago (1906) of this phenomenon as the 'expression of case by the verb', rather than its usual locus on the noun or in the noun phrase.

Blake's description, while very insightful, is, however, not complete. In addition to the verbal affixes, Tagalog does possess true case markers, as is clear from the glosses given to the prepositions *ng* and *sa* above. Although there are some complications to be discussed below, the basic Tagalog case system is a simple binary one, contrasting core NPs, those prototypically subcategorised by verbs like actors and undergoers, with oblique NPs, not so subcategorized, such as locations, beneficiaries, goals, etc. NPs are divided into [±proper] and case marked as follows:

(2)

	CORE	OBL
[+proper]	ni Juan	kay Juan
[-proper]	ng lalake	sa lalake

PROnominal NPs are inflected for case:

		CORE	OBL
SG	1	*ko	akin
	2	mo	iyo
	3	niya	kaniya
PL	1EX	natin	atin
	1IN	namin	amin
	2	ninyo	inyo
	3	nila	kanila
PROX		nito	dito
NEAR DIST		niyan	diyan
FAR DIST		niyon/noon	doon

The core pronominals never occur with the preposition *ng* or *ni*, but the oblique pronominals when functioning as clause level constituents typically do.

If the core/oblique distinction, *ng/sa* etc., is the basic NP case marking system in Tagalog, then what exactly is the function of *ang*? Note that it too, has its [+proper] NP variant and a full set of corresponding pronouns (i.e. those that can replace an *ang* NP and syntactically function identically):

(3) NP

		[+proper]	si Juan
		[-proper]	ang lalake
PROnominals			
		1	*ako*
SG		2	*ka/ikaw*
		3	*siya*
PL		1 EX	*tayo*
		1 IN	*kami*
		2	kayo
		3	*sila*
PROX			*ito*
NEAR DIST			*iyan*
FAR DIST			*iyon*

The set of grammatical distinctions in (3) exactly parallels that found in (2), which realizes the basic core/oblique case distinction in the language. This had led some analysts to dub the *ang* forms nominative case forms, noting the fact that it is nominative forms which show agreement with the verb via the affixation of *-um-*, *-in*, etc, and, cross-linguistically, it is the nominative case forms in languages which prototypically show agreement with the verb, as in English:

(4)

		NOM	ACC
1	SG	I	me
	PL	we	us
3	SG	she	her
	PL	they	them

a. I(SG) *am* (SG) going to visit them (PL)
b. *I (SG *are* (PL) going to visit them (PL)
c. We (PL) *are* (PL) going to visit her (SG)
d. *We (PL) *is* (SG) going to visit her (SG)

This analysis would then suggest a three way nominal case system for Tagalog: CORE-[+NOM], CORE-[-NOM], and OBL.

2 What the Philippine Voice System is Not

2.1 Arguments against the Active-Passive Analysis

While there are good reasons to question whether *ang* is a case marker at all (for example the fact that in recent perfective clause types (Schachter and Otanes 1972: 371-375) there are no *ang* form NPs at all, a highly typologically unexpected situation if, as claimed above, they do bear nominative case, the unmarked case form in a clause), let's follow where the analysis leads us. If *ang* in the examples in (1) really represents a nominative case, then the contrast between (1a) and (1b) looks very much like an active-passive alternation in English: the actor is marked as nominative by *ang* in (1a), while the undergoer is marked as nominative in (1b). But there are two immediate problems with this analysis. First, the actor of the so-called passive sentence in (1b) remains a core NP marked by *ng* in marked contrast to the obliquely marked actors of canonical passives cross-linguistically (compare the use of the preposition *by* in English). Second, again contrary to canonical passives, there is no unmarked active form, but both the putative active and passive voices are indicated by verbal morphemes: -*um*- for active and -*in* for passive. This is highly unusual; normally the active voice is morphologically and syntactically unmarked, the basic inflectional form of the verb, while the passive is marked; compare English *buy* versus *be bought*. Finally, examples (1c) through (1e) present still further problems for the analysis. In each of these cases it is erstwhile oblique NPs, locatives, instrumentals or benefactives, arguments not subcategorized by the verb, which have assumed nominative case and the verb appears with specific affixes indicating their semantic function. Again, these are non-actor NPs in nominative case, so following the above analysis these need to be analyzed as passives. This would require postulating that Tagalog has four passive voices in contrast to English's one (actually rather more than that because there are a number of other voice types which also allow non-subcategorized arguments to assume nominative case not illustrated here; see Schachter and Otanes (1972)). This is typologically a highly marked situation. It is true that many languages (e.g. Bantu) allow non-subcategorized arguments to assume nominative case in passives, but they do this first via applicativization which makes the non-subcategorized argument a core NP of the verb and then by passivization which allows it to assume nominative case, as in this Indonesian example:

(5) *sawah*   *itu*   *di-tanam-i*   *padi*   *oleh*
     rice fields   DET   PASS-plant-APPL   rice   by
     Hasan
     PN
     'The rice field was planted with rice by Hasan.'

First, the applicative suffix -*i* allows the non-subcategorized erstwhile locative argument *sawah* 'rice field' to assume core NP status and then the prefix *di-*, PASS, allows it to assume nominative case, assigned to the preverbal position in Indonesian. Note the actor in the passive follows the verb and is marked with the oblique agentive preposition *oleh*. This is cross-linguistically the expected pattern, but the Tagalog situation is fundamentally different. For example in (1c) there is only the voice affix -*an*. This would need to be analyzed as doing double duty, both applicativization and passivization. But outside of Philippine languages, languages simply don't do this, and this typological fact must force us to question seriously whether the passive analysis is really the right one for these languages.

It is important to note that this unusual typological picture is not restricted just to the geographical area of the Philippines, but is widespread among the Western Austronesian languages from Taiwan to Western Indonesia and is diagnostic of what is known as 'Philippine-type' languages among Austronesian specialists. There are good reasons to suspect that proto-Austronesian was itself a language of this type (Wolff 1973, 1979; Starosta, Pawley and Reid 1982). Atayal of Taiwan (Egerod 1965, 1966; Rau 1992; Huang 1993) and Kimaragang of Sabah (Kroeger 1988, 1996) both illustrate the same structural patterns of voice as Tagalog (nominative case NPs are bolded):

(6)   Atayal (Huang 1993)

  a.   *t-**m**-tu*   *tali*   **ghuniq**
       VC-crush   PN   tree
       'The tree crushed Tali.'

  b.   *t-ʔ-**un***   *ghuniq*   **tali**
       crush-VC   tree   PN
       'The tree crushed Tali.'

  c.   *byiq-**an**-mu*   *hira*   *gulih*   **tali**
       give-VC-1SG.CORE   yesterday   fish   PN
       'I gave a fish to Tali yesterday.'

    d.   **s-ʔagan-mu**   *gulih*   **sgari?**   **gani**
         VC-take-1SG.CORE   fish   net   this
         'I caught the fish with this net.'

    e.   **s-ʔagan-mu**   *gulih*   **Tali**
         VC-take-1SG.CORE   fish   PN
         'I'll catch a fish for Tali.'

In this dialect of Atayal there are no obligatory NP case marking prepositions (although other dialects do have them), so that word order is much more rigidly fixed than in Tagalog. The actor always immediately follows the verb (if it is a pronoun it is encliticized as in (6c)-(e)), unless it is nominative, in which case, it is clause final (6a). The verb is affixed with the usual voice affixes, all of which are in fact cognate with their Tagalog equivalents (-*um*-: -*m*-: -*in*; -*un* < PAN*-ˊn; -*an*: -*an*; *i*-: *s*- < PAN *Si-). The same basic patterns are found: (1) subcategorized arguments remain core NPs (i.e. Ø case marked) in all voice forms of the verb; (2) there are no unmarked verbal forms, i.e. an active form; and (3) nonsubcategorized arguments can freely assume nominative case without going through an applicative derivation first via the affixes -*an* or *s*-. While it might be objected that the verb 'give' does subcategorize a recipient argument, as in (6c), such an analysis seems wrong for Atayal and Tagalog, as may be the case for many Austronesian languages. Returning to (6c), if *Tali* were not nominative, it could occur with an overt case marker and that case would be the oblique *te*, not the core *na ʔ*, indicating that the recipient argument is probably not subcategorized. In other words verbs like 'give' in Tagalog and Atayal, and quite probably in Austronesian languages quite generally, are transitive verbs, not ditransitive ones, subcategorizing only two core arguments, the actor and the transferred object; the recipient is a nonsubcategorized oblique argument. Also, there are other examples of verbs affixed with -*an*, in which the locative argument could not be plausibly argued to be subcategorized:

(7)   **nanu?**   *ʔby-**an**   *tali*
       what   sleep-VC   PN
       'Where does Tali want to sleep?'

Now consider examples from Kimaragang (Kroeger 1988):

(8)   a.   *momoli*   ***okuh***   *do*   *tasin*
             m-poN-boli   1SG   CORE [-DEF]   salt
             VC-TR-buy
             'I am going to buy some salt.'

       b.   *amu*   *kuh*   *bili-**on***   ***itih***   ***tasin***   ***ditih***
             NEG   1SG.CORE   buy-VC   this   salt   this
             'I won't buy this salt.'

       c.   ***siongah***   *pinomolian*   *nuh*   *dilo*
             where   -in-poN-bili-*an*   2SG.CORE   that.CORE
                             PST-TRNS-buy-VC
             gampa   *nuh*
             machete   2SG.POSS
             'Where did you buy your machete?'

       d.   *n-**i**-boli*   *kuh*   ***it***   ***siin***
             PST-VC-buy   1SG.CORE   [+DEF]   money
             ku   *dot*   *tasin*
             1SG.POSS   CORE [-DEF]   salt
             'I bought salt with my money.'

       e.   ***isai***   *boli-**an***   *nuh*   ***ditih***   *tubat*   *ditih*
             who   buy-VC   2SG.CORE   this   medicine   this
             'Who will you buy medicine for?'

Kimaragang, like Tagalog and unlike Atayal, has NP case markers and like Tagalog has a three way contrast: e.g. *it* CORE-[+NOM], *dit* CORE-[-NOM] and *sid* OBL; or *okuh* 1SG.CORE-[+NOM], *kuh* 1SG.CORE-[-NOM] and *dogon* OBL (the CORE case markers also distinguish [±DEF], *it* CORE-[+NOM] [+DEF] versus *ot* CORE-[+NOM] [-DEF]; see table in Kroeger 1996:35). Again, the general typological picture is like that of Tagalog and Atayal: (1) subcategorized arguments remain core in all voice forms of the verb (the forms *kuh* and *nuh* in (7b)-(e); (2) all verbal forms are overtly marked for voice, i.e. the semantic role of the nominative NP, there being no unmarked verbal form corresponding to the English active voice; and (3) non-subcategorized arguments again directly assume nominative through a single verbal affix, *-an* or *i-*, there being no intermediate applicative derivation. Again, the affixes involved are directly cognate with the Tagalog ones: *-um-: m-~-um-; -in: -on* < PAN *- ´n*; *-an: -an*; and *i-: i-*. The only seemingly significant difference between Kimaragang and the other two languages concerns the example in which the beneficiary is

marked nominative (7e). In the Tagalog and Atayal examples this participant type was marked with the prefix *Si- (Tagalog i-, Atayal s-), the same
affix used for instruments, but in Kimaragang, it occurs with -an, the locative voice marker. But the beneficiary voice marker actually shows considerable variation among Philippine type languages (and within them!) between *-an and *Si-; even in Tagalog a number of stems will show beneficiary voice with -an.

These three languages, drawn from widely disparate areas, present a
consistent typological picture of Philippine type languages, and one which
seems quite incompatible with an active-passive analysis of these clausal
alternations. Many other arguments against such an analysis have been presented by previous researchers, so I will not repeat them here, but for some
of these see Schachter's justly famous papers on Tagalog grammatical relations (Schachter 1976, 1977).

2.2 Arguments against the Ergative-Antipassive Analysis

In recent years, problems of this sort have led researchers to propose an
alternative, an ergative-absolutive analysis of Philippine clausal structure
(Cena 1977, De Guzman 1979, Gerdts 1988). In this analysis, the NPs
which were described as bearing nominative case in the active-passive
analysis, are now claimed to carry absolutive case (this is typologically
plausible, because absolutive NPs are the ones most likely to agree with the
verb in ergative-absolutive languages) and the erstwhile non-nominative
core NPs are now actually taken to be ergatively marked. Example (1b)
would now be analyzed as:

(9) *bi-bilh-in*   *ng*   *lalake*   *sa*   *tindahan*   *ang*
     IRR-buy-VC   ERG   man   OBL   store   ABS
     isda
     fish
     'The man will buy the fish in the store.'

As this is now an ergative language, the form with the undergoer
marked with *ang* would be the basic clause type, with it in absolutive case
and the actor in ergative case. The clause type in which the actor is in absolutive case is now a derived form, the antipassive, a functional equivalent of
passive in ergative languages: the absolutive NP of (9) becomes ergative
and the ergative NP, absolutive:

(10) b-**um**-ili   ng   isda   sa   tindahan   ang
      ANTI-buy   ERG   fish   OBL   store   ABS
      lalake
      man
      'The man bought fish in the store.'

The -um- is analyzed as an antipassive marker which derives an intransitive verb from the transitive bilh-in in (9). Note that -um- prototypically occurs with intransitive verbs:

(11) p-**um**-unta   ang   lalake
      go   ABS   man
      'The man went.'

Note that while both the actor in (9) and the undergoer in (10) are case marked with ng, glossed ergative, this actually belies a quite different syntactic status for the two NPs. (9) is a normal transitive clause, so isda is an ergatively case marked core NP. (10), on the other hand, is an antipassive, and antipassives as claimed here are *intransitive* clauses. Hence the sole core argument in (10) is the absolutive lalake 'man'; the ergatively case marked isda is necessarily oblique. It is very important to distinguish in what follows between core ergatively marked NPs of transitive clauses and oblique ergatively marked NPs of antipassives.

The ergative analysis has a great advantage over the active-passive one in that it neatly accounts for why non-subcategorized arguments can assume absolutive status without a prior applicative derivation (examples (1c)-(e)). It is well known that true ergative languages have a global constraint against double absolutive NPs in a clause. As a result, whenever applicativization applies to give core NP status, specifically absolutive case, to a previously non-subcategorized oblique NP, a simultaneous antipassive applies to force the prior absolutive to assume oblique case, as in these Chamorro examples (Cooreman 1988):

(12) a. hu-tuge'   i   katta
          1SG.ERG-write   ABS   letter
          'I wrote the letter.'

      b. hu-tugi'-i   i   patgon   ni   katta
          1SG.ERG-write-APPL   ABS   child   OBL   letter
          'I wrote the child the letter.'

(12a) presents *tuge* 'write' as a simple transitive verb with two subcategorized arguments: *hu-* 1SG.ERG and *i katta* ABS letter. (12b) presents a derived applicative verb form with *-i* APPL 'to/for'. The newly introduced core participant *i patgon* ABS child now assumes absolutive case, and due to the global blocking constraint against double absolutive NPs, this derivation now simultaneously forces the previous absolutive NP *i katta* to appear as oblique *ni katta*, an antipassive process. Because the whole process is one simultaneous derivation, there is no need for a separate antipassive morpheme: APPLicativization is antipassivization, pure and simple.

Adapting this to the Tagalog examples in (1c)-(e) and *ceteribus paribus* the Atayal and Kimaragang examples in (6c)-(e) and (8c)-(e), we would now claim that *-an* and *i-* are not voice markers at all, simply applicative affixes, and the case marking exhibited in the examples is simply the result of a process parallel to that described for Chamorro:

(13) a. *bi-bilh-in*   *ng*   *lalake*   *sa*   *tindahan*   *ang*
          IRR-buy   ERG   man   OBL   store   ABS
          isda
          fish
          'The man will buy the fish in the store.'

      b. *bi-bilh-an*   *ng*   *lalake*   *ng*   *isda*   *ang*
          IRR-buy-APPL   ERG   man   ERG   fish   ABS
          tindahan
          store
          'The man will buy fish in the store.'

Here *-an* is simply an applicative marker which makes *tindahan* a non-actor core argument, hence case marked absolutive, and forces the prior absolutive NP *isda* into ergative case, via the no double absolutive constraint (note that the two ergatively case marked NPs have different syntactic status: the first is core but the second is oblique via antipassivization as a result of the applicativization requirement).

As attractive as the ergative analysis might be, it too runs into serious descriptive problems. First, if examples like (10) are really antipassives they should exhibit the cross-linguistically well attested typological properties of antipassives. Unfortunately they do not. Comparing the verb forms of (10) and (11), we see that the antipassive and true intransitive verbs are morphologically identical. This is virtually never true of antipassives. While the verbs of antipassive constructions *are* intransitive, they always carry morphological markers of derivation to indicate that they have been derived from transitive verbs, and these are always distinct from simple intransitive verb inflection, as in Dyirbal (Dixon 1972):

(14) a. Intransitive verb

bayi	*yara*	*bani-nyu*
DET.ABS	man.ABS	come-TNS

'The man came.'

      b. antipassive *derived* intransitive verb

bayi	*yara*	*bugun*	*jugumbil-gu*
DET.ABS	man.ABS	DET.DAT	woman-DAT

*bural-**ng**-nyu*
see-ANTI-TNS
'The man saw the woman.'

Note the prototypical Dyirbal antipassive contains the obligatory derivational suffix -*Na(y)* which the intransitive verb necessarily lacks. (Some languages like Eskimo may have zero allomorphs of antipassive affixes, but these are *allomorphs* of morphemes overt in other environments, so they do not constitute a counterexample to the claim that derived antipassive verb forms are never identical with true underived intransitive verbs.) This is quite different from the situation in Tagalog and suggests that (10) is not a true antipassive construction.

Continuing along these lines, the prototypical effect of an antipassive is to delink the undergoer of the verb from the status of core argument and reassign it to an oblique function. Note above in (14b), the antipassive construction forces the seen participant to appear in the dative case, an oblique case in Dyirbal. Now again consider Tagalog example (10), repeated here as (15):

(15)

*b-**um**-ili*	*ng*	*isda*	*sa*	*tindahan*	*ang*	*lalake*
ANTI-buy	ERG	fish	OBL	store	ABS	man

'The man bought fish in the store.'

If (15) is to be considered a true antipassive, then *ng isda* must be construed as an oblique constituent. There is, however, an argument that suggests that *ng* marked undergoers are not oblique constituents, but core NPs like *ng* marked actors. Tagalog allows true oblique constituents to precede the verb in a topicalization construction:

(16) | *sa* | *tindahan* | *bi-bilh-in* | *ng* | *lalake* | *ang* | *isda* |
|---|---|---|---|---|---|---|
| OBL | store | IRR-buy | ERG | man | ABS | fish |

'In the store the man will buy the fish.'

This construction is completely prohibited for core NPs like ergatively marked actors:

(17) | **ng* | *lalake* | *bi-bilh-in* | *sa* | *tindahan* | *ang* | *isda* |
|---|---|---|---|---|---|---|
| ERG | man | IRR-buy | OBL | store | ABS | fish |

And it is equally prohibited for *ng* marked undergoers in putative antipassive constructions like (15):

(18) | **ng* | *isda* | *b-um-ili* | *sa* | *tindahan* | *ang* | *lalake* |
|---|---|---|---|---|---|---|
| ERG | fish | buy | OBL | store | ABS | man |

This strongly argues that *ng* marked undergoers are still core arguments of the verb and not truly oblique NPs as an antipassive analysis of (15) would require. This constraint cannot be put down to a simple constraint against *ng* marked NPs in clause-initial position. For example, verbs in putative antipassive constructions assign either ergative or oblique case to the non-actor argument, depending on its definiteness:

(19) | *um-akyat* | *ng/sa* | *puno* | *ang* | *bata* |
|---|---|---|---|---|
| climb | ERG/OBL | tree | ABS | child |

'The child climbed a/the tree.'

However, regardless of whether the NP is marked with *ng* or *sa*, it remains a core argument, for in neither case can it assume the preverbal topicalization position of true oblique NPs:

(20) a. | **ng* | *puno* | *um-akyat* | *ang* | *bata* |
|---|---|---|---|---|
| ERG | tree | climb | ABS | child |

b. | **sa* | *puno* | *um-akyat* | *ang* | *bata* |
|---|---|---|---|---|
| OBL | tree | climb | ABS | child |

(Grammatical in the meaning 'The child climbed *up* the tree'.)

This conclusively demonstrates that the *ng* marked NPs of constructions like (15) are not oblique and therefore these constructions cannot be true antipassives.

While the evidence in Tagalog for the core status of *ng* marked NPs is somewhat indirect, in some other Philippine type languages it is much more transparent and hence persuasive. For example, in Kimaragang (Kroeger 1996), there is the normal pattern of multiple voices with different verbal affixes to mark voice (see examples in (8)). If the system is a true ergative-absolutive one, then again the form with *-m-* marking the actor as absolutive would have to be taken as an antipassive. These putative antipassives, however, co-occur with an additional derivational suffix lacking in all other voice types:

(21) a.   *mangalapak*   *okuh*   *do*   *niyuw*
         m-poN-lapak
         VC-?-split   1SG.ABS   ERG [-DEF]   coconut
         'I will split a coconut.'

      b.   *lapak-**on***   *kuh*   *it*   *niyuw*
         split-VC   1SG.ERG   ABS[+DEF]   coconut
         'I will split the coconut.'

      c.   *lapak-**an***   *kuh*   *do*   *niyuw*
         split-VC   1SG.ERG   ERG[-DEF]   coconut
         it   *wugok*
         ABS[+DEF]   pig
         'I will split a coconut for the pigs.'

Crucially, these prefixes *poN-* and *po-* occur in sentences like (21a), voice constructions in which the actor is marked ABS, putative antipassives. But remarkably the function of these prefixes is to mark alternations in the semantic role of the non-actor argument. Kimaragang, like English, exhibits alterations in the choice of the undergoer NP like *load hay in the truck* and *load the truck with hay*. Constructions like the former, with the theme as core undergoer and the locative as oblique occur with the prefix *po-* (glossed here as UNDR), while constructions with both arguments as core undergoer NPs take *poN-*:

(22) a.   *ϕ-po-suwang*   *okuh*   *ditih*   *sada*   *sid*
         -UNDR-enter   1SG.ABS   This.ERG   fish   OBL
         pata'an
         basket
         'I will put this fish in the basket.'

    b.   *monuwang*   *okuh*   *do*
        m-*poN-suwang*
        -UNDR-enter   1SG.ABS   ERG [-DEF]
        pata'an   *do*   *sada*
        basket   ERG [-DEF]   fish
        'I will fill a basket with fish.'

(23) a.   *ɸ-pa-ta'ak*   *okuh*   *do*   *siin*
        -UNDR-give   1SG.ABS   ERG [-DEF] money
        tanak   *kuh*
        child   1SG.POSS
        'I give money to my child.'

    b.   *mana'ak*   *okuh*   *di*   *tanak*
        m-*poN-ta'ak*
        -UNDR-give   1SG.ABS   ERG [+DEF] child
        kuh   *do*   *siin*
        1SG.POSS   ERG [-DEF]   money
        'I will give my child money.'

PoN- is also used to mark patients as undergoer, as (21a) demonstrates. Sentences like (21a) and (22)-(23) present a strong challenge to the ergative analysis and specifically the analysis of -(*u*)*m*-marked verbs as antipassives. In antipassive constructions, the undergoer must be an oblique constituent, yet in Kimaragang the verb is obligatorily marked in -(*u*)*m*- inflected verbs for the specific semantic role of the undergoer. Cross-linguistically, verbal marking is exclusively restricted to core arguments, so the Kimaragang undergoer in (21a) must be a core argument. But if it is, again on cross-linguistic evidence, (21a) cannot be properly analyzed as an antipassive construction.

Nor will an analysis of *poN-* as an applicative marker work either. First, why would an applicative marker be needed in (21a)? The verb *lapak* 'split' is already a transitive verb subcategorizing an actor and an undergoer, as (21b) clearly shows. Why would an applicative be needed in (21a) with only the same two arguments? Consider, then, for the sake of argument that there are two *poN-*'s, a verbal derivational prefix in (21a) and a true applicative in (22b) and (23b). *PoN-* in the latter two examples is taken as an applicative suffix deriving a ditransitive verb from a formerly monotransitive root by presenting a formerly oblique locational argument as a core argument. The main problem with this analysis is that it sacrifices what we saw with Tagalog data is the strongest evidence for the ergative analysis in the first place: namely, that given the universal one absolutive NP per clause constraint operative in true ergative languages, an applicative derivation will necessarily trigger antipassive, forcing the previous absolutive NP into oblique case. Kimaragang has examples parallel to Tagalog -an marked verbs that seem to fit this description:

(24) a.   *itih*   *pe'es*   *i-ta'ak*   *dih*   *kamaman*
             this.ABS   knife   give   ERG [+DEF]   uncle
             sid   *dogon*
             OBL   1SG.OBL
             'My uncle will give this knife to me.'

      b.   *taak-**an***   *okuh*   *dih*   *kamaman*
             give   1SG.ABS   ERG [+DEF]   uncle
             do   *pe'es*
             ERG [-DEF]   knife
             'My uncle gave me a knife.'

(24a) is the basic construction if the language is analyzed as ergative, with the actor in the ergative case, the theme in the absolutive, and the recipient in the oblique. The suffix -an is analyzed as an applicative promoting the recipient to core status and deriving a ditransitive verb. Due to the one absolutive per clause constraint, a simultaneous antipassive applies, throwing the theme into an oblique case, in this case, the ergative, as with Tagalog *ng* (see discussion above re example (10)). Note importantly, no *poN-* is used in the derivation: the antipassive is implicated and simultaneous with applicative formation, and the single suffix -an is sufficient. Now note what happens with -*m*- marked verbs:

(25)   *mana'ak*   *okuh*   *dih*   *kamaman*
         m-poN-ta'ak
         -UNDR-give   1SG.ABS   ERG [+DEF]   uncle
         do   *pe'es*
         ERG [-DEF]   knife
         'I gave my uncle a knife.'

Note that there are two ergative NPs, the theme and the recipient, and the prefix *poN-*, but no suffix -*an*. Example (25) is extremely hard to account for in the ergative/antipassive analysis. Note that the recipient occurs in the ergative case, not oblique. In order for that to be possible it needs to have gone through a stage of being a core argument, i.e. licensed by -*an* (as in (24b)), but -*an* is nowhere to be found, only *poN-*. It begs credibility to suppose *poN-* is an allomorph of *-an*; one a prefix, the other a suffix. Further they can actually co-occur in certain verbal forms *poN-lapak-an* 'split things someplace'.

Finally, there are verb forms with *poN-* which occur in basic clauses, i.e. clauses in which the undergoer is in absolutive case:

(26) *nunuh*   *ot*   *pana'ak*   *nuh*
                          poN-ta'ak
      what   ABS   UNDR-give   2SG.ERG
      'What would you give?'

nunuh 'what' is in absolutive case, but if *poN-* is an applicative then by the one absolutive NP per clause constraint *nunuh* should be ergative with the understood but ellipsed recipient in absolutive. The fact that this is not the case suggests either that *poN-* is not an applicative or Kimaragang is not an ergative language. So (25) as an antipassive is now wholly unaccounted for; we would expect by normal derivational processes (27) instead:

(27) **t-**um**-aak-an*   *okuh*   *dih*   *kamaman*
      give-APPL   1SG.ABS   ERG [+DEF]   uncle
      do   *pe'es*
      ERG [-DEF]   knife
      'I gave my uncle a knife.'

in which the antipassive triggered by the applicative *-an* first forces the theme *pe'es* 'knife' into ergative case, and the second antipassive with the voice affix *-(u)m-* delinks the formerly absolutive recipient argument *kamaman* 'uncle' from core status and places it in oblique ergative case. Of course (27) is not what we really get; instead we find (25), with a prefix *poN-* that seems to verbally cross-reference NPs as undergoers, a function of core grammatical relations no less! This all leads to the single conclusion that Kimaragang should not be analyzed as an ergative language.

Other Philippine type languages too present arguments against the ergative analysis via interactions with applicative derivations. Consider these data from Sama (Walton 1986):

(28) a. *b'lli*   *ku*   *taumpa*   *ma*   *onde'*
          buy   1SG.ERG   shoe(s)   OBL   child
          'I bought the shoes for the child.'

b. *N-b'lli*   *aku*   *taumpa*   *ma*   *onde'*
ANTI-buy   1SG.ABS shoes   OBL   child
'I bought shoe(s) for the child.'

On the face of it, Sama would seem to be the ideal Philippine candidate for an ergative language. For the first time, we find a φ marked underived verbal form, one used with the undergoer as absolutive, a putative basic ergative construction, and another form derived with *N-*, presenting the actor as absolutive, and hence, an antipassive. But (28b) presents one obvious immediate problem for the antipassive analysis: the undergoer remains φ case marked as it was when it was the absolutive NP in (28a); it completely fails to take the oblique case marker *ma*. Again, it is cross-linguistically the case that antipassives force undergoer NPs into oblique cases, and it is overwhelmingly the case that oblique NPs are marked by some overt predicator/adposition/case marker, not by φ. φ marking is a property of core NPs and the fact that *taumpa* 'shoe(s)' in (28b) is so marked suggests that it indeed is a core NP and hence (28b) is not an antipassive.

Further evidence comes from interaction with applicative derivations. Consider these examples:

(29) a.   *b'lli*   *ku*   *taumpa* *ma*   *si*   *Andi*
          buy   1SG.ERG shoe(s)   OBL ART PN
          'I bought the shoes for Andy.'

     b.   *N-b'lli*   *aku*   *taumpa* *ma*   *si*   *Andi*
          ANTI-buy 1SG.ABS shoe(s) OBL ART PN
          'I bought shoes for Andy.'

(30) a.   *b'lli-an*   *ku*   *si*   *Andi*   *taumpa*
          buy-APPL 1SG.ERG ART PN   shoe(s)
          'I bought Andy some shoes.'

     b.   *N-b'lli-an*   *aku*   *si*   *Andi* *taumpa*
          ANTI-buy-APPL 1SG.ABS ART PN shoe(s)
          'I bought Andy some shoes.'

(29a) and (b) are the expected basic ergative and antipassive constructions respectively. (30a) is a common example of applicative derivation: *si Andi* which was oblique in (29), marked with *ma* is promoted to core status by the suffix *-an*. (30b) is the crucial example; it is the Sama equivalent of the unattested Kimaragang example (27). First applicativization applies, marked by *-an*, and then antipassivization with *N-*. While it is true that the no double absolutive constraint holds for (30b), i.e. only *aku* 1SG is absolutive, it remains problematic why both the beneficiary and the themes remain φ case marked, i.e. behave like core arguments, when the double operation of two antipassives should put both into oblique cases. It is typologically highly implausible to claim that the beneficiary and theme are obliquely case marked, first, because oblique cases are never φ marked, but require an overt marker; and second, because the Sama oblique case marker is in fact an overt preposition *maka*. We must conclude therefore that the antipassive analysis fails for Sama as it has for Tagalog and Kimaragang.

Returning to Tagalog now, there are a couple of other arguments that can be advanced against the ergative analysis. Proponents of the ergative analysis claim that forms in which the actor of the clause is marked by *ang*, ABS, are antipassives, and antipassivization is accomplished through deriving intransitive verbs from basic transitive ones. There are a number of serious problems with this view. First, it depends on a sharp, well defined notion of transitivity, dividing verbs into transitive and intransitive classes. Unfortunately, this notion is anything but clear in Philippine languages. Not a few semantically intransitive verbs occur with voice suffixes diagnostic of transitive verbs, namely *i-*, *-in* and *-an*: *i-kasal* 'get married', *pawis-an* 'sweat', *kilabot-an* 'be terrified', *antuk-in* 'feel sleepy', *langgam-in* 'be infested with ants', *ma-lamig-an* 'feel cold'. Nor is this restricted to Tagalog: witness the Kimaragang intransitive verbs *tuuw-an* 'be thirsty', *losu-an* 'feel hot', *sogit-on* 'feel cold', *o-weeg-an* 'be flooded' (Kroeger 1988), Thus, we cannot gloss *-um-* as simply 'intransitive' and be done with it: there are a number of different voice affixes that semantically intransitive verbs take. This is because the voice affixes signal subtle semantic properties of the NP marked by *ang*, as well as semantic properties of the verb (see Ramos 1974; de Guzman 1978). They are not global markers of a syntactic distinction of transitivity, which is in fact very problematic in Tagalog.

Related to this fact are the particular semantics supplied to roots by *-um-*. It occurs in paradigmatic alternation with a number of other affixes for the derivation of verbal forms, all of which mark their sole core argument with *ang*:

(31) a. pula 'red' → *ma*-pula 'be reddish' → p-*um*-ula 'become red'
 → *mam*-(p)ula 'blush'

b.	***um****-abot*	'reach for'	***mag****-abot*	'hand to'
	bangka	'boat'	***mam****-(b)angka*	'go boating'
	bus	'bus'	***mag****-bus*	'ride a bus'
	payat	'thin'	*p-**um**-ayat*	'become thin'

Again simply glossing an affix like *-um-* or any of the other affixes in (31) as 'intransitive' ignores the rich derivational and semantic functions they serve. These data cast grave doubt on the claim that *-um-* is an intransitivizer or antipassivizer for it is clearly in paradigmatic alternation with the other affixes in (31), so that if *-um-* has that function, then the others must have it also. But while some languages may have more than one antipassive, the differences are largely syntactic, not the semantic subtleties expressed, for example, in the contrast between *-um-*, *mag-*, *ma-* and *maN-*. This strongly suggests that *-um-* is not a marker of antipassive, but simply a verbal derivational suffix, subject to semantic conditions and in paradigmatic contrast to other such affixes.

2.3 Evidence against the Unergative-Unaccusative Analysis

I have now considered both an active-passive and ergative-antipassive analysis of the Philippine type voice alternations typified by Tagalog (1), Atayal (6) or Kimaragang (8) and marshalled a number of arguments to reject both. The question remains where does this now leave us in trying to understand these languages? There is, of course, a third type, the unergative-unaccusative split type language, and while Tagalog and Kimaragang (Kroeger 1990) unquestionably do have some properties of such languages in their patterns of verbal morphology (Drossard 1984), it is clear that this type is also inappropriate because both unergative and unaccusative intransitive verbs mark their single core argument with *ang*, although they commonly do take different verbal affixes, typically *-um-* for unergatives and *ma-* for unaccusatives:

(32) a. unergative *punta* 'go'
   p-***um***-unta   ***ang***   lalake
   go   man
   'The man went.'

   b. unaccusative *lanta* 'wither'
   ma*-la-lanta*   ***ang***   mga   bulaklak
   IRR-wither   PL   flower
   'The flowers will wither.'

While the hypothesized unergative-unaccusative split does explain some of the variations we find in verbal morphology (as it should if, as we claimed earlier, verbal morphology reflects subtle semantic differences in verbal meaning and the semantics of participants), the fact that the sole core argument of both verb types is marked with *ang* indicates that Tagalog is not *syntactically* of this type. Again Philippine languages seem to slip through the crack of the available syntactic typologies for voice and case marking systems.

3 Conclusion

Let me offer now the possibility that Philippine languages actually belong to a distinct syntactic type, one not covered by any of the three investigated thus far. I will call these languages the symmetrical voice type. To understand more clearly what this type entails, let me summarize first the properties of asymmetrical voice languages typified by nominative-accusative English and ergative-absolutive Dyirbal. Both of these languages have a single NP per clause, the nominative in English and the absolutive in Dyirbal which is selectively treated grammatically vis-a-vis all the other NP types; let's call this type of NP, the pivot (see Dixon 1979 and Foley and Van Valin 1984 for further discussion and justification of this notion). There is a marked preference in each language as to which NP should function as the pivot; this is the actor for a nominative-accusative language like English and the undergoer for an ergative-absolutive language like Dyirbal. This is indicated by the fact that the clause type is the basic form if these NPs are selected as pivot and the verb is morphologically unmarked for voice. If any other NP type, i.e. undergoer for English or actor for Dyirbal, is selected as pivot, a marked clause type occurs and a special voice affix on the verb must be used, passive or antipassive. Hence, voice choice in English and Dyirbal is asymmetrical, because one NP is selectively preferred for pivot choice over all others, a preference clearly signalled in (the lack of) verbal morphology and congruent NP case marking.

Philippine type languages contrast in being symmetrical voice languages. No one NP type is preferred for pivot choice (i.e. *ang* marked NPs in Tagalog); regardless of which choice is made, all are signalled by some overt verbal voice morpheme (e.g. *-um-*, *-in*, *-an*, *i-*, etc). Further, other than the superposition of *ang* marking on the NP choice for pivot, no alterations accrue to the case marking of the NPs in the clause, in marked contrast to the radical rearrangements of case marking required by marked voice options like passive or antipassive in asymmetrical languages. There is no need for such alterations, because symmetrical voice languages do not have unmarked predication orientations toward a particular NP type, nominative or absolutive, as do asymmetrical languages; all options are equally marked (or unmarked as the case may be, the standard terminology fails us here). This suggests that there may be important ramifications of a symmetrical voice system in other aspects of the syntax of these languages. There are indeed, but that is the topic for another paper.

4 References

Blake, F. 1906. The expression of case of the verb in Tagalog. *Journal of the American Oriental Society* 27:183–189.

Cena, R. 1977. Patient primacy in Tagalog. Paper presented at the Annual Meeting of the Linguistic Society of America, Chicago.

Cooreman, A. 1988. The antipassive in Chamorro: variations on the theme of transitivity. In *Passive and voice* ed. M. Shibatani. 561–593. Amsterdam: John Benjamins.

De Guzman, V. 1978. *Syntactic derivation of Tagalog verbs* Oceanic Linguistics Special Publications 16. Honolulu: University of Hawai'i Press.

De Guzman, V. 1979. Morphological evidence for primacy of patient as subject in Tagalog. Paper presented at the Annual Meeting of the Linguistic Society of America, Los Angeles.

Dixon, R. 1972. *The Dyirbal language of North Queensland.* Cambridge: Cambridge University Press.

Dixon, R. 1979. Ergativity. *Language* 55:59–138.

Drossard, W. 1984. *Das Tagalog als Repräsentant des aktivischen Sprachbaus.* Tübingen: Narr.

Egerod, S. 1965. Verb inflection in Atayal. *Lingua* 15:251–282.

Egerod, S. 1966. Word order and word classes in Atayal. *Language* 42:346–369.

Foley, W. & R. Van Valin. 1984. *Functional syntax and universal grammar.* Cambridge: Cambridge University Press.

Gerdts, D. 1988. Antipassives and causatives in Ilokano: evidence for an ergative analysis. In *Studies in Austronesian Linguistics* ed. Richard McGinn. 295–321. Athens, Ohio: Ohio University Center for Southeast Asia studies.

Guilfoyle, E., H. Hung & L. Travis. 1992. SPEC of IP and SPEC of VP: two subjects in Austronesian languages. *Natural Language and Linguistic Theory* 10:375–414.

Huang, L. 1993. *A study of Atayal syntax.* Taipei: Crane Publications.

Kroeger, P. 1988. Verbal focus in Kimaragang. In *Papers in Western Austronesian Linguistics No. 3* ed. Hein Steinhauer. 217–240. Canberra: Pacific Linguistics (A-78).

Kroeger, P. 1990. Stative aspect and unaccusativity in Kimaragang Dusun. *Oceanic Linguistics* 29:110–131.

Kroeger, P. 1993. *Phrase structure and grammatical relations in Tagalog.* Stanford: Center for the Study of Language and Information.

Kroeger, P. 1996. The morphology of affectedness in Kimaragang Dusun. In *Papers in Austronesian Linguistics No. 3* ed. Hein Steinhauer. 33–50. Canberra: Pacific Linguistics (A-84).

McGinn, R. 1988. Government and case in Tagalog. In *Studies in Austronesian linguistics* ed. R. McGinn. 275–293. Athens, Ohio: Ohio University Center for Southeast Asia studies.

Ramos, T. 1974. *The case system of Tagalog verbs.* Canberra: Pacific Linguistics (B-27).

Ramos, T. & M. Bautista. 1986. *Handbook of Tagalog verbs: inflections, modes and aspects.* Honolulu: University of Hawai'i Press.

Rau, D. 1992. *A grammar of Atayal.* Taipei: Crane Publications.

Schachter, P. 1976. The subject in Philippine languages: topic, actor, actor-topic or none of the above. In *Subject and Topic* ed. Charles Li. 491–518. New York: Academic Press.

Schachter, P. 1977. Reference-related and Role-related properties of subject. In *Syntax and Semantics 8: Grammatical Relations* ed. Peter Cole & Jerrold Sadock. 279–306. New York: Academic Press.

Schachter, P. & F. Otanes. 1972. *Tagalog reference grammar.* Berkeley: University of California Press.

Shibatani, M. 1988. Voice in Philippine languages. In *Passive and voice* ed. M. Shibatani. 85–142. Amsterdam: John Benjamins.

Starosta, S., A. Pawley & L. Reid. 1982. The evolution of focus in Austronesian. In *Papers from the Third International Conference on Austronesian Linguistics* vol. 2. ed. Amram Halim, Lois Carrington & S. A. Wurm. 145–170. Canberra: Pacific Linguistics (C-75).

Walton, C. 1986. *Sama verbal semantics: classification, derivation and inflection.* Manila: Linguistic Society of the Philippines.

Wolff, J. 1973. Verbal inflection in Proto-Austronesian. In *Parangal kay Cecilio Lopez* ed. A. Gonzales. 71–91. Philippine Journal of Linguistics Special Monographs 4. Quezon City: Linguistic Society of the Philippines.

Wolff, J. 1979. Verbal morphology and verbal sentences in Proto-Austronesian. In *Austronesian studies: papers from the Second Eastern Conference on Austronesian languages* ed. P. Naylor. 152–168. Ann Arbor: Center for South and Southeast Asian Studies, University of Michigan.

3

Voice and Grammatical Relations in Indonesian: A New Perspective

I WAYAN ARKA AND CHRISTOPHER D. MANNING

1 Grammatical Relations in Indonesian and Theoretical Background

This paper deals with the voice system of Indonesian, and argues that certain of the constructions traditionally analysed as passives should be given a different treatment, parallel to arguments by Kroeger (1993) for Tagalog. We examine the role of different conceptions of subject and their place in binding. We show that, unlike other Western Austronesian languages, the *logical* subject (i.e., the semantically most prominent argument) plays little role in binding: being a logical subject alone does not make an argument a binder. Syntactic prominence is crucial, and in particular the data on binding in Indonesian presented here further confirms the notion of syntacticised argument structure first proposed in Manning (1996b) and also adopted in Arka (2003), wherein a central role is given to the notion of *a-subject*. Like other Austronesian languages, the (surface) *grammatical subject* plays little role, especially in the binding of morphologically complex

Voice and Grammatical Relations in Austronesian Languages.
Simon Musgrave and Peter Austin
Copyright © 2007, CSLI Publications.

reflexives. The data from binding is supported by other syntactic tests such as topicalisation with pronominal copy.

1.1 Grammatical Relations in Indonesian in Brief

Indonesian transitive verbs can appear prefixed with *meN-* or *di-* or without a prefix.[1] With *meN-* verbs (henceforth referred to as agentive voice or AV forms), there is evidence that the logical subject (i.e., the semantically most prominent argument, abbreviated as the l-subject), such as the agent *Amir* in (1), is syntactically the surface grammatical subject (or gr-subject for short, that is, the SUBJ in terms of LFG's f-structure).

(1)   a.   *Amir*   *mem-baca*   *buku*   *itu.*
              Amir   AV-read   book   that
              'Amir read the book.'

Among the important properties of the gr-subject in Indonesian (Vamarasi 1999) are: (a) appears canonically in a preverbal position; (b) the only function that can be questioned by a clefted question word, relativised on or clefted; and (c) the only function that can be controlled, either as an equi-target of certain verbs or as the gapped function in controlled adverbial clauses. An additional test of a morphosyntactic character is that the 3SG pronoun can optionally be just *ia* rather than the usual *dia* when it is functioning as the gr-subject of a clause (adding adverbs etc. shows that this form is indeed grammatically not phonologically conditioned).

Thus, *Amir* in (1a) is the *gr-subject* because it comes preverbally, and it can be **relativised** in a cleft sentence (to give a slightly different pragmatic implication):

(1)   b.   *Amir*   *yang*   *mem-baca*   *buku*   *itu.*
              Amir   REL   AV-read   book   that
              'It is Amir who read the book.'

It can be an equi-target:

        c.   *Amir*   *ingin*   *[__*   *membaca*   *buku*   *itu]*
             Amir   want   AV-read   book   that
             'Amir wants to read the book.'

It can be replaced by *ia*:

---

[1] The meN- prefix takes forms homorganic with a following consonant.

d. *Ia*   *mem-baca*   *buku*   *itu.*
   3SG   AV-read   book   that
   'He read the book.'

It is also widely agreed that the agent of *di-* verbs expressed by a PP, as in (2), is an oblique, while the theme has grammatical subject properties. The grammatical relations in (2) thus mirror an English passive, and one might presume that *di-* is a passive marker. But actually the situation is a little more complicated, as we discuss below.

(2)   *Buku*   *itu*   *di-baca*   **oleh**   **Amir**
      book   that   di-read   by   Amir
      'The book was read by Amir.'

The situation is less clear in other constructions where the *l*-subject is not the gr-subject, namely when it is expressed by the pronominals *saya/kamu/dia* or the clitics *ku-/kau-/-nya*, in the sentences shown in (3).

(3)   a.   *Buku*   *itu*   **saya/kamu/dia**   *baca*
         book   that   1SG/2/3   read
         'The book, I read.'

    b.   *Buku*   *itu*   **ku-/kau-***baca*
         book   that   1SG-/2-read
         'The book, you read.'

    c.   *Buku*   *itu*   *di-baca-nya*
         book   that   di-read-3
         'The book, (s)he read.'

Here the verbs lack the *meN-* (i.e., the AV) marker, being either bare, or prefixed with *di-*. Many studies in Indonesian syntax are unclear as to quite what syntactic status to give such sentences. As suggested by the glosses, such sentences are normally appropriately translated into English with active sentences, but syntactically they have been analysed as passives by previous studies (Chung 1976a; Vamarasi 1999, among others). We discuss these constructions in much more detail below.

1.2   A-structure and Binding Theory in Brief

LFG has proposed a model of parallel representations, and in general prominence can be defined on any level. Accounts such as Dalrymple (1993) and Mohanan (1990) have made use of this to propose that some parts of binding theory may be sensitive to one level, and other parts to another level. In contrast, Manning (1996a) has argued that the principal constraints of binding theory can be defined on a level of syntacticised argument structure (a-str), while admitting that some anaphors may require additional constraints, such as also requiring the binder to be a gr-subject. Within this theory, term or core arguments (that is subjects and various kinds of objects) outrank obliques in a-str, and within each of those groupings, prominence is based on thematic or Lexical Conceptual Structure prominence (following Hellan 1988). Derived forms like passives have a derived argument structure, with different argument structure mappings, while the kind of 'voice' alternations commonly seen in Western Austronesian languages have no effect on argument structure.

2   Binding in the AV Constructions

In the AV constructions marked by meN-, the *l-subject, a-subject and gr-subject* are identical. For example, the relativization test shows that the agent *saya* in (4) is the gr-subject in (4b). By way of contrast, the reflexive object cannot be relativised (4c). It is also the *a-subject*, a-commanding the *reflexive* theme *diri saya* (i.e. the object) in (4a), which we assume to have an argument structure as in (4d)—where the vertical bar is used to separate core or term arguments from obliques. By way of contrast, an attempt to make the gr-subject an anaphor fails as is shown in (4e).

(4)   a.   *Saya*   *menyerahkan*   **diri saya**   *ke*   *polisi.*
             1SG   AV.surrender   self 1   to   police
             'I surrendered myself to the police.'

       b.   *Saya*   **yang**   *menyerahkan*   **diri saya**   *ke*   *polisi.*
             1SG   REL   AV.surrender   self.1   to   police
             'It is me who surrendered myself to the police.'

       c.   * **Diri saya**   **yang**   *saya*   *menyerahkan*   *ke*
             Self.1   REL   1SG   AV.surrender   to
             polisi.
             police
             'It is myself that I surrendered to the police.'

       d.   < *saya, diri saya | polisi* >

       e.   * *Diri saya*   *menyerahkan*   *saya*   *ke*   *polisi*
             Self.1   AV.surrender   1SG   to   police
             * 'Myself surrendered I to the police.'

In short, the l-subject/agent in the AV construction is an *a-subject* (and also a *gr-subject*). Binding in (4) is straightforward and exactly as one would expect from well-known accusative type languages. The data thus far does not serve to isolate any particular analysis.

3 The Status of the Actor in Non-AV Constructions

Binding properties show that non-AV verbs cannot be lumped together as a homogenous class, traditionally simply called passives. In what follows, we discuss a variety of non-AV verbs and examine the syntactic status of their l-subjects based on evidence from reflexive binding.

3.1 The Status of the Actor in Passive Constructions: Evidence from Binding

As shown in (5), an *l-subject* appearing as an oblique PP cannot bind a reflexive functioning as a *gr-subject*. This is consistent with a passive analysis of this construction, with the l-subject being an oblique.

(5)   a.   ?***Dirinya**   *di-serahkan*   *ke*   *Polisi*   *oleh*   *Amir*
           self.3   di-surrender   to   police   by   Amir
           'Himself was surrendered to the police by Amir.'

      b.   ??*Dirinya*   *di-ajukan*   *sebagai*   *calon*   ***oleh***
           self.3   di-nominate   as   candidate   by
           Amir
           Amir
           'Self was nominated as a candidate.'

The same is true for pronominal agents which can appear either as an enclitic to the preposition (*oleh-nya*) or as a prepositional object (*oleh dia*). They cannot bind a reflexive *gr-subject* as shown by the contrast between (6a) and (6b)—(6b) is discussed further below.

(6)   a.   ??***Dirinya***   *yang*   *di-ajukan*   *sebagai*   *calon*
           self.3   REL   di-nominate   as   candidate
           oleh-nya/oleh dia.
           by-3/by 3SG
           'It is himself that is nominated as a candidate by him/her'.
           <'self.3', '3'>

b. | **Dirinya** | yang | dia | ajukan | sebagai | calon |
|---|---|---|---|---|---|
| self.3 | REL | 3 | nominate | as | candidate |

'It is himself that he nominated as a candidate.'
<'3', 'self.3'>

The failure of binding in (5) and (6a) shows that 'semantic' binding does not apply in Indonesian. It is not the case that all l-subjects are possible binders and can bind thematically lower arguments within their clause. Rather, it seems to be the case that, although the passive agent is an l-subject, the crucial fact is that it does not a-command the reflexive, since the reflexive gr-subject is higher in the a-str, because it is promoted in the passive (Manning 1996b; Manning and Sag 1999).[2]

It is not that the passive agent is inert with respect to the binding theory, however. Examine the following sentences with a three-place predicate 'ask':

(7) a. | Amir/dia | menanyai | saya | tentang | dirinya |
|---|---|---|---|---|
| Amir/3SG | AV.ask | 1 | about | self |

'Amir/he asked me about himself.'

b. | Saya | di-tanyai | oleh | Amir/dia/-nya | tentang |
|---|---|---|---|---|
| 1 | di-ask | by | Amir/3SG/3SG | about |

dirinya
self

'I was asked by Amir/him about himself.'

As expected according to the theory of Manning (1996b), the agent oblique can bind other oblique arguments, such as the oblique theme in (7b), because it a-commands such arguments. The argument structure of (7b) would be as in (7c):

(7) c. $<Saya_i, <Amir, -_i, dirinya>>$

Di- verbs cannot appear with a non-third-person agent:

---

[2] Under the theory of Pollard and Sag (1994), or Manning and Sag (1999), the reflexive in (5) or (6a) is an *exempt* anaphor, and should be able to be bound by a suitable discourse referent, but at any rate, binding by the oblique agent does not seem possible here. Other Austronesian languages such as Balinese (Arka 2003) do allow a non-a-commanded exempt reflexive to be bound by the oblique agent.

(8) * *Buku* *itu* *sudah* *di-baca* **oleh-ku/mu**
     book   that   already   di-read   by-1SG/2
     'The book was already read by me/you'

Backgrounding of non-third persons is not possible with the *di-* passive, but it is possible with an otherwise similar construction: the *ter-* verb prefix. The prefix *ter-* has various functions such as expressing a sense of ability or possibility, which generally appears in negative sentences, as in (9a), or an accidental event with a non-volitional doer as in (9b).

(9) a. *Buku*   *itu*   **(tidak)**   *ter-baca*
         book   that   (NEG)   ter-read
         oleh-ku/oleh-mu/oleh-nya
         by-1SG/by-2/by-3
         'The book was (not) readable by me/by you/by him/her.'

     b. *Obat*   *itu*   *ter-makan*   *oleh*   *anak*   *itu*
         medicine   that   ter-eat   by   child   that
         'The medicine was unintentionally taken by the child.'

In all these cases the agent is backgrounded and can be expressed in a PP. In these constructions, the agent again appears to be an oblique, as is shown by the inability to form (10b):

(10) a. *Ia*   *ter-tembak*   *(oleh)*   *teman-nya*
          3   ter-shoot   by   friend-3.POSS
          'He was accidentally shot by his friend.'

      b. * *Dirinya*   *ter-tembak*   *(oleh)*   *Amir*
          self.3   ter-shoot   by   Amir
          *'Amir accidentally shot himself.'

3.2 Verbs with Preverbal Pronominals: Objective Voice Verbs

What is the syntactic status of the NP and pronominal arguments in sentences of the sort represented by (3a)–(b), repeated below?

(3) a. *Buku*   *itu*   **saya/kamu/dia**   *baca*
         book   that   1SG/2/3   read
         'The book, I read.'

     b. *Buku*   *itu*   **ku-/kau-baca**
         book   that   1SG-/2-read
         'The book, you read.'

Cartier (1979) and Alsagoff (1992) treat the pronominal agent of this construction as subject and the patient as a (preposed) object (OBJ in LFG). However, note that the *l-subject* of this type of sentence must be a pronominal (though it can be of any person). A common noun cannot appear in this construction:[3]

(11) a. * *Buku*　*itu*　*orang*　*itu*　*baca*
        book　　that　　man　　the　　read
        'The book, the man read.'

    b. * *Buku*　*itu*　*akan*　*ayah*　*beli*
        book　　that　　FUT　　father　　buy
        'The book, father will buy.'

There are two forms for 1SG and 2SG, and the orthography writes the shorter, perhaps reduced ones as attached clitics, but all of them must appear immediately preceding the verb. (We are unsure at this point whether there is good phonological evidence for regarding any of them as phonologically attached.) Nothing can intervene in between: sentence (12b) is bad because the auxiliary *akan* intervenes; (12c) is bad because an adverb intervenes. This suggests these words occupy a position at the left edge of the VP reserved for pronouns or pronominal clitics rather than the usual subject position.

(12) a. *Rumah*　*itu*　*akan*　*saya*　*jual*
        house　　that　　FUT　　1SG　　sell
        'The house, I will sell.'

    b. * *Rumah*　*itu*　*saya*　*akan*　*jual*
        house　　that　　1SG　　FUT　　sell

    c. * *Rumah*　*itu*　*akan*　*saya*　*besok*　*jual*
        house　　that　　FUT　　1SG　　tomorrow　　sell

The restricted nature and special position of the expression of the l-subject in this construction already raises questions about the viability of the preposed object analysis of Cartier and Alsagoff. Evidence from the subject tests that we introduced in section 2 further serves to demonstrate that it is the patient that is the gr-subj, for it is the one that can be relativised. Recall

---

[3] We exclude a few titles that are used vocatively equivalently to 2nd person pronouns; see Verhaar (1988:353).

that relativisation is an exclusive property of subjects. A preposed object can never be relativised. Sentence (13a) shows a preposed OBJ of the AV verb (acceptable), (13b) shows that relativization of this preposed object is unacceptable, while (13c) shows that the sentence-initial patient of an OV verb can be relativised. The acceptability of (13c) shows clearly that we are dealing with a subject and not a preposed OBJ in this construction.

(13) a. *Orang   itu,   saya   mengajak   kesini*
          person   that   1SG   AV-take   here
          'As for the person, I took (him/her) here.'

      b. **Orang   itu   yang   saya   mengajak   kesini*
          person   that   REL   1SG   AV-take   here
          *'The person, I took (him/her) here.'

      c. *Orang   itu   yang   saya   ajak   kesini*
          person   that   REL   1SG   OV-take   here
          'As for the person, it is me who took (him/her) here.'

A number of further good arguments that the sentence-initial NP in these examples is the gr-subject, rather than just some kind of preposed topic, are presented by Chung (1976a,b).[4] For instance, it is this NP that is the equi-target:[5]

(14) *Saja   mem-bawa   surat   itu   untuk   (dapat)   kau-baca*
      I   AV-bring   letter   the   for   can   you-read
      'I brought the letter to (be able to) be read by you.'

So we conclude that these sentences have the undergoer as gr-subject, appearing in the regular subject position.

Consequently, Vamarasi (1999), roughly following Chung's analysis (1976a), explicitly claims that the *l-subject* or the *initial subject* (i.e. the *initial-1* in Relational Grammar terminology) in a sentence of the type in (3) is a *final 1*-chomeur (i.e. a non-core argument, basically an oblique). However, in what follows we show evidence that the pronominals immediately preceding the verb (3a), the proclitic (3b), and also the enclitic (3c) are still term/core arguments. The evidence is mainly from binding, with some sup-

---

[4] Although, immediately below we disagree with her resulting conclusion that the construction is a passive one.

[5] Facts regarding control targets are however more complex in Austronesian languages; see discussion in Arka and Simpson, this volume.

porting evidence from a pronominal copy test, control, and discourse properties. Hence, in our view, the passive analysis for (3) is untenable.[6]

Before considering the binding evidence, let us note that if the bare form of the verb is used, as in the above examples, then the pronominal form cannot be omitted:

(15) * *Rumah*   *itu*   *akan*   __   *jual*
         house   that   FUT   sell

The fact that the agent must be present already suggests that it is a term, rather than an oblique. Note that sentence (15) is not acceptable in any interpretation, e.g. it cannot be interpreted as having a first or second person l-subject.

3.2.1 Binding Evidence

Evidence from binding further shows that the agent pronominal in this construction has a very different status to a passive agent. Indeed, we argue that it is really a term, hence an *a-subject*. In the following sentences, the reflexive *gr-subjects* can be bound by the preverbal pronominals (16). Evidence that the reflexives are *gr-subjects* comes from their appearance in the canonical subject position and the possibility of cleft formation by *yang* (17). Attempts to cleft a non-subject reflexive (i.e. by making the verbs appear in AV) fail (18)–(19).

(16) a. ***Diri saya***   ***saya***   *serahkan*   *ke*   *polisi*
              Self.3   1SG   surrender   to   police
          'I surrendered myself to the police.'

       b. ***Dirimu***   *mesti*   ***kau***   *serahkan*   *ke*   *polisi*
              Self.2   must   2   surrender   to   police
          'You must surrender youself to the police.'

       c. ***Dirinya***   *mesti*   ***dia***   *serahkan*   *ke*   *polisi*
              Self.3   must   3SG   surrender   to   police
          '(S)he must surrender herself/himself to the police.'

---

[6] That this is not a passive (i.e. the agent is not an oblique) has been recognised by other work such as Cartier (1979) and Alsagoff (1992), however, as we saw above, that led them to regard the undergoer as simply preposed, while the agent remains the gr-subject. We present more evidence to support the termhood of the agent, but denying this latter claim leads us to argue that we are dealing with a syntactically ergative construction, as also suggested (somewhat informally) in Verhaar (1988). Under our proposal, the role of *di-* is simply as marker showing a mapping of undergoer onto subject, a property shared by passive and ergative.

(17) a. **Diri saya**   **yang**   *saya*   *serahkan*   *ke*   *polisi*
               Self.1   REL   1SG   surrender   to   police
               'It is myself that I surrendered to the police.'

      b. **Dirimu**   **yang**   *mesti*   *kau*   *serahkan*   *ke*   *polisi*
               Self.2   REL   must   2   surrender   to   police
               'It is yourself that you must surrender to the police.'

      c. **Dirinya**   **yang**   *mesti*   **dia**   *serahkan*   *ke*   *polisi*
               Self.3   REL   must   3SG   surrender   to   police
               'It is herself/himself that (s)he must surrender to the police.'

(18) a. (self = OBJ)
           Dia   *menyerahkan*   **dirinya**   *ke*   *polisi*
           3SG   AV-surrender   self.3   to   police
           '(S)he surrendered herself/himself to the police.'

      b. * **Dirinya**   **yang**   *dia*   *meny-(s)erahkan*   *ke*   *polisi*
               Self.3   REL   3SG   AV-surrender   to   police
               'It is herself/himself that (s)he surrendered to the police.'

(19) a. (self = OBL)
           Dia   *tidak*   *ingat*   *dengan*   **dirinya**
           3   NEG   remember   with   self.3
           '(S)he did not remember herself/himself.'

      b. (relativisation of OBL)
           * **dengan**   **dirinya**   **yang**   *dia*   *tidak*   *ingat*

Alsagoff (1992:39) claims that reflexives in Malay never appear in the subject position themselves because they require their antecedents to be subjects. According to this analysis, the constraint on the reflexive *diri*-poss, for instance, is that it must be an object (see also Chung 1976b). Thus, the acceptability of reflexives in (16) supports the idea that these are object preposing constructions. However, we regard this view as untenable given the relativisation data in (17)–(18).

    Crucially, note that the binding behaviour here differs from that with the oblique agent appearing in a PP headed by *oleh*, of the type that was shown in (6). This suggests that the syntactic status of the *l-subject* appearing as a preverbal pronominal in a non-AV verb exemplified in (16)–(17) differs from that of an l-subject appearing in the PP with the *di-* verb in (6). The *di-*verb with the PP agent is a passive construction with the agent/l-subject being an oblique. The verb without *meN-* with a preverbal pronominal is not a passive verb. The *l-subject* is a term, and hence an a-subject. This corresponds to the idea that the sentence feels semantically 'active'—it is usually translated as an active—despite the fact that the non-agent argument is the surface gr-subject.

A construction with a cross mapping where an agent a-subject is not a gr-subject, but still a term, and the gr-subject is a non-agent core argument, is an ergative construction (Dixon 1994; Manning 1996b). Following the terminology for Tagalog from Kroeger (1993) and Balinese from Arka (2003) and Wechsler and Arka (1998), the Indonesian verbs with cross-mapping exemplified in (16)-(17) can be labelled as objective voice (OV) verbs. But this 'voice' should really be interpreted as an ergative construction within the language. Given the pervasive evidence from binding cross-linguistically (Manning1996a, 1996b; Arka 2003), it is misleading to collapse OV/ergative constructions with passives, or indeed any of the traditional 'voices'.

3.2.2 Control of Complex Arguments

Additional evidence for preverbal pronouns being terms comes from control of complex arguments. It has been observed that the functional controller of a complex argument is restricted to a term (Bresnan 1982,[7] Arka and Simpson, this volume). For example, the sentence *To go there was asked of John by me* is unacceptable because the controller (*of John*) is not expressed as a term argument. Like Balinese (Arka and Simpson, this volume), Indonesian allows control into a complex argument, including one acting as gr-subject, and crucially the controller must be a term:

(20) a. *Saya/kamu/mereka*   *sudah*   *men-coba*   *[__*
          1SG/2/3pl   PERF   AV-try
          mencari   *kerja*   *di*   *kota]*
          AV-search   job   at   city
          'I/you/they have tried to look for a job in the city.'

      b. *[__*   *men-cari*   *kerja*   *di*   *kota]*   *yang*   *sudah*
                    AV-search   job   at   city   REL   PERF
          saya/kamu/mereka   *coba*
          1SG/2/3pl   try
          'Looking for a job in the city is what I/you/(s)he has tried.'

---

[7] In fact Bresnan's claim was that the functional controller be a semantically unrestricted function, among which she included subject, object and secondary object.

c. ?* [__   men-cari   kerja   di   kota]   yang
                AV-search   job   at   city   REL
    sudah   *di-coba*   *oleh*   *saya/kamu/mereka/Amir*
    PERF   di-try   by   1SG/2/3pl/name
    'Looking for a job in the city is what has been tried
    by me/you/them/Amir.'

Coba 'try' semantically has two arguments: a *trier* (a simple argument) and
the thing tried (a proposition, a complex argument). It is a commitment type
of verb (Sag and Pollard 1991), characterised by having a committer (i.e.
the *trier*) as a controller. (20a) shows the AV construction with the controller as gr-subject (acceptable), (20b) shows the OV construction with the
controller as a preverbal pronoun (acceptable), (20c) shows the controller as
a non-term (oblique) and, crucially, the sentence is then unacceptable. This
test again shows the preverbal pronoun grouping with other terms as opposed to obliques.

3.2.3 Topicalization with a Pronominal Copy

A little further evidence for the pronouns before the verb being term arguments can be derived from examining the construction where an NP becomes an external topic at the left margin of the clause, and then is repeated
by a pronoun within the clause. This is possible when the pronoun is a term
argument, as in (21a), but it is not possible with clear obliques such as the
objects of prepositions, see (21b):

(21) a. *Orang*   *itu,*   *dia*   *tidak*   *mau*   *datang*
          person   that   3SG   NEG   willing   come
          'That person, (s)he refused to come.'

      b. ?* *Orang*   *itu,*   *saya*   *yang*   *di-cari-cari*
          person   that   1   REL   di-search-search
          oleh   *dia*
          by   3SG
          'As for that person, it is me who (s)he is looking for.'

Note now that topicalization with pronominal copy is possible with the pronominal arguments that precede the verb, supporting our regarding them as
term arguments:

(22) *Orang*   *itu,*   *saya*   *yang*   *dia*   *cari-cari*
      person   that   1   REL   3SG   OV.search-search
      'As for the person, it is me who he is looking for.'

3.3 The Distribution and behaviour of -nya

The enclitic *-nya* attached to a head verb always expresses a core argument that is not the gr-subject (what we might call an OBJ or a term-complement to avoid associations between object and patient). It can express an l-subject/agent as in (3c), repeated as (23a), or a patient functioning as an object as in (23b). In this respect the enclitic *-nya* is rather special, since the other enclitics *-ku* '1', *-mu* '2' and *-kau* '2' cannot be understood as l-subjects (23c), but only as undergoers (23d):

(23) a. *Buku   itu   di-baca-nya*
          book   that   di-read-3
          'The book, (s)he read.'

      b. *Dia   men-jelaskan-nya*
          3   AV-explain-3
          'S(he) explained it.'

      c. * *Buku   itu   (di-)baca-ku/-mu*
          book   that   (di-)read-1/-2
          'I/you read the book.'

      d. *Amir   me-lihat-ku/-mu*
          name   AV-see-1/2
          'Amir saw me/you.'
          *'I/you/ saw Amir.'

The enclitic *-nya* cannot however be the *gr-subject* (23e). That is, the structure in (23e) is forced to be an OV construction by dropping *meN-* making the preverbal pronominal agent *dia* a non gr-subject. We attempt to force the enlitic patient *-nya* to act as the gr-subject instead. It fails. In other words, although both the agent and patient arguments of the transitive verb are present in sentence (23e), the sentence is bad because it lacks a gr-subject; neither argument can act as the gr-subject. Note that a normal pronominal gr-subject *can* come post verbally (23f). The point is that *-nya* can appear attached to the verb only when another argument is the gr-subject: in the AV verb (marked by *meN-*, as in (23b)) where *-nya* is the undergoer, or else in the di- verb as in (23a) where *-nya* is the actor.

      e. * *dia   jelaskan-nya*
          3   OV.explain-3
          '(S)he explained it.'

f. *Akan   saya   cari   **dia***
    FUT   1   search 3SG
    'I'm going to look for him/her.'

The enclitic *-nya* can also appear attached to the preposition expressing an oblique agent (24a). As noted previously, the pronominal *dia* is also possible. These forms must again appear with a *di-* verb, hence the unacceptability of (24b). The enclitic *-nya* cannot be doubled with the appearance of the preverbal pronominal *dia* (24c)–(d). (Thus, the contrast between (24a) and (24c)–(d) suggests that *di-* is not really a pronominal, *pace* Vamarasi (1999) who suggests that *di-* is a shortened form of *dia*.)

(24) a. *Buku   itu   sudah   **di**-baca   **oleh-nya** /   **oleh***
         book   that   already di-read   by-3   by
         dia
         3SG
         'The book was already read by him/her.'

     b. * *Buku   itu   sudah   baca   **oleh-nya** /   **oleh***
         book   that   already read   by-3   by
         dia
         3SG

     c. * *Buku   itu   sudah   **dia**   baca-**nya***
         book   that   already 3SG   read-3

     d. * *Buku   itu   sudah   **dia**   baca   **oleh-nya***
         book   that   already 3SG   read   by-3

3.3.1 Binding by an Enclitic -nya Hosted by the Head Verb

The binding behaviour of the enclitic *-nya* attached to the head verb contrasts strongly with the binding behaviour of a passive agent expressed in a PP. Consider:

(25) a. ***Dirinya***   *tidak*   *di-perhatikan-**nya***   <'3', 'self.3'>
         self.3   NEG   di-care-3
         '(S)he didn't take care of himself/herself.'

     b. ***Dirinya***   *selalu*   *di-utamakan-**nya***
         self.3   always   di-prioritise-3
         '(S)he always giving priority to herself/himself.'

It can be concluded that the third person agent appearing in PP is an oblique, whereas the pronominal clitic hosted by the head verb is not, but rather a term complement in an ergative construction. It is still a term and an *a-subject* and so can bind the reflexive *gr-subject*. This perhaps in part motivates its interesting discourse function briefly mentioned below.

3.3.2 Pronominal copy with -nya

The binding evidence supporting *-nya* as a term in a transitive clause is again backed up by evidence for the possibility of topicalization with a pronominal copy, which as we have seen is only possible with term arguments:

(26) Orang   itu,   saya   yang   menolong-nya
      person   that   1   REL   AV.help-3
      'As for the person, I helped him/her.'

3.4 Binding by a Postverbal NP

There is one final complication in the discussion of verbs with a *di-* prefix. Until now, we have shown examples with the agent expressed within a PP. But, somewhat surprisingly, *di-* verbs can also take a postverbal NP agent as in (27). Indeed, when the NP is indefinite as in (27a), the agent NP is preferred to the PP. Some accounts suggest that this is possible because the preposition is in some sense optional, but this does not seem to be correct as a postverbal agent NP is only possible when it is adjacent to the verb (Myhill 1988). Hence the acceptability contrast in (28a)–(d). This suggests that the agent NP occupies a different phrase structure position to the agent PP.

(27) a. Saya   di-pukul   { orang /   ?* oleh   orang }
          1   di-hit   man /   by   man
          'I was hit by someone.'

      b. Saya   di-marah-i   (oleh)   Amir/Ayah
          1   di-angry-APPL   (by)   Amir /father
          'I was scolded by Amir/father.'

(28) a. Saya   di-beli-kan   baju   **oleh**   **Amir**
          1   di-buy-APPL   shirt   by   Amir
          'I was bought a shirt by Amir.'

      b. Saya   di-beli-kan   **Amir**   baju
          1   di-buy-APPL   Amir   shirt
          'I was bought a shirt by Amir.'

c.   * *Saya*   *di-beli-kan*   *baju*   **Amir**
      1   di-buy-APPL   shirt   Amir

d.   ?**Saya*   *di-beli-kan*   **oleh**   **Amir**   *baju*
      1   di-buy-APPL   by   Amir   shirt

The question is, what is the status of the postverbal NP agent? The fact that it occurs without a preposition suggests that it is a term argument. On the other hand, it cannot bind the gr-subject reflexive:

(29)   a.   ?**Dirinya*   *tidak*   *di-perhatikan*   *Amir*
          self.3   NEG   di-care   Amir
          'Himself was not taken care of by Amir.'

      b.   ?* *Dirinya*   *selalu*   *di-utamakan*   *Amir*
          self.3   always   di-prioritise   Amir
          'Amir is always giving priority to himself.'

Furthermore, it cannot bind the theme object:

      c.   *Amir$_i$*   *di-perlihatkan*   *Ayah$_j$*   *foto*   *dirinya$_{i/*j}$*
          Amir   di-show   father   picture   self.3
          'Amiri was shown the picture of himselfi/*j by fatherj.'

If the agent NP *ayah* is a term, it should be a possible binder for *dirinya* because the agent is the thematically most prominent item. This suggests that a bare agent NP following the verb should be regarded as an oblique.

     Further evidence comes from (possessor) topicalisation with a pronominal copy. Consider the possessor topicalisation of the subject (30a), of the object (30b) and of the postverbal agent NP (30c). Only the first two are acceptable. (Sentence (30d) shows the non-topicalised version of (30c).)

(30)   a.   *Orang*   *itu,*   *ayah-**nya***   *mencari-cari*
          person   that   father-3.POSS   AV.search-search
          kamu
          2
          'The person$_i$, his/her$_i$ father is looking for you.'

      b.   *Orang*   *itu,*   *saya*   *yang*   *menolong*
          person   that   1SG   REL   AV.help
          *ayah-**nya***
          father-3.POSS
          'The person$_i$, it is me who helped his/her$_i$ father.'

c. ?*Orang   itu,   kamu   di-cari-cari
    person   that   2   di-search-search
    ayah-**nya**
    father-3.POSS
    'The person$_i$, you are wanted by his/her$_i$ father.'

d. Kamu   di-cari-cari   ayah   orang   itu
    2   di-seach-search   father   person   that
    'You are wanted by the father of the person.'

Myhill (1988) in fact argues that the agent noun is incorporated in this construction. It is unclear to us whether we would want to say that—Myhill is basing this analysis on the loose definition of incorporation from Mithun (1984:849) which covers cases where 'a verb and its direct object are simply juxtaposed to form an especially tight bond. The verb and noun remain separate words phonologically, but ... the N loses its syntactic status as an argument of the sentence, and the VN unit functions as an intransitive predicate'. But it is interesting to note that in this case there is some evidence of the agent noun preceding enclitic particles which are semantically modifying the verb. For example, Myhill gives the example in (31), where the particle -*lah* is giving emphasis to the temporal sequencing of the verb, and not to the agent noun.[8]

(31) Sebuah   talam   yang   berisi   penganan   diangkat
      a   tray   that   full   snacks   brought
      orang-**lah**   ke   hadapan   Sutan   Menjinjing   Alam
      person-**lah**   to   honorific S.   M.   A.
      'A tray full of snacks was brought (by a person) to Sutan
      Menjinjing Alam.'

On the other hand, this construction is definitely not the canonical case of noun incorporation widely discussed in the syntactic literature, since, as Myhill discusses, multiword agent NPs can appear in this construction. At any rate, all the available evidence suggests that the postverbal NP agent is not a term but an oblique, and so we will analyse it thus.

---

[8] This example appears to be from an old text or perhaps Malay. At any rate, it sounds odd to the first author. In contemporary Indonesian -**lah** seems to be in complementary distribution with a post-verbal agent NP.

4 Analysis

To summarize the discussion so far, binding suggests that an agent/*l-subject* can have the syntactic expressions shown in Table 1. Given the a-str based binding theory, only the *l-subject* in AV (row a), OV (row b), and di-verb-nya (row c.i) is a possible binder of term arguments within the same clause in Indonesian.

Table 1: Expression of *l-subject*

	Types of verbs	Nominal types/Category	Syntactic Status
a.	AV verb	non-pron, pron, not -nya	gr-subject & a-subject
b.	OV verb (no di-)	pronominal, proclitic, not non-pronominal	Not gr-subject but a-subject (i.e. still a term)
c.	di- verb	i. -nya hosted by the head V	Not gr-subject but a-subject
		ii. -nya hosted by a P	oblique (i.e. not a-subject)
		iii. (non)-pron expressed in PP/NP	oblique (i.e. not a-subject)
d	ter- verb	NP / PP	oblique (i.e. not a-subject)

In the examples we have seen, the l-subject can be expressed in any of five ways: (i) as a preverbal pronoun; (ii) as a pronominal prefix; (iii) as *-nya* as a suffix to the verb; (iv) as a prepositional phrase headed by *oleh* (and involving either a noun/pronoun or *-nya* again); or (v) as a postverbal oblique NP. Note now that the presence of *di-* in conjunction with *-nya* (i.e. row (c.i.) in Table 1, example (25)) argues that *di-* is not really a passive marker, because clauses with *di-* and *-nya* represent an ergative construction, which is still transitive. Rather, *di-* seems to be best analysed as simply encoding the mapping of an undergoer term to SUBJ (which is only part of what a passive marker does). *Di-* leaves the status of the *l-subject* unspecified, allowing other specifications such as the information structure to determine the exact syntactic expression of the *l-subject*.

While there are various other possibilities, such as gr-subject postposing, it seems that the basic phrase structure for Indonesian that we have to work with is the following:

(32)

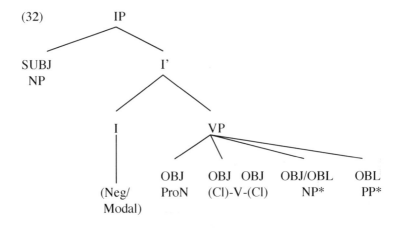

All the verbal clitic positions, including the preceding full pronouns, must be immediately adjacent to the verb and are reserved for words with pronominal meaning that express the object/term-complement of the clause. These are used when the verb remains transitive. As shown by (32), the preverbal positions are positions for agent term complements only. When these positions are occupied, the clause is in the objective voice. The post verbal clitic position is not restricted to an agent. We have observed that -nya appearing in this position can be an agent (example (3c)) or a non agent (example (23a)). However, we note that -nya is somewhat exceptional in this regard, since the other enclitics that appear in this slot only express an undergoer term complement. When the verb has been passivized, these slots cannot be used, but the agent can be realized as an oblique, either as an NP oblique, which again must be adjacent to the verb, or as a PP oblique, which need not be.

These informal remarks raise some questions about how to treat and constrain the alternation between a syntactically active and ergative transitive construction and the passive construction. The most revealing approach appears to be to say that various morphemes serve merely to place constraints on the mapping between argument structure and grammatical relations. Using the terms actor and undergoer as convenient if informal shortcuts for the first two term arguments in the argument structure, and α as a correspondence function picking out the argument structure, we could then suggest the following constraints:

(33) a.   meN-: $(\uparrow \text{SUBJ}) = (\uparrow \alpha \text{ actor})$
      b.   di-: $(\uparrow \text{SUBJ}) = (\uparrow \alpha \text{ undergoer})$
      c.   ter-: $(\uparrow \text{OBLag}) = (\uparrow \alpha \text{ actor})$
      d.   *saya/kamu/dia ku-/kau-* $\downarrow = (\uparrow \alpha \text{ actor})$
           preceding verb:

                                    $(\downarrow \text{PRED}) = \text{'pro'}$
      e.   -ku/-mu/-kau: $\downarrow = (\uparrow \alpha \text{ undergoer})$
      f.   NP inside VP: Cannot express actor
                                    term-complement

These constraints, together with a constraint on mapping to the effect that
there must be a gr-subject (Bresnan and Kanerva 1989) are sufficient to
ensure that only the observed patterns of linking actually occur. The constraint (33f) is somewhat unsatisfactory but reflects that Indonesian does
not allow the free appearance of NP actor term-complements. In this respect
it is like English, and unlike, say, Balinese (Arka 2003). However, actor
term-complements can be expressed by the various pronouns and verbal
clitics. To work through some of the possibilities, in turn:

1. If *meN-* is prefixed to the verb, then the actor must be the subject. The
    other term in a transitive argument structure must become the object
    and can be expressed either as an object NP or via a enclitic suffix on
    the verb.
2. If *di-* is prefixed to the verb, then the subject is the undergoer. This
    could be either because the verb is passivized or because the ergative
    construction is being used.
    a.   If the verb is passivized, then the optional agentive oblique
         can be expressed either as a PP headed by *oleh* or in the im-
         mediately postverbal position for realization of agentive
         obliques that we discussed in 3.3.4.
    b.   If the verb is not passivized, then the actor remains a term ar-
         gument, and must be expressed in the sentence. Since the pre-
         verbal slot for expression is already taken, and an NP inside
         the VP and most of the enclitics cannot express an actor, the
         only possibility is when the agent is realized by *-nya*.
3. If *saya/kamu/dia* immediately precedes the verb or *ku-/kau-* appear as
    proclitics on the verb, then they express the agent, but as an object/term
    complement. Therefore, the undergoer must fill the subject slot. How-
    ever, these are pronominal clitics, and therefore they cannot co-occur
    with another expression of the agent, such as a PP headed by *oleh*.

5   Discourse Implications

Before closing, we will briefly touch on one of the interesting consequences of this analysis for a theory of information structuring, and in particular how it challenges even the simple theory of information structure that is commonly accepted in LFG. This section is largely based on material from McCune (1979). As has already been noted, ergative sentences with *-nya* are naturally translated with actives in English. For example, consider the following text:

(34) *Pe-muda*   *kakatua*   *juga*   *hidup*   *kembali.*
      AG.NR-young   cockatoo   also   alive   return

      Di-pandang-nya   *wajah*   *Peggy*   *dan*   *Peggy*
      di-look-3   face   Peggy   and   Peggy
      me-mandang-nya   *pula.*
      AV-look-3   again

      Di-ambil-nya   *lagi*   *se-helai*   *serbet*   *kertas*   ...
      di-take-3   again   one-sheet   napkin   paper
      dan   ...
      and

   'The young Mr Cockatoo also came back to life. He *looked* at Peggy's face and she looked at him, too. He *took* another paper napkin ... and ...'

The verbs in italics in the free translation are ergative clauses with *-nya* in the original. Note firstly that a passive translation of either of these sentences is implausible. But then note further that the discourse structure here thus goes against what is commonly assumed. Bresnan (2001) suggests that the grammatical subject is universally optionally identified as the default topic of the clause. But in Indonesian narratives, of which this one is quite typical, the subject is not used as a default topic. Rather, after the first sentence, the topic of this excerpt is young Mr Cockatoo, and he is consistently referred to by the term-complement enclitic *-nya*. The subject actually expresses new information, a pattern that is common in Indonesian (and Balinese). In both cases the verb appears before the subject. This option is generally available in Indonesian, and taking it here fits with the general tendency for new information to appear later in the sentence.

It is somewhat unclear whether to view this alternative as subject postposing or verb preposing, but we are tempted to analyse it as the latter because the verb receives some kind of pragmatic prominence in such sentences. On such an analysis, we might propose the structure in (35) for a simplified version of the last sentence in (34):

(35)

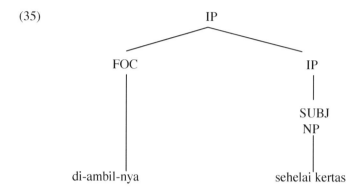

At any rate, this use of the subject position to express new information, which is not the *theme* of the narrative, challenges most existing theories of information structuring, including that of LFG.

Recognising that these sentences with -*nya* are not passives seems part of the solution to the problem, in that we would expect a term argument to have greater discourse prominence than an oblique agent. Recall that the agent of the di-V-nya verb is definite and is not backgrounded. And, at the same time, the syntactic expression (i.e. the c-structure) of the di-V-nya verb being a unit allows the possibility of its fronting to the focus position as shown in (35). This explains the typical ergative word order in Malay/Indonesian observed by Hopper (1983), where the OV verb is followed by the theme NP. But clearly much more work on this topic remains to be done.

6 Conclusion

We have shown that the Indonesian 'passive' should be divided between constructions that are genuinely comparable to an English passive, and ergative constructions that are not. In the ergative construction, we find that term-complement a-subjects can bind gr-subjects, as for Toba Batak (Manning 1996a) and Balinese (Arka 2003). Within the passive constructions, although the oblique agent cannot bind any of the term arguments, it remains a logical subject and can bind other obliques. The Indonesian data presented here thus provide further congruent evidence in support of mixed mappings between argument structure and grammatical relations in Western

Austronesian languages. Finally, the ergative analysis of clauses with *di-V-nya* verbs sheds some light on their use in narrative texts, but raises new challenges for information packaging.

7 References

Alsagoff, L. 1992. Topic in Malay: the other subject. PhD thesis, Department of Linguistics, Stanford University.

Arka, I Wayan. 2003. *Balinese morphosyntax: a lexical-functional approach*. Canberra: Pacific Linguistics (PL 547).

Bresnan, J. 2001. *Lexical Functional Syntax*. Malden MA/Oxford UK: Blackwell.

Bresnan, J. & J. Kanerva. 1989. Locative Inversion in Chichewa: A Case Study of Factorization in Grammar. *Linguistic Inquiry* 20:1–50.

Cartier, A. 1979. Devoiced transitive verb sentences in formal Indonesian. In *Ergativity: Towards a theory of grammatical relations* ed. F. Plank. 161–183. New York: Academic Press.

Chung, S. 1976a. On the Subject of Two Passives in Indonesian. In *Subject and Topic* ed. Charles Li. 57–98. New York: Academic Press.

Chung, S. 1976b. An Object-Creating Rule in Bahasa Indonesia. *Linguistic Inquiry* 7:41–87.

Dalrymple, M. 1993. *The Syntax of Anaphoric Binding*. Stanford: CSLI.

Dixon, R. M. W. 1994. *Ergativity*. Cambridge: Cambridge University Press.

Hellan, L. 1988. *Anaphora in Norwegian and the Theory of Grammar*. Dordrecht: Foris.

Hopper, P. J. 1983. Ergative, passive, and active in Malay narrative. In *Discourse perspectives on syntax* ed. F. Klein-Andreu. 67–88. New York: Academic Press.

Kroeger, P. 1993. *Phrase Structure and Grammatical Relations in Tagalog*. Stanford: CSLI.

Manning, C. D. 1996a. Argument Structure as a Locus for Binding Theory. In *Proceedings of the 1st LFG conference* Grenoble, France.

Manning, C. D. 1996b. *Ergativity: Argument Structure and Grammatical Relations*. Stanford: CSLI.

Manning, C. D. & I. A. Sag. 1999. Dissociations Between Argument Structure and Grammatical Relations. In *Lexical and Constructional Aspects of Linguistic Explanation* ed. G. Webelhuth, A. Kathol & J.-P. Koenig. 63–78. Stanford: CSLI.

McCune, K. 1979. Passive Function and the Indonesian Passive. *Oceanic Linguistics* 18:119–169.

Mithun, M. 1984. The evolution of noun incorporation. *Language* 60:847–894.

Mohanan, T. 1990. Arguments in Hindi, PhD thesis, Department of Linguistics, Stanford University. Published in 1994 as *Argument Structure in Hindi*. Stanford: CSLI.

Myhill, J. 1988. Nominal agent incorporation in Indonesian. *Journal of Linguistics* 24:111–136.

Pollard, C. & I. A. Sag. 1994. *Head-Driven Phrase Structure Grammar*. Chicago: University of Chicago Press.

Sag, I. A. & C. Pollard. 1991. An integrated theory of complement control. *Language* 67:63–113.

Vamarasi, M. A. Kana. 1999. Grammatical Relations in Bahasa Indonesia. Canberra: Pacific Linguistics (D-93).

Wechsler, S. & I Wayan Arka. 1998. Syntactic Ergativity in Balinese: an Argument Structure Based Theory. *Natural Language and Linguistic Theory* 16:387–441.

Verhaar, J. W. M. 1988. Syntactic Ergativity in Contemporary Indonesian. In *Studies in Austronesian Linguistics* ed. Richard McGinn. 347–384. Athens, Ohio: Ohio Center for Southeast Asia Studies.

4

Voice and the Syntax of =a/-a Verbs in Balinese

I WAYAN ARKA

1 Introduction

This paper discusses the syntax of verbs followed by the formative *a* in Balinese. Such verbs are always transitive and have the less agentive argument as subject. In some cases, the agent is omitted as in (1a) and in other cases it is expressed by a PP as in (1b). These two constructions, together with the *ka-* verb (1c), will be contrasted with the AV (agentive voice) construction, in which the verb is marked with a nasal prefix, shown in (1d):

(1)   a.   *Nyoman*   *baang=a*   *pipis*
           PN   OV.give=3   money
           '(S)he gave Nyoman (not someone else) money.'

       b.   *Nyoman*   *baang-a*   *pipis*   *(teken Wayan)*
           PN   give-PASS   money   by Wayan
           'Nyoman was given money (by Wayan).'

Voice and Grammatical Relations in Austronesian Languages.
Simon Musgrave and Peter Austin
Copyright © 2007, CSLI Publications.

c. | *Gumi-ne* | *ka-prentah* | *(antuk/teken* | *bangsa* |
|---|---|---|---|
| country-DEF | PASS-govern | by | people |

gelah)
own
'The country is governed (by our own people).'

d. | *Ia* | *maang* | *Nyoman* | *pipis* |
|---|---|---|---|
| 3 | AV.give | PN | money |

'(S)he gave Nyoman money.'

There is evidence that the verb with the *ka-* prefix (1c) is the real passive in Balinese (Arka and Wechsler 1996; Artawa 1994). Traditionally, (1a-c) are all analysed as passives (Barber 1977; Hunter 1988; Kersten 1970), in contrast to the 'active' sentence (1d), without any clear supporting argument as to why this is the case (except, apparently, the fact that the subject is not an actor). While it is made explicit in Arka and Wechsler (1996) and Artawa (1994) that the *-a* verb without PP (1a) is not passive, there has not been explicit discussion of the status of the *-a* verb with a PP (i.e. constructions of the type (1b)).

In what follows, I argue that the bound form *-a* leads a double life, as a pronominal clitic, and also as a grammatical marker functioning as a passive marker; this is reflected in my glossing of =a in (1a) and *-a* (1b). My view therefore differs from Artawa (1994) and Clynes (1995) in that I analyse the *-a* verbs as *real* passive verbs in certain circumstances. The presence of the PP agent (oblique) renders the construction grammatically passive. In the absence of the PP oblique, out of context, it may be ambiguous between passive and non- passive (more precisely, objective voice or OV) verb. My view also differs from the traditional analysis of Balinese (Barber 1977; Hunter 1988; Kersten 1970) in that I do not share the view that all *-a* verbs are passives. Nor do I follow these scholars in collapsing the grammatically distinct voice which I call objective voice (OV) with passive. A non-third person agent of OV appears as a free (i.e. not bound) form and there is convincing evidence that such free pronominals are not obliques. Evidence that such arguments are not obliques comes from a number of tests, e.g. they can bind a subject reflexive and they can take quantifier float (see Arka 2003, Wechsler and Arka 1998). Hence it is wrong to analyse the construction as passive. I argue below that many of the occurrences of *-a* verbs in real texts belong to the objective voice, not to the passive.

The purpose of this paper is to show that the *-a*/=a verbs belong to two distinct voices. First, I will present evidence showing that the free pronoun *ia* is in complementary distribution with *a*. This evidence forces the conclusion that *a* can be a bound pronominal in certain contexts. Then, I discuss the status of the bound pronominal marker =a, giving evidence from grammatical tests showing that =a is a core argument of the OV verb. Finally, I argue that grammaticalization has resulted in -a being reinterpreted as a passive marker in another context. A number of syntactic tests are given to support the passive analysis.

2 Distribution of the Free Pronoun *ia* '3' and its Corresponding Bound Form =a

The distributions of the clitic =a and the free pronoun *ia* '3rd person' are mutually exclusive. The clitic appears only on the OV verb if it is the OV agent, as in (1a), repeated as (2a). The corresponding non-clitic pronoun agent *ia* is not possible (2b). Elsewhere, the pronoun *ia* must be used, and the enclitic =a is not allowed; e.g. as the AV patient in (3), as the non-subject benefactive or the theme of the ditransitive verb, as in (4)-(5), or as the single argument of an intransitive verb irrespective of the intransitive type, as in (6).

(2) a. *Nyoman*   *baang=**a***   *pipis*
      PN   OV.give=3   money
      '(S)he gave Nyoman (not someone else) money.'

    b. **Nyoman*   *baang*   *ia*   *pipis*

(3) a. *Nyoman*   *ningalin*   *ia*
      PN   AV.see   3
      'Nyoman saw him/her.'

    b. **Nyoman*   *ningalin=**a***

(4) a. *Nyoman*   *nyemak-ang*   *ia*   *jaja*
      PN   AV.take-APPL   3   cake
      'Nyoman took cake for him/her.'

    b. **Nyoman*   *nyemak-ang=**a***   *jaja*

(5) a. *Nyoman*   *alih-ang*   *cang*   *ia*
      PN   OV.look.for-APPL   1   3
      'I searched him/her for Nyoman.'

    b. **Nyoman*   *alih-ang*   *cang=a*

(6)   a.   *Ia   ulung/ malaib*
           3   fall/ run
           '(S)he fell/ran.'

      b.   *Ulung=**a** /   malaib=**a***

The following show that the free pronoun *ia* is used for obliques, =*a* is not possible:

(7)   a.   *Nyoman   pedih   teken   ia*
           PN   angry   with   3
           'Nyoman was angry with him/her.'

      b.   * *Nyoman   pedih   teken=**a***

(8)   a.   *Nyoman   ngentung-ang   yeh   sig   **ia**-ne*
           PN   AV.throw-APPL   water   to   3-DEF
           'Nyoman threw water to him/her.'

      b.   **Nyoman   ngentung-ang   yeh   sig=**a**-ne*

The free pronoun *ia*, not the clitic =*a*, is also used as the possessor:

(9)   a.   *umah   **ia**-ne*   b.   * *umah=**a**(ne)*
           house   3-DEF
      c.   *umah-**ne***
           house-3.POSS
           'his/her house'

It should be noted that the actual definite suffix in Balinese is -*e*. It gets a linker (-*n*-), when the preceding noun ends in a vowel, as in (9a). The possessive pronoun itself is -*ne*, hence definite -*ne* (9a) and possessive -*ne* (9c) are homophones. The possessive suffix can also get the linker when the preceding noun ends in a vowel, e.g. as in *lima-n-ne* 'his/her hand'.[1]

    Clitic =*a* can, however, appear (optionally) with the preposition *ajak* 'with' in the complex quantifier *ajak(=a) liu/makejang* 'with many/all of them' when the referent is animate. Even in this context, it is mutually exclusive with *ia* (?**ajak ia liu/makejang*). The distribution of clitic =*a* with a preposition seems to be restricted to this possibility.

---

[1] Presumably -*ne* might have come from *n*+*ia* (i.e. the convergence of the proto Austronesian genitive maker *n- and the vowel 'sandhi' of -*e* (<*ia*).

3   Double Function of =a/-a

The bound form =a/-a has a double function in contemporary Balinese: (i) it is a clitic with a referential meaning, and (ii) it is a passive marker. It may be the case that the second function develops from (i.e. is a grammaticalization of) the first:[2] the clitic has lost its syntactic status as an independent argument (having semantic content) to become a syntactic marker.[3] The shift appears to be functionally motivated in the grammatical system of Balinese (to be discussed shortly).

3.1   The Pronominal Clitic =a

I now present the evidence for the claim that =a is a pronominal clitic bearing a syntactic function.

First, it is a (pronominal) clitic because, unlike free pronouns, it must be attached to a host and cannot stand by itself. Additionally, it is a clitic, not a suffix, because it has four out of six common properties of clitics as opposed to inflectional suffixes which are cited in Zwicky (1985), Zwicky (1987), and Zwicky and Pullum (1983): it is not only attached to verbs, there is no gap in the relevant set of combinations, it is morphophonologically regular,[4] and it is semantically regular. In terms of its position in word structure, it must be outside all other formatives (i.e. in outermost or final position). Thus, for example, it must appear after the applicative/causative suffixes such as -in and -ang:

(10)   a.   tegak-in=a
            sit-APPL=3
            '(S)he sits on something.'

       b.   *tegak=a-in

---

[2] The grammaticalization is not yet complete, however, because the -a passive still retains the third-person feature restriction. That is, the -a passive cannot take a first or second person oblique agent. See example (21c).

[3] Hunter (1988) has a similar view (based on pragmatic reasons). However, he does not give any syntactic evidence to support his stance. His approach also differs from mine in that he does not distinguish the grammatically distinct voice labelled here as OV.

[4] Morpho-phonologically its form is shorter than the free pronoun ia, from which it is undoubtedly derived historically. In standard Balinese, -na (instead of =a) is used when the host is vowel-final (e.g. beli=na 'buy=3') but in the Badung dialect, the clitic =(n)a is invariably =a (i.e. the vowel/consonant final of the host is not a condition). The -n- is a reflect of the Proto-Austronesian genitive marker (Ross 2004; Kikusawa 2001).

    c.   *tegeh-ang=a*
           high-CAUS=3
           '(S)he made it high.'

    d.   *tegeh=a-ang*

Also, unlike the free pronoun, it cannot be stressed. These are typical morpho-phonological properties of clitics cross-linguistically.

    Second, though morpho-phonologically it looks like an affix (i.e. in being bound to an OV host), semantically and syntactically it is like a free pronoun. It contains an index (i.e. it is referential) and it functions as a syntactic unit (i.e. as an argument of the head verb). The evidence comes from binding. Example (11) shows that the third-person pronoun can bind the reflexive *awakne* in either form: as free pronoun (11a), or as enclitic (11b):

(11)   a.   *Ia*   *tusing*   *ngrungu-ang*   *awakne*
                  3   NEG   AV.care-APPL   self.3

        b.   *Awakne*   *tusing*   *rungu-ang=a*
                 self.3   NEG   OV.care-APPL=3
                 '(S)he did not care about himself/herself.'

        c.   *ia*   *=a*
                      | |
        'care < '3'$_i$, 'refl.3'$_i$>'   'care < '3'$_i$, 'refl.3'$_i$>'

It has been argued (Manning 1996a, b) that the two sentences of the type shown in (11a) and (b) share an argument structure (a-structure), shown as having its arguments within angle brackets in (11c). I am assuming a syntacticised a-structure as discussed in Arka 2003; Manning 1996a, b; Wechsler and Arka 1998. Crucially, the a-structure contains syntactic information specifying the termhood, i.e. whether an argument is term/core or not. A core outranks a non-core and within a set of cores/non-cores, the arguments are ranked thematically. Crucially, in both (11a) and (11b), the 3rd person pronominal binds the reflexive. Therefore, it must be a core argument in both cases in order that it can a-command the reflexive. X a-commands Y roughly means: 'X is more prominent than Y, and X and Y are arguments in the same a-structure'. The only differences are the morphological realisations and grammatical functions of the third-person argument: the preverbal free pronoun *ia* (11a) is subject whereas the clitic *=a* (11b) is not subject because the subject in this sentence is the reflexive *awakne*. The evidence for *ia* in (11a) and *awakne* (11b) being subject comes from relativisation:

(12) a. *Ia   ane   tusing   ngrunguang   awakne*
          3   REL   NEG   AV.care   self.3
          'It is him/her who does not care of himself/herself.'

     b. *Awakne   ane   tusing   runguang=a*
          self.3   REL   NEG   OV.care=3
          'It is himself/herself that (s)he does not care for.'

In short, the enclitic =*a* in (11b), just like the free pronoun *ia* (11a), bears an index (a semantic referent) and is linked to a core argument position in the a-structure.

   Third, the evidence that the pronominal clitic has an index comes from its 'anaphoric' function (in the general sense of referring back in a text). Sentence (13b) appears after sentence (13a) in the quoted text:

(13) a. *Keto   masih   Nyoman Santosa   tanpa   bayu*
          that   same   PN   without   energy
          nglantas   ngelut   Made Arini   (TLS: 104) [5]
          then   AV.embrace   PN
          'Similarly then Nyoman Santosa could not resist hugging Made Arini.'

     b. *Tekek-ang=a   pesan,   buka   tusing   lakar*
          tight-CAUS=3   very   as.if   NEG   FUT
          lebang=a   buin.   (TLS: 104)
          OV.release=3   again
          'He tightly hugged her as if he would not release her again.'

In (13a), two persons are mentioned, *Nyoman Santosa* (a boy) and *Made Arini* (a girl).[6] In (13b), the two persons are referred to by a zero pronominal (i.e. the subject of *tekek-ang=a* 'make tight') and a clitic =*a*. The zero pronominal refers to *Made Arini* and the clitic refers to *Nyoman Santosa*, not the other way around. The pronominal clitic does not distinguish between male and female referents, but generally there is no ambiguity about its anaphoric relation because it must refer to the agent. One can therefore easily track down which is the agent and which is the patient depending on

---

[5] Throughout this paper, the sources of texts are shown after the examples. The abbreviations are explained at the end of the paper, and the numbers refer to page numbers in the sources.

[6] In the Balinese naming system, a male person's name generally ends in -*a* (e.g. *Santosa*, *Putra* etc.) and a female's name ends in -*i* (e.g. *Arini*, *Putri*, etc.).

the flow of the discourse. Since the clitic must be an OV agent and the sentences describe the event of 'hugging', the clitic =a must refer to *Made Santosa*, the agent of (13a), the person who hugged the girl.

Fourth, like a free pronoun, it can take a quantifier *ajak makejang* 'with all' to mean 'all of them':

(14) a. *Ia*   *ajak*   *makejang*   *nyilih*   *buku*
          3   with   all   AV.borrow   book

      b. *Buku*   *silih=a*   *ajak*   *makejang*
          book   OV.borrow=3   with   all
          'They all borrowed books.'

Note that in both cases we get the third-person plural meaning. Here is another example of quantification with a different quantifier:

(15) *I Ubuh*   *paksa=na*   *ajaka*   *liu*   (SB)
      ART PN   OV.force=3   with   many
      'Many of them forced I Ubuh.'

That the free and bound pronominals can be pluralised/quantified in the same way suggests that the bound pronominal clitic has semantic content. The real (*ka-*) passive, on the other hand, cannot have quantifier modification in this way, as shown by (16). Sentence (16) suggests that *ka-* is really a passive marker having no referential content. *Sareng sami/akeh* '(lit.) with all/many' is the high-register[7] variant of *ajak makejang/liu*:

(16) ?**Cakepan*   *ka-selang*   *sareng*   *sami /akeh*   (h.r.)
      book   PASS-borrow   with   all/many
      'Books were borrowed by all/many of them.'

Fifth, the clitic cannot be doubled by a clause-internal free pronoun or a clause-internal NP, as exemplified by (17a). This supports the idea that the agent clitic is linked to the a-subject argument. There can be only one a-subject/logical subject, so the addition of another free pronoun makes the sentence unacceptable because the free pronoun *ia* (or NP *Wayan*) is left dangling. However, doubling it with a clause external NP functioning as topic is acceptable as in (17b).

---

[7] Balinese basically has two registers (high and low). High register is indicated with (h.r.) after the relevant example. Low register is unmarked.

(17) a.   *Nyoman   tusing   tingalin=a   ia/   Wayan
              PN   NEG   OV.see=3   3   PN
              '(S)he/Wayan did not see Nyoman.'

      b.   *I*   *Bapa,*   *I*   *Nyoman*   *ane*   *pedih-in=a*
           ART father   ART PN   REL   angry-APPL=3
           'As for Father, it was Nyoman who he was angry at.'

The *ka-* passive, on the other hand, although commonly followed by a PP, may appear with an NP. Although rare, this usage is attested in real texts. (18) shows that the *ka-* passive formed out of the same stem *temah* 'curse' is found with an agent NP (a) as well as with an agent PP (b) in the same text:

(18) a.   *Yan*   *saja*   *ka-temah*   *Widi,*   *ngenken*   *nu*
           If   really   PASS-curse   God   why   still
           masliweran   *di*   *gumi-ne*   *tenenan?*   (KA:115)
           wandering   in   world-DEF   this
           'If he has really been cursed by God, why is he still wandering around here?'

      b.   *Ane*   *terang*   *gati*   *ia*   *suba*   *ka-temah*
           REL   clear   very   3   already   PASS-curse
           ban   *Widi*   (KA: 127)
           by   God
           'What is very clear is that he has been cursed by God.'

Finally, *=a* (19c), like the free pronoun *ia* (19a,b), can function as a resumptive pronoun. The real (*ka-*) passive, however, cannot serve as a resumptive pronoun (19d).

(19) a.   *I*   *meme,*   *ia*   *suba*   *teka*
           ART   mother   3   already   come
           'As for Mother, she has come.'

      b.   *I*   *meme,*   *apa*   *Nyoman*   *ningalin*   *ia ?*
           ART   mother   what   PN   AV.see   3
           'As for Mother, did you (Nyoman) see her?'

      c.   *I*   *meme,*   *apa*   *jakan=a*   *di*   *paon?*
           ART   mother   what   OV.cook=3   at   kitchen
           'As for Mother, what is she cooking in the kitchen?'

d.	*?*I biyang,	napi	ka-tumbas	ring	pasar?
	ART mother	what	PASS-buy	at	market

'As for Mother, what did she buy in the market?' (h.r.)

Note that example (19d) is fine if *biyang* 'Mother' (i.e. without the article *I*) is used vocatively to mean 'you, Mother': 'Mother, what is being bought (by you) in the market?' This use of passive is motivated by politeness (i.e. it is an avoidance strategy against addressing the second person directly).

To conclude, the *=a* clitic has the properties shown in (20), where the points in (b-e) distinguish it from the (real) *ka-* passive:

(20) a. It is a pronominal clitic, morphologically bound to a host (OV verb).

b. It has referential content (an index); it can be quantified by *ajak makejang* 'all', it can function as a resumptive pronoun, and it can refer back in a discourse.

c. Semantically, it is the OV actor; since it is itself an argument, doubling with another clause internal (agent) free pronoun/NP is not possible.

d. Syntactically, it cannot be the grammatical subject of the OV.

e. It is a term (core argument, an a-subject/logical subject), not an oblique, because it can bind another argument item (e.g. the grammatical subject).

3.2 The -a Passive: Grammaticalization

Evidence from binding and other properties summarised in the preceding section shows that the clitic is an argument (i.e. a-subject). However, there is evidence that the *-a* verb followed by a PP agent shows the properties of a passive construction. What must have happened is that the bound form has changed to become a passive-like suffix. There is a functional reason for this, which I deal with presently. I claim that the bound form *=a/-a* leads a double life in contemporary Balinese. More correctly, there are two kinds of *a*: enclitic *=a* and passive *-a*.[8]

---

[8] The development of a person marker to become a passive marker is not unique to Balinese. Indonesian passive *di-* may have developed from the pronominal *dia* '3', although there is no clear evidence for this (Guilfoyle, Hung, and Travis 1992; Kana 1999; Shibatani 1994), but see Ross (2002) for different hypotheses of its historical development. Other languages reported to show similar development are Ainu, Kimbundu (Bantu), and Trukic (Austronesian) (Shibatani 1994).

The view that both the =*a* clitic and the -*a* passive are historically related is supported by the fact that the -*a* passive is constrained to have a third-person actor (see example (21c) below). Hence, the grammaticalization to become passive is not complete yet. Nevertheless, syntactically speaking, the -*a* passive has more in common with the *ka*- passive (and passives in other languages) than with its clitic counterpart (i.e. the =*a* clitic in the OV construction). Evidence will be given shortly.

The grammaticalization of -*a* to become a passive marker is motivated by the grammatical system of Balinese. The real passive (i.e. the *ka*- passive) is generally used in the high register.[9] Since the low register has no passive, there is a need to fill in the gap for backgrounding the agent, a need which is handled by the *ka*- passive in the high register. In the low register, -*a* followed by a PP agent comes to the rescue and functions just like a passive construction. I will argue that, for syntactic reasons, in such a case, the bound form -*a* *is* a passive marker.

3.3   Syntactic Evidence for the -a Passive

The following evidence shows that the -*a* verb followed by a PP agent is syntactically passive. (The -*a* verb also shows the semantics/pragmatics of passives, see Arka (2003)).

First, there is the categorial expression of the agent. As is normal in passive constructions cross-linguistically (and the *ka*- passive in Balinese), the agent is marked by a preposition. The preposition for the *ka*- passive is normally *antuk*, but it can also be *teken* (e.g. (21a)). The same preposition is used to mark the agent of the -*a* passive (21b). However, it should be noted that, unlike the *ka*- passive as in (21a), the -*a* passive cannot take a non-third person agent. Hence, (21c) is not acceptable.

(21)	a.	*Bli*	*Man*	*sida*	*masih*	*ka-tepuk*	*teken*
		Brother	PN	can	still	PASS-see	by
		tiang.	(TLS:103)				
		I	(h.r.)				

'(Lit.) Brother Man can still be seen by me.'
'I can still see Brother Man.'

---

[9] Historically, it was borrowed from Old Javanese (Clynes 1995; Hunter 1988).

b. | *Bli* | *Man* | *nyidaang* | *masih* | *tepuk-a* |
|---|---|---|---|---|
| Brother | PN | can | still | see-PASS |

    teken   *Made Arini*
    by   PN

    'Brother Man can still be seen by Made Arini.'

c. | **Bli* | *Man* | *nyidaang* | *masih* | *tepuk-a* |
|---|---|---|---|---|
| Brother | PN | can | still | see-PASS |

    teken   *tiang*
    by   I

    'Brother Man can still be seen by me.'

Second, the PP agent of the *-a* passive is not simply doubling the bound form *-a*. The PP agent following the *-a* verb is indeed an argument. Therefore, the *-a* affix, like its high-register counterpart *ka-*, is a passive marker. This analysis is supported by the evidence showing that the PP agent of the *-a* passive behaves in the same way as the PP agent of the *ka-* passive with respect to binding. The point is that the agent is grammatically an oblique, not a core/term argument. (Recall that the pronominal clitic *=a* is a core argument, see example (11)). To illustrate the point, consider the following contrast where we have a cliticised OV verb (22a), an *-a* passive (22b) and a *ka-* passive (22c):

(22) a. | *Anak-e* | *cenik* | *ento*$_i$ | *edengin=a*$_j$ | *awakne*$_{i/j}$ |
|---|---|---|---|---|
| person-DEF | small | that | OV.show=3 | self.3 |

    di   *kaca-ne*
    at   mirror-DEF

    'He$_j$ showed the child$_i$ himself$_{i/j}$ in the mirror.'

b. | *Anak-e* | *cenik* | *ento*$_i$ | *edengin-a* | *awakne*$_{i/*j}$ |
|---|---|---|---|---|
| person-DEF | small | that | show-PASS | self.3 |

    di   *kaca-ne*   *teken*   *ia*$_j$
    at   mirror-DEF   by   3

    'The child$_i$ was shown himself$_{i/*j}$ in the mirror by him$_j$.'

c. | *Anak-e* | *alit* | *punika*$_i$ | *ka-edengin* | *ragane*$_{i/*j}$ |
|---|---|---|---|---|
| person-DEF | small | that | PASS-show | self.3 |

    ring   *kaca-ne*   *antuk*   *ida*$_j$
    at   mirror-DEF   by   3

    'The child$_i$ was shown himself$_{i/*j}$ in the mirror by him$_j$.'

The enclitic *=a* (22a) is the a-subject (core) and can bind the reflexive (i.e. it can be interpreted as indexed with *j*). The appearance of a PP agent *teken* *ia* in the *-a* passive (22b) gives rise to a different binding where co-indexation by *j* is not possible. Precisely the same situation is observed in the corresponding *ka-* passive (22c). This supports the view that the agent PP (22b,c) does not have the same syntactic status as the enclitic agent *=a* in (22a). That is, the passive agent in (22b,c) is an oblique, not a core argument.

More evidence that the PP agent of the *-a* passive is an oblique comes from quantifier binding. Example (23a) shows the *-a* passive and (23b) the *ka-* passive. They exhibit the same pattern with respect to binding of the pronominal *-ne/ipun* by the quantifier *sabilang* 'every':

(23)   a.   *Sabilang*   *anak*   *cenik$_i$*   *beli-ang-a*   *teken*
            every   person   child   buy-APPL-PASS   by
                           [core]&[ben]

            bapan-ne$_i$ *tas*
            father-3.POSS   bag
            [obl]&[agent]
            'A bag was bought for every child$_i$ by his$_i$ father.'

       b.   *Sabilang*   *anak*   *alit$_i$*   *ka-ambil-ang*
            every   person   small   PASS-take-APPL
                           [core]&[ben]

            ajengan   *antuk*   *reraman*   ***ipun$_i$** -e*
            food   by   parents   3.POSS-DEF
                           [obl]&[agent]
            'Food was taken for every child$_i$ by his$_i$ parents.'   (h.r.)

The pronominals *-ne* (*-a* passive, 23a) and *ipun* (*ka-* passive, 23b) are associated with the agent PPs. The binder (i.e. the quantifier *sabilang*) is associated with benefactive/goal NPs (*sabilang anak cenik / alit* 'every child'). Given the constraint on quantifier binding that the binder must be syntactically more prominent than the bindee (Bresnan 1995a; Bresnan 1995b; Bresnan 2001), we can conclude that the agent PPs in the two sentences above must be obliques, less prominent than the NPs containing the quantifier (which are core arguments).

The same also holds for the following locative applicative *-a* passive (24):

(24) a. *Sabilang*   *banten $_i$*   *jang-in-a*   *teken*
      Every   offering   put-APPL-PASS   by
      *penyuun-**ne** $_i$*   *pinget*
      carrier-3.POSS   mark
      'On every offering$_i$, a mark was put by its $_i$ carrier.'

     b. **Pinget*   *jang-in-a*   *teken*   *penyuun-**ne** $_i$*
       mark   put-APPL-PASS   by   carrier-3.POSS
       sabilang   *banten $_i$*
       every   offering
       'A mark was put by its $_i$ carrier on every $_i$ offering.'

Sentence (24a) is fine because the pronominal *-ne* of *penyuun-ne* 'its car-rier' in the PP agent oblique is bound by the quantifier in the applied loca-tive NP *sabilang banten* 'every offering'. This suggests that the applied locative NP is a core argument. (A core argument is more prominent than a non-core argument (Bresnan 2001; Manning 1996a,b; Wechsler and Arka 1998)). Note that, if we assume that the agent is also a core argument, bind-ing would fail because the agent is thematically higher than the locative argument. (Within a set of core or non-core arguments, prominence is de-termimed by thematic prominence (Manning 1996b).) Sentence (24b) is bad because the word-order constraint on operator binding is violated.

    Now, if the analysis (that the PP agent is OBL) is correct, three predic-tions follow. First, a quantifier associated with the agent PP must not be able to bind a pronominal associated with the benefactive or theme core argument. This prediction is borne out. In the *-a* passive (25a,b) below, linear order is respected; but the sentences are bad because the quantifier *sabilang* is associated with an oblique and the pronominal *-ne* that it binds is associated with a core argument.

(25) a. **Buku*   *baang-a*   [*teken*   *sabilang*   **guru** $_{i}]_{obl}$*
      book   give-PASS   by   every   teacher
      [*murid-**ne** $_{i}]_{core}$*
      student-3.POSS
      'Books were given by every teacher $_i$ to his $_i$ student.'

     b. **Pinget*   *jang-in-a*   [*teken*   *sabilang*
       mark   put-APPL-PASS   by   every
       penyuun $_{i}$ $]_{obl}$*   [*banten-**ne** $_{i}]_{core}$*
       carrier   offering-3.POSS
       'A mark was put by every carrier $_i$ on his $_i$ offering.'

The same prediction holds for the *ka-* passive, as in:

(26) *Ajengan   ka-ambli-ang   [antuk   sabilang
      food   PASS-take-APPL   by   every
      rarama$_i$] $_{obl}$ [anak alit-**ipun** $_i$ -e]$_{core}$
      parents   person small-3-DEF
      'Food was taken by every parent $_i$ for his $_i$ child.'   (h.r.)

Second, given the idea that within the group of obliques, a passive agent oblique is more prominent than other obliques, then the quantifier associated with the agent oblique is predicted to be able to bind a pronominal in the other obliques. This is also confirmed. Consider *jang-a* (27a), which is the non-applicative counterpart of *jang-in-a* in (24). Note that this sentence, in contrast to (25b), is acceptable: the pronominal in the locative item *banten-ne* 'his offering' can be bound by the quantifier of the agent oblique. The same holds for the *ka-* passive, as shown by (27b):

(27) a.   *Pinget*   *jang-a*   *teken*   *sabilang*   *panyuun* $_i$
           marker   put-PASS   by   every   carrier
                                              agent-OBL

           di/sig   *banten-**ne*** $_i$
           in   offering-3.POSS
                       LOC-OBL
           'A mark was put by every carrier $_i$ on his $_i$ offering.'

      b.   *Jinah-e*   *ka-tarik*   *antuk*   *sabilang*   *nasabah* $_i$
           money-DEF   PASS-draw   by   every   customer
                                                    agent-OBL

           ring   *bank*   *ipun* $_i$ (h.r.)
           at   bank   3
                      LOC-OBL
           'The money was drawn by every customer $_i$ at his $_i$ bank.'

Third, if the voice marking is switched to AV, binding must be acceptable because the agent is now a core (i.e. a-subject/SUBJ) and the most prominent item. Crucially, it must be able to bind a pronominal in any other argument of the verb. This prediction is borne out (28)-(30). In these double-complement constructions, the quantifier in the subject (agent) NP can systematically bind the pronominal in the two complements (OBJs and OBLs):

(28) a.   *Sabilang*   *guru*$_i$ *maang*   *murid-ne*$_i$
              Every   teacher   AV.give   student-3.POSS
              buku
              book
              'Every teacher$_i$ gave his$_i$ student a book.'
              (binding of 1st complement)

      b.   *Sabilang*   *guru*$_i$ *maang*   *murid-e*
              Every   teacher   AV.give   student-DEF
              bukun-ne$_i$
              book-3.POSS
              'Every teacher$_i$ gave the student(s) his$_i$ book.'
              (binding of 2nd complement)

(29) a.   *Sabilang*   *panyuun*$_i$ *nyang-in*   *banten-ne*$_i$
              Every   carrier   AV.put-APPL   offering-3.POSS
              pinget
              mark
              'Every carrier$_i$ put a mark on his$_i$ offering.'
              (binding of 1st complement)

      b.   *Sabilang*   *panyuun*$_i$ *nyang-in*   *bante-ne*
              Every   carrier   AV.put-APPL   offering-DEF
              pinget-ne$_i$
              mark-3.POSS
              'Every carrier$_i$ put his$_i$ mark on the offering.'
              (binding of 2nd complement)

(30) a.   *Sabilang*   *nasabah*$_i$ *narik*   *jinah*   *ipun*$_i$*-e*
              every   customer   AV.draw   money   3.POSS-DEF
              ring   *bank*   *(h.r.)*
              at   bank
              'Every customer$_i$ drew his$_i$ money from the bank.'
              (binding of 1st complement)

      b.   *Sabilang*   *nasabah*$_i$ *narik*   *jinah*   *ring*
              every   customer   AV.draw   money   at
              bank   **ipun**$_i$*-e*
              bank   3.POSS-DEF
              'Every customer$_i$ drew money from his$_i$ bank.'
              (binding of 2nd complement)

That the agent PP is an oblique is further supported by the Quantifier Float (QF) test. (QF is restricted to core arguments in Balinese, see Arka 2003). Consider:

(31) a. *Guru-ne*   *maang*   *murid-e*   *buku*   *makejang*
          teacher-DEF   AV.give   student   book   all
          (i) 'All the teachers gave the students books.'
          (ii) 'The teacher(s) gave all the students books.'

      b. *Murid-e*   *baang-a*   *teken*   *Guru-ne*
          student-DEF   give-PASS   by   teacher-DEF
          buku   *makejang*
          book   all
          (i) 'All the students were given books by the teacher(s).'
          ?*(ii) 'The student(s) was/were given books by all the teachers.'

      c. *Guru-ne*   *ka-aturang*   *teken*   *murid-e*
          teacher   PASS-give   by   student-DEF
          jinah   *sami*   (h.r.)
          money   all
          (i) 'All the teachers were given money by the students.'
          ?*(ii) 'The teacher(s) was/were given money by all the students.'

Example (31a) shows the AV verb, (31b) the *-a* passive and (31c) the *ka-* passive. Note that the two passives (31b,c) pattern the same in contrast to the AV (31a). In the AV form (31a), the agent 'the teachers' is subject (i.e. a core). The quantifier *makejang* can float, so two readings are possible. In the corresponding *-a* and *ka-* passives (31b,c), by contrast, the QF cannot be associated with the PP agent (i.e. reading (ii) is not possible). This is what is expected if the agent is an oblique in the passives because QF is a property of cores in Balinese. In short, the QF test suggests that *-a*, just like *ka-*, gives rise to a passive construction where the agent is an oblique, not a core argument.

A resumptive pronoun test also confirms the oblique status of a PP agent (example (32a) is identical to example (19c)):

(32) a. *I*   *Meme,*   *apa*   *jakan=a*   *di*   *paon?*
          ART   mother   QW   OV.cook=3   at   kitchen
          'As for Mother, what is she cooking in the kitchen?'

b.   *?*I*   *Meme,*   *apa*   *jakan-a*   *teken*   *ia*
      ART   mother   QW   cook-PASS   by   3
      di   *paon?*
      at   kitchen
      'As for Mother, what is being cooked by her in the kitchen?'

Without the PP agent, (32a) can be interpreted as an OV verb with clitic
=*a*. The clitic is an a-subject, a core; it can therefore function as a resumptive pronoun. (Only cores can function as resumptive pronouns in Balinese
(Arka 2003).) The presence of the PP agent, however, forces the -*a*-passive
interpretation of the -*a* verb whereby the agent is an oblique. Being an
oblique, the third-person pronoun agent cannot function as a resumptive
pronoun. The badness of (32b) is expected.

To conclude, there is convincing syntactic evidence to support the view
that the verb with bound -*a* is another passive construction in Balinese, in
addition to the *ka-* passive.

4 Conclusion

The following points emerge from the study of syntax of the =*a*/-*a* verbs in
Balinese. First, they are both non-active verbs where the subject is a non-
agent item. Second, there are two kinds of -*a*: enclitic =*a* and passive -*a*.
Third, the enclitic =*a* patterns with the OV verb, where =*a* is not a syntactic
marker but an argument of the head verb. It is a term or core argument of
the verb; it is the a-subject (i.e. the most prominent item in the a-structure
of the predicate). This explains why in reflexive and quantifier binding, it
can bind the reflexive/pronominal associated with any other argument(s).
Also, the clitic =*a* has a referential index (i.e. it refers) and can therefore
function as a resumptive or anaphoric pronominal, as shown by the evidence in actual texts. Fourth, the passive -*a* patterns with the passive *ka-*.
Their grammatical properties conform to passive properties cross-
linguistically. The argument of the verb is the agent PP, not the bound form
-*a* or *ka-*. Syntactically, the PP agent is an oblique, not a core argument.
Categorially, the agent is marked by a preposition (the typical marking for
obliques in Balinese and other languages lacking case morphology). The
crucial property of this agent PP is that it is syntactically not the most
prominent item in the a-structure of the predicate, as shown by reflexive
and quantifier binding data. Hence, grammatically the -*a* and *ka-* verbs are
passive verbs, in contrast to the AV and OV verbs.

5 Sources of Examples

KA = Dharna, G. 1978. Kobaran Apine. In *Kembang rampe kesusastraan Bali Anyar*, edited by I G. N. Bagus and I K. Ginarsa Denpasar: Yayasan Saba Sastra Bali.

TLS = Santha, J. 1981. *Tresnane Lebur Ajur Satonden Kembang*. Denpasar.

SB = Raka, A.A. G. et al. 1989. *Satua Bali*. Denpasar: Dinas Pendidikan Dasar Propinsi Daerah Tingkat I Bali.

6 References

Arka, I Wayan 2003. *Balinese morphosyntax: a lexical-functional approach*. Canberra: Pacific Linguistics (PL 547).

Arka, I Wayan & S. Wechsler. 1996. Argument Structure and Linear Order in Balinese Binding. Paper presented at the Lexical-Functional Grammar workshop, Grenoble, France, August 1996.

Artawa, K. 1994. Ergativity and Balinese Syntax. Ph.D thesis, La Trobe University.

Barber, C. C. 1977. *A Grammar of Balinese Language*. Vol. I and II. Aberdeen: Aberdeen University.

Bresnan, J. 1995a. Linear Order, Syntactic Rank, and Empty Categories: On Weak Crossover. In *Formal Issues in Lexical-Functional Grammar* ed. R. M. Kaplan, M. Dalrymple, J. T. Maxwell III & A. Zaenen. 241–274. Stanford: CSLI.

Bresnan, J. 1995b. Morphology Competes with Syntax: Explaining Typological Variation in Weak Crossover Effects. Ms., Stanford.

Bresnan, J. 2001. *Lexical Functional Syntax*. Oxford: Blackwell.

Clynes, A. 1995. Topics in the Phonology and Morphosyntax of Balinese. Ph.D thesis, Australian National University.

Guilfoyle, E., H. Hung & L. Travis. 1992. SPEC of IP and SPEC of VP: two subjects in Austronesian languages. *Natural Language and Linguistic Theory* 10.3:375–414.

Hunter, T. M. 1988. *Balinese Language: Historical Background and Contemporary State*. Michigan: Michigan University.

Kana, M. A. 1999. *Grammatical Relations in Bahasa Indonesia*. Canberra: Pacific Linguistics (D-93).

Kersten, J. 1970. *Tatabahasa Bali*. Flores: Arnoldus.

Kikusawa, R. 2001. The development of the Indonesian pronominal system. MS., Linguistics Department, Research School of Pacific and Australian Studies, Canberra.

Manning, C. D. 1996a. Argument Structure as a Locus for Binding Theory. Paper presented at the Lexical-Functional Grammar workshop, Grenoble, France, August 1996.

Manning, C. D. 1996b. *Ergativity: Argument Structure and Grammatical Relations.* Stanford: CSLI.

Ross, Malcolm D. 2002. The history and transitivity of Western Austronesian voice and voice marking. In *The Historical and Typological Development of Western Austronesian Voice Systems* ed. F. Wouk and M. D. Ross. Canberra: Pacific Linguistics (PL 518).

Ross, Malcolm D. 2004. Notes on the prehistory and internal subgrouping of Malayic. In *Papers in Austronesian subgrouping and dialectology* ed. John Bowden & Nikolaus Himmelmann. 97–109. Canberra: Pacific Linguistics (PL 563).

Shibatani, M. 1994. Voice. In *The Encyclopedia of Language and Linguistics* ed. R. E. Asher and J. M. Y. Simpson. Oxford: Pergamon Press.

Wechsler, S. & I Wayan Arka. 1998. Syntactic Ergativity in Balinese: an Argument Structure Based Theory. *Natural Language and Linguistic Theory.* 16:387–441.

Zwicky, A. M. 1985. Clitics and Particles. *Language* 61:283–305.

Zwicky, A. M. 1987. Suppressing the Zs. *Journal of Linguistics* 23:133–148.

Zwicky, A. M. & G. K. Pullum. 1983. Cliticization vs. Inflection. *Language* 59:502–513.

5

Objective Voice and Control into Subject Clauses in Balinese[1]

I WAYAN ARKA AND JANE SIMPSON

1 Introduction

Split expression (using Jespersen's (1969) term) refers to a construction where a state of affairs (SOA)[2] argument gets expressed in two parts in a clause; that is, where one semantic argument corresponds to two syntactic arguments. Subject-raising and object-raising constructions are the classic manifestations of such split expression. We are particularly interested in what happens to these parts in Balinese[3] because Balinese exhibits an ob-

[1] Earlier versions of this paper were presented to the Argument Structure Group, Max Planck Institute for Psycholinguistics and to the Lexical Functional Grammar Workshop, Brisbane 1998, and appeared in the proceedings of the latter. The authors wish to thank the participants, in particular Melissa Bowerman, Joan Bresnan, Bill Foley, Paul Kay, Sotaro Kita, Simon Musgrave, and Pieter Seuren, for helpful comments.

[2] We take this useful term from Sag and Pollard (1991), as a way of avoiding controversial terms such as 'proposition' and 'event'.

[3] Balinese is a language in a sub-group of western Austronesian, spoken by around three million speakers, mainly on the islands of Bali and Nusa Penida, but also in the western part of

Voice and Grammatical Relations in Austronesian Languages.
Simon Musgrave and Peter Austin

jective voice (OV) alternation treating a SOA—which is a complex argument—as a non-agent argument, similar to a simple argument.

Consider the equi example in (1).[4]

(1) *Tiang   negarang   [__ naar   ubad   ento]*
     1   AV.try   AV.eat   medicine   that
     'I tried to take the medicine.'

The meaning of a clause containing an active voice (AV) verb *negarang*, like its English counterpart 'try', requires a trier (an entity), and some action that they try (eating in (1), a state of affairs).[5] In both Balinese and English the trier is expressed overtly as the subject of the higher verb. In both Balinese and English the action is expressed overtly as a clause, nonfinite in English, unmarked for finiteness[6] in Balinese. We assume that this clause is embedded in the higher clause. In both languages the subject of the lower clause, the eater, is left unexpressed, but is understood to be coreferent with (i.e. controlled by) the trier, the subject of the higher clause.

In terms of grammatical functions and syntactic realisation, the Balinese sentence and its English translation exemplify control, a phenomenon which has received much attention in the generative grammar literature. Modifying Bresnan (1982:317) we define control as a relation of referential dependence between an unexpressed argument in an embedded clause (controlled argument) and an expressed or unexpressed argument (the controller) in a matrix clause. The controller determines the referential properties of the controlled element, which may indeed have an arbitrary referent.

Existing theories of control would have no trouble representing the Balinese example in (1). But Balinese has another version of (1) which English lacks. In (1) the verb *n/tegarang* is in the active voice, in which (roughly) the argument with the actor or agent semantic role maps to subject, and the argument with the theme semantic role maps to object. (2)

Lombok, and in some transmigration areas in other parts of Indonesia, such as Sumatra and Sulawesi.

[4] The first author is a native speaker of Balinese, and the judgments in this paper are his, confirmed by Ni Luh Adnyawati and I Nyoman Arthanegara (all are speakers of the Badung dialect).

[5] For the effect of voice alternations on grammatical relations in Austronesian languages, see among others Schachter (1977); Foley and Van Valin (1984); Durie (1985); Kroeger (1993); Manning (1996b); Vamarasi (1999). For the historical development of voice and voice marking in Austronesian languages, see Ross (1995; 2004); Starosta, Pawley, and Reid (1982); Wolff (1996).

[6] However, *n/tegarang* is not compatible with an overt future marker *lakar*. As we shall show later, tense and finiteness are not really relevant to issues of control in Balinese. For example, raising takes place regardless of whether there is an overt tense marker.

shows the same verb in the objective voice; note that clefting is required to provide an appropriate English translation:[7]

(2)　　[__ naar　　ubad　　　ento]SUBJ　　tegarang　　tiang
　　　　　AV.eat　　medicine　　that　　　　　OV.try　　　　I
　　　　'To take the medicine is what I tried.'
　　　　(*'To take the medicine was tried.')

In this sentence the clause representing the action (which we suppose bears the theme semantic role) maps to subject, while the trier (bearing the actor or agent semantic role) is expressed as a pronoun following the verb. We claim that this construction shows control into subject, and we will show later that this actor is not an adjunct, (as a demoted agent is in an English passive) but a core or term argument, expressed as a term-complement of the verb (as opposed to a subject). Both (1) and (2) are complex sentences, consisting of two clauses, one embedding the other, and sharing a common element. They differ in the morphological shape of the verb (active voice or objective voice), in the phrase structure position of the embedded clause (initially or finally), and in the grammatical function of the controller (subject or term-complement).

Control into subject is also exhibited by the raising verb *tawang* in the following example:

(3)　　[__ nagih　　pipis　　dogen]SUBJ　　tawang=a
　　　　　AV.ask　　money　　only　　　　　　OV.know=3
　　　　'Just asking for money is what (s)he knows.'
　　　　* 'Just asking for money is known by her.'

The asker (i.e. the controlled argument) in (2) is the knower (realised by the third person clitic =a). Crucially, the whole clause is the subject because the third person clitic =a cannot be subject in Balinese (Arka 2003, see also Arka in this volume).

Existing theories of control do have trouble representing the Balinese examples in (2)-(3), because, by and large, they have inbuilt mechanisms to rule out the English counterpart, the passive of subject-controlled verbs like *try*. In this paper we extend existing representations of control to capture (1), (2) and (3) in Balinese.

---

[7] For simplicity we do not represent the ∅- prefix of OV verbs, thus the OV verb ∅-*daar* is shown as *daar* and glossed as 'OV.eat'. Likewise we gloss AV verbs without segmenting the form: *naar* 'eat' (from the stem *daar*) is glossed as 'AV.eat', unless the AV prefix can be clearly segmented, as with the vowel initial stem, e.g. *ejuk* 'arrest' → *ng-ejuk* 'AV-arrest'.

1.1 How Languages Express 'State of Affairs' Arguments

Languages vary as to whether verbs can semantically select states of affairs as arguments, and as to how selected SOAs are represented, both categorially and functionally. These three properties are often linked; for example, Warlpiri, like many Australian languages (e.g. Dixon 1995 for Dyirbal), has very few verbs that select SOA arguments (Hale 1982), a categorial restriction only allowing nominals to act as arguments of sentences (Simpson 1991), and no grammatical function equivalent to the English COMP (Bresnan 1982), the grammatical function assigned to a clause such as *that Sue fell* in *I know that Sue fell.*

But unlike Warlpiri, many languages allow clauses (finite or non-finite) to act as arguments of a verb. For convenience, we list the syntactic expressions of SOA arguments in a top-bottom line:[8]

TENSED CLAUSES	That Peter was dismissed shocked me	
WITH EXPLETIVE ANAPHOR	I love it that you can do it so easily	In many languages these can be expressed by serial verb constructions of varying degrees of tightness, in which one verb and its arguments may or may not constitute an argument of the other verb.
ANAPHORIC CONTROL	Mary signalled (for us) to leave	
EQUI	John tried to go. We persuaded John to go	
RAISING	John seemed to like Mary. We believe Mary to like John.	
COMPLEX PREDICATES (FRENCH)	Je ferai manger les pommes à Jean	

The topmost share the least number of features with the matrix clause; the lowest share the most. Thus, at the top, no argument of a finite sentential subject in English is expected to be an argument of the matrix clause. At the bottom, all arguments of certain complex predicates have been taken as arguments of a single clause (see also Urdu permissive constructions discussed by Butt 1997). In between are several kinds of clauses that can act as arguments, but which share one (or sometimes more than one) argument and perhaps other properties, with the main clause (see Andrews (1982) for

---

[8] See Foley and Van Valin (1984) for hierarchies of Juncture and Nexus that represent this information, and also include combinations in which what is embedded is not an argument but some kind of adverbial modifier.

Icelandic raising and equi constructions, and Neidle (1982) for similar facts in Russian).

As the line suggests, raising constructions share some but not all properties with complex predicates. They contain one argument which is shared in a very tight way between both predicates.

Work in recent years in Head-driven Phrase Structure Grammar (HPSG) and Lexical Functional Grammar (LFG) has led to the positing of a syntactic level of argument structure at which many kinds of complex predicates are formed by argument sharing (Alsina 1996, Wechsler 1995, Manning and Sag 1999, Mohanan 1995, Butt 1997). Moreover, some of the LFG mechanisms which Bresnan (1982) used to explain control phenomena, in particular functional control equations and the use of lexical rules to change functional control equations, no longer exist, or now have analogues in argument structure. So it seems worth exploring the possibility that control phenomena (in which we include both raising and equi constructions) should be handled at argument structure. Balinese provides a useful place to explore this, because the system of active, objective and passive voice provide rich material for exploring the syntactic status of the constructions.

1.2   Bresnan's Account of Control

Within Lexical Functional Grammar (LFG), Bresnan (1982) argues that representing control phenomena involves both semantics (via the lexical entries of verbs), and syntax (via the grammatical functions of the controller and the controlled argument). She gives a detailed account of control phenomena in English, addressing the four central properties that need to be accounted for:

1. How are the two clauses linked?

For control phenomena Bresnan assumes that the clauses are linked by embedding. One clause acts as an argument of the other. The subject of the lower clause is understood to be shared between the two clauses. Otherwise the clauses are independent. There are two kinds of sharing, absolute identity (functional control) and referential identity (anaphoric control).

In functional control, the phrasal category representing the controlled clause is an XP with a missing subject identified obligatorily with some function in the higher sentence. In anaphoric control, the clause is a full sentence with an invisible zero pronominal subject which may be identified anaphorically with some element of the higher clause (and sometimes understood to refer outside the sentence), or may be treated generically:

(4)   a. At the moment, the goal of the police is to try to prevent a riot.
       b. At the moment, the goal is to try to prevent a riot.

The unexpressed subject of *try* is anaphorically controlled by *the police* in (4a) but is arbitrarily controlled in (4b) (that is, the referent is determined in context). The unexpressed subject of *prevent* is functionally controlled by the unexpressed subject of *try* in both sentences.

2. What are the functions of the two clauses in the sentence?
The higher clause is taken to provide the argument-taking predicate. The lower clause is assigned the function XCOMP or COMP, depending on whether the shared element is absolutely (XCOMP) or referentially identical (COMP) to some element in the higher clause.

XCOMP is a special kind of grammatical function, distinct from other functions such as subject, object, adjunct. The X of the name is intended to show it could be expressed by any lexical category (N, V, A, P), and the COMP of the name shows that it expresses a complement of the verb. XCOMP is an 'open' grammatical function—that is, XCOMP can only be assigned to a phrasal category XP, where XP does not include an element representing the subject. In English, XCOMP is assigned to a particular place in the VP, following the object if there is one. In this way Bresnan captured Bowers' (1973) insight that English has a predicate constituent following the verb (or the object of a transitive verb) in its phrase structure, which does not behave like an object.

The embedded clause headed by *prevent* in (4) is an instance of XCOMP and the one headed by *try* is an instance of COMP. This difference may have syntactic manifestations–for example an adjunct agreeing with the understood subject of an XCOMP should have the same case as the controller of that XCOMP, while an adjunct agreeing with the understood subject of a COMP would normally have the same case as an overt subject of that COMP (Andrews 1982, Neidle 1982, Simpson 1983).

3. How is the shared element represented in the sentence?
The shared element is realised once, as an argument of the higher verb.

4. How do we know what is the shared element?
Referential identity can be assigned in a variety of ways, both lexical and pragmatic. For purely referential identity (i.e. when the SOA argument is expressed as a COMP), the missing element in the lower clause is assumed to be a null anaphor, hence the name anaphoric control. For absolute identity (i.e. when the SOA argument is expressed as an XCOMP), the lexical entry of the higher verb tells us what the grammatical function of the shared element is both in the higher clause and in the lower clause. That is, information about possible controllers is represented as functional equations in

lexical entries of verbs. Hence the name functional control. Thus for *Sue believed Mary to have left* the lexical entry for *believe* states that the subject of the lower clause is identical to the object of the higher clause. In this way Bresnan captured both the claim that, in English, and many languages, only subjects are controlled and the claim that only arguments of the verb could act as controllers. Such functional control equations could be altered by the operation of lexical rules such as passive, allowing for the change of function of the controller in *Mary was believed to have left*. In this way Bresnan captured Visser's (1963–1973) generalisation that subject control verbs can't be passivised, **I was promised to leave*. If they were passivised, their controller would be an adjunct.

Bresnan's approach accounts very well for the structures discussed above in which one clause represents a complex argument of another clause, one argument is shared between two clauses, that argument is the subject of the lower clause.

In what follows, we show that, while surface grammatical relations or f-structures still play a role in control, there is evidence from Balinese voice marking and mapping that:

(a) control relations involve syntax-semantic interactions, where the notion of a syntacticised argument-structure (a-structure) is crucial.

(b) complex arguments, like simple arguments, can be either terms (core) or non-terms, and participate in regular voice/function alternations (just like simple arguments), suggesting that they are not necessarily expressed as (X)COMPs.

(c) Bresnan's explanation of Visser's generalisation makes an interesting and correct prediction about the possible voice alternations in control structures in Balinese.

Bearing in mind that there are non-functional constraints involved, we still maintain the distinction between 'functional control' (i.e. obligatory control) and 'anaphoric control' (i.e. optional control), because these two types of control are syntactically distinguishable.

1.3 Grammatical Functions and Argument Structure in Brief

The levels of representation that we adopt here are:
- Lexical semantic structure (sem-structure): arguments, argument-taking predicates and decomposition of these into Jackendoff-style structures
- Syntactic argument structure (a-structure): (see below)
- Functional structure (f-structure): a set of grammatical functions (subject, object, xcomp, adjunct etc.) and constraints on what constitutes a well-formed functional structure

- Constituent structure (c-structure): morphological or syntactic realisations of grammatical functions

We summarise the properties of the version of a-structure, which we are adopting (Arka 2003; Arka and Manning, this volume; Manning 1996a; Manning 1996b; Wechsler and Arka 1998):

a-structure

    a.   It carries information about the syntactic valency of a predicate (i.e. number of arguments: one-place predicate, two-place predicate, etc.)

    b.   It carries information about termhood (i.e. whether an argument is a term or not; hence syntactic transitivity: intransitive, monotransitive, etc.)

    c.   It contains syntactic arguments having the following prominence:

        (i)   terms outrank non-terms

        (ii)   within sets of terms/non-terms, prominence reflects semantic prominence

Manning (1996b:27) has proposed that 'universally there are features of language that are sensitive to each of the two levels of grammatical relations and argument structure'. The kinds of features that are sensitive to grammatical relations include word order, the realisation of discourse functions (in Balinese the appearance of the particle *(s)ane* is such a feature) and what can be raised. Features sensitive to argument structure are often 'construal processes' including reflexive binding, equi target and complex predicate formation. Construal features are often sensitive to 'termhood' properties. The property of being a 'term' captures much of what was previously captured by the grammatical function feature [-restricted], a natural class which encompasses subjects and objects.

In Balinese, as we shall argue, the objective voice alternation changes the grammatical functions borne by the actor and theme, but not their termhood status. Both are term arguments.

2   Introduction to Voice-Marking in Balinese

2.1   Voice Marking and Term Arguments

We begin with a brief overview of voice marking in Balinese. Three concern us here, active voice (AV), objective voice (OV) and passive, as shown in (5):

(5) a. *Tiang* *ng-alih* *Nyoman*
         1   AV-search name
         'I searched for Nyoman.'

     b. *Nyoman* *alih*   *tiang*
         name   OV.search   1
         'Nyoman, I searched for.'

     c. *Nyoman* *sampun* *ka-rereh*   *(antuk*   *ida)*
         name   PERF   PASS-search   by   3
         'Nyoman has been searched for (by him/her).'   (h.r.)[9]

We translate the objective voice as far as possible by fronting, rather than by passive, because the fronting of objective voice has a pragmatic effect, and because Balinese has a passive anyway. Sentence (5a) shows the AV verb, marked by a homorganic nasal prefix replacing the initial consonant, whereas sentence (b) shows the OV counterpart.[10] The unmarked form can be thought of as having a zero prefix because there seems to be no convincing syntactic reason to regard either AV or OV as more basic than, or as derived from, the other.

Balinese canonically has SVO[11] order (Arka 2003; Artawa 1994; Wechsler and Arka 1998), hence the subject in (5a) is the AV actor *tiang*, while the OV theme *Nyoman* in (5b) is the subject (hereafter grammatical function subject (GF-subject), to distinguish it from other kinds of subjects).[12] Arguments for claiming that a particular constituent acts as a GF-subject come from a number of syntactic properties: word-order, exclusive access to relativisation with *(s)ane*, exclusive access to raising and control, exclusive access to fronting as a question word, privileged access (among term arguments) to extraposition to sentence-final position and contrastive focus with *anak* (see Arka 2003 for details).

---

[9] Balinese basically has two registers—high and low. They mainly differ in their lexical items, not in syntax. High register is indicated with (h.r.) after the relevant example. Low register is unmarked.

[10] |*ng*| is the form of the AV prefix for a vowel-initial or liquid-initial stem, although in the latter a schwa may be inserted: *lempag* 'OV.hit' → *ng-lempag* or *ng-e-lempag* 'AV.hit'

[11] Initial position has discourse import. However, the unmarked order for clauses with objective voice verbs is undergoer verb actor, while the unmarked order for clauses with active voice verbs is actor verb undergoer. Only in very marked structures would this be changed.

[12] The OV verb in Balinese represents the ergative mapping (Arka 2003). Artawa (1994) claims that Balinese is an ergative language, but Artawa, Artini, and Blake (1997) and Arka (2003) adopt the view that Balinese shows ergative properties without implying that it is an ergative language.

Note that Balinese has two passives,[13] one used in high register, which involves prefixing *ka-* to the verb and can used with an agent of any person, optionally expressed by a PP, and the other used in low register, which involves suffixing *-a* to the verb and expressing the agent as a PP (what the P is can vary):

(6)   *Gusti Aji   lunga   kija,   Gusti Biang?*
      name   go   where   name
      'Where is Gusti Aji going, Gusti Biang?'
      Ka   Badung.   Mara   gati   alih-a   teken
      to   name   just   very   escort-PASS   by
      timpal-ne.
      friend-3.POSS
      '(He's going) to Badung. (He was) just picked up by his friends.'

(7)   *Nyoman Santosa   tau   teken   tingalin-a   baan*
      name   know   with   see-PASS   by
      Made Astiti
      name
      'Nyoman Santosa was aware of being seen by Made Astiti.'

(8)   *Nglemeng   tiang   ka-duka-in   ring   I*
      Every day   1   PASS-angry-APPL   by   ART
      guru
      teacher
      'Every day, the teacher was angry with me.'   (h.r.)

The objective voice and passive voice differ with respect to the function of the agent. In the passive voice, the agent has some low-end grammatical function, oblique or adjunct, as it does in English. It is expressed as a PP in both the high and low register. In the objective voice, Arka (2003) argues that at the level of syntactic argument-structure, the agent is a term argu-

---

[13] There is evidence that the verb with the *ka-* prefix (5c) is the real passive in Balinese (Arka 2003, Wechsler and Arka 1998; Artawa 1994). The *ka-* passive is generally used in the high register. Since the low register has no passive, there is a need to fill in the gap for backgrounding the agent, a need which is handled by the *ka-* passive in the high register. In the low register, *-a* followed by a PP agent comes to the rescue and functions just like a passive construction. Without the PP agent and out of context, the construction may be ambiguous between OV verb and passive. However not all *-a* verbs are passives. Many occurrences of *-a* verbs in real texts belong to the objective voice (OV), not to the passive. See Arka (this volume) for the evidence that an *-a* verb can be an OV form.

ment. At the functional level, it acts as a kind of object, which we will call term-complement.[14] Categorially it is expressed as an NP.

Properties of terms in Balinese include launching quantifier float, providing an antecedent for a resumptive pronoun, controlling certain depictive predicates, and being the understood (actor) argument of imperatives (Arka 2003).[15] Only one (quantifier float) is shown here. (9a) shows the quantifier phrase *ajak makejang* modifying a term argument agent expressed as subject in an AV verb construction. (9b) shows it modifying a term argument bearing the sematic role actor/agent and expressed as a term-complement in an OV verb construction. And (9c) shows it modifying a (theme) object.

(9)   a.   *Tiang*   *ng-alih*   *Nyoman*   *ibi*   *ajak*
          1   AV-search   name   yesterday   with
          makejang
          all
          'We all searched for Nyoman yesterday.'

     b.   *Nyoman*   *alih*   *tiang*   *ibi*   *ajak*
          name   OV-search   1   yesterday   with
          makejang
          all
          'For Nyoman we all searched yesterday.'

     c.   *Ketut*   *ng-ajak*   *anak-e*   *ento*   *ibi*
          name   AV-take   person-DEF   that   yesterday
          ajak   *makejang*
          with   all
          'Ketut took all of the people there yesterday.'

---

[14] With an OV verb, the actor term-complement must follow the verb. It cannot be fronted, nor can any material come before it. Contrast the acceptability of (i) with (ii) and (iii). (Arka 2003 Ch.4:19a-c).

(i)   *Ooh,*   *enggih,*   *niki,*   *kopi-ne*   *tunas*   **tiang**
       Oh   yes   this   coffee-DEF   OV.take   1
       'Oh well, this, the coffee...I have it' (TLS:100)

(ii)*   *Ooh,*   *enggih,*   *tiang*   *niki*   *kopi-ne*   *tunas*
       oh   yes   1   this   coffee-DEF   OV.take

(iii)*   *Ooh,*   *enggih,*   *niki,*   *kopi-ne*   *tunas*   **enggal-enggal**
       Oh   yes   this   coffee-DEF   OV.take   quick-quick
       tiang
       1
       'Oh well, this coffee...I take it quickly.'

[15] Properties of terms in Tagalog include control of participial clauses and restrictions on 'adjunct fronting' (Kroeger 1993:41-46).

That is, quantifier float can be associated with the agent, regardless of whether it is the subject in active voice, or a term complement in objective voice. Many different verbs can appear with this quantifier float. Contrast this with the high register passive.

(10) | *Guru-ne* | *ka-aturang* | *teken* | *murid-e* | *jinah* |
teacher-DEF	PASS-offer	by	student-DEF	money
sareng	*sami*			(h.r.)
with	all			

    i. 'All the teachers were given money by the students.'
    ii. * 'The teacher(s) was/were given money by all the students.'

(*Sareng sami/akeh* '(lit.) with all/many' is the high-register variant of *ajak makejang*). The PP agent *teken muride* 'by the students' in the passive is not a term argument, and so cannot be quantified by a free quantifier. (Complex quantifiers with *ajak/sareng* are for animate nouns only, hence *sareng sami* in (10) cannot modify *jinah* 'money'.)

2.2   Objective Voice and 'Symmetrical' System

We must briefly discuss the relation of applicativisation[16] to voice alternations, especially the one that yields a ditransitive verb to show that Balinese exhibits some properties of what Foley (1998) calls a symmetrical voice system—ability to have more than one non-subject core argument, and for free assignment of subject function to arguments of the verb. Most importantly, the assignment of subject function to a non-actor argument does not cause a demotion of the actor argument to non-term status. However, western Austronesian languages differ as to which elements can be subject; some are claimed to allow certain non-subcategorised elements (e.g. locative) to act as subject (Foley and Van Valin 1984, Kroeger 1993, Foley 1998); others, like Balinese, allow only core arguments (whether basic or derived by applicativisation) to act as subject. Thus, a locative argument in Balinese must be first promoted to core (by means of applicativisation) in order to be eligible for subject. This is illustrated by the verb *n/tanem* 'plant' in (11). We analyse all three arguments of the applicative verb—a planter, something planted, and a place where things are planted—as term/core arguments because all three appear as NPs and, crucially, in ob-

---

[16] An applicative verb in Balinese can be formed out of an intransitive base or a transitive base with either *-ang* or *-in*. The *-ang* form is associated with benefactive, instrumental and stimulus roles, while the *-in* form is associated with goal, source and locative roles.

jective voice (11b-c), either of the two postverbal NPs can be expressed as the preverbal NP, the subject.[17]

(11)   a.   *Ia*   *nanem-in*   *teban-ne*   *kasela-kutuh*
         3   AV.plant-APPL   backyard-3.POSS   cassava
         '(S)he planted cassava in his/her backyard.'

      b.   *Kasela-kutuh*   *tanem-in=a*   *teban-ne*
         cassava   OV.plant-APPL   backyard-3.POSS
         '(S)he planted cassava (i.e. nothing else) in his/her backyard.'

      c.   teban-ne   tanem-in=a   kasela-kutuh
         backyard-3.POSS   OV.plant-APPL   cassava
         'In his/her backyard, (s)he planted cassava.'

To conclude, the objective voice alternation does not demote the actor argument in the way the passive does in English and Balinese. AV/OV voice-marking differences reflect different mapping alternatives for the term arguments onto surface grammatical relations. The mapping between semantic roles, arguments and grammatical functions is summarised below (from Arka 2003).

(12)   Balinese mapping and marking:
    I.Subject selection:
        a. AV marking: map an agent term argument onto subject
        b. OV marking: map a non-agent term argument onto subject
        c. Passive: map a non-agent term argument onto subject
    II.Complement function:
        Map the other term(s) onto term-complement(s) (which include object)
    III.Oblique non-term:
        Passive: treat an agent as a non-term, map onto oblique

These mapping rules make the prediction that if a clausal complement is a term argument, it should be able to appear sentence-initially in OV verb clauses, while if it is not it should not be able to appear there. But before

---

[17] Indonesian, however, is 'less symmetrical' than Balinese in that it does not allow the third term argument of a ditransitive verb to be linked to subject in the OV verb. In other words, it is non-symmetrical with respect to 'object doubling'. Thus, the Indonesian equivalent of (11) would allow only the promoted locative (term) argument to be linked to subject because the promoted locative argument is the second in rank (after the actor argument). Therefore, the equivalent of sentence (11b) would be unacceptable in Indonesian.

considering what voice alternations reveal about the grammatical functions borne by the states of affairs arguments, we must first consider the properties of the expression of states of affairs arguments as controlled clauses, in particular their categories, what can be controlled, and what are possible controllers.

3   General Properties of Control in Balinese

3.1   The Category of the Embedded Clause

Although a Balinese verb is not inflected in the same way as an English verb, the finiteness distinction is still relevant for some verbs. For example *edot* 'want' takes a non-finite complement so that an auxiliary item such as *lakar* future cannot appear with it. However, the tense/non-tense distinction does not appear to be relevant to whether or not the clause can be controlled. Raising can apply from tensed complements in Balinese (see Arka 2003).

3.2   What can be controlled?

It is claimed that, cross-linguistically, the shared argument can only bear the subject function in the lower clause. Austronesian languages appear to show variations in this respect. Tagalog (Kroeger 1993:38-39) shows that non-subjects can be controlled. Balinese, however, shows that only subjects can be controlled (Artawa 1994, Arka 2003).

(13)   a.   *Tiang   tawang=a   [__   ng-alih   Luh Sari]*
          1   OV.know=3   (1)   AV-look.for   name
          'Of me (s)he knew I was looking for Luh Sari.'

      b.   **Tiang   tawang=a   [Luh Sari   alih   __]*
          1   OV.know=3   name   OV.look.for
          'Of me (s)he knew that Luh Sari was being looked for by me.'

      c.   *Luh Sari   tawang=a   [__   alih   tiang]*
          name   OV.know=3   OV.look.for   1
          'Of Luh Sari (s)he knew that she was being looked for by me.'

      d.   **Luh Sari   tawang=a   [tiang   alih   __]*
          name   OV.know=3   1   OV.look.for
          'Of Luh Sari (s)he knew that I was looking for her.'

Sentence (13a) has a controlled agent as GF-subject in the lower clause (in parentheses), (acceptable), whereas sentence (13b) has the controlled argument agent as a non-GF-subject (unacceptable). Sentence (13c) shows the acceptable version of (13b) where the matrix and the embedded verbs are in OV, and crucially the controlled non-agent argument (Luh Sari) must be the GF-subject. Thus, (13d) is unacceptable.

3.3   What Can Be a Controller?

It is generally accepted that the meanings of verbs which take part in equi constructions and those which take part in raising constructions are important in determining what gets controlled and what controls it (Kiparsky and Kiparsky 1971, Jackendoff 1972, Foley and Van Valin 1984; Sag and Pollard 1991, Van Valin 1993, Dixon 1995). Arka (2003) follows the classification of equi verbs in Sag and Pollard (1991) and Pollard and Sag (Pollard and Sag 1994), and, as a first cut, divides Balinese verbs into the orientation type, the commitment type and the influence type. As well, there are verbs which participate in raising constructions. The relevant ones that we shall discuss are verbs of seeming (subject raising) and verbs of thinking and knowing (object raising).

The orientation verbs (e.g. *edot, makita* 'wish', *makeneh* 'desire', *perlu* 'need' and *demen* 'like (to do something)) are, in Pollard and Sag's terms, those in which the experiencer is oriented towards some state of affairs, the SOA. Unsurprisingly they are characterised by having an experiencer as controller.

Consider the sentences in (14), high and low register counterparts of the same sentence. In each the verb has two semantic arguments, a wanter and a state of affairs, what they want. The controlled argument of the state of affairs argument, the subject, is identical with the wanter. In each, the clause has two syntactic arguments, an NP realising the wanter, and a verb realising the desired state of affairs.

(14) a. *Ia   edot   [__   teka]*
          3   want   come
          'He wants to come.'

      b. *Tiang   tan   makita   [__   merika]*
          1   NEG   wish   go.there
          'I do not wish to go there.'   (h.r.)

The influence verbs (e.g. *tunden* 'ask, require', *ongkon* 'ask, request, *orahin* 'tell', *perintah* 'order', *paksa* 'force', *baang* 'allow, let' and *larang* 'prohibit') are those in which the influenced person is influenced by someone to bring about a state of affairs. They are characterised by having the influenced argument (e.g. the person asked, not the asker) as controller. They also have a semantic constraint on the shared argument in the lower clause that the referent be able to carry out the action, or bring about the state of affairs.

The influence verb in (15) has three semantic arguments, an asker, a person asked and a state of affairs, what is asked. The meanings of influence verbs indicate that the controlled argument of the state of affairs, the subject, is identical with the person asked and not the asker. In (15) the three semantic arguments correspond to three syntactic arguments: an NP which acts as GF-subject, as an NP which acts as object, and a partial clause, whose GF-subject is identical to the matrix object.

(15) *Tiang*   *nunden*   *ipun*   *maang*   *Nyoman*   *pipis*
      1   AV. ask   3   AV.give   name   money
      'I asked him to give Nyoman money.'

The commitment verbs (e.g. *majanji* 'promise', *masumpah* 'swear, vow', *nyak* 'agree' and *negarang* 'try, attempt') are those in which the committer commits him or herself to bring about some state of affairs. There may or may not be a person to whom they commit themselves. The committer is thus the controller (i.e. the promiser, the swearer, etc.). In (16a) the two semantic arguments correspond to two syntactic arguments: an NP (*ia*, the promiser) which acts as GF-subject and a partial clause, whose GF-subject is identical to the matrix GF-subject. Balinese appears to allow the construction like English *Pat was promised to be allowed to leave*, as in (16b), where on the surface syntax the controller of the missing embedded GF-subject is not the promiser. This is acceptable presumably due to '(semantic) causative coercion' (Sag and Pollard 1991, Pollard and Sag 1994) because it means 'I promised that I would cause it to come about that (s)he was allowed to go home'. Thus, semantically, the promiser is still the 'controller' of the thing promised.

(16) a. *Ia*   *majanji*   *[__ lakar*   *ng-aba-ang*   *tiang*
           3   promise   FUT   AV.bring-APPL   1
           kamben]
           clothes
           '(S)he promises that (s)he will bring clothes for me.'

      b. *Ia*   *janjiang*   *cang*   *[__ baang-a*
           3   OV.prominse   1   3   allow-PASS
           __ mulih]
           3   go.home
           'I promised him/her that (s)he would be allowed to go home.'

To summarise this section, we have the following constraints:

- Syntactic constraint on control
- The lower argument must bear the grammatical function subject.
- Semantic constraints
- Orientation verbs require the experiencer to be the controller.
- Commitment verbs require the committer to be the controller.
- Influence verbs require the undergoer to be the controller.

Influence and commitment verbs both place a restriction on the argument representing the subject of the lower clause that it be one that could bring about the state of affairs.

The semantic description is very rough, but it is adequate for the purpose at hand.[18] For example, the influence verb *tunden* 'ask' has the following the partial specification:

$$sem\text{-}str\text{: (asker, askee}_i, \text{ (doer}_i, \text{ (thing to be DONE)))}$$

Here, DO just stands for something that the asker can expect the person asked to carry out. The indices show that the askee and the DO-er are linked in semantic structure; they must be identical. We turn now to the alternations caused by voice-marking.

4 Control and Voice Alternations in Balinese

4.1 Verbs with Three Semantic Arguments

Underived verbs with three arguments show objective voice alternations. (17) shows an influence verb *n/tunden* 'ask', first in active voice, then in objective voice.

(17) a.

Tiang	*nunden*	*ipun*	*maang*	*Nyoman*	*pipis*
1	AV.ask	3	AV.give	name	money

'I asked him to give Nyoman money.' (h.r.)

b.

Ipun	*tunden*	*tiang*	*maang*	*Nyoman*	*pipis*
3	OV.ask	1	AV.give	name	money

'Him I asked to give Nyoman money.'

Both are quite acceptable. They both respect the semantic constraint on the shared argument that in the higher clause the controller is the person asked, and, in the lower clause, the syntactic constraint that the controlled

---

[18] See Van Valin and Wilkins (1993) for arguments that a more fine-grained decomposition of semantic structure should allow for an explanatory account of control relations.

argument be the GF-subject, and the semantic constraint that it be an agent. This last is achieved by having the lower verb in active voice. The grammatical realisations of the matrix controller (as GF-object in (17a) or as subject in (17b)) are expected, because they are licensed by the mapping and marking principle stated in (12).

The following two sentences violate the syntactic constraint, in that the shared argument is not the GF-subject of the lower clause.

(18)   a.   * *Ipun*   *tunden*   *tiang*   *pipis*   *baang* __
            3   OV.ask   1   money   OV.give
            Nyoman
            name
            'He I asked money to be given to Nyoman by'

       b.   * *Ipun*   *tunden*   *tiang*   *Nyoman*   *baang* __
            3   OV.ask   1   name   OV.give
            pipis
            money
            'He I asked money to be given to Nyoman by'

Now consider (19), in which the lower verbs are in objective voice. The GF-subject of the lower verb is the non-agent argument—recipient in (19a) and the patient in (19b). Both sentences violate the (Balinese) semantic constraint that the shared argument be the one in control of the state of affairs described by the embedded verb. Note that (19b) is roughly the equivalent of the (acceptable) English sentence with an embedded passive verb. To express the idea in (19b), the embedded verb in AV form must be used as in (19c).[19]

---

[19] The fact that we cannot get a 'semantic causative coercion' here is rather surprising. This is perhaps associated with the INFLUENCE type of control verb we have in (19) where *nunden* is immediately followed by an embedded VP without any subordinate marker. In this way, it is interpreted as involving a direct control over the SOA. When the embedded verb of *n/tunden* takes a subordinator marker *apang* '(roughly) so that' then it is possible to have such a semantic coercion:

       Tiang   *nunden*   *apang* __ *periksa-na*   *teken*   *dokter-e*
       1   AV.ask   apang   examine-PASS   by   doctor-DEF
       '(Lit.) I asked (someone) to cause it to come about that I would be examined by a doctor.'

As noted, even in this interpretation, the controller of the SOA is still the 'influenced' argument, not the 'asker'.

(19) a. *Tiang   nunden   Nyoman   [__ baang   ipun
          1   AV.ask   name   OV.give   3
          pipis]
          money
          ?? 'I asked Nyoman to be given money by him'

      b. *Tiang   nunden   [__   periksa-na   teken
          1   AV.ask   examine   by
          dokter-e]
          doctor-DEF
          'I asked to be examined by the doctor.'

      c. Tiang   nunden   dokter-e   [__ meriksa
          1   AV.ask   doctor-DEF   AV.examine
          tiang]
          1
          'I asked the doctor to examine me.'

Thus, satisfaction of the syntactic constraint alone does not seem to be enough: the sentence must also satisfy the semantic constraint that the GF-subject must be perceived to have a degree of control over the state of affairs.

The commitment type also shows a similar semantic restriction.

(20) *Tiang   majanji   [__ baang   ipun   pipis]
      1   promise   OV.give   3   money
      ?? 'I promised to be given money by him.'

The shared argument is the GF-subject of the lower clause, but also the recipient in that lower clause. But for the argument to be shared, it must have the meaning in the lower clause that it represents a person who is in control of the state of affairs (that (s)he is promising to bring about), not a recipient. And as a result, the sentence is bad. (However, see possible 'causative coercion' and its restrictions when it takes the embedded verb 'allow' in (27)-(28).)

To conclude, for the influence type and commitment type of control verbs in Balinese, the controlled argument must be not simply a GF-subject, but specifically a GF-subject linked to an argument with the actor semantic role. Therefore the lower clause must be in active voice. In this they contrast with an orientation verb like *edot*, which doesn't place any actor restriction on its shared argument, and so the lower clause can be in active or objective voice.

We turn now to the question of what grammatical function the clause bears. For the examples we have seen so far, we could adopt Bresnan's (1982) analysis of functionally controlled Equi clauses in English, and treat them as XCOMPs. However, there is some evidence against this. This comes from a second objective voice alternation. We saw earlier that, in ditransitives (example (11)), either the theme or the location argument can become the GF-subject in the objective voice alternation. Exactly the same is true for these constructions. The controlled clause can alternate with *Nyoman* as the GF-subject if the verb is in objective voice:

(21)   *[__ teka   mai   prajani]   ane   orahin   tiang*
       come   here   immediately REL   OV.ask   1
      Nyoman
      name
      'Coming here immediately is what I asked Nyoman to do.'

The sentence-initial presence of the clause in (21) and the presence of *(s)ane* argue for the clause *teka mai prajani* being not only a term argument of the sentence but also the GF-subject. The question then arises, what is the relation between *Nyoman* and the clause? Bresnan (1982)'s account of functional control in such clauses has two parts, first, that there cannot be functional control into the GF-subject of a sentence, only into XCOMPs and XADJs. The permitted equation should be, for example, (- XCOMP SUBJ) = (- SUBJ), and not (- SUBJ SUBJ) = (- OBJECT) (Zaenen and Engdahl 1994). And second, the controller must be a semantically unrestricted function (i.e. term or core in our terminology here).

If (21) is a true case of functional control, we would expect:
(i)   No possibility of an overt GF-subject in the *teka mai prajani* clause
(ii) No possibility of omitting *Nyoman* in the clause
(iii) *Nyoman* must be a term, in order to be a functional controller
As for (i), an overt subject (*ia*) renders the sentence unacceptable:

(22)   *[Ia   teka   mai   prajani]   ane   orahin*
      3   come   here   immediately   REL   OV.ask
      tiang   Nyoman
      1   name
      'Coming here immediately is what I asked Nyoman to do.'

As for (ii), the controller can occasionally be omitted, but is understood as someone specific/definite, not generic.

(23) [__teka   mai   prajani]   ane   orahin   tiang
     come   here   immediately   REL   OV.ask   1
     'Coming here immediately is what I asked him/her/them to do.'

As for (iii), there is evidence that the three arguments are all terms. Consider the simultaneous tests of termhood: relativisation, topicalisation with a pronominal copy, and QF shown by (24).

(24) Nyoman   [__ teka   mai   prajani]   ane   orahin
     Name   come   here   immediately REL   OV.ask
     tiang   ia   ibi   ajak   makejang
     1   3   yesterday   with   all
     'As for Nyoman, coming here immediately is what we all asked him to do yesterday.'

Note that the three semantic arguments (one being a SOA) are all treated equally as terms: relativisation shows that the SOA/controlled clause is the GF-subject, topicalisation with a resumptive pronoun shows that *Nyoman*/the askee is a term, and the quantifier float shows that the agent *tiang* is also a term. In short, we need to capture control by an object of the subject of a subject, which was prohibited in Bresnan (1982) and Zaenen and Engdahl (1994).

The upshot is that the data supports one part of Bresnan's account, but not the other. Bresnan's claim was that the functional controller be a semantically unrestricted function (i.e. a term argument), among which she included subject, object and secondary objects. Functional control into an embedded clause acting as the GF-subject of the sentence argues against restricting functional control to XCOMPs and a particular class of adjunct. However, if *Nyoman* is a term argument, not an oblique or a chomeur, then Bresnan's account predicts correctly that as a term argument it should be eligible as a controller, in contrast to the corresponding English sentence: **To go there was asked of John by me.* This is unacceptable because we cannot express the controller *of John* as a term argument.

Furthermore, Bresnan's proposal that only term arguments can be functional controllers makes the correct prediction that Balinese commitment verbs, such as *promise*, which have committer controlled complements, should be able to appear in objective voice, in contrast to their English counterparts, which reject subject control. This rejection in English is part of what Bresnan (1982) called Visser's generalisation.

(25) a.   **John was promised by Mary to buy herself a spaceship.*

b. *Ci   nyanjiang   ia   [__ meli   montor]*
   2   AV-promise 3   AV.buy   motor-bike
   'You promised him to buy a motor bike.'

c. *Ia   janjiang   ci   [__ meli   montor]*
   3   OV.promise 2   AV.buy   motor-bike
   'Him you promised to buy a motor bike.'

d. *[__ meli   montor]   janjiang   ci   ia*
   AV.buy   motor-bike   OV.promise 2 3
   'Buying a motor bike is what you promised him.'

The English form (25a) is unacceptable because the controller, the promiser, is an adjunct, expressed as a PP. The Balinese form is acceptable,[20] because the promiser controller is a term argument: the GF-subject in the AV construction (25b) and a term complement in the OV construction (25c)–(d). Passivisation demotes the agent controller into a non-term, hence the following contrast is expected:

(26) a. *Ia   nyanjiang   I Bapa   [__ lakar*
   3   AV.promise ART father   FUT
   enggal-enggal   nganten]
   quick-quick   get.married
   '(S)he promised Father to get married quickly.'

    b. *?* [__ lakar   enggal-enggal   nganten   ane*
          FUT   quick-quick   get.married   REL
    janjiang-a   I   Bapa   teken   ia
    promise-PASS ART   father by   3
    '*Getting married quickly is what is promised Father by him/her.'

Recall that Balinese allows 'semantic causative coercion' where, as shown by example (16b), the controller of the commitment is indeed semantically the 'committer' even though the GF-SUBJ of the embedded verb appears to be controlled by a non-committer argument on the surface syntax. However, there are two restrictions in this respect: the controller (i.e. the promiser) has to be a term argument and the embedded verb must have

---

[20] Some Balinese speakers consider the intransitive counterpart (*majanji*), where the promisee appears as an oblique, is more natural than the one with the applicative (*janji-ang*):
Ci   ma-janji   teken   ia   [__ meli   montor]
2   ma-promise to   3   AV.buy   motor-bike
'You promised (to) him to buy a motor bike'
Since *majanji* is an intransitive verb, it does not have AV/OV voice alternation.

the verb 'allow'; otherwise the acceptability of the sentence decreases as shown by (27)-(28). Only (27a) is acceptable because the clitic =a of *janjianga* can be understood as the OV agent term argument (see footnote 14, also Arka this volume for the status double life of –a verbs). (27b), in contrast, is bad because of the presence of the PP *teken Nyoman* forcing the PASS structure of *janjianga* and also the absence of the embedded verb *baang*. Control relation with the *ka-* passive in (28a) and (b) is as expected not acceptable, even when it appears with the embedded verb *icen* 'allow' (28a).

(27) a. *Ia   janjiang=a   __ baang-a   __ kema*
          3   OV.promise=3   allow-PASS   go.there
          '(S)he was promised to be allowed to go there.'
          (or, (S)he$_i$ promised him that (s)he$_i$ would make it possible for him/her to go there.')

      b. *?? ia   janjiang-a   __ kema   teken   Nyoman*
          3   promise-PASS   go.there   by   name
          *'He was promised to go there by Nyoman.'

(28) a. *?? Ipun   ka-janjiang   __ ka-icen   __ merika*
          3   PASS-promise   PASS-allowed   go.there
          '(S)he was promised to be allowed to go there.'   (h.r)

      b. *?? Ipun   ka-janjiang   __ merika*
          3   PASS-promise   go.there
          *(S)he was promised to go there.'

The difference between commitment verbs and influence verbs can therefore be shown by the argument sharing in their a-structures:

(29) a. Influence verbs: e.g. *orahin* 'ask'

asker	askee$_i$	State of affairs (DOer$_i$ (thing to be DONE))	*semantic structure*
term	term	term	*syntactic argument structure*

b. Commitment verbs: *janjiang* 'promise'

promiser$_i$	promisee	State of affairs (DOer$_i$, (thing to be DONE))	*semantic structure*
term	term	term	*syntactic argument structure*

Both kinds of verbs semantically and syntactically have three arguments: two simple arguments and one complex argument with obligatory control. All of them are terms. Thus, by the mapping principles in (12), any of them can be GF-subject. The two verbs differ in choice of controller, which is semantically determined. The mapping principles result in the controller bearing different grammatical functions. Crucially, since a controller must be a term, Balinese allows a non-subject controller with the commitment verb *promise* but the verb must be in OV because the controller, the promiser, is still a term in this clause. In its passive counterpart, however, a non-subject controller is prohibited because the promiser is not a term.

4.2   Verbs with Two Semantic Arguments

4.2.1   *edot*, an orientation verb

With a verb of desire like *edot* 'want', the embedded verb can be in active or objective voice, because the meaning of the verb doesn't require that the GF-subject of the lower clause be an agent. In (30) the complement clauses differ only in the voice markings, which therefore cause the controllee *cai* '2' to be associated with different grammatical functions. The controllee is the agent-subject in the AV verb (30a) and patient-subject in the OV-verb (30b). Note that simply switching the marking but retaining word-order in effect triggers different control relations and, as the translations suggest, different meanings.

(30) a. *Cai   edot   [__   nyakitin   bapa]?*
          2   want   AV.hurt   father
          'Do you want to hurt me (Father)?' (KA:127)

      b. *Cai   edot   [__   sakitin   bapa]?*
          2   want   OV.hurt   father
          'Do you want to be hurt by me (Father)?'

In contrast to (30), the following are unacceptable because the controlled argument would not be linked to subject, even though in (31a) it is the agent.

(31)   a.   * *Bapa*   *sing*   *edot*   *[cai*   *sakitin* __ *]*
             father   NEG   want   2   OV.hurt
             'I (Father) do not want to hurt you.'

       b.   * *Bapa*   *sing*   *edot*   *[cai*   *nyakitin* __ *]*
             father   NEG   want   2   AV.hurt
             'I (Father) do not want you to hurt me.'

Edot doesn't show any alternation between active and objective voice (but see its applicative form in (34) below). The controlled clause cannot act as the subject. Thus, in contrast to (30), the following is not acceptable:

(32)   * *[* __   *nyakitin*   *bapa]*   *ane*   *edot*   *cai?*
             AV.hurt   father   REL   want   2
       'Hurting me (Father) is what you want?'

This fits with the fact that *edot* doesn't take an NP argument, but rather a PP argument, and so doesn't show active/objective voice alternations.

(33)   *Ia*   *edot*   *[teken*   *poh]*
       3   want   to   mango
       '(S)he wants a mango.'

In other words, *edot* is syntactically intransitive with the SOA being treated as a non-term argument. We analyse it as bearing XCOMP. The evidence for its non-term status comes from its inability to be linked to GF-SUBJ as in (32) and its possible promotion to term status by means of applicativisation. Thus, the acceptable version of (32) is the one with the verb *edotin* as in (34):

(34)   *[* __   *nyakitin*   *bapa]*   *ane*   *edot-in*   *cai?*
             AV.hurt   father   REL   OV.want-APPL   2
       'Hurting me (Father) is what you want?'

The proposed parallel structures of the intransitive orientation verbs such as *edot* are therefore the following:

(35)　Orientation verbs: e.g. *edot* 'want' (Intransitive)

wanter$_i$	State of affairs (DOer$_{i,}$ (thing to be DONE))	*semantic structure*
term	non-term	*syntactic a-structure*
subject	XCOMP (i.e. non-term complement)	*f-structure*

4.2.2　*n/tegarang*, a commitment verb

Edot contrasts with another class of verbs with two semantic arguments, the *n/tegarang* class, a kind of commitment class.[21] These verbs are transitive and show the active/objective voice alternation.

(36)　a.　*[Tiang]*$_{SUBJ}$　　*negarang*　　*[__　naar　　ubad*
　　　　　1　　　　　　AV.try　　　　　　AV.eat　　medicine

　　　　　ento] $_{OBJ}$
　　　　　that
　　　　　'I tried to take the medicine.'

　　　b.　*[__　naar　　ubad　　　ento]*$_{SUBJ}$　*tegarang　　tiang*
　　　　　　　AV.eat　medicine　　that　　　　　OV.try　　　1
　　　　　　'Taking the medicine is what I tried.'

We claim that in (36b) *naar ubad ento* is indeed the subject of *tegarang*. The presence of a relativiser *(s)ane* bears this out.

(37)　*[__　naar　　ubad　　　ento]* $_{SUBJ}$　*ane　　tegarang　　tiang*
　　　　　　AV.eat　medicine　　that　　　REL　　OV.try　　　1
　　　'It is taking the medicine that is what I tried.'

Thus, like the clausal complement of influence and commitment verbs, and indeed like any non-subject term argument, the clausal complement of *n/tegarang* can become the subject in the objective voice mapping. We sug-

---

[21] The difference between the two has nothing to do with the tense of the complement. Like *edot*, *tegarang* cannot appear with tense marking.

(i)　　*[__ lakar naar　　ubad　　ento]　　tegarang　tiang*
　　　　　FUT　AV.eat　medicine　that　　OV.try　　1
　　　　*'To take that medicine was tried by me.'

(ii)　　*tiang　　tegarang [__　　lakar　　naar　　ubad　　ento]*
　　　　　1　　　OV.try　　　FUT　　AV.eat　medicine　that
　　　　*'I tried to take the medicine.'

gest therefore that it is a term argument.[22] The verb *n/tegarang* thus contrasts with the verb *edot*, whose clausal complement is a non-term argument. It also contrasts with English *try* which cannot be passivised. That is, Balinese *n/tegarang* has two terms whereas English *try* has one term. The proposed structures for *tegarang* in (37) are shown below:

(38)   Commitment verbs: e.g. *n/tegarang* 'try'

trier$_i$	State of affairs (DOer$_i$, (thing to be DONE))	*semantic structure*
term	term	*syntactic a-structure*
term-complement	subject	*f-structure*

Bresnan (1982) argues that *To go there was tried by me* is unacceptable as functional control because the controller *by me* is an adjunct, not a grammatical function such as subject or object. In the Balinese example however, the controller *tiang* is not an adjunct, but a term complement. So it doesn't violate the constraint on functional control.

4.2.3   Raising verbs

The verb *n/tawang* 'know' has two semantic arguments, a knower and a SOA, what is known. It has several realisations of these arguments. First, the semantic SOA can be realised as a single syntactic argument. This argument can appear as the subject in an objective voice construction.

(39)   a.   *Tiang*   *nawang*   *[Nyoman Santosa*   *ng-alih*
              1   AV.know   name   AV-look.for
              Luh Sari]
              name
              'I knew that Nyoman Santosa was looking for Luh Sari.'

        b.   *[Tiang*   *ng-alih*   *Luh Sari]* $_{SUBJ}$ *tawang=a*
              1   AV-look.for   name   OV.know=3
              'That I was looking for Luh Sari, (s)he knew.'

But (39a) is actually ambiguous in structure, because *n/tawang* has a second realisation—as a raising verb:

---

[22] Evidence from binding further confirms that the OV agent is a term not an oblique. We do not repeat the discussion here (see Wechsler and Arka 1998, Wechsler 1999 for details).

(40) *Tiang   nawang   [Nyoman Santosa]   [ng-alih*
      1   AV.know   name   AV-look.for
      Luh Sari]
      name
      'I knew Nyoman Santosa to be looking for Luh Sari.'

Semantically the (whole) state of affairs 'Nyoman Santosa looked for Luh Sari' is *what is known*. Syntactically, however, as shown by the bracketing in (40), the embedded subject *Nyoman Santosa* is taken as a syntactic dependent NP of the matrix verb. This is not obvious in (40) where it occurs in its usual position before the embedded verb. But it becomes obvious as soon as we look at the voice alternations.

Unlike *edot*, *n/tawang*[23] can appear in both objective voice and active voice. In (41a) and (41b) the shared argument acts as the GF-subject of the higher clause.

(41) a. *Nyoman Santosa   tawang   tiang   [__ ng-alih*
          name   OV.know   1   AV-look.for
          Luh Sari]
          name
          'Of Nyoman I knew him to be looking for Luh Sari.'

      b. *Tiang   tawang=a   [__ ng-alih   Luh Sari]*
          1   OV.know=3   AV-look.for   name
          'Of me (s)he knew that I was looking for Luh Sari.'

Hence, syntactically there are three arguments in the sentences, corresponding to two semantic arguments. Thus *n/tawang* parallels English raising-to-object verbs like *believe*. That *tiang* really is the GF-subject in (41b) is shown not only by its initial position, but also by the fact that it can be relativised, as in (42):

(42) *Tiang   ane   tawang=a   [__ ng-alih   Luh Sari]*
      1   REL   OV.know=3   AV-look.for   name
      'It is me who is known by him to have looked for Luh Sari.'

(43) shows that *any* combination of embedded subject argument can raise, for all four combinations of AV and OV on the matrix and embedded predicates are attested (all four sentences have the same logical relations, indicated by the translation below):

---

[23] Note also that unlike *edot* and *n/tegarang*, *n/tawang*'s complement can be marked for future via the *lakar* particle.

(43) a. *Ia   nawang   Wayan   lakar   tangkep   polisi*
            3   AV.know   name   FUT   OV.arrest   police
            'He knew that Wayan would be arrested by the police.'
            (Wayan=lower subject (theme) raised to object)

      b. *Wayan   tawang=a   lakar   tangkep   polisi*
            name   OV.know=3   FUT   OV.arrest   police
            'Of Wayan he knew that he would be arrested by the police.'
            (Wayan=lower subject (theme) raised to subject)

      c. *Ia   nawang   polisi   lakar   nangkep   Wayan*
            3   AV.know   police   FUT   AV.arrest   name
            'He knew that the police would arrest Wayan.'
            (Police=lower subject (agent/actor) raised to object)

      d. *Polisi   tawang=a   lakar   nangkep   Wayan*
            police   OV.know=3   FUT   AV.arrest   name
            'Of the police he knew that they would arrest Wayan.'
            (Police=lower subject (agent/actor) raised to subject)

(44) shows that only the GF-subject of the lower clause can raise; that is, only the agent/actor of an active voice verb, and the undergoer/theme of an objective voice verb can raise to be in the main clause:

(44) a. * *Ia   nawang   polisi   Wayan   lakar   tangkep* __
              3   AV.know   police   name   FUT   OV.arrest
            * 'He knew that as for the police Wayan would be arrested.'

      b. * *Polisi   tawang=a   Wayan   lakar   tangkep* __
            police   OV.know=3   name   FUT   OV.arrest
            * 'Of the police he knew that Wayan would be arrested.'

      c. * *Ia   nawang   Wayan   polisi   lakar   nangkep* __
              3   AV.know   name   police   FUT   AV.arrest
            * 'He knew that as for Wayan the police would arrest.'

      d. * *Wayan   tawang=a   polisi   lakar   nangkep* __
            name   OV.know=3   police   FUT   AV.arrest
            * 'Of Wayan he knew that the police would arrest'

More interesting, however, is the second objective voice alternation. We have seen earlier that the clausal complements to *n/tegarang* 'try' and *orahin* 'ask' can become the GF-subject in the objective voice alternation. Like them, the clausal complement in a raising construction can occur sentence-initially. And it can occur with *(s)ane* indicating it is the GF-subject. And there is control by the agent term-complement.

(45) [__ *ng-alih*   *Luh Sari*]_{SUBJ}   *ane*   *tawang=a*   *tiang*
      AV-look.for   name   REL   OV.know=3   1
      'Looking for Luh Sari is what (s)he knows of me.'

A parallel in English would be the unacceptable *To have gone was known (of) me by her.* Again the English is unacceptable because the controller cannot be expressed as an NP following the verb,[24] while the Balinese is acceptable because the controller is a term argument expressed as an NP.

The following show that the raising can occur with a tensed complement including the future *lakar*.

(46) a. *Tiang*   *ngaden*   *Nyoman*   *lakar*   *kema*
         1   AV.think   name   FUT   go.there
         'I think that Nyoman will go there.'

     b. *Nyoman*   *kaden*   *tiang*   *lakar*   *kema*
         name   OV.think   1   FUT   go.there
         'Nyoman, I think, will go there.'

     c. *lakar*   *kema*   *kaden*   *tiang*   *Nyoman*
         FUT   go.there   OV.think   1   name
         'That Nyoman will go there is what I think about Nyoman.'

We propose that raising verbs such as *n/tawang* 'know' and *ng/kaden* 'think' have the a-structure shown in (47). It explicitly shows the split where a single argument (i.e. the SOA) corresponds to two term arguments, with one of them being athematic and shared with an embedded argument, y (not necessarily an agent). Then, by mapping principles any of these terms can be selected as GF-subject as shown by the examples in (43) and (45).

(47) *n/tawang* 'know'

knower		state of affairs (....y$_i$ ....)	*semantic structure*
term	term$_i$	term	*syntactic* *argument structure*

---

[24] The failure of passive with a clausal subject in English is comparable to the failure in many dialects of English of passive with theme subjects and NP recipients in ditransitives: ??*An apple was given John.*

5 A Typological Aspect of GF Realization of Complex Arguments

Traditionally in LFG, an oblique function is distinguished from a non-oblique function of subject/object (i.e. core argument) on one hand for being semantically restricted ([+r]) compared with core arguments, and from an XCOMP (i.e. a complex non-core argument) on the other, for being simple, that is, having no argument-taking predicate of its own. In short, although both oblique and XCOMP are semantically restricted ([+r]), they differ in their internal structure; an XCOMP is a complex argument containing an argument-taking predicate whereas an oblique is a simple argument. This can be seen in (48):

(48)

terms [-r]		non-terms [+r]	
subject	object	oblique	xcomp
simple / complex	simple / complex	simple	complex

However, the data from Balinese showing control into subject suggest that a complex argument can be classified as semantically unrestricted (i.e. [-r]), syntactically as a term/core argument, against the view adopted by Zaenen and Engdahl (1994). Thus, a complex argument does not always get expressed as an XCOMP. Indeed, a *that*-clause in English can be subject[25] as in *That he is a liar is well known*, although a clause with a controlled argument functioning as subject is not possible: **To fix the car is tried (by me)*. As (48) shows, internally simple and complex structuring is only relevant for the classification of non-terms, not that of terms. It seems reasonable to simplify the function classification in (48) into (49), where the distinction of the non-core functions is collapsed giving rise to the following systematic classification:

(49)

terms [-r]		non-terms [+r]
subject	object	oblique
simple / complex	simple / complex	simple / complex

---

[25] But see Bresnan (2001:116) for an argument that sentential subjects appear syntactically in the position linked with topic, not with the position linked with subject.

(49) shows that, like a simple argument, a complex argument can be mapped onto any function. This captures cross-linguistic variations, exemplified by Balinese and English.

The question now is what determines the range of possibilities that a complex argument can or cannot be a term. It appears that it is lexically determined. Evidence comes from cross-linguistic variations of syntactic realization of semantically equivalent verbs. For example, Balinese *n/tawang* 'know' is always transitive but the Indonesian counterpart can be intransitive. The intransitive *tahu* 'know' has its complex argument expressed as a non-term argument marked by the complementizer *bahwa*:

(50) a. | *Aku* | *sudah* | *tahu* | *[bahwa* | *ia* | *berbohong]* |
|---|---|---|---|---|---|
| 1SG | already | know | that | 3SG | lie |

'I already know that (s)he tells lies.'

b. | *?*[bahwa* | *ia* | *berbohong]* | *sudah* | *ku=tahu* |
|---|---|---|---|---|
| that | 3SG | lie | already | 1SG=know |

'That (s)he tells lies, I already know.'

Indonesian is an SVO language. (50b) is not acceptable because the complex clause is forced to become subject by fronting it and by using the pronominal clitic *ku=*, instead of a (free) pronoun *aku*. (A pronominal clitic cannot be subject in Indonesian, see Arka and Manning this volume).

The attempt to have the embedded clause of (50) controlled with *bahwa* present yields an unacceptable sentence:

(51) a. | * *Dia* | *sudah* | *tahu* | *[bahwa* __ | *berbohong]* |
|---|---|---|---|---|
| | 3SG | already | know | that | lie |

b. | *Dia* | *sudah* | *tahu* | *[*__ | *berbohong]* |
|---|---|---|---|---|
| 3SG | already | know | | lie |

'(S)he already knows (how) to lie.'

Its transitive counterpart *ketahui* shows that the complex argument is treated as a term:

(52) a. | *Aku* | *sudah* | *mengetahui* | *[bahwa* | *dia* | *sering* |
|---|---|---|---|---|---|
| 1SG | already | know | that | 3SG | often |

berbohong]
lie

b. *[bahwa   dia   sering   berbohong]   sudah*
    that   3SG   often   lie   already
ku=ketahui
2SG=know
'I already know that (s)he often lies.'

The Indonesian *bahwa*-clause is therefore like the English *that*-clause in that it can be subject. Moreover, like English, Indonesian allows a raising version (i.e. with control) where the complementizer *bahwa/that* cannot show up:

(53) a. *Dia   sudah   ku=ketahui   [__ sering   berbohong*
          3SG   already   2SG=know   often   lie

    b. **Dia   sudah   ku=ketahui   bahwa   [__ sering*
         3SG   already   2SG=know   often
         berbohong]
         lie

(54) a. (S)he has been known to frequently tell lies.
    b. * (S)he has been known that __ frequently tell lies.

Recall that Balinese *tawang* 'know' can have its controlled clause mapped onto subject (45). The controlled clause of Indonesian 'know' (53a) (and that of English) lack this possibility:

(55) *??[__ sering   berbohong   sudah   ku=ketahui   dia*
          often   lie   already   2SG=know   3SG

    The unacceptability of (55) might be taken as evidence that the SOA argument is not a term. However, it is possible that the SOA argument may be a term, but that the structure (55) is not permitted simply because Indonesian is, unlike Balinese, asymmetrical in that only one non-agent term can be subject in the OV verb. This is shown in (56), which has a three-place verb with simple arguments:[26]

---

[26] (b) may be acceptable for speakers of some varieties of Bahasa Indonesia, perhaps influenced by particular local languages.

(56) a. *Adik*   *saya*   *beri-kan*   *buku*   *baru*
     younger.sibling   1SG   give-APPL   book   new
     itu
     that

    b. *?? buku*   *baru*   *itu*   *saya*   *beri-kan*
        book   new   that   1SG   give-APPL
     adik
     younger.sibling
     'I gave (my) little brother/sister the new book.'

Summing up, we have so far shown five possibilities for expressing the SOA of the equivalents of 'know' in Balinese, English and Indonesian:

i.   a non-term in an intransitive structure with or without control (57a),
ii.   a term in a transitive structure without control (57b),
iii.   a term in a transitive structure with control (57c),
iv.   a non-term in a syntactically three-place structure with control (57d),
v.   a term in a syntactically three-place structure with control (57e).

The inside angle brackets represent grouping of arguments into terms (the left group) and non-terms (the right group). A dash represents a thematically empty argument (position) to which an embedded argument is raised.

(57) a. *know* << knower><SOA.known>>   (with or without
     Indonesian   control)

    b. *know* <knower, SOA.known>   (no control)
     Balinese, Indonesian, English

    c. *know* <knower, SOA.known>   (with control)
     Balinese

    d. *know* <knower, __ ><SOA.known>   (raising/with control)
     Indonesian, English

    e. *know* <knower, __ , SOA.known>   (raising/with control)
     Balinese, (?Indonesian)

Control into subject is not unique to Balinese, however. Indonesian does allow control into subject with a different verb. Consider *ingin* 'want' (intransitive) (58) and *ingin-kan* (transitive) in (59). (58b) shows control into subject (unacceptable) and (59b) (acceptable).

(58) a. *Aku*   *ingin*   *[___*   *menjadi*   *orang*   *kaya]*
             1SG   want   become   person   rich

      b. * *[___*   *menjadi*   *orang*   *kaya]*   *ku=ingin*
                   become   person   rich   2SG=want

(59) a. *Aku*   *mengingin-kan*   *[___*   *menjadi*   *orang*
             1SG   AV.want-APPL   become   person
             kaya]
             rich

      b. *[___*   *menjadi*   *orang*   *kaya]*   *yang*
               become   person   rich   REL
             ku=ingin-kan
             2SG=want-APPL

The English counterpart * *To be a rich man is wanted by me* may be prohibited by a language-particular constraint that control into subject is not allowed. Or it may simply be blocked because of the lack of objective voice which allows an agent/experiencer to be a non-subject term, and thus a legitimate controller. If this last is correct, we expect control into subject not to be unusual in languages with objective voice (or with syntactically ergative mapping), because the requirement that a functional controller be a term is satisfied. This is an empirical question for further research.

6   Summary

We have demonstrated how complex arguments involving control can be accounted for by having a syntacticised a-structure as an intermediate level between semantic and surface syntax. It provides a natural account for change in the surface grammatical function assignment of a controller in connection with changes in voice marking. The alternation follows the general mapping and marking principles applicable to simple arguments. The analysis presented here correctly predicts that there may be a number of alternative syntactic expressions of such arguments. Crucially, an argument representing a SOA can be either a term or non-term. As a term, it can be the GF-subject of an intransitive verb or of an OV transitive verb. Syntactically, the SOA can be split, with one of its arguments being 'raised' to subject or object. Our analysis accounts for control into subject which is barred in earlier analyses (Bresnan 1982, Zaenen and Engdahl 1994) and further confirms Bresnan's proposal (1982) that, in functional control, a controller is restricted to core/term arguments.

7 References

Alsina, Alex. 1996. The role of argument structure in grammar. Stanford: CSLI.

Andrews, Avery. 1982. Long distance agreement in Modern Icelandic. In The Nature of Syntactic Representation ed. Pauline Jacobson & Geoffrey Pullum. 1–33. Dordrecht: D. Reidel Publishing Company.

Arka, I Wayan. 2003. Balinese morphosyntax: a lexical-functional approach. Canberra: Pacific Linguistics (PL 547).

Artawa, Ketut. 1994. Ergativity and Balinese syntax. Ph.D thesis, La Trobe University, Melbourne.

Artawa, Ketut, Artini, & Barry Blake. 1997. Balinese grammar and discourse. Ms, Udayana University, Denpasar/ La Trobe University, Melbourne.

Bowers, John. 1973. Grammatical relations. Ph.D thesis, Massachusetts Institute of Technology, Cambridge, Massachusetts.

Bresnan, Joan. 1982. Control and complementation. Linguistic Inquiry 13.3:343–434.

Bresnan, Joan. 2001. Lexical-functional syntax. Oxford: Blackwell.

Butt, Miriam. 1997. Complex predicates in Urdu. In Complex predicates ed. Alex Alsina, Joan Bresnan & Peter Sells. 107–149. CSLI Lecture Notes 64. Stanford: CSLI.

Dixon, Robert M. W. 1995. Complement clauses and complementation strategies. In Grammar and meaning: Essays in honour of Sir John Lyons ed. Frank R. Palmer. 175–220. Cambridge: Cambridge University Press.

Durie, Mark. 1985. A grammar of Acehnese on the basis of a dialect of North Aceh. Dordecht/Cinnaminson: Foris.

Foley, William A. 1998. Symmetrical voice systems and precategoriality in Philippine languages. Ms, University of Sydney.

Foley, William A. & Robert D. Van Valin Jr. 1984. Functional syntax and universal grammar. Cambridge Studies in Linguistics. Cambridge: Cambridge University Press.

Hale, Kenneth. 1982. Some essential features of Warlpiri main clauses. In Papers in Warlpiri grammar: in memory of Lothar Jagst ed. Stephen Swartz. 217–315. Berrimah, Australia: Summer Institute of Linguistics.

Jackendoff, Ray S. 1972. Semantic interpretation in generative grammar. Linguistic Inquiry Monograph. Cambridge, Massachusetts: MIT Press.

Jespersen, Otto. 1969. Analytic syntax. Transatlantic series in linguistics. New York: Holt, Rinehart and Winston.

Kiparsky, Paul & Carol Kiparsky. 1971. Fact. Semantics: an interdisciplinary reader in philosophy, linguistics, and psychology ed. D. D. Steinberg & L. A. Jakobovits. 345–369. Cambridge, UK: Cambridge University Press.

Kroeger, Paul. 1993. Phrase structure and grammatical relations in Tagalog. Stanford: CSLI.

Manning, Christopher D. 1996a. Argument Structure as a Locus for Binding Theory. Paper presented at the Lexical-Functional Grammar workshop, Grenoble,
France, August 1996.

Manning, Christopher D. 1996b. Ergativity: argument structure and grammatical
relations. Dissertations in linguistics. Stanford: CSLI.

Manning, Christopher D. & Ivan A. Sag. 1999. Dissociations between Argument
Structure and Grammatical Relations. In Lexical And Constructional Aspects of
Linguistic Explanation ed. Gert Webelhuth, Jean-Pierre Koenig & Andreas
Kathol. 63–78. Stanford: CSLI.

Mohanan, Tara. 1995. Argument structure in Hindi. Dissertations in linguistics.
Stanford: CSLI.

Neidle, Carol. 1982. Case agreement in Russian. In The Mental Representation of
Grammatical Relations ed. Joan Bresnan. 391–426. Cambridge, Massachusetts:
MIT Press.

Pollard, Carl & Ivan A. Sag. 1994. Head-driven phrase-structure grammar. Studies
in contemporary linguistics. Chicago/Stanford: University of Chicago
Press/CSLI.

Ross, Malcolm D. 1995. Reconstructing Proto-Austronesian verbal morphology:
evidence from Taiwan. In Austronesian studies relating to Taiwan ed. Paul J..
Li. Taipei: Institute of History and Philology, Academia Sinica.

Ross, Malcolm D. 2004. Notes on the prehistory and internal subgrouping of Malayic. In Papers in Austronesian subgrouping and dialectology ed. John Bowden
& Nikolaus Himmelmann. Canberra: Pacific Linguistics (PL 563).

Sag, Ivan A. & Carl Pollard. 1991. An integrated theory of complement control.
Language 67:63–113.

Schachter, Paul. 1977. Reference-related and role-related properties of subjects. In
Grammatical relations (Syntax and semantics 8) ed. P. Cole & J. M. Sadock.
279–306. New York: Academic Press.

Simpson, Jane. 1983. Aspects of Warlpiri morphology and syntax. Ph.D thesis,
Massachusetts Institute of Technology.

Simpson, Jane. 1991. Warlpiri morphosyntax: a lexicalist approach. Studies in Natural Language and Linguistic Theory. Dordrecht: Kluwer.

Starosta, Stanley, Andrew K. Pawley & Lawrence A. Reid. 1982. The Evolution of
focus in Austronesian. Paper presented at the Third International Conference on
Austronesian Linguistics, Bali.

Vamarasi, Marit Kana. 1999. Grammatical relations in Bahasa Indonesia. Canberra:
Pacific Linguistics.

Van Valin, Robert D. 1993. A synopsis of role and reference grammar. In Advances
in role and reference grammar ed. Robert D. Van Valin Jr. 1–164. Amsterdam:
John Benjamins.

Van Valin, Robert D. & David P. Wilkins. 1993. Predicting syntactic structure from
semantic representations: Remember in English and its equivalents in

Mparntwe Arrernte. in Advances in role and reference grammar ed. Robert D. Van Valin Jr. 499–534. Amsterdam: John Benjamins.

Visser, F. 1963–1973. An historical syntax of the English language. Leiden: F. J. Brill.

Wechsler, Stephen. 1995. The semantic basis of argument structure. Stanford: CSLI.

Wechsler, Stephen. 1999. HPSG, GB, and the Balinese Bind. In Lexical and constructional aspects of linguistic explanation ed. A. Kathol, J.-P. Koenig & G. Webelhuth. 179–195. Stanford: CSLI.

Wechsler, Stephen & I Wayan Arka. 1998. Syntactic ergativity in Balinese: an argument structure based theory. Natural Language and Linguistic Theory 16.2:387–441.

Wolff, John U. 1996. The development of the passive verb with pronominal prefix in Western Austronesian languages. In Reconstruction, Classification, Description: Festschrift in Honor of Isidore Dyen, ed. Bernd Nothofer. 15–40. Hamburg: Abera. (Asia-Pacific; 3).

Zaenen, Annie & Elisabet Engdahl. 1994. Descriptive and theoretical syntax in the lexicon. In Computational approaches to the lexicon ed. B. T. S. Atkins & A. Zampolli. 181–212. Oxford: Oxford University Press.

6

The Grammatical Function OBJ in Indonesian

SIMON MUSGRAVE

1 Introduction

This paper argues that the status of the grammatical function of object (OBJ) in Indonesian is ambiguous. There are a variety of clause types with two direct arguments in the language, which can be divided into two categories: those with unprefixed verbs and those with prefixed verbs. The prefixed verb type has traditionally been treated as the basic transitive clause type of the language, with the non-subject argument analysed as an object (see for example Chung 1976a,b, Sneddon 1996 among others). In the prescriptive standard of the language, unprefixed verbs are restricted to a class of verbs denoting emotional and cognitive states, and much of the data in this paper will use these verbs to exemplify this clause type. However, in less formal registers, all two argument verbs can be used without a prefix and in this usage they share properties with emotion and cognition verbs rather than with their prefixed derivatives. I argue here that if the non-

Voice and Grammatical Relations in Austronesian Languages.
Simon Musgrave and Peter Austin

subject argument of the prefixed verb clauses is taken as OBJ, then there is no satisfactory analysis of the non-subject argument of the emotion and cognition verbs within the inventory of grammatical functions allowed by Lexical Functional Grammar (LFG, see Kaplan and Bresnan 1982, Bresnan 2001). The possible alternatives are that such arguments have the grammatical function OBJ_θ, or that the inventory of grammatical functions must be expanded. I argue that both of these alternatives are unsatisfactory, and suggest instead that it is preferable to analyse the non-subject argument of unprefixed verbs as OBJ, and to treat the prefixed verbs as a special case. This approach is justified by the fact that morphological processes in Indonesian are exclusively derivational.

The paper is organised as follows. Section 2 presents basic data on Indonesian clauses, introducing both the prefixed verb clause types and the emotion and cognition verbs. Section 3 gives detailed argumentation as to the best analysis of the non-subject argument of the emotion and cognition verbs, on the assumption that the non-subject argument of a prefixed verb is an OBJ. Section 4 argues that a configurational analysis of the Indonesian data either in the spirit of Belletti and Rizzi (1988) or in the spirit of Larson (1988) cannot accommodate the data. Finally, section 5 discusses the reasons for rejecting the assumption that the non-subject argument of prefixed verbs are OBJs, and sketches the alternative analysis.[1]

2 Clausal syntax in Indonesian

2.1 Two-Place Verbs

The overwhelming majority of two-place verbs in Indonesian can appear in the following three types of clause:[2]

(1) *Dia*   *membaca*   *buku*   *itu*
     3SG   *meN*-read   book   that
     'S/he read the book.'

---

[1] Examples in this paper which are not taken from texts reflect the judgments of M. Umar Muslim and Katerina Sukamto, for whose patience I am very grateful. I am also grateful to Helen McKay for providing me with numerous examples drawn from the corpus of Indonesian journalism which she has collected. Several discussions with Peter Austin and one with Bill Foley were important in shaping this material, as was the feedback of an audience at The University of Melbourne particularly that of Nick Evans and Rachel Nordlinger. Remaining errors are my own responsibility.

[2] The verbal prefixes *meN*- and *di*- are left unglossed throughout this paper. The abbreviations used for sources of examples are explained at the conclusion of the paper.

(2) *Buku itu dibaca (oleh) Ali*
     book   that   *di*-read (by)   Ali
     'The book was read by Ali.'

(3) *Buku itu saya baca*
     book   that   1SG   read
     'The book, I read.'

In example (1), the verb stem is prefixed with the morpheme *meN-* tradi-tionally analysed as marking active voice. This prefix ends with a nasal segment which assimilates to a following consonant. When the consonant is unvoiced, the nasal fuses with it (in the case of *s* the result is a post-alveolar nasal *ny*), except in the case of the affricate *c*. Before a vowel, the form of the prefix is *meng-*, and before a liquid the nasal segment deletes. The fol-lowing examples illustrate this allomorphy:

(4) | **Base** | **Prefixed form** |
|------|---------------|
| *anggap* | *menganggap* |
| *baca* | *membaca* |
| *dapat* | *mendapat* |
| *ganggu* | *mengganggu* |
| *peras* | *memeras* |
| *tulis* | *menulis* |
| *kasih* | *mengasih* |
| *seluruh* | *menyeluruh* |
| *curiga* | *mencuriga* |
| *lihat* | *melihat* |

There are no restrictions on the use of this prefix, aside from lexical ones. That is, if a verb stem allows the prefix, then a clause using the prefixed form will be grammatical with any type of nouns as arguments.[3] This is not true of the clause types seen in examples (2) and (3). Both of these clause types are conventionally treated as passives (Chung 1976b) and they are in quasi-complementary distribution depending on the nature of the nominals instantiating the more agent-like argument. Clauses such as example (3) are only possible with a pronoun filling this role, or with a name or address term used as a pronoun substitute, while clauses such as example (2) are only possible with a third person agent. In clauses with *di-* prefixed verbs, the preposition *oleh* is obligatory before the agent except where the agent

---

[3] It should also be noted here that there are a small number of one-place verbs which take the prefix *meN-*, for example *menangis* 'weep', from the root *tangis* 'weeping'.

immediately follows the verb when it is optional. In clauses such as example (3), nothing can intervene between the pronoun agent and the verb including auxiliaries and modals which normally immediately precede the verb:

(5) *Buku   itu   akan   saya   baca*
    book   that   FUT   1SG   read
    'The book, I will read.'

Recent work has argued that clauses such as example (3) are not passive, nor are some clauses with *di-* prefixed verbs (Arka and Manning, this volume, Musgrave, 2001b). Therefore, in this paper I will use the term undergoer-subject clause to cover both these types, and I will describe clauses with *meN-* prefixed verbs as actor-subject clauses.

There is one additional clause type in which two-place verbs appear:

(6) *Dia   baca   buku   itu*
    3SG   read   book   that
    'S/he read the book.'

This construction is not recognised in prescriptive grammars, but is common in general use (Voskuil 1996:Appendix to Ch.8, see also Benjamin 1993 on verb morphology as a sociolinguistic marker in the Malay world). This type is another actor-subject clause type, and can be distinguished from the undergoer-subject type in example (3) in two ways. Firstly, there is no restriction on the type of nominal which may appear as agent, and secondly, auxiliaries and modals appear between the agent (including pronouns) and the verb in this clause type:

(7) *Dia   akan   baca   buku   itu*
    3SG   FUT   read   book   that
    'S/he will read the book.'

A clause such as example (3), in the absence of an auxiliary, is ambiguous when written between the undergoer-subject reading and a reading as an unprefixed actor-subject clause (example (6)) with a left-dislocated second argument. In speech, the intonation associated with the two possibilities is distinct and no ambiguity exists (Chung 1978).

2.2 Emotion and Cognition Predicates

Emotion and cognition predicates in Indonesian form a coherent group not only by virtue of their meaning but also by their syntactic behaviour. Syntactically, these predicates appear to be intransitive in that they do not take the 'transitive' verb prefixes *meN-* and *di-*, but they can have a second argument which is coded as a prepositional phrase. Semantically, there is only one exception to the generalisation that these predicates denote emotional and cognitive states, which is the predicate *mirip* 'resemble'. Typical examples are the predicates *puas* 'content, satisfied' and *salut* 'respect, admire':

(8) | *Dan* | *mereka* | *juga* | *sudah* | *puas* | *dengan* |
     |-------|----------|--------|---------|--------|----------|
     | and | 3PL | also | PERF | content | with |

kasus	*wanita*	*yang*	*hilang*	*itu?*
case	woman	REL	lost	that

     'And were they also satisfied with the case of the woman who disappeared?' (SDPGS:128)

(9) | *ia* | *bangga* | *dan* | *salut* | *akan* | *kesadaran* |
     |------|----------|-------|---------|--------|-------------|
     | 3SG | proud | and | respect | about | NR-aware-NR |

     Sandy
     Sandy

     'She was proud and respected Sandy's attention.' (PYD:19)

Some of these predicates can also appear in a construction where the second argument, which I will refer to as the stimulus (of the emotion or cognition), is coded as a simple NP. That is, the clause has what look like two direct arguments as seen in the following examples:

(10) | *Kamu* | *lupa* | *rumahku?* |
     |--------|--------|------------|
     | 2SG | forget | house-1SG |

     'You have forgotten my house?' (SDM:96)

(11) | *Ia* | *kuatir* | *suratnya* | *tidak* | *sampai* |
     |------|----------|------------|---------|----------|
     | 3SG | fear | letter-3 | NEG | arrive |

     'She was afraid her letter would not arrive.' (ES:313)

(12) | *Aku* | *takut* | *wanita* | *yang* | *aku* | *cintai* |
     |-------|---------|----------|--------|-------|----------|
     | 1SG | fear | woman | REL | 1SG | love-APPL |

ternyata	*tidak*	*mencintaiku*
apparently	NEG	*meN-*love-APPL-1SG

     'I am afraid of the woman that I love, apparently she doesn't love me.' (PYD:12)

(13) | Cuma | aku | tidak | suka | omongannya |
|---|---|---|---|---|
| only | 1SG | NEG | like | gossip-3 |

yang   *sok*   *suci*
REL   as.if   pure
'I just don't like his gossip that takes the moral high ground.' (PYD:87)

(14) | Saya | nggak | senang | wartawannya |
|---|---|---|---|
| 1SG | NEG | like | journalist-3[4] |

'I don't like journalists.' (McKay)

However, as will be shown in detail below, such clauses do not have the same syntactic properties as those discussed in the previous section. The question this paper seeks to answer then is what grammatical function is assigned to the stimulus argument in clauses such as examples (10) to (14)?

I attempt to answer this question using the theoretical resources of Lexical Functional Grammar (LFG; Kaplan and Bresnan 1982, Bresnan 2001). This framework assumes a constrained list of grammatical functions: subject (SUBJ), object (OBJ), oblique (OBL_θ) and second object (OBJ_θ). This inventory is defined in a principled fashion; it is the result of the interaction of two binary features: +/- o(bjective) and +/- r(estricted), where a restricted function must be assigned a semantic role. These features generate a four-celled matrix as follows:

(15) | | **-r** | **+r** |
|---|---|---|
| **-O** | SUBJ | OBL_θ |
| **+O** | OBJ | OBJ_θ |

The last two grammatical functions are subscripted with a theta because in the case of OBJ_θs their thematic role is assumed to be restricted within any particular language (Bresnan and Kanerva 1989), and in the case of OBL_θs their thematic role is indexed by the adposition or case marker which licenses them. These grammatical functions are not configurationally defined. They are elements of f(unctional)-structure, a structure which is distinct from but parallel to c(onstituent)-structure (Bresnan, 2001:55-63). Syntactic properties other than configurational ones are therefore of primary interest in this investigation.

The group of predicates of interest here includes the following words:

---

[4] The possessive clitic -*nya* is used here to indicate that the referent is identifiable.

(16)

berang	angry, irate	*mimpi*	dream
bosan	bored	*mirip*	resemble
gila	crazy, obsessed	*peduli*	care about, pay attention
kangen	miss, long for	*percaya*	believe
kasih	love	*sayang*	love, pity
kasihan	love, pity	*senang*	happy, like
kuatir	fear	*suka*	like
lupa	forget	*takut*	fear
marah	angry	*yakin*	sure

This list is not exhaustive; rather it includes just those words for which I have clear examples from texts. Also, several words are left out of this list which might have a claim to be included. These words (*benci* 'hate', *ingat* 'remember' and *percaya* 'believe') all occur in the construction of examples (8) and (9). But they also all have related prefixed verbs which are not derived with an applicative suffix (*membenci, mengingat* and *mempercaya*). Therefore it is not possible to say whether clauses with these predicates and a NP stimulus are examples of the construction seen in examples (10) to (14), or whether they are rather examples of the unprefixed actor-subject verb construction exemplified in example (6) above. Given this unclarity, it is preferable to omit these predicates from my discussion.

The translations given above suggest that many of these words have an adjectival character. Whether Indonesian has adjectives as a lexical category or not is a disputed question (see Cumming 1991 and Mahdi 1998 for differing views), and the evidence is particularly unclear for the words under consideration. For example, *ter-* prefixation derives adjectival superlatives for most of the words with which it is possible (e.g. *tergila* 'most crazy', *termarah* 'most angry'), but some verbal derivatives occur also (e.g. *terlupa* 'forget accidentally'). Indonesian allows all major phrasal categories to function as the predicate of a clause, that is verbs (see examples above), nouns, prepositions and putative adjectives can all head the predicate constituent:

(17) *Ini   keputusan   saya*
      this   NR-decide-NR   1SG
      'This is my decision.'

(18) *Mereka   di   Jakarta   sekarang*
      3PL   LOC   Jakarta   now
      'They are in Jakarta now.'

(19) *Mencari*   *pekerjaan*   *di*   *kota*   *tidak*   *begitu*
      meN-find   NR-work-NR   LOC   city   NEG   like that
      mudah
      easy
      'Finding work in the city isn't very easy.'

However, the only type of NP dependent allowed by a nominal predicate is a possessor. The interpretation of clauses such as examples (10) to (14) is incompatible with a reading in which the subject is equated with a possessed emotion. The only case in which words which are *prima facie* adjectives in Indonesian take NP dependents is when the comparative morpheme *se-* is prefixed to them:

(20) *Dia*   *tidak*   *setakut*   *saya*   *dengan*   *anjing*
      3SG   NEG   *se*-afraid   1SG   with   dog
      '(S)he is not as afraid of dogs as me.'

Clearly the clauses in examples (10) to (14) are not of this type. The other examples of a NP dependent of the head of a predication all involve verbs, and it is therefore reasonable to conclude that in the clause type of examples (10) to (14) the emotion and cognition predicate is verbal. In the case of examples such as (8) and (9), the correct analysis is not obvious, and no position as to this question is taken here.[5]

The data presented in this paper does not represent standard Indonesian. Many of the examples are drawn from contemporary, popular novels, one set in Jakarta (SDM) and one set in Surabaya (PYD). The majority of the characters in both novels are educated people, and in conjunction with the judgments of the native speakers with whom I have worked, this data may be said to represent the careful speech of educated Indonesians.[6]

3 NP Stimuli—What Grammatical Function?

The system constituted by the clause types in examples (1) to (3) (and (6)) covers the vast majority of two-place clauses in Indonesian. The null hypothesis therefore must be that this is the transitive system of the language, and that a clause such as example (1) has both subject and object grammati-

---

[5] There is also the possibility that clauses such as examples (17), (18) and (19) should be analysed as containing a zero copula, a possibility which I ignore here.

[6] The two native speakers whose judgments are reported here are both Javanese. The issue of whether the phenomena discussed here are affected by the speaker's first language (if that is not Indonesian) remains for future research.

cal functions in the associated f-structure. The arguments of the following sections will assume that this is the case and I will refer to verbs which participate in this system as transitive verbs; the assumption will however be re-examined later in the paper.

3.1 SUBJ and OBJ

Clauses with emotion predicates look the same as the type exemplified in (6), but the other, related clause types are not possible for these predicates:

(21) *Aku*   *bosan*   *hidup*   *terus-menerus*   *di*
       1SG   bored   life   continue-*meN*-continue   LOC
       Surabaya
       Surabaya
       'I am fed up with monotonous life in Surabaya.' (PYD:180)

(22)   **Aku membosan hidup terus-menerus di Surabaya.*

The type of clause illustrated in example (2) is not possible with a first person actor, but substitution of a third person actor does not make this construction possible with this predicate:

(23) **Hidup*   *terus-menerus*   *di*   *Surabaya*
       life   continue-*meN*-continue   LOC   Surabaya
       dibosannya
       di-bored-3

The type exemplified in (3) is not possible either, although the direct manipulation of example (21) yields a sentence which does have a reading:

(24) *Hidup*   *terus-menerus*   *di*   *Surabaya*
       life   continue-*meN*-continue   LOC   Surabaya
       aku   *bosan*
       1SG   bored
       'This monotonous life in Surabaya, I am fed up with it.'

This clause requires an intonation distinct from that associated with clauses of the type seen in example (3) with a pause after the initial NP which is a topicalised constituent (Chung 1978), and the addition of an auxiliary verb to the sentence makes the distinction absolutely clear. In a construction of the type in example (3), the actor pronoun remains adjacent to the main verb even when an auxiliary or modal is included, but in emotion predicate clauses, the actor pronoun appears to the left of an auxiliary:

(25) | *Buku* | *itu* | *akan* | *saya* | *baca.* |
|------|--------|--------|--------|---------|
| book | that | PROG | 1SG | read |

'I will read that book.'

(26) | *Hidup* | *terus-menerus* | | *di* | *Surabaya* |
|---------|----------------|--|------|-----------|
| life | continue-*meN*-continue | | LOC | Surabaya |
| *aku* | *akan* | *bosan* | | |
| 1SG | FUT | bored | | |

'This monotonous life in Surabaya, I will be fed up with it.'

(27) | **Hidup* | *terus-menerus* | | *di* | *Surabaya* |
|-----------|----------------|--|------|-----------|
| life | continue-*meN*-continue | | LOC | Surabaya |
| *akan* | *aku* | *bosan* | | |
| FUT | 1SG | bored | | |

This evidence shows that these predicates do not participate in the system described in section 2.1.

This status alone may be enough to show that the stimulus argument of an emotion predicate is not an OBJ. If OBJ is defined as the non-SUBJ argument of a transitive verb, then stimuli are not objects because the predicate that they are associated with is not syntactically transitive.[7] A more stringent test requires an OBJ be able to become the SUBJ of a related clause, typically a passive. Leaving aside the issue of whether the related clause types in Indonesian should be described as passive, it is clear that stimuli also fail this test as seen in example (23). Many of the emotion predicates derive transitive verbs with an applicative suffix, and a comparison of their properties with the basic predicates is instructive. The applicativised verbs appear with both *meN-* and *di-* prefixes, with the alternatives used to make an argument available for relativisation as in the following examples:

(28) | *Kamu* | *punya* | *ibu* | *yang* | *menyayangimu.* |
|--------|---------|--------|--------|-----------------|
| 2SG | have | mother | REL | *meN*-love-APPL-2SG |

'You have a mother who loves you.' (SDM:84)

---

[7] I assume that, as SUBJ and OBJ are syntactic concepts, syntactic transitivity is the relevant notion for this argument.

(29) | *Untuk* | *menemui* | | *anak* | *yang* | *begitu* |
| for | *meN*-meet-APPL | | child | REL | so |

disayanginya.
di-love-APPL-3
'In order to meet a child who is so loved.' (SDM:208)

The contrast in syntactic behaviour between the derived transitive verb which does have an OBJ and the emotion predicate is clear. These examples also show a further difference between transitive verbs and emotion and cognition predicates. A verb prefixed with *meN*- or *di*- can have a bound pronoun as its non-subject argument. In the case of *di*- prefixed verbs, this can only be the third person pronoun form *-nya*, given the restriction on the nature of the agent argument for such verbs, but for *meN*- prefixed verbs, the full range of bound pronouns is possible. However, emotion verbs can never have bound pronouns as the stimulus argument, except in cases such as examples (28) and (29) where a transitive verb has been derived:

(30) | **Kamu* | *punya* | *ibu* | *yang* | *sayangmu.* |
| 2SG | have | mother | REL | love-2SG |

(FOR: 'You have a mother who loves you.')

This property has been taken as a criterion for objects in Indonesian by Vamarasi (1999). This position is too strong, but the data nevertheless show another distinction between transitive verbs and emotion and cognition predicates.

The possibility that the stimulus is the SUBJ of its clause can also be eliminated for various reasons. Firstly, it would be surprising that an argument alternated between being an OBL and a SUBJ with no verbal morphology. Secondly, it can be seen from example (28) that the experiencer is the SUBJ of the corresponding applicative verb with *meN*- prefix, the clause type which corresponds to an active clause. Applicativization does not affect SUBJs, therefore the experiencer should be the SUBJ of the basic predicate. A clause can only have one SUBJ, therefore the stimulus cannot be one. Finally, Indonesian has a third person pronoun, *ia*, which is restricted (more or less) to appear in SUBJ position. This pronoun can occur as experiencer of an emotion predicate clause:

(31) | *Ia* | *kuatir* | *suratnya* | *tidak* | *sampai* |
| 3SG | fear | letter-3 | NEG | arrive |

'She was afraid her letter would not arrive.' (ES:313)

Once again, the fact that a clause can only have one SUBJ forces the conclusion that the stimulus cannot be SUBJ.

This section has demonstrated that emotion predicates are not transitive verbs in Indonesian. Therefore, a bare NP stimulus argument following such a predicate cannot be an OBJ. And the (remote) possibility that such arguments are SUBJs has also been eliminated.

3.2 OBL$_\theta$

Having established that a NP stimulus of an emotion predicate cannot be assigned the grammatical functions SUBJ or OBJ, I now turn to examine the arguments as to whether such elements might be classified as OBL$_\theta$. The following pair of examples, which are adjacent in the text in which they occur, suggests that there is no clear semantic difference between the two constructions for speakers:

(32) *Papa   sayang   padamu,   Risa.*
      father   love   to-2   Risa
      'Father loves you, Risa.'

(33) *Risa   juga   sayang   Papa.*
      Risa   also   love   father
      'Risa loves Father too.' (SDM:293)

In many cases, where an argument can be coded either with or without a preposition, the non-prepositional possibility is more directly affected by the event. As that is not the case here, it might be possible to argue that the stimulus in example (33) and similar clauses is still an OBL$_\theta$, but one with non-standard coding. There are two pieces of evidence which suggest that this would be a wrong conclusion.

Before turning to these, there is once more a definitional issue. Indonesian is not a case-marking language, and therefore the obvious distinction between core and non-core arguments is the presence of prepositions. This is not a definitive criterion however. The literature includes examples both of NPs with the coding properties of obliques being treated as direct arguments, and of NPs with the coding properties of direct arguments being treated as obliques. Examples of the first type are animate, referential objects in Spanish, which are preceded by the preposition *a*:

(34) *Busco   a   mi   amigo*
      seek-1SG   a   1SG-POSS   friend
      'I'm looking for my friend.' (Hopper and Thompson 1980:ex 11b)

and various subjects in Icelandic with 'quirky' case-marking:

(35) *Henni   hefur   alltaf   þótt   Ólafur*
      she.DAT   has   always   thought   Olaf-NOM
      leiðinlegur
      boring-NOM.SG
      'She has always considered Olaf boring.'
      (Zaenen, Maling and Thráinsson 1985:ex 13))

An example of the second type is the use of accusative case in Icelandic to mark some temporal adjuncts (Smith 1996:40-42):

(36) *Ég   var   þar   tvo   daga*
      1SG.NOM   was   there   two.ACC   days.ACC
      'I was there for two days.' (Smith 1996:41, ex 49)

Also relevant here is the syncretism of ergative case, which I assume marks terms, with some oblique case, typically instrumental or genitive, in many languages with ergative-absolutive morphology (Blake 1977:60). Such examples show that coding properties alone are not sufficient to establish the syntactic status of an argument. Behavioural tests are necessary also, and I now turn to two such tests which show that the stimulus of example (33) and similar clauses does not have the properties of an oblique argument.

The first way in which NP stimuli behave like direct arguments is that a quantifier can be floated from them. This is not possible with a PP stimulus, or a PP which is an adjunct:

(37) *Anak-anak   itu   suka   gula-gula   itu   semuanya.*
      child-RED   that   like   sugar-RED   that   all
      'All the children like the sweets.' OR
      'The children like all the sweets.'

(38) *Anak-anak   itu   suka   dengan   gula-gula ·   itu*
      child-RED   that   like   with   sugar-RED   that
      semuanya
      all
      'All the children like the sweets.' NOT
      'The children like all the sweets.'

(39) *Orang-orang*   *Sasak*   *datang*   *dengan*   *anak-anaknya*
      man-RED   Sasak   come   with   child-RED-3
      semuanya
      all
      'All the Sasak people came with their children.' NOT
      *'The Sasak people came with all their children.'

In each case, the quantifier can be read as having floated from the SUBJ, and evidence to be presented below will show that other direct arguments also have this property. But only with the NP complement of an emotion verb can the quantifier be read as having floated from the other NP in the clause; when that NP is within a PP the quantifier cannot be construed with it.[8]

    The second piece of evidence comes from extraction facts. Indonesian subjects can always be extracted leaving a gap and this generalisation is agreed on by all sources. The facts regarding other arguments of transitive verbs are in dispute and will be discussed below. For emotion verbs, I am only aware of one discussion of extraction in the literature, Stevens (1970), and this source claims that extraction of NP stimuli is grammatical.[9] This judgment is shared by the native speakers I have consulted. Gapped extraction from PPs is completely impossible however,[10] neither preposition-stranding nor pied-piping is available in Indonesian. The status of the PP involved, selected or not, is not relevant:

(40) *gula-gula*   *yang*   *anak-anak*   *suka*   *itu*
      sugar-RED   REL   child-RED   like   that
      'The sweets that the children like.'

(41) **gula-gula*   *yang*   *anak-anak*   *suka*   *dengan*   *itu*
      sugar-RED   REL   child-RED   like   with   that

(42) **gula-gula*   *dengan*   *yang*   *anak-anak*   *suka*   *itu*
      sugar-RED   with   REL   child-RED   like   that

---

[8] One of my consultants allows both readings of example (37), but the second reading seems to be marginal and is strongly rejected by the other consultant.

[9] Vamarasi (1999) discusses emotion predicates in some detail (see also below), but does not consider extraction.

[10] Extraction with a resumptive pronoun is possible: see Sneddon (1996:289-291), but the native speakers I consulted disallowed this possibility for PP stimuli.

(43) *anak-anak yang orang Sasak datang dengan itu*
      FOR: 'the children that the Sasak people came with.'

Clearly, the behavioural properties of NP stimuli are different from those associated with the grammatical function OBL$_{\theta}$ in Indonesian. It is not possible to maintain an analysis which treats these constituents as obliques with unusual coding properties. Therefore, it seems that the only possible analysis within LFG's inventory of grammatical functions is to treat the stimuli as OBJ$_{\theta}$s and I turn to an examination of the evidence for this position in the following section.

Although not part of the main argument being developed here, it is of interest to note that even when stimuli are coded as PPs, in the construction of examples (8) and (9), they have some properties which are not typical of obliques in general. In this construction, for any one predicate various prepositions are possible introducing the second argument:

(44) | tak | percaya | akan | diri | sendiri |
      |-----|---------|------|------|---------|
      | NEG | believe | about | self | self.INT |

      'lack self-confidence' (E&S:422)

(45) | Kau | kira | sekarang | | orang | akan | percaya |
      |-----|------|----------|---|-------|------|---------|
      | 2SG | guess | now | | man | FUT | believe |

dengan	bualmu	itu?
with	boasting-2	that

      'Do you think anyone will believe your boasting now?' (PYD:200)

(46) | Kami | tidak | percaya | kepada | mereka. |
      |------|-------|---------|--------|---------|
      | 1PL.EX | NEG | believe | to | 3PL |

      'We don't believe (in) them.' (McKay)

(47) | Salahnya, | dulu | saya | tidak | percaya |
      |-----------|------|------|-------|---------|
      | mistakenly | formerly | 1SG | NEG | believe |

padamu
to-2

      'Mistakenly, I did not believe you previously.' (SDM:168)

This behaviour is seen across the whole group of predicates involved, including those which never occur with a NP stimulus, and there does not appear to be any meaning difference depending on the preposition choice. Two factors do influence the choice of preposition. If the following NP is human, then *kepada* or *pada* is preferred.[11] Register is the other factor which has consistent effects on preposition choice with, for example, *akan* only occurring in formal registers and *sama* (not exemplified here) only occurring in informal registers. These data suggest that in this construction the stimulus is being assigned a semantic role directly by the predicate, with the preposition making no semantic contribution. This behaviour is not typical of true OBL_θs, which display semantic interdependence with the preposition or case-marker which licenses them.

3.3. OBJ_θ

As mentioned above, OBJ_θ is the grammatical function of the second object of ditransitive verbs for LFG. Indonesian has a small number of underived verbs which are ditransitive, and a large number derived with the applicative suffixes -*i* and -*kan*. I will discuss here three properties of the second objects of such verbs—access to SUBJ in a related clause, quantifier float and extraction—and compare them with the properties of NP stimuli.

The second object of a ditransitive clause with a *meN*- prefixed verb cannot become subject of a clause with a *di*- prefixed verb:

(48) **Surat   itu   dikirimi   wanita   itu*
      letter   that   *di*-send-APPL   woman   that
      'The letter was sent the woman.' (Chung 1976a:ex 63a)

In the case of derived ditransitive verbs such as that in example (48), the same thematic argument would be OBJ in a related clause with an underived, *meN*-prefixed verb and has access to SUBJ position in the related clause with a *di*-prefixed verb:

(49) *Surat   itu   dikirim   kepada   wanita   itu*
      letter   that   *di*-send   to   woman   that
      'The letter was sent to the woman.'

The motivation for applicative is to make the third argument available to syntactic processes which require core status; there is no motivation to maintain the status of other arguments. In respect of access to SUBJ, the behaviour of the OBJ_θs and the NP stimuli is similar. NP stimuli cannot become SUBJ of a related clause either unless the verb is morphologically altered. They can then become SUBJ of a related clause headed by a *di*-prefixed derived verb (example (29)) and the behaviour of the two argu-

---

[11] One consultant reports that this is taught as a prescriptive rule in the Indonesian education system.

ment types diverges here. Second objects cannot be SUBJ or OBJ with derived verbs while stimuli can. However, the relevant verbal derivation, applicative, promotes an oblique argument to core status, therefore the source of the applicativised emotion verbs must be the construction with a PP stimulus and the comparison between the two types is not in fact direct on this point.[12]

In the previous section, examples were given which showed that a quantifier could float from a SUBJ. This is also possible from OBJs and from OBJ_θs:

(50)   *Saya*   *pukul*   *anak-anak*   *itu*   *kemarin*   *semuanya*
       1SG   hit   child-RED   that   yesterday   all
       'I hit all the children yesterday.'

(51)   *Saya*   *memberinya*   *hadiah*   *itu*   *semuanya*
       1SG   *meN*-give-3   gift   that   all
       'I gave her all the presents.'

The descriptive generalisation is that quantifiers can float from any direct argument in Indonesian. And as previously shown, a quantifier can also float from an NP stimulus (example (37), repeated here):

(52)   *Anak-anak*   *itu*   *suka*   *gula-gula*   *itu*   *semuanya.*
       child-RED   that   like   sugar-RED   that   all
       'All the children like the sweets.' OR
       'The children like all the sweets.'

In this case, the stimuli behave like direct arguments; they are not SUBJ or OBJ, so OBJ_θ is the remaining possibility.

Many descriptions of Indonesian state that extraction (relative clause formation and question formation) is only possible with SUBJs. The facts are a good deal more complicated than this as soon as anything other than the prescriptive standard is investigated; a more complete account is given by Voskuil (1996:ch 8). For the purposes of this discussion, I will assume that all direct arguments can be extracted in the absence of verb affixa-

---

[12] I ignore here the issue of applicative derivations in Indonesian which take a transitive verb and derive another transitive verb with a different meaning e.g. *memergok* 'catch someone by surprise', *memergoki* 'catch someone redhanded'.

tion.[13] Thus an OBJ can be extracted from a clause of the type seen in example (6) (auxiliary added to disambiguate the construction):[14]

(53)	buku	yang	dia	akan	baca	itu
book	REL	3SG	FUT	read	that
'the book that she will read'

As for OBJ$_\theta$s, judgments vary. As might be expected, such arguments cannot be extracted when the verb carries a prefix, and no native speaker I have consulted will allow extraction when the verb is derived with an applicative suffix. In the case of underived, unprefixed ditransitive verbs, judgments vary. At least some speakers will permit extraction of the second object from clauses of this type:[15]

(54)	Saya	akan	beri	dia	buku	itu
1SG	FUT	give	3SG	book	that
'I will give him the book.'

(55)	?buku	yang	saya	akan	beri	dia	itu
book	REL	1SG	FUT	give	3SG	that
'the book that I will give him'

As demonstrated above (example (40)), this type of extraction is also possible with a NP stimuli:

(56)	orang	yang	saya	suka	itu
person	REL	1SG	like	that
'the person that I like'

On this test, the NP stimulus possesses the syntactic properties of a direct argument more clearly than OBJ$_\theta$s. I have demonstrated that NP stimuli cannot be plausibly assigned any of the other three grammatical functions recognised by LFG, and that their syntactic properties are very similar to those of OBJ$_\theta$s. Within the theory as currently formulated, this would seem to be the only possible analysis. The only alternative is to add a grammati-

---

[13] The construction seen in example (3) is a special case: despite the lack of a verb affixes, only the SUBJ can be extracted. Musgrave (2001b) offers a tentative account of why this should be so.

[14] Michael Ewing (p.c.) informs me that he has observed numerous examples of such constructions in recorded conversation of educated Indonesians.

[15] This is not true for the verb *ajar* 'teach' for my primary consultant. I have no explanation of this fact.

cal function to the inventory, and the final section of this paper examines which of these two possibilities is preferable from a theoretical point of view. First, I consider whether a configurational account of the data might be more satisfactory.

4   Principles and Parameters Analyses—VP Shells and Internal Arguments

The previous sections have argued that the bare NP complement of an emotion or cognition verb has syntactic properties which resemble those of a second object, an OBJ$_\theta$ in LFG terms. This grammatical function is given equal status to SUBJ and OBJ (and OBL) in LFG, but other syntactic theories do not accord it the same status. In particular, principles and parameters syntax, since Larson (1988), analyses second objects as the result of DP-movement in a particular VP configuration. The aim of this section is to show that such an analysis of the Indonesian data under consideration is implausible.

In Larson's analysis of the double object construction (1988, afterwards ODOC), ditransitive verbs project nested VP configurations. The basic structure for a clause containing such a verb is the following:

(57)

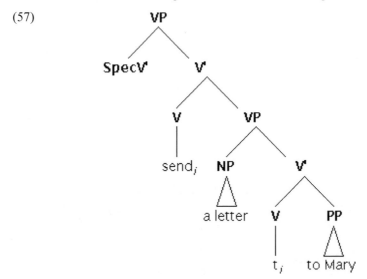

The double object configuration is the result of an operation in the lower VP which ODOC describes as similar to passive in that the specifier or subject position becomes athematic. By Burzio's generalisation (Burzio 1986), the verb therefore is not able to assign case to its complement; that argument moves to the specifier position and the other argument (the theme) is realised as a V' adjunct:

(58)

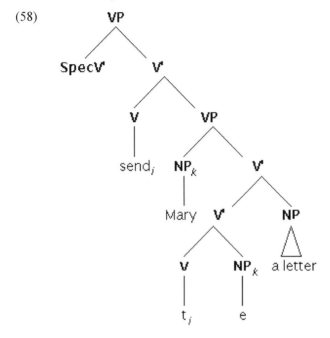

In all cases, the verb raises from the lower VP to the higher VP (before moving to a higher functional head if necessary).

The first problem in applying this type of analysis to the Indonesian data is to decide what the lexical characteristics of the verb should be, that is, what d-structure does it project? If a layered VP is only projected by a verb with two internal arguments, then we must conclude that Indonesian emotion verbs are of this type. Further, we must conclude that in their basic configuration, these verbs project the experiencer argument to a lower structural position than the stimulus. This must be the case as it is the stimulus which will end up as the second object and it must therefore originate as the specifier of the lower VP. Then a passive-like operation must obligatorily apply in the lower VP, and, following this, the experiencer must move to subject position. These instances of DP movement are not the problematic part of the analysis. An unaccusative verb does not assign a thematic role to a subject position, and as noted by Burzio (1986), does not assign case to its object. It is plausible to extend these generalisations to the question of two-place unaccusatives by assuming that such verbs cannot assign case from either of the positions they occupy within VP. Thus, in a structure such as (57) with a two-place unaccusative verb, the conditions are met for Larson's PASSIVE operation: no thematic role is assigned to the specifier of the lower VP. This results in a structure like (58), and on the assumption suggested here, the verb in its higher position cannot case-mark the DP in the lower specifier position. Therefore this DP has no option but to move upward again, finally to the case position, specifier of IP. The second object can receive case from the verb if Belletti and Rizzi's (1988) revision of Burzio's generalisation is adopted. Their version of this principle states that a verb which does not assign a thematic role to its subject cannot assign structural case to an object. Thus, the second object can be assigned inherent case by the verb without affecting the other elements of the analysis.[16] There is a possible analysis that gives the desired result: that the stimulus argument is a second object derived by movement in the lower VP of a layered structure.

However, such an analysis can be ruled out on both empirical and theoretical grounds. Firstly, the empirical evidence as to the unaccusative status of these verbs is unreliable. Vamarasi (1999:chapter 3) proposes that -*kan* suffixation is a test for the status of intransitive verbs in Indonesian. The claim is that where -*kan* has applicative effect, the base verb is unergative, and where the suffix has causative effect, the base verb is unaccusative. But when applied to emotion and cognition verbs, this test does not give unequivocal results (Musgrave 2001a:chapter 4). On one interpretation, the test is not reliable at all and there is no reason to accept that any of the emotion and cognition verbs are two-place unaccusatives. On an alternative interpretation, some emotion and cognition verbs are unaccusative, but there are some which are not. In this case, the Larsonian analysis would be unable to account for the fact that there are Indonesian emotion and cognition verbs which are not unaccusative on the test proposed, but which nevertheless have second arguments which have the same properties as those which are unaccusative on the same test.

Theoretically, there is a consensus across all versions of the thematic hierarchy that experiencers are high on the thematic hierarchy, certainly higher than stimuli (or themes). Where surface syntactic relations do not reflect this ranking, for example with a verb such as English *frighten*, various sorts of special pleading have been considered necessary. For example, Pesetsky (1995) claims that in such cases the stimulus is not a theme, it does not have the same semantic role as the second argument of *fear*. He

---

[16] ODOC claims that the lowest V' bar is reanalysed as a V for this, but the details are not relevant here.

argues for a more fine-grained analysis of semantic roles, specifically that the role *causer* is important for inverse psych verbs. The question of what is the correct level of detail at which to make generalisations about semantic roles is an important one, but one which is beyond the scope of this study.[17] Another approach is that of Grimshaw (1990), who accepts the thematic hierarchy, but dissociates thematic and aspectual information. In the case of verbs such as *frighten*, Grimshaw argues that information from the event structure conflicts with the thematic hierarchy, that is, the stimulus has a causal role and is more prominent in the event that the experiencer, and that this information is treated as more important in argument structure. Note however that Indonesian has only the one type of emotion and cognition verb—there is no syntactic evidence requiring us to propose more fine-grained distinctions here, either in thematic or aspectual structure.

The claim that some verbs have two internal arguments and no external argument, that they are two-place unaccusatives, has been made by Belletti and Rizzi (1988) for two of the three classes of psych verbs in Italian. However, the essential feature of their analysis is that the d-structure for such verbs reflects the thematic prominence of the arguments although the surface relations are reversed (that is, the stimulus is the surface subject).[18] For the remaining class of verbs (the *temere* class), the experiencer is subject and the theme is object. The null hypothesis in this case must be that that if surface thematic relations are as we expect, then so are relations at any other level. Belletti and Rizzi do not question this assumption and argue for an analysis of the *temere* class which respects it, that is, that the experiencer is an external argument. The facts give no reason not to accept a similar analysis for emotion and cognition verbs in Indonesian: there is only one class of verbs, and surface thematic relations do not diverge from assumed underlying relations.[19]

5 Theoretical and Empirical Problems

The previous sections have argued that, given the assumption that transitive verbs are those which participate in the system seen in examples (1) to (6),

---

[17] Dowty 1991 and Foley and Van Valin 1984 present arguments for only recognising two roles as relevant to syntax. At the other extreme, McRae, Ferretti and Amyote (1997) present psycho-linguistic evidence suggesting that no such generalisations are used in comprehension.

[18] Belletti and Rizzi's analysis is thus a P&P reworking of the Relational Grammar inversion analysis of such constructions (Blake 1990:46-50)

[19] There is another possible analysis in Belletti and Rizzi's scheme which captures the Indonesian facts—that the verbs are two-place unaccusatives which assign case inherently to the theme argument, explaining its second-object properties and also why it is the experiencer which must move—but this is also ruled out by the considerations just discussed.

the grammatical function which is most appropriate for the NP stimulus argument of an emotion and cognition verb is OBJ_θ. I now turn to the question of whether this analysis sits comfortably within the broader LFG framework, more specifically, whether the use made of the grammatical function OBJ_θ is consistent with the theory. I argue that the analysis is consistent with the theory but is also typologically surprising, and that this is contrary to the spirit of LFG, and that emotion and cognition verbs provide empirical evidence for questioning the assumption made about the transitive system of Indonesian.

5.1 The Status of OBJ_θ in LFG

Classic LFG (Kaplan and Bresnan 1982) admitted OBJECT-2 as a basic grammatical function. The grammatical function was necessary for the analysis of, for example, English double object constructions such as:

(59)   Mary baked James a cake.

But in a theory where the inventory of grammatical functions did not depend on any other theoretical construct, the status of this grammatical function could be marginal; it could be a necessary evil with no theoretical consequences. However, with the introduction of Lexical Mapping Theory (LMT) (Bresnan and Kanerva 1989), the grammatical function OBJ_θ has a rather different theoretical status. The apparatus of LMT predicts that four grammatical functions, and only four, must exist. The four are placed in a markedness hierarchy, but the theoretical apparatus accords them all equal legitimacy. The restricted role played by OBJ_θ is then somewhat surprising, as is the fact that not all languages have this grammatical function. This point can be made clear by considering the asymmetry between the two markedness relations established by LMT. SUBJ is the unmarked grammatical function with the other three grammatical functions all more marked (they all have a + value for at least one feature, OBJ_θ is the most marked with + values for both features). Typologically, this plausibly translates as the claim that SUBJs appear more freely in a language than the other grammatical functions, but not as a claim that there are languages which have SUBJs but which lack all other grammatical functions. Any such claim would be incoherent to the extent that SUBJ is a relational notion: it is the grammatical function of the most prominent or most syntactically privileged DP in the clause and this clearly implies that it must be possible for there to be other DPs in the clause with some other grammatical function.[20] But the relation between OBJ and OBL_θ on the one hand and OBJ_θ on the other is different: in this case the increase in markedness can mean that the most marked function is optional. This does not follow from the apparatus of LMT, where the theoretical difference in markedness is the same in the two cases.

It might be suggested that the evidence presented here justifies proposing a more fine-grained analysis of non-subject arguments in Indonesian than is allowed by LFG. The syntactic properties of DP stimuli and OBJ_θs are not identical, and the considerable overlap might be due only to the fact that both are types of direct argument. There might be more than three types of non-subject argument in the language. However, the LMT offers a strong theory-internal argument against adopting such an analysis. Two binary-valued features allow exactly the four grammatical functions assumed by the theory and introducing a new grammatical function would disrupt this aspect of the theory. To do so must mean that the two features used thus far do not exhaust the relevant information, and another feature would be required. This in turn would mean that rather than adding one grammatical function, at least two would have to be added, on the assumption that the new feature would be dependent on one of those already assumed. If the new feature was independent of the existing ones, then four new grammatical functions would be added to the system. To my knowledge, there is no empirical support for reducing the constraints on the theory in this way. This consideration suggests that LFG should either seek an explanation of the asymmetry discussed in the previous paragraph, or should seek analyses, such as that proposed here, which accord a greater importance to the OBJ_θ grammatical function.

Against this is the aim of LFG to be what might be called a 'typologically responsible' framework. That is, the framework aims to deal with the full typological range of languages without doing violence to the facts. And the typological facts are that second objects are not used in all languages and that where they do exist their occurrence is limited. There is empirical evidence from a number of languages, some referred to in previous sections, that subject and indirect object, or a nominative and dative case array, is a diathesis that occurs in many languages and that this is associated with predicates of low transitivity (see Blume 1998 for a partial survey). The data under consideration here might be thought to fall under this category, but the match is in fact poor. Indonesian is very similar to English in its treatment of three-place events (modulo the presence of morphological ap-

---

[20] This argument applies in cases such as Mel'cuk's analysis of Lezgian (1983) as a language without transitive verbs. The non-subject DPs still have to have some grammatical function, in this case oblique.

plicative). Recipients and beneficiaries, the prototypical semantic roles which receive dative case in case-marking languages, are coded either as obliques or as direct objects; they are never second objects. Some of the examples of this clause type in other languages are restricted to verbs denoting psychological processes, and these might be considered particularly relevant. But as discussed in previous sections, such verbs have the experiencer in dative case. There is then a double mismatch with the Indonesian data: dative is not the relevant semantic relation and experiencer is not the semantic role which is treated in nonstandard fashion. Therefore on typological grounds the proposed analysis of Indonesian emotion and cognition verbs is extremely unusual. The fact that the apparatus of LFG can accommodate the analysis is not a sufficient reason for accepting it without examining alternatives.

5.2 Empirical Issues

A basic assumption that has guided the discussion above is that a two-place verb which does not enter into the system given in examples (1) to (6) is not a transitive verb in Indonesian. The analysis of the second argument of emotion and cognition verbs as a second object is a direct result of this assumption. However, in addition to the concerns discussed in the preceding section there are empirical reasons to be uncomfortable with the analysis and to question the assumption.

Firstly, the syntactic properties of the arguments in question are not identical to those of second objects. Relative clause constructions with the stimulus argument as head are accepted by all speakers as fully grammatical, as noted by Stevens in 1970 (see example (40) above). On the other hand, relative clauses with second objects as head are impossible for many speakers, and marginal for some speakers, but subject to lexical idiosyncrasy even for them (see example (55)). Secondly, the type of clause in which emotion and cognition verbs appear is strikingly similar to the type of clause seen in example (6). In this clause type, an unaffixed verb appears and the actor is always subject. In particular, extraction of the second argument is fully grammatical from this type of clause:

(60)   *Inilah*   *buku*   *yang*   *Badu*   *sudah*   *baca*
        this-EMPH   book   REL   Badu   PERF   read
        'This is the book which Badu has read already.'
        (Voskuil 1996:189, ex4)

Also, unprefixed verbs of this type can never have a bound pronoun as their second argument:

(61) *Dia*   *baca*   *buku*   *itu*
      3SG   read   book   that
      'S/he read the book.'

(62) **Dia*   *bacanya*
      3SG   read-3
      (FOR: 'S/he read the book.')

On the assumptions adopted to this point, the second argument is an OBJ in one case and an OBJ$_\theta$ in the other case, despite the great similarity in their syntactic properties.

In addition to the reasons discussed thus far, there is a further reason to question the assumption that the prefixed verb system is the transitive system of Indonesian. Morphology in Indonesian is exclusively derivational; the language systematically lacks inflectional morphology, with perhaps one exception. There is no morphological marking of tense, aspect or mood, no agreement or cross-referencing markers (bound pronouns can never be doubled) and no morphological marking of number. The only partial exception to this generalisation is the use of reduplication. Reduplication of a noun can indicate plurality, and reduplication of a verb can indicate repeated action. But in both cases, other meanings are possible also (Sneddon 1996:15-21). Prefixed verbs must therefore be considered as less basic, in some sense, than unprefixed verbs. I have argued elsewhere (Musgrave 2001b) that the function of the prefixes is to specify directly the linking of one semantic argument of the verb to the SUBJ grammatical function, and that this represents a continuation of the older Austronesian system seen in Philippine languages. LMT has only limited application is such a system. In contrast, unprefixed verbs behave as would be predicted by LMT, with the more agent-like argument consistently being mapped to the SUBJ grammatical function. In a cross-linguistic perspective, it therefore is more perspicuous to treat unprefixed verbs as true transitive verbs, and to maintain a picture of Indonesian syntax which allows for two different types of clausal organisation for verbs with two arguments. In one case, the verb is underived, the mapping of its arguments to grammatical functions is mediated by LMT and I propose that the non-subject arguments of such verbs should be treated as OBJs. In the other case, the verb is morphologically derived, the linking of its arguments to grammatical functions is not mediated by LMT and the status of the non-subject argument is unclear. The following table summarises the relevant properties of the two types:

(63) | Property | Prefixed-V | Unprefixed-V |
|---|---|---|
| **Derived** | X | |
| Linking | Direct | LMT |
| **Non-subject argument**: | | |
| Quantifier float | X | X |
| Bound pronoun | X | |
| Extraction | | X |

On this account, emotion and cognition verbs are regular transitive verbs with one oddity: they do not form derived (prefixed) verbs directly like other two-place verbs, but require the intermediate step of applicative derivation first. As noted in the discussion of section 4, it is not uncommon for verbs in this semantic field to have unusual properties in the transitivity system of a language. Whether this is a sufficient explanation for the behaviour of Indonesian emotion and cognition verbs is a question remaining for future research.

6 Sources of Examples

E&S - Echols, Jason M. and Hassan Shadily (1994) *Kamus Indonesia-Inggris* (3rd ed) Jakarta: Penerbit PT Gramedia.

McKay - Corpus of Indonesian journalism collected by Helen McKay.

PYD - Fredy S. (1991) *Perasaan yang ditinggalkan* Jakarta: Gultom Agency.

SDM - Mira W. (1995) *Sekelam dendam Marisa* Jakarta: Penerbit PT Gramedia.

7 References

Belletti, Adriana & Luigi Rizzi. 1988. Psych verbs and θ-theory. *Natural Language and Linguistic Theory* 6:291–352.

Benjamin, Geoffrey. 1993. Grammar and polity: The cultural and political background to Standard Malay. In *The Role of Theory in Language Description* ed. William A. Foley. 341–392. Berlin/New York: Mouton de Gruyter.

Blake, Barry J. 1977. *Case-marking in Australian Languages*. Canberra: Australian Institute of Aboriginal Studies.

Blake, Barry J. 1990. *Relational Grammar*. London/New York: Routledge.

Blume, Kerstin. 1998. A contrastive analysis of interaction verbs with dative complements. *Linguistics* 36:253–280.

Bresnan, Joan W. 2001. *Lexical-Functional Syntax*. Oxford: Blackwell.

Bresnan, Joan W. & Jonni Kanerva. 1989. Locative inversion in Chichewa: A case study of factorization in grammar. *Linguistic Inquiry* 20:1–50.

Burzio, Luigi. 1986. *Italian Syntax: a Government and Binding approach.* Dordrecht: Reidel.

Chung, Sandra. 1976a. An Object-Creating Rule in Bahasa Indonesia. *Linguistic Inquiry* 7:41–87.

Chung, Sandra. 1976b. On the subject of two passives in Indonesian. In *Subject and Topic* ed. Charles Li. 57–98. New York: Academic Press.

Chung, Sandra. 1978. Stem sentences in Indonesian. In *Second International Conference on Austronesian Linguistics: Proceedings Fascicle 1* ed. S. Wurm & L. Carrington. 335–365. Canberra: Pacific Linguistics (C-61).

Cumming, Susanna. 1991. *Functional Change: The case of Malay constituent order.* Berlin: Mouton de Gruyter.

Dowty, David R. 1991. Thematic proto-roles and argument selection. *Language* 67:547–619.

Foley, William A. & Robert D. Van Valin Jr. 1984. *Functional syntax and universal grammar.* Cambridge, UK: Cambridge University Press.

Grimshaw, Jane. 1990. *Argument Structure.* Cambridge, Massachusetts: MIT Press.

Hopper, Paul & Sandra Thompson. 1980. Transitivity in grammar and discourse. *Language* 56:251–299.

Kaplan, Ronald M. & Joan Bresnan. 1982. Lexical-Functional Grammar: A formal system for grammatical representation. In *The Mental Representation of Grammatical Relations* ed. J. Bresnan. 173–281. Cambridge, Massachusetts: MIT Press.

Larson, Richard K. 1988. On the Double Object construction. *Linguistic Inquiry* 19:335–391.

Mahdi, Waruno. 1998. Adjectives. Posting to *Bahasa* list 13 February 1998, available at http://w3.rz-berlin.mpg.de/~wm/PAP/BHS-L/BHS-adjectives.html.

McCrae, Ken, Todd R. Ferretti & Liane Amyote. 1997. Thematic roles as verb-specific concepts. *Language and Cognitive Processes* 12:137–176.

Mel'cuk, Igor. 1983. Grammatical subject and the problem of the ergative constructions in Lezgian. *Folio Slavica* 5:246–293.

Musgrave, Simon. 2001a. *Non-subject Arguments and Grammatical Functions in Bahasa Indonesia* Ph.D Thesis, University of Melbourne.

Musgrave, Simon. 2001b. Pronouns and morphology: undergoer subject clauses in Indonesian. In *Yearbook of Morphology* ed. G. Booij & J. van Marle. 155–186. Dordrecht/Boston/London: Kluwer Academic Publishers.

Pesetsky, David. 1995. *Zero Syntax.* Cambridge, Massachusetts: MIT Press.

Smith, Henry. 1996. *Restrictiveness in Case Theory.* Cambridge, UK: Cambridge University Press.

Sneddon, James Neil. 1996. *Indonesian Reference Grammar.* St Leonards, NSW: Allen and Unwin.

Stevens, Alan M. 1970. Pseudo-transitive verbs in Indonesian. *Indonesia* 9:67–72.

Vamarasi, M. A. Kana. 1999. Grammatical Relations in Bahasa Indonesia. Canberra: Pacific Linguistics (D-93).

Voskuil, Jan. 1996. *Comparative Morphology: Verb Taxonomy in Indonesian, Tagalog and Dutch* HIL Dissertations 21. The Hague: Holland Academic Graphics.

Zaenen, Annie, Joan Maling & Hoskildur Thráinsson. 1985. Case and grammatical function: the Icelandic passive. *Natural Language and Linguistic Theory* 3:441–483.

7

Grammatical Properties of the Ergative Noun Phrase in Tongan

MICHAEL DUKES

1 Introduction

What is the grammatical status of the ergative case-marked NP in Tongan (and, by extension, in the other ergative languages of Polynesia)? It has been treated as a subject by some linguists (e.g. Churchward 1953, Chung 1978, Anderson 1976) and as an oblique by others (Lynch 1972, Biggs 1974, Dukes 1996, 1998a). On the basis of recent accounts of grammatical relations in Western Malayo-Polynesian (WMP) (Schachter 1984, Artawa and Blake 1997, Wechsler and Arka 1998) and recent proposals regarding the treatment of ergativity (Manning 1996), it is also not out of the question that it might be analysed as a complement of some sort. The question is of interest to grammarians for several reasons.

Firstly, the treatment of the Tongan ergative bears directly on the very issue of how to define the terms 'subject', 'complement', etc. It requires us to make choices about which criteria will be considered diagnostic for the

Voice and Grammatical Relations in Austronesian Languages.
Simon Musgrave and Peter Austin

grammatical categories that linguistic theories make available and it also provides an interesting test case for formalizing these notions.

Secondly, as in the case of 'patient-prominent' languages in WMP (such as Balinese (Artawa and Blake 1997, Wechsler and Arka 1998) and Malagasy (Keenan 1999, Dukes 1998b) the treatment of the Tongan ergative bears on the proper treatment of constraints on linking between semantic roles and grammatical relations. If the ergative is not the subject in a transitive sentence, then the linking patterns in the language are not the canonical ones that are often assumed to constitute the default for human languages (i.e. that unmarked grammatical prominence correlates directly with thematic prominence (Givón 1984, Bresnan and Kanerva 1989, amongst a multitude of others).

Thirdly, the facts of the Tongan ergative bear on recent hypotheses about the nature of ergativity; in particular, the recent claim (Manning 1996) that genuinely syntactically ergative languages should all be analyzed as having 'inverse' grammatical relations. This approach postulates that the ergative argument (i.e. the transitive agent) is in fact the direct object of a transitive predicate. Thus the characteristics of the Tongan ergative appear to bear directly on the extent to which the inverse analysis of ergativity can be maintained.

In this paper I will argue for an analysis which differs somewhat from all of those referred to above but which is most closely related to the view that the Tongan ergative noun phrase is syntactically an oblique. In general, its properties are strikingly similar to those of the English passive *by*-phrase, which is analyzed in both LFG and HPSG as an optional oblique complement (Bresnan 1982, Pollard and Sag 1987). However, in order to account for certain word order facts that distinguish the ergative from other arguments, I will actually end up treating the ergative as a kind of agentive adjunct, an analysis which I believe will extend naturally to account for the properties of 'verb-adjacent agents' in some WMP languages such as Malagasy. Just as some analyses within HPSG have gone as far as treating negatives and other adverbs as grammatically selected complements (e.g. Kim and Sag 2002), despite the fact that these elements are not semantically selected in any obvious sense by the head which they modify, I will argue that the Tongan ergative represents the opposite possibility—that a semantically selected element is not grammatically selected by the head. If correct, this analysis is problematic for Manning's inverse analysis of ergativity. The analysis also employs a list-based notion of argument structure (a-structure) that has become standard in recent HPSG (Manning and Sag 1999, Wechsler and Arka 1998, Dukes 1998a). The a-structure feature allows us to account for certain nominative properties displayed by the ergative while maintaining the view that the 'surface' syntax is significantly ergatively oriented.

2 A Description of Some Key Properties of the Ergative Argument

While Tongan has frequently been held up as an archetype of the 'surface ergative' or 'morphologically ergative' language (e.g. Anderson 1976, 1992), I have previously argued that its syntax has substantial ergatively organized properties (Dukes 1996, 1998a), following some widely held views in the Polynesianist literature (Biggs 1974, Clark 1976, 1981, Hooper 1993).[1] The main predicate types underlying any analysis of grammatical relations in Tongan, either ergative or accusative, are outlined below.

2.1 Predicate Classes Selecting Ergative NPs in Tongan

The ergative NP in Tongan has a number of distributional characteristics that distinguish it from other noun phrases in the language. Firstly, it may only appear in a sentence as an argument of a *canonical transitive* (or *ergative*) predicate, which constitute a large class of semantically two-place predicates.

(1) *Na'e huo 'e Siale 'a e ngoué*
    PST hoe ERG Siale ABS DET garden
    'Siale hoed the garden.'   [ergative predicate]

Ergative predicates select an ergative argument and an absolutive argument, in contrast to the other two main predicate classes in Tongan; *middle* predicates, which select an absolutive argument and a goal or locative marked argument, and *intransitive* (or *absolutive*) predicates, which select just an absolutive NP.

(2) *Na'e muimui 'a Siale ki he tangatá*
    PST follow ABS Siale Goal DET man
    'Siale followed the man.'   [middle predicate]

(3) *Kuo 'alu 'a Siale*
    PST go ABS Siale
    'Siale has left.'   [intransitive predicate]

---

[1] See also Dixon 1994, Manning 1996 for critiques of some of the key criteria that have been used to support the surface ergative view.

Ergative predicates denote a prototypically transitive event (Hopper and Thompson 1980) in contrast to the other two-place predicate class, the middle predicates, which primarily denote psychological states or activities that lack most of the entailments typical of fully transitive predicates (Dowty 1991). The ergative NP thus usually denotes a prototypical agent acting on the entity denoted by the absolutive, though it may also denote an entity that is more instrument-like than agentive.

(4) | *Pea* | *ko* | *e* | *papa* | *na'e* | *'ikai* | *lava* | *'o* |
     |--------|-------|-------|--------|--------|---------|--------|--------|
     | CONJ | TOP | DET | wood | PST | NEG | able | CONJ |
     | *tutu'u* | *e* | *he* | *ki'i* | *tutu'ú.* | | | |
     | cut | ERG | DET | DIM | chisel | | | |

'But the wood was not able to be cut by the the little chisel.'   [MR][2]

A smallish number of two-place predicates in Tongan are labile (e.g. *vakai* 'seek', *kai* 'eat') meaning that they may appear either as ergative or middle predicates, depending largely on the pragmatics of the particular situation in which a token happens to be used. Furthermore, ergative predicates may be derived from middle ones quite freely via a process that attaches some allomorph of the so-called Polynesian 'transitive suffix' (usually realized as -*'i*) to the middle predicate. Thus, in many circumstances, Tongan speakers can make an active choice whether or not to use an ergative or middle predicate, as contextual circumstances dictate.[3]

(5) | *Na'e* | *sio* | *'a* | *Mele* | *ki* | *he* | *va'inga* |
     |--------|-------|------|--------|-------|------|-----------|
     | PST | see | ABS | PN | Goal | DET | game |

'Mary saw the game.'

(6) | *Na'e* | *sio'i* | *'e* | *Mele* | *e* | *va'inga* |
     |--------|---------|------|--------|------|-----------|
     | PST | watch | ERG | PN | DET | game |

'Mary watched the game.'

---

[2] Sources for examples given in brackets after free translations. Abbreviations are explained at the end of this paper.

[3] In view of the fact that this suffix can also be applied to an ergative verb to derive an 'executive form' of the verb (Churchward 1953:241) it is not itself a relation-changing affix.

In addition to ergative predicates that take two nominal arguments there is also a small class of communication predicates (reporting speech of various sorts) that take an ergative NP and a clausal argument.[4]

(7)   *... pea*   *tala*   *mai*   *'e*   *Tevita*   *ko*   *e*
        CONJ   say   DIR1   ERG   PN   TOP   DET
        hingoa   *'o*   *e*   *hakaú*   *ko*   *"Minerva Reef"*.
        name   GEN   DET   reef   TOP
        'and then Tevita told us that the name of the reef was
        "Minerva Reef".'   [MR]

At present it is not entirely clear to me whether these should be treated as a subtype of the ergative predicate class or as a completely distinct set of verbs. Whichever path turns out to be the most enlightening one, it is certainly the case that, in terms of simple token counts in Tongan text, ergative case-marked NPs appear far more frequently with this small set of verbs than with ordinary ergative predicates.

2.2   The Relationship of the Ergative NP to the Predicate

Since ergative case-marked NPs can only appear as arguments of ergative predicates, they are clearly 'selected' in some obvious sense by those predicates. Prima facie, this might lead us to one of two conclusions: either that ergatives are complements of ergative predicates or that they are subjects. However, there are problems with both these approaches, which I will now review (see also Dukes 1998a for further discussion).

In the first place, while the ergative argument is clearly semantically linked to the predicate that selects it, it is not the case that the ergative argument *must* be realized in the sentence. It is essentially an optional modifier of the predicate, as the following examples indicate.

(8)   *Ne*   *fai*   *'ema*   *kai*   *'i*   *he*   *funga*
        PST   do   1PL.GEN   eat   LOC   DET   TOP
        sima.
        concrete
        '(We) ate our food on top of the concrete (tank).'   [FHJ]

---

[4] Tongan directionals code direction by person: 'toward speaker', 'toward hearer' and 'toward another person'. These forms are glossed here as e.g. DIR1 = 1st person directional, towards speaker.

(9)   *...na'e*   *tamate'i*   *'a*   *e*   *Misini*   *ka*
        PST   kill   ABS   DET   engine   CONJ
        mau   *folau*   *lā*   *pē, ...*
        1PL.EX   sail   sail   only
        '(We) turned off the engine and we just travelled by sail.' [MR]

In both examples above it is possible to reconstruct a missing pronoun as fulfilling the semantic role of the subject, but the sentences could just as well be translated in English by a passive. As Biggs (1974) points out for the case of East Futunan (and basically the same facts seem to apply in the other ergative languages of Polynesia), native speakers feel that a sentence is 'incomplete' if it lacks an absolutive argument but not if it lacks an ergative. When omitted, the absolutive argument is understood as picking out a predetermined referent, typically overtly realized in the local linguistic context. Missing ergatives on the other hand may simply fail to denote any element in the discourse and an existential interpretation is frequently inferred. This behaviour illustrates a striking parallel with the *by*-phrase in an English passive, which is similarly licensed semantically by the predicate it modifies but at the same time is completely optional. Furthermore, when the *by*-phrase is unexpressed, the agentive semantic role may be left unlinked to any element in the discourse and is typically interpreted existentially.

2.3   On the Nonsubjecthood of the Ergative

The behaviour described above counts against the idea that the ergative is a subject because subjects are prototypically obligatory referential arguments, particularly in Austronesian. Indeed the datum supports the idea that the absolutive is the subject because it does accord with these subject properties in all three clause types (i.e. ergative, middle and absolutive). The possible complementhood of the ergative also looks questionable, given its across-the-board optionality. Indeed, the optionality of the ergative is considerably more extreme than the discussion so far may have suggested because there is in fact a strong tendency to omit the ergative argument whenever possible, even in circumstances where there may be some uncertainty about the exact identity of the inferred agent. This tendency leads in Samoan to what Duranti and Ochs (1990) have called the 'two constituent bias', in which the large majority of clauses tend to be realized as a predicate followed by an absolutive argument. Furthermore, the occurrence of clauses headed by an ergative predicate containing overt tokens of both the ergative and the absolutive argument are quite uncommon.

Despite the discussion above, several additional pieces of evidence have been put forward in support of the hypothesis that the Polynesian ergative is the subject.[5]

Firstly, the ergative is clearly the most agentive argument of the predicate. Under the assumption that linking to grammatical relations is determined according to a thematic hierarchy, we expect the ergative to be the subject. However, if this view of linking were correct there would hardly be any empirical issue to discuss. That there is such an issue implies that the linking generalizations can only be taken as suggestive, not definitional. Alternatively, the thematic hierarchy may be understood as constraining the linking of semantic roles to argument structure without implying anything about the spelling out of 'surface' grammatical relations (as proposed for Balinese by Wechsler and Arka 1998).

A second, much stronger, argument for the subjecthood of the ergative is that a pronominal ergative is obligatorily doubled by a preverbal clitic pronoun, which has the same form as the preverbal pronoun that doubles an absolutive pronoun in an absolutive clause.

(10) Na'á   ku   'alu   ki   kolo   'aneafi.
      PST   1SG   go   Goal   town   yesterday
      'I went to town yesterday.'

(11) Na'á   ku   sio'i   ('e   au)   'a   e
      PST   1SG   watch   ERG   1SG   ABS   DET
      va'inga   'aneafi.
      game   yesterday
      'I watched the game yesterday.'

Note that when the preverbal pronoun appears, the postverbal pronoun is typically deleted, unless contrast or emphasis is required. This nominative parallelism is historically one of the key facts supporting the surface ergative analysis of Tongan and any analysis of Tongan grammatical relations must be able to account for it. However, both the facts themselves and the conclusion that they have been used to justify are less robust than might first appear.

In the first place, while Tongan does display a strong parallelism between the ergative and intransitive absolutive, the data in other ergative Polynesian languages is less supportive. In East Futunan, absolutive argu-

---

[5] For discussion of some other arguments that have been put forward in support of the claim that the ergative is the subject, see Chung 1978, Dukes 1998a.

ments of ergative predicates (i.e. accusative arguments under the surface ergative analysis) may also be doubled by preverbal pronouns (Moyse-Faurie 1994), while in Tokelauan by contrast, only ergative NPs may be doubled by preverbal pronouns (Hooper 1993).[6] Thus while the preverbal pronoun facts presented above must be modelled in a grammar of Tongan, they cannot in general be held as diagnostic of the gross characteristics of Polynesian ergativity.

A second more general problem is the issue of whether the existence of the preverbal pronouns is actually diagnostic of syntactic subjecthood. While such an analysis is the most natural one, there is another approach available that accords nicely with the data.

Within the Malayo-Polynesian family, there are a number of languages which exhibit agreement of various sorts between semantically two-place predicates and agentive obliques. In Chamorro (WMP, Marianas Islands), passive verbs display prefixal number agreement with what is clearly an oblique agentive phrase (examples below from Gibson 1992).

(12) [prefixal plural agreement]

Ma-dulalak	*si*	*Jose*	*nu*	*i*	*famagu'un*
PASS.PL-follow	PN		OBL	the	children

'Jose was followed by the children.'

(13) [infixal singular agreement]

D-in-ilalak	*si*	*Jose*	*as*	*Juan.*
PASS.SG-follow	PN		OBL	

'Jose was followed by Juan.'

In Sasak (WMP, Lombok; Austin 1998, Kroon 1998), third person oblique agents marked with the preposition *isiq* 'by' trigger person/number agreement on sentence-initial inflectional particles of the same sort as surface subjects (examples from Kroon 1998).

(14) [ordinary subject agreement]

Mu-n	*bèng-k*	*kelambi*	*nó.*
ACT.TR-3	give-1	shirt	that

'S/he gave me that shirt.'

---

[6] In Niuean, the preverbal pronouns have been completely lost, probably under the influence of contact with the nonergative languages of Eastern Polynesia (Seiter 1980).

(15)   [agreement with the *isiq* phrase]
Mu-n	*bèng-k*	*kelambi*	*nó*	*isiq*	*inaq*
ACT.TR-3	give-1	shirt	that	by	mother

       'Mother gave me that shirt'
       (Lit: 'She_j gave me that shirt by mother_j')

And in Bimanese (Central MP, Sumbawa; Owens 2000), agentive obliques
marked with the preposition *b'a* 'by' freely trigger the appearance of pronominal agreement on the verb of the same sort as (preverbal) surface subjects.

(16)   [ordinary subject agreement]
Nahu	*ka-lao*	*d'i*	*Surabaya*	*wura*	*satando*
1SG	1SG-go	to		moon	next

       'I'm going to Surabaya next month.'

(17)   [agreement with the *b'a* phrase]
...wa'u	*ede*	*ka-totaku*	*b'a*	*nahu*	*kai*
before	then	1SG-cut	by	1SG	with

       cilamboko!
       machete
       '...and then I'll cut you up with my machete!'

Thus, the Tongan pronominal clitic data is equally consistent with the idea
that it is the argument-structure subject that triggers the appearance of preverbal clitics rather than the syntactic subject, just as appears to be the case
in the languages illustrated above. This distinction between (at least) two
notions of subjecthood is an important one which I will rely on in the analysis presented below.

   A third piece of evidence that has been suggested in favour of the view
that the ergative is a subject revolves around the word order facts. When
both the ergative and absolutive arguments of a predicate are overt in the
clause, the ergative generally precedes the absolutive. Under the assumption that subjects tend to precede other kinds of arguments, the linear
precedence facts favour the view that the ergative is the subject.[7]

   There are several problems with this line of argumentation. Firstly,
there are numerous verb-initial Austronesian languages (e.g. Malagasy,
Tagalog, Toba Batak) in which postverbal nonsubject agents appear much

---

[7] This argument rests on somewhat outdated Greenbergian assumptions about the relative
order of subject and object in the world's languages.

closer to the verb than might be expected cross-linguistically (Dukes 1998b). Thus the generalization that subjects precede other constituents is only a statistical one that is of dubious value in the analysis of Austronesian grammar. Indeed, it might be argued that the generalization can be turned on its head with respect to verb-initial languages in this particular family.

Secondly, as with the issue of the preverbal clitics, the generalization that ergatives precede absolutives is a property of Tongan but not necessarily a property of other Polynesian languages with ergative/absolutive case-marking. In East Futunan for example, the absolutive shows a very strong tendency to precede the ergative (Biggs 1974, Moyse-Faurie 1992). The criterion would lead us to one conclusion for Tongan and another for Futunan. While it is not out of the question that the subject NP might actually be ergative in one language but absolutive in the other, other criteria suggest that the general properties of ergatives and absolutives in Tongan and East Futunan are actually quite similar (Biggs 1974). Thus the naive word order argument tends to lead to a conclusion that runs counter to other criteria.

The postverbal word order facts of Tongan can in fact be used to support a further argument *against* the subjecthood of the ergative. Churchward (1953:67) provides the following description:

> ...when both the subject [for Churchward, the ergative; MD] and object [the absolutive; MD] of a verb are nouns, either the subject or the object may be placed first, in Tongan, according to the emphasis desired.

Thus the claim is that relative word order of postverbal ergative and absolutive is rather free and dependent as much on pragmatic factors as on purely grammatical ones.

I had previously believed Churchward's generalization to be correct and my earlier analyses of Tongan syntax were designed to allow for the free order of the postverbal arguments as a natural consequence (Dukes 1996). And indeed, in elicitation work, speakers seem reasonably happy to accept suggested examples in which the absolutive precedes the ergative (though often noting that it is 'more correct' or 'sounds better' to reverse the order). This word order generalization suggests a flat structure of the general sort illustrated in (18), with underspecified ordering of the postverbal arguments.

(18)   VP

       [Verb complex]   Ergative   Absolutive

However, on the basis of the examination of a corpus consisting of texts from a range of genres (recorded conversation, folktales, narratives, short stories and sociohistorical material) I believe that Churchward's claim regarding the free order of postverbal NPs must be rejected.[8] Across all genres, it appears that no phrasal constituent may intervene between the ergative NP and the verb complex, which at the right boundary consists of a verb followed optionally by a small number of grammatical particles, most notably, the incorporating instrumental preposition 'aki, a small class of lexical adverbs, 'bare' absolutive pronouns (i.e. which must lack an overt case marker) and the oblique pronoun ai. Thus, phrasal absolutive NPs may not precede the ergative. Nor can any other phrasal category. In this regard, Tongan appears to be much more like Niuean (which requires ergative to precede absolutive (Seiter 1980)) than previously thought. Some examples below illustrate the general pattern:

(19)   *... pea*   *fusi*   *mai*   *ia*   *'e*   *Lōisi*   *'o.*
       CONJ   pull   DIR1   3SG   ERG   CONJ
       'and she was pulled towards (it) by Loisi.'   [LMU]

(20)   *Na'e*   *fai*   *ai*   *pē*   *'e*   *Taufulifonua*   *'ene*
       PST   do   then   just   ERG   3SG.GEN
       Tala Fatongiá,.
       'Then Taufulifonua did his Tala Fatongia.'   [Ef]

(21)   *Na'e*   *toe*   *fakatupu*   *mai*   *leva*   *'e*   *Piki*
       PST   more   grow   DIR1   next   ERG
       mo   *Kele*   *ha*   *fonua.*
       CONJ   DET   land
       'Next Piki and Kele made more land rise up.'   [Ef]

The strength of this word order generalization can be illustrated on the basis of a sample text count. In a small set of Tongan texts consisting of about 12,000 words, there were 72 occurrences of the ergative NP. In 70 of these occurrences, the ergative was immediately adjacent to the verb complex. There were only two cases in which a phrasal category intervened between the ergative and the verb complex. In one of these cases (from a recorded

---

[8] Shumway (1988:184) also notes that the ergative 'usually follows immediately the verb phrase, except when the object of the verb is a pronoun'. Interestingly, he refers to the absolutive case marker as a 'focus marker'.

conversation), the unexpected order clearly arises from the fact that the speaker has simply lost track of her stream of speech. In the other case there is clear motivation for the postposing of the ergative due to the juxtaposition of a presentative NP that •reasserts the identity of the agent and is tacked on to the end of the sentence. There are no cases in which the ergative is postposed simply for emphasis or contrast and there is certainly no question of free ordering.

The required adjacency of the ergative to the verb complex, while not conclusive, suggests that they together form a constituent which excludes the absolutive and other phrasal modifiers, giving the hierarchical structure for the verb complex and postverbal domain illustrated in (22).

(22)

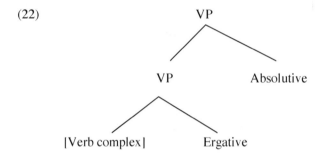

This structure suggests a striking parallel with the configurational properties of some Western MP languages, such as Malagasy and Toba Batak, which display postverbal agent phrases that are either morphologically 'glued' to the verb or that must be immediately adjacent to it (Schachter 1984, Keenan 1999, Dukes 1998a). Taking the parallel a little further, the word order facts provide further evidence that the absolutive, being the 'least oblique' argument of the verb, should be positioned higher in the tree than the ergative, and treated as the subject in Tongan. This proposal is also supported by the rather free positioning of the absolutive in the post-verbal field as compared to the ergative. The absolutive may appear immediately after the ergative (on those rather rare occasions when both are present in the sentence) or be interleaved between oblique phrases of various sorts, much as is the case in the VOS language, Malagasy (Keenan 1999). Some notion of 'heaviness' does seem to play a part in determining the relative position of the absolutive.

(23) | Na'e | tauhi | foki | 'e Hikule'o | 'i Pulotu | 'a |
      | PST | keep | back | ERG | LOC | ABS |

      | 'ene | ongo | koloa | tupu'a... |
      | 3SG.GEN | dual | possession | old |

      'Hikule'o kept his ancient possessions in Pulotu.'   [Ef]

(24) | ...ke | 'oange | 'e | Kinikinilau | ha | kuli | 'i |
      | SUBJ | bring | ERG | | DET | dog | LOC |

      | he | 'ene | fa'a | 'alu | ange. |
      | DET | 3SG.GEN | often | go | DIR3 |

      '(told) Kinikinilau (not) to bring his dogs in his fre-   [TPF]
      quent visits to see her.'

These facts would be expected if the absolutive is excluded from the constituent containing the verb complex and the ergative, as proposed above.

Alongside the rather weak arguments for the subjecthood of the ergative outlined above, there are a number of others with more teeth. However, all of these arguments revolve around 'deep' or 'role-related' properties determined by agenthood (Schachter 1977). Thus, as has been discussed elsewhere (Chung 1978, Dukes 1996), 'controlled' ergative NPs in complement clauses tend to delete quite freely and in some Polynesian languages they undergo raising more often than other NP types (e.g. Samoan; Mosel and Hovdhaugen 1992). But as Dixon (1994) and Manning (1996) point out, such properties tend to operate in accusative fashion even in languages that are clearly syntactically ergative. They do not provide direct evidence for the structural organization of the sentence under typical lexicalist assumptions.

Additional tests that target 'surface' or 'reference-related' properties of subjects suggest that the ergative is not the syntactic subject in Tongan. For example, quantifier float is restricted to absolutives, absolutive case markers are frequently omitted (while the ergative marker is obligatory) and, most obviously, the absolutive argument is obligatory in all species of transitive and intransitive clauses. In those languages that retain vestiges of number agreement in ergative clauses (e.g. Samoan), the verb agrees with the absolutive argument but not with the ergative. The properties of surface clausal organization that Schachter's criteria pick out illustrate the role of the ergative/absolutive distinction in Tongan syntax and demonstrate that it is not simply a morphological curiosity lacking functional load.

2.4 Possible Arguments for the Inverse Analysis

Having concluded on the basis of the discussion above that the ergative is not a subject, we seem to be left with two choices: it is either a complement or an oblique. However, on the face of it, the arguments presented so far seem to point both ways at once. In particular, the constituency facts suggest that the ergative fulfills the standard *structural* definition of 'complement', being a sister to the verb complex, while the standard semantic and distributional criteria suggest that it is an optional modifier on a par with the English *by*-phrase.

The parallel with agent phrases in Western MP is again instructive here. Agent phrases in Malagasy also form a constituent with the verb, in fact a much 'tighter' constituent than the one observed in Tongan, since the agent phrase must be morphologically bound to the verb (Keenan 1999). Like the Tongan ergative, the Malagasy agent phrase is essentially optional (though it actually appears in text far more often than its Tongan equivalent). On the face of it, the Malagasy agent phrase also looks like a complement from the point of view of constituency. However, if the Malagasy agent phrase is a complement, it is rather a strange one, for the reason that it actually appears *too close* to the predicate in comparison with other constituents that are more uncontroversially complements. The verb *ome* 'give' for example, takes two typical (accusative) complement NPs in active voice, but in the 'passive' voice, it forms a constituent with the agent phrase, thus apparently excluding the remaining complement from being sister to the head.

(25)   *N-an-ome*   *ny*   *vola*   *an-dRakoto*   *Rabe*
       PST-ACT-give   the   money   ACC-Rakoto   Rabe
       'Rabe gave Rakoto the money.'

(26)   *N-omen-dRabe*   *an-dRakoto*   *ny*   *vola*
       PST-give-Rabe (GEN)   ACC-Rakoto   the   money
       'The money was given to Rakoto by Rabe.'

If the agent-phrase really is a structural complement then accusative NPs will only be complements when there is no agent phrase present, a rather unappealling conclusion given that the grammatical properties of accusative NPs don't appear to change at all depending on the presence or absence of a genitive agent. Furthermore the (genitive) agent phrase can be omitted, while the accusative object cannot.

(27)   *N-omena*   **(an-dRakoto)*   *ny*   *vola*
       PST-give   ACC-Rakoto   the   money
       'The money was given to Rakoto.'

In both cases, Tongan and Malagasy, the agent phrase behaves like an adjunct which simply requires adjacency to and constituency with the verb. It is not at all like a typical complement. Nevertheless, despite the unusual properties of such agent phrases, some linguists prefer to treat them as a special kind of complement, the evidence for which we will now review as it applies to Tongan.

Manning (1996) advocates the idea that the agentive argument in ergative languages is always a 'core' complement (i.e. an object), an approach which he terms the 'inverse analysis', in contrast to another approach, the 'oblique analysis', which treats the agent as an oblique (as advocated for Tongan in Dukes 1998a and in the discussion above).

Under the inverse analysis, ergative case can be viewed as a kind of accusative case that is restricted to underlying agents. In contrast, a particular consequence of the oblique analysis is that ergative languages lack grammatically transitive clauses. This distinction provides a useful diagnostic for assessing these competing views. Thus Manning demonstrates, in the case of Dyirbal, that the language does indeed have transitive clauses. He presents several pieces of evidence for the transitivity of Dyirbal clauses, some of which are considered below with respect to their applicability to the Tongan case (the remaining points are not relevant to Tongan).[9]

Clause Chaining Manning points out that clause chaining, in which a missing subject (i.e. 'pivot') in a consequent clause is obligatorily understood as coreferent with a particular argument in a main clause can shed light on the relative prominence of the arguments in a clause. He proposes that only terms (i.e. subjects and objects) may be antecedents for such processes.

The kind of grammaticized clause-chaining restrictions observed in Dyirbal are difficult to identify in Polynesian languages due to the rather free use of zero pronouns in almost all grammatical functions.[10] There is certainly no doubt that ergative NPs can antecede zero subjects in conjoined clauses, but the issue is whether there is actually any evidence that a grammatical notion of pivothood (in Dixon's (1994) sense) is involved in determining possible antecedents. The default interpretation for missing arguments is undoubtedly that they involve semantically 'core participants', but the criteria for deciding the appropriate antecedent in any given case are

---

[9] Manning does not discuss the case of Lezgian (probably for lack of available data), which, as he notes (pp. 66-8), contrasts in several important ways with Dyirbal. My (lack of) knowledge of Dyirbal does not allow me to pass judgement on Manning's evidence for the inverse analysis of that language.

[10] A similar problem dogs attempts to identify grammaticized processes of 'control by deletion' in Polynesian (Hooper 1993, Dukes 1996).

largely pragmatic and dependent on the semantics of the particular conjunction word involved.

Dixon (1994:176) claims that the Tongan conjunction *mo* 'with' (implying simultaneity of action) operates with an S/A (accusative) pivot, while *'o* 'and (as a result)' operates with an S/O (ergative) pivot. Such conclusions may be the outcome of testing a small set of constructed examples, but they are hard to come by in examining a larger corpus of naturally occurring text. The conjunction *'o* for example can certainly embed a missing subject with a (null) ergative antecedent (in the case of example (28) this may be interpreted as a genitive antecedent inside the absolutive) or it may simply lack an overt antecedent altogether, particularly when used in a complementizer-like fashion (as in (30)):

(28)   *...pea   fai   hake   pē   'a   'ema   ō   hake*
       CONJ   do   up   just   ABS   1PL   go   up
       'amaua,   'o   hangatonu   pē   ki   he
       1PL.GEN   CONJ   direct   just   Goal   DET
       me'a.
       thing
       '...and we continued on up and went directly towards (the crying that we could hear).'

(29)   *Pea   u   hanga   leva   'e   au   ia*
       CONJ   1SG   turn   then   ERG   1SG   now
       'o   li'aki   'a   'emau   tangai   vala.
       CONJ   throw   ABS   1PL.GEN   bag   clothes
       '...and so then I went and threw our bag of clothes (into the water).'

(30)   *Pea   'oku   'ikai   ke   malava   'o*
       CONJ   PRES   NEG   SUBJ   possible   CONJ
       fakamatala'i   'a   e   fakailifia.
       describe   ABS   DET   fear
       'It's not possible to describe the fear.'

[All examples from FHJ]

The assertion that *'o* operates with an S/O pivot is simply incorrect, as the above examples demonstrate. Furthermore, the example which Dixon provides involving *mo* is quite unidiomatic and not at all typical of the way in which *mo* is used in Tongan discourse.[11] In short, the constraints on the interpretation of such missing arguments appear to be almost exclusively pragmatic and shed no light on pivothood in Tongan.

Conjugation classes Dyirbal has rather strict conjugation classes for verbs, which, it is argued, strongly distinguish transitive from intransitive. This is not the case in Tongan however, which has a small number of labile verbs and which also freely allows the omission of ergative NPs. Under the inverse analysis, this omission either implies that all ergative predicates have complements that are completely optional (a rather odd conclusion from a crosslinguistic perspective) or it would have to be treated as a change in transitivity (a rule of antipassivization that removes the ergative complement) despite the lack of any morphological (or other) reflexes of the operation. Under this latter approach to ergative omission, the inverse analysis would unavoidably mimic the main claim of the oblique analysis; namely that all ergative predicates are (or can be) intransitive.

Pronominal Case Marking Manning notes that Dyirbal nominative subject pronouns would have to appear in one form with verbs that license an agentive oblique and in another form with those that don't. As noted above, a similar problem arises in Tongan, where absolutive subjects of absolutive clauses trigger the same preverbal pronoun forms as ergatives. But the inverse analysis would not fare any better on this point, since now the preverbal pronouns would be subject agreeing in one case (i.e. with the absolutive in absolutive clauses) and object agreeing in the other (i.e. with the ergative complement). Furthermore, since there clearly *are* other Austronesian languages in which agentive obliques trigger agreement, the oblique analysis looks distinctly preferable as an approach to this problem. In any case, even in English there must be two classes of intransitive verbs (at least on a lexicalist analysis), those that license *by*-phrases and those that don't. The possibility that the grammar of some languages might be morphologically sensitive to this distinction shouldn't come as too much of a shock, particularly if one considers the likely historical origins of such a system (Clark 1976, Chung 1978, Dixon 1994).

In short, Manning's arguments for the applicability of the inverse analysis to Dyirbal do not naturally extend to Tongan. With the exception of the verb adjacency problem, the oblique analysis looks distinctly preferable as a descriptive approach to the facts of the Tongan ergative.

---

[11] Tongan speakers I have consulted note that it simply doesn't make sense to use *mo* in the sentence which Dixon provides. *Mo* is in fact used very rarely as a predicate or clause level connector and appears most often as an NP conjunction.

3   A Lexicalist Analysis of the Tongan Ergative

Given the data reviewed above, a grammatical analysis of the data must account for the following cluster of facts:

1. the ergative NP apparently forms a constituent with the verb to the exclusion of other arguments and modifiers of the predicate. At the very least, the analysis must guarantee adjacency of the verb and ergative.
2. the ergative is neither a subject nor an object but has similar general properties to an oblique adjunct of much the same sort as the English *by*-phrase (apart from the constituency facts).
3. it must satisfy the semantic role of the agent of the ergative predicate and participate in the hierarchy of arguments that determine constraints on pronominal binding in the language, which, following much recent work, I take to be argument structure (a-structure).[12]

There are at least two possible approaches to dealing with the properties of the Tongan ergative within HPSG, depending upon whether we take the verb to be a functor selecting the ergative or vice versa.[13] While the first of these approaches is definitely the more standard treatment of obliques, I believe that the second analysis has a number of benefits that deserve consideration.

Under the first approach, the ergative can be treated as an (optional) oblique element on the COMPS list of the verb, distinguished from core arguments using some appropriate notational convention (e.g. the 'bar' (|) employed in Manning 1996 and elsewhere). This analysis would strongly parallel standard lexicalist representations of passive verbs in English (Bresnan 1982, Pollard and Sag 1987). It is appealingly straightforward but there are considerations that count against it.

Firstly, in order to ensure that the ergative is adjacent to the verb, we would need to impose a constraint on the linear ordering of the verb's complements. This is certainly easy to do but it begs the question of why this particular oblique should be required to precede all other elements on the COMPS list (including the absolutive, which for various reasons I analyse as the 'least oblique' element on the COMPS list). Since all other postverbal constituents appear to be fairly permutable, it is odd that this one element requires a specific position. The ad hoc linear order requirement provides a weaker analysis than one in which the ergative actually forms a

---

[12] See Dukes 1998a for discussion of why this should be.

[13] See Pollard and Sag 1994, Kim and Sag 2002 for some discussion of the issue of direction of selection in the treatment of modifiers within HPSG.

constituent with the verb, thereby guaranteeing adjacency to it. In any case, the latter approach will certainly be required for Malagasy, where the evidence of verb/agent constituency is extremely strong. Thus the straightforward oblique analysis will not extend to Malagasy.

A second problem with the standard oblique analysis is that it requires us to specify that the ergative oblique is completely optional. This is essentially the same problem noted above with regard to the inverse analysis. But if an argument type associated with an entire class of predicates is completely optional it is hard to see in what sense the predicate really *selects* the argument, as opposed to simply being semantically and grammatically *compatible* with it. While the dividing line between oblique complements and adjuncts is a notoriously difficult one, elements that are completely optional certainly appear to be likely candidates for an adjunct analysis.[14]

Rather than treating the Tongan ergative as an oblique element on the COMPS list, I propose to treat it as a kind of adjunct. The analysis falls into the general class of approaches that seek to explain mismatches between semantic and syntactic selection via the use of an HPSG analog of categorial type-raising. Kim and Sag (2002) for example, use a 'type-raising' analysis to account for the complement-like behaviour of certain lexical adverbs (particularly negative ones) in English and French. Such adverbs are provided with a semantic functor type that seeks a predicative argument but are optionally added to the COMPS list of the verbal head. Thus while the adverb selects the predicate semantically, the predicate selects the adverb at the grammatical level.

The case of the Tongan ergative can be seen as an inverse of the Kim and Sag analysis. While the ergative verb semantically (and at a-structure) seeks an agent, the ergative argument seeks to modify a lexical ergative verb. Such an analysis will also straightforwardly extend to the case of Malagasy and potentially to other Western MP languages of the patient-prominent type with verb-adjacent agents.

Following the notational conventions of Sag and Wasow 1999, I supply ergative verbs with the following category.

---

[14] The same line of reasoning could also be applied to the analysis of the English *by*-phrase, the optionality of which implies its adjuncthood.

(31)

$$
\begin{bmatrix}
word \\[4pt]
\text{SYN} \begin{bmatrix} \text{HEAD } verb\text{–}erg \\ \text{SUBJ} \langle\ \rangle \\ \text{COMPS} \langle \boxed{1}\text{NP[abs]} \rangle \end{bmatrix} \\[12pt]
\text{ARG–ST} \quad \langle \boxed{2}_i, \boxed{1}_j \rangle \\[8pt]
\text{SEM} \begin{bmatrix} \text{RELN } verbing \\ \text{VERBER} \quad i \\ \text{VERBEE} \quad j \end{bmatrix}
\end{bmatrix}
$$

Note that the absolutive argument is defined as 'subject' in terms of least obliqueness on the COMPS list (as in earlier versions of HPSG and as proposed for certain VSO languages in Borsley 1995) not as the value of the SUBJ feature.[15] No mention is made of the ergative argument in the lexical entry of the predicate. The agent (or agentlike) semantic role is linked to the argument structure subject (i.e. the least oblique element on the a-structure list).

The lexical entry for the ergative case marker, which for argument's sake I will treat as a kind of preposition, is given in (32).

(32)

$$
\left\langle \text{'e,} \begin{bmatrix}
word \\
\text{HEAD} \qquad prep \\
\text{COMPS} \quad \langle \boxed{1}\text{NP} \rangle \\[6pt]
\text{MOD} \begin{bmatrix} word \\ \text{HEAD } verb\text{–}erg \\ \text{ARG–ST} \quad \langle \boxed{1}, ... \rangle \end{bmatrix}
\end{bmatrix} \right\rangle
$$

The ergative preposition is thus analyzed simply as a category that provides grammatical 'glue' for sticking together agentive noun phrases with ergative verbs. It does nothing else. Since it has a modifier (MOD) specification

---

[15] The reasons for this approach are not directly relevant to the topic of this paper but mainly revolve around the treatment of the preverbal (nominative) subject pronouns which in earlier work I have analyzed as the value of the SUBJ feature (Dukes 1996). It is for this reason that I have refrained from referring to the absolutive argument as 'nominative'.

for combining with the ergative verb, the constituent created will be a phrase of sort *head-adjunct-structure* (*head-adj-struc*) which is licensed via Pollard and Sag's Immediate Dominance Schema 5 (1994:56).[16] Note in addition that the NP complement of the preposition is structure-shared with the argument-structure subject of the verb. This use of structure-sharing allows us to guarantee that the agent participates in hierarchical binding constraints affecting the arguments of the verb without having to treat the agent phrase itself as an argument of the verb.

Employing the categories above, a sentence such as (1), repeated here as (33), will have the VP structure in (34):[17]

(33)   *Na'e*   *huo*   *'e*   *Siale*   *'a*   *e*   *ngoué*
       PST   hoe   ERG   ABS   DET garden
       'Siale hoed the garden.'

---

[16] Note that, as Pollard and Sag point out, we must make the additional proviso that the COMPS value of the adjunct daughter must be fully discharged, a condition which probably must be added to the statement of Schema 5.

[17] I omit discussion of the tense markers here for reasons of space. There is ample evidence that they are somewhat higher in the structure of the sentence and do not form a close constituent with the verb (Dukes 1996).

(34)

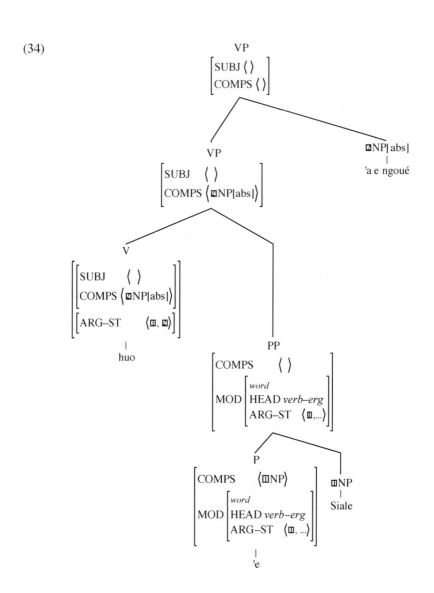

4   Some Conclusions

The analysis of the Tongan ergative as a head-seeking adjunct has a number of advantages over the ordinary oblique complement approach, to which it is nevertheless quite closely related. Firstly, it simplifies the lexical entry for the ergative verb, obviating the need to specify the optionality of an oblique complement on the COMPS list of the predicate. At the same time, the analysis provides a natural account of the complete grammatical optionality of the ergative argument in Tongan because adjuncts are not grammatically selected and need not show up in the sentence.

A second advantage of the adjunct analysis is that it accounts for the word order and constituency facts of the ergative argument via one straightforward mechanism without requiring recourse to ad hoc linear order constraints on the elements in the COMPS list of the predicate. The word order results fall out from the fact that the ergative forms a constituent with the head.

A third advantage of the adjunct analysis is that it builds the grammatical contribution of the ergative preposition directly into the structure of the sentence. Rather than simply being a lexical diacritic on the COMPS list of the predicate, the ergative marker is provided with a category that describes exactly what its combinatoric potential in a sentence is, thus giving a natural account of what it means for an argument to be 'ergative' in the grammar of Tongan.

Finally, the adjunct analysis has the potential to extend, with some minor variations, to other languages in the Malayo-Polynesian family. The case of Malagasy can be dealt with in an almost entirely parallel fashion by providing a similar head-seeking adjunct category for the genitive agent. The prenominal genitive marking that 'bonds' the agent to the verb can be assigned much the same category as the Tongan ergative preposition. This 'adjunct agent' type can be seen as one of several variations in the linking of semantic roles to grammatical functions that have evolved in the MP family as a result of gradual shifts in clausal organization and associated predicate category types through time.

5   Sources of Examples

TPF = Fanua, Tupou Posesi. 1976. *Po Fananga: Folk Tales of Tonga.* Nuku'alofa: Friendly Islands Bookshop.

LMU = Fonua, Pesi. *La'a mo 'Uha (Sun and Rain).* Nuku'alofa: Friendly Islands Bookshop.

MR = Hafoka, Loseli (ed.). 1992. *Minerva Reef.* Tonga: Friendly Islands Bookshop.

Ef = Moala, Masiu. *Efinanga.* Nuku'alofa: Vava'u Press.

FHJ= Rogers, Garth (ed.). 1986. *The Fire Has Jumped.* Suva: USP.

6   References

Anderson, Stephen. 1976. On the Notion of Subject in Ergative Languages. In *Subject and Topic* ed. Charles Li. 1–23. New York: Academic Press.

Anderson, Stephen. 1992. *A-morphous morphology.* Cambridge UK: Cambridge University Press.

Artawa, Ketut & Barry Blake. 1997. Patient Primacy in Balinese. *Studies in Language* 21:483–508.

Austin, Peter. 1998. Relativisation in Sasak, Lombok, Indonesia. Paper presented at the 1998 Australian Linguistics Society Conference, Brisbane.

Biggs, Bruce. 1974. Some Problems of Polynesian Grammar. *Journal of the Polynesian Society.* 83:401–426.

Borsley, Robert. 1995. On Some Similarities and Differences between Welsh and Syrian Arabic. *Linguistics* 33:99–122.

Bresnan, Joan. 1982. The Passive in Lexical Theory. In *The Mental Representation of Grammatical Relations* ed. Joan Bresnan. 3–86. Cambridge: MIT Press.

Bresnan, Joan & Jonni Kanerva. 1989. Locative Inversion in Chichewa. *Linguistic Inquiry* 20:1–50.

Chung, Sandra. 1978. *Case Marking and Grammatical Relations in Polynesian.* Austin: University of Texas Press.

Churchward, C. Maxwell. 1953. *Tongan Grammar.* London: Oxford University Press.

Churchward, C. Maxwell. 1959. *Tongan Dictionary.* London: Oxford University Press.

Clark, Ross. 1976. *Aspects of Proto-Polynesian Syntax.* Auckland: Linguistics Society of New Zealand.

Clark, Ross. 1981. Review of Chung 1978. *Language* 57:198–205.

Dixon, R. M. W. 1994. *Ergativity.* Cambridge: Cambridge University Press.

Dowty, David. 1991. Thematic Proto-Roles and Argument Selection. *Language* 67:547–619.

Dukes, Michael. 1996. *On the Non-existence of Anaphors and Pronominals in the Grammar of Tongan.* Ph.D thesis, UCLA.

Dukes, Michael. 1998a. Evidence for Grammatical Functions in Tongan. In *Proceedings of the LFG98 Conference.* ed. Miriam Butt & Tracy Holloway King. http://www-csli.stanford.edu.publications.

Dukes, Michael. 1998b. Valence, Voice and Argument Structure in Austronesian. In *Proceedings of the 1998 Conference of the Australian Linguistics Society* ed. John Ingram. http://lingua.cltr.uq.edu.au:8000/als98/als98papers/.

Duranti, Alessandro & Elinor Ochs. 1990. Genitive Constructions and Agency in Samoan Discourse. *Studies in Language* 14:1–23.

Gibson, Jeanne. 1992. *Clause Union in Chamorro and in Universal Grammar.* New York: Garland.

Givón, Talmy. 1984. *Syntax: A Functional-Typological Introduction.* Amsterdam: John Benjamins.

Hooper, Robin. 1993. *Studies in Tokelauan Syntax.* Ph.D thesis, University of Auckland.

Hopper, Paul & Sandra A. Thompson. 1980. Transitivity in grammar and discourse. *Language* 56:251–299.

Keenan, Edward. 1999. Morphology is Structure: A Malagasy test case. In *Formal Issues in Austronesian Linguistics* ed. Ileana Paul, Vivianne Philips & Lisa Travis. 27–48. Dordrecht: Kluwer.

Kim, Jong-Bok & Ivan Sag. 2002. French and English negation without Head Movement. *Natural Language and Linguistic Theory* 20:339–412.

Kroon, Yosep B. 1998. The *isiq* construction and its grammatical relations. In *Working Papers in Sasak, volume 1* ed. Peter K. Austin. 105–118. Department of Linguistics and Applied Linguistics, University of Melbourne.

Lynch, John. 1972. Passives and Statives in Tongan. *Journal of the Polynesian Society* 81:5–18.

Manning, Christopher D. 1996. *Ergativity: Argument Structure and Grammatical Relations.* Stanford: CSLI.

Manning, C. D., and I. A. Sag. 1999. Dissociations Between Argument Structure and Grammatical Relations. In G. Webelhuth, A. Kathol and J.-P. Koenig (eds) *Lexical and Constructional Aspects of Linguistic Explanation.* Stanford: CSLI Publications.

Mosel, Ulrike & Even Hovdhaugen. 1992. *Samoan Reference Grammar.* Oslo: Scandinavian University Press.

Moyse-Faurie, Claire. 1992. Verb Classes and Argument Structure Variation in Futunan. *Oceanic Linguistics* 31:209–227.

Moyse-Faurie, Claire. 1994. Syntactic and Pragmatic Functions of Futunan Preverbal Pronouns. Paper presented at the International Conference on Austronesian Linguistics, Leiden.

Owens, Melanie. 2000. *Agreement in Bimanese.* M.A. Thesis, University of Canterbury.

Pollard, Carl & Ivan Sag. 1987. *Information-based Syntax and Semantics, volume 1.* Stanford: CSLI.

Pollard, Carl & Ivan Sag. 1994. *Head-driven Phrase Structure Grammar*. Chicago: University of Chicago Press.

Sag, Ivan & Thomas Wasow. 1999. *Syntactic Theory: a formal introduction*. Stanford: CSLI.

Schachter, Paul. 1977. Reference-related and Role-related properties of subject. In *Syntax and Semantics 8: Grammatical Relations* ed. Peter Cole & Jerrold Sadock. 279–306. New York: Academic Press.

Schachter, Paul (ed.). 1984. *Studies in the Structure of Toba Batak*. Occasional Papers in Linguistics, No. 5. California: Department of Linguistics, UCLA.

Seiter, William. 1980. *Studies in Niuean Syntax*. New York: Garland Publishing.

Shumway, Eric B. 1988. *Intensive course in Tongan*. Laie, Hawaii: Institute for Polynesian Studies, Brigham Young University.

Wechsler, Stephen and I Wayan Arka. 1998. Syntactic Ergativity in Balinese: an Argument Structure Based Theory. *Natural Language and Linguistic Theory* 16:387–441.

8

Voice and Being Core: Evidence from (Eastern) Indonesian Languages *

I WAYAN ARKA

1 Introduction

The paper deals with the significance of core argument status and associated (pragmatic) prominence in (eastern) Indonesian languages of the Nusa Tenggara region covering the provinces of Bali, West Nusa Tenggara, and East Nusa Tenggara. There are tens of languages in this area but the present analysis is mainly based on Balinese,[1] Bima,[2] Manggarai, Lio, Sikka[3] and

* I thank Bill Foley, Simon Musgrave, Peter Austin, Marian Klamer and other participants at the AFLA7 Conference Amsterdam for their comments that led to the revision of the paper. Part of the data in this paper come from an on-going project of core arguments in Eastern Indonesian languages, funded through the University Research Graduate Education (URGE) grant, contract no. 065/HTTP-IV/URGE/1999.

[1] Balinese is mainly spoken in the island of Bali (with around 3 million speakers). For detailed discussion on Balinese linguistics, see (Arka 2003; Artawa, Artini, and Blake 1997; Artawa 1994; Beratha 1992; Clynes 1995; Hunter 1988; Pastika 1999; Wechsler and Arka 1998).

[2] Bima is spoken in the eastern part of Sumbawa island with around 600,000 speakers. See Jauhary (2000) for discussion on passive in this language.

3 Manggarai, Lio and Sikka are three languages spoken in the island of Flores with around 500,000, 200,000, and 250,000 speakers respectively. See further details in Kosmas (2000) for Manggarai, Sawardi (2000) for Lio and Sedeng (2000) for Sikka.

Voice and Grammatical Relations in Austronesian Languages.

Simon Musgrave and Peter Austin

Lamaholot.[4] Balinese belongs to the Western Malayo-Polynesian subgroup of Austronesian and the other languages belong to the Central-Eastern subgroup. The discussion is also supported by Indonesian data.

The issues to be discussed are: (i) how core status is determined; (ii) how core status might be changed; (iii) what motivates the change; and (iv) what parameter can be formulated to account for typological variations associated with the answers of the foregoing questions.

The present research suggests that being core is a complex matter involving morphosyntax-semantic interaction and, crucially, pragmatic prominence. The investigation in these languages confirms the notion of prominence in language system, particularly in argument-structure (Arka 2003; Arka and Manning this volume; Foley 1998a, 1998b; Manning 1996). Data from the languages other than Balinese (which have an isolating morphological structure) lead to the proposal that mapping and core status may be determined, not only by lexicon/morphology, but also by pragmatics via syntax. The analysis, couched within Lexical Functional Grammar (LFG), is an argument-structure based version of the parameterized properties in voice systems and object doubling as discussed in Foley (1998a, b).

The paper is organized as follows. First of all, a short typological description of the basic facts is given, which includes word order (2.1) and other means of coding (2.2). The important data on core alternations and the associated pragmatic functions follow (2.3). Then, in section 3, the analysis is given. It covers the discussions on voice and argument structure in LFG (3.1), mapping and coding strategies (default and marked), their relation with parametric principles of voice system and object doubling, and evidence for voice alternations as mapping alternations (3.2–3-3). Further support for the significance of being core in voice alternations is given from the restriction it places on possible binding relations (3.4). Finally, some conclusions are given in section 4.

---

4 Lamaholot is spoken in the islands east of Flores such as Adonara, Solor and Lembata (around 200,000 speakers). The present study is based on the Nusa Tadon dialect spoken in the island of Adonara, as discussed in Japa (2000).

2 Basic Facts about the Languages under Investigation

2.1 Word Order

The languages discussed here are all have subject verb object word order on the basis of a variety of tests to be discussed below; the following examples show typical actor voice active clauses.[5]

(1)   a.   Balinese (h.r.)[6]

Tiang	numbas	tamba
1	AV.buy	medicine

'I bought medicine.'

        b.   Indonesian

Dia	me-lihat	saya
3SG	AV-see	1SG

'(S)he saw me.'

        c.   Bima

Sia	na-weli-ku	baju.
3SG	3-buy-ADV	shirt

'(S)he really bought the shirt.'

        d.   Manggarai

Hia	ongga	ami
3SG	hit	1PL.EX

'(S)he hit us.'

        e.   Lio

Ata	nuwamuri	ghea	pai	ema
person	young	that	call	father

'The young person called father.'

---

5 AV in (1) stands for agentive/active voice, where the agent is the grammatical subject. Voice is marked differently across the languages under investigation. In the languages of the synthetic type such as Balinese, it is morphologically marked, and consequently there is morphological opposition of verbal forms signaling different voices. A verb form in this language is therefore glossed showing the relevant voice, as in Balinese example (1a), where the verb-initial nasal is the AV marker. In the languages of the analytic type there is no such morphological opposition. The verb is not therefore glossed for the relevant voice.

6 h.r. = high register; low register is not marked.

    f.   Sikka
        Mame   *rena*   *naruk*   *ia*
        uncle   hear   news   that
        'Uncle heard the news.'

    g.   Lamaholot
        Go'e   *plei*   *Budi*
        1SG   hit   PN
        'I hit Budi.'

In these sentences, the head predicates are transitive verbs with the agent arguments appearing preverbally functioning as the grammatical subjects (henceforth, SUBJ). The evidence of their being SUBJs comes from relativization, a property unique to the grammatical subject in these languages. The following contrast from Lio, for example, shows that relativizing the SUBJ *ata nuwamuri* 'young man' is fine (2a) (the relevant clause being within brackets) whereas relativizing the object *ema* 'father' is prohibited (2b):

(2)   Lio
    a.   *Ata*   *nuwamuri*   *[eo*   ___   *pai*   *ema]*
        person   young   [REL   call   father]
        mai
        come
        'The young man who called Father came.'

    b.   **Ema*   *[eo*   *ata*   *nuwamuri*   *pai*   __]*
        father   [REL   person   youth   call   __]
        mai
        come
        'Father whom the young man called came.'

SVO is the canonical order (i.e. pragmatically unmarked). Word order variation is highly constrained and is sometimes not possible. An alternative ordering with patient coming sentence-initially, particularly in the isolating group (to be discussed shortly in section 2.2), gives rise to a pragmatically marked construction. This is not simply an object preposing construction; rather it is an objective voice construction with the patient being SUBJ.

2.2 Marking

2.2.1 Head marking: Indonesian, Balinese, Bima and Lamaholot (relatively rich in morphology)

The AV verb in Balinese and Indonesian is morphologically marked whereas the AV counterpart in Lamaholot is morpologically unmarked. In Balinese, the AV is marked by a (homorganic) nasal prefix (*ng-* as in (3a)) and in Indonesian by *meN-* (as in (3b)). In all of these AV constructions, the agent is the grammatical subject coming before the verb and the patient is the object coming after the verb.

(3) a. Balinese (h.r.)

Tiang	*ng-lempag*	*ipun*	(agent–verb–patient)
1	AV-hit	3	

'I hit him.'

  b. Indonesian

Saya	*mem-(p)ukul*	*dia*	(agent–verb–patient)
1SG	AV-hit	3SG	

'I hit him/her.'

  c. Lamaholot

Na'e	*na'a*	*go'e*	(agent–verb–patient)
3SG	hit.AV	1SG	

'S/he hit me.'

The three languages allow another alternative structure shown in (4), labelled here as objective voice (OV). The OV verb is, like the AV verb, syntactically transitive because the patient of the OV verb is core. The patient is the grammatical subject (SUBJ), coming sentence-initially), and crucially, the agent is still core, not demoted to non-core status.[7] As in the AV verb marking, the OV marking in Balinese/Indonesian and Lamaholot shows an opposite strategy: the OV verb in Lamaholot is morphologically marked whereas the OV verb in Balinese/Indonesian is not. The following are the OV versions of (3):

---

7 That the agent of the OV verb is still core (hence the OV verb is not a passive verb) has been argued at length in Arka (2003) for Balinese. Binding provides evidence for this (see 8.3.3).

(4)   a.   Balinese

Ipun	*lempag*	*tiang*	(patient–verb–agent)
3	OV.hit	1	

'Him/her, I hit.'

      b.   Indonesian

Dia	*saya*	*pukul*	(patient–agent–verb)
3SG	1SG	OV.hit	

'Him/her, I hit.'

      c.   Lamaholot

Go'e	*na'e*	*na'a-nek*	(patient–agent–verb)
1SG	3SG	hit-OV.1SG	

'Me, (s)he hit.'

The set of the OV markers in Lamaholot and the corresponding free pronouns are shown in the following table:[8]

Table 1: OV Suffixes and their Corresponding Free Pronouns in Lamaholot

	1SG	1PL.EX	1PL.IN	2SG	2PL	3SG	3PL
Free ProN	*go'e*	*kame*	*tite*	*mo'e*	*mio*	*na'e*	*ra'e*
OV-marker	*-k*	*-m*	*-t*	*-o*	*-e*	*-o'*	*-we*

Unlike Balinese and Lamaholot, Bima does not have OV; it has passive verbs showing active voice (AV) and passive (PASS) voice in Bima are equally marked (Jauhary 2000). The active voice (AV) is marked by verbal affixes showing agreement with the SUBJ, with the prefix signalling irrealis and the suffix signalling realis (perfective aspect):

---

8 The suffixes may have allomorphs: the ones that are expressed by consonants -k, -m, and -t may have a schwa inserted if the verb base ends with a consonant (e.g. -ək '1SG' in wətot-ək 'kick-1SG') and another additional nasal -n- if the verb base ends with a vowel (e.g. -n k as in sika-nək 'expell'). However, there may be variation with -r- as in tobo-nək or tobo-rək 'sit-1SG'. Simon, a native speaker of this language (p.c.), suggests that this variation is dialectal. Further examination is needed to confirm this claim.

(5) a. Bima

 Sia *na–mbei* *ana* *dou* *ede* *buku*
 3SG 3.IRR-give child person that book
 '(S)he is going to give the child a book.'

 b. *Nahu* *nduku-ku* *sia*
   1SG hit-1SG.RL 3SG
   'I have hit him/her.'

The prefix *na-* in *namebi* (5a) agrees with the agent-SUBJ *sia*, which comes preverbally. Likewise, the verbal suffix *-ku* in (5b) agrees with the SUBJ *nahu*. The other arguments appearing after the verb are the objects.

 Passive is marked by a prefix: *di-* is for irrealis and *ra-* for realis.[9] The prefix shows no agreement with the SUBJ. The following is an example of the *ra-* passive:

(6) *Mbe'e* *ede* *ra-nduku* *ba* *ompu*   *sia*
   goat that PASS.RL-hit by grandfather 3SG
   'The goat was hit by his/her grandfather.'

In short, a verbal affix in Bima may simultaneously express (i) modality/aspect, and (ii) grammatical function mapping (possibly with SUBJ agreement). The set of verbal affixes showing voice in Bima are shown in the following table:

Table 2: Verbal Affixes in Bima

Function-mapping	(1) Actor = SUBJ (core)		(2) Actor = OBL (non-core)
⇓ Modality /Aspect	(1a) PREFIX	(1b) SUFFIX	PREFIX
IRREALIS	*ka-* '1SG/1PL.IN' *ta-* '1PL.EX' *na-* '3'		*di-*
REALIS		*-ku* '1SG/1PL.IN' *-ta* '1PL.EX' *-mu* '2' *-na* '3'	*ra-*

---

9 Passive in Manggarai may have no verbal marking. It is only signalled by the syntactic appearance of the agent as an oblique, expressed in a PP. In such a case, it is like voice in the neighbouring isolating languages where voice is analytically encoded.

2.2.2 Non-head marking: analytic group, poor in morphology: Manggarai, Sikka, and Lio

This group of languages (Lio, Sikka, and Manggarai) relies on word order to encode grammatical relations. Voice appears to be analytically encoded. That is, verbs with different grammatical relations/voices have different linear ordering with respect to their arguments; morphologically the verb forms are the same.

Manggarai, for example, which has no OV, makes use of the same verb form *ongga* 'hit' in two different grammatical relations/voices, in the active construction (7a) and in the passive construction (7b).

(7)   Manggarai

    a.   *Hia*   ***ongga***   *ami*   (active)
         3SG   hit   1PL.EX
         '(S)he hit us.'

    b.   *Ami*   ***ongga***   *le*   *hia*   (passive)
         1PL.EX   hit   by   3SG
         'We were hit by him/her.'

Sentence (7b) is syntactically passive, with the agent PP being a non-core argument (i.e. an oblique), and the patient *Ami* is the grammatical subject (see also evidence from binding discussed later in section 3.4) and further details about subjecthood in Manggarai in Kosmas 2000).

Unlike Manggarai, Lio and Sikka have no passive. They appear to have the analytic OV construction; that is, the OV construction that is marked by different linear order. The OV verb is morphologically the same as that in the AV construction. Thus, there is no verbal morphology which correlates with voice alternations in these isolating languages. For example, the verb *tebo* 'hit' in Lio (8) and *rena* 'hear' in Sikka (9) are associated with AV and OV. The (a) sentences are equivalent to the AV construction in Balinese and Lamaholot whereas the (b) constructions are equivalent to the corresponding OV construction.

(8)   a.   Lio   (AV)   (agent–verb–patient)
         Kai   *ghea*   ***tebo***   *aji*
         3SG   that   hit   younger.sibling
         'S/he hit the little brother/sister.'

b. (OV)   (patient–agent–verb)
   Aji   *kai*   *ghea*   ***tebo***
   younger.sibling   3SG   that   hit
   'The little brother/sister, s/he hit.'

(9) a. Sikka (AV)   (experiencer–verb–theme)
         Mame ***rena*** *naruk* *ia*
         uncle   hear   news   that
         'Uncle heard the news.'

     b. (OV)   (theme–experiencer–verb)
         Naruk *ia*   *mame*   ***rena***
         news   that   uncle   hear
         'The news, Uncle heard (or the news was heard by Uncle).'

All the clause-initial NPs are SUBJs. The evidence for their being subject in these sentences comes from a number of tests exclusive to SUBJ in these languages such as relativization, adverbial insertion, control, and possessor ascension/topicalization. The following is the evidence from Lio (Sawardi 2000). Basically the same evidence holds for Sikka (see Sedeng 2000).

(10) Lio
      Relativization:
      a. *Kai*   *[eo*   __   *tebo*   *aji]*   *mera*   *leka*
          3SG   [REL   __   hit   little.sibling]   sit   on
          kedera
          chair
          '(S)he, who hit (our) brother sat on the chair.'

      b. **Aji*   *[eo*   *kai*   *ghea*   *tebo*   __]   *mera*
          little.sibling   [REL   3SG   that   hit   __]   sit
          leka   *kedera*
          on   chair
          '(Our) little sibling whom (s)he hit sat on the chair.'

      Adverbial insertion:
      c. *Aji*   *[eo*   *(meremai)* *kai*   *ghea*   *(*meremai)*
          little.sibling   [REL   yesterday   3SG   that   yesterday
          tebo   __]   *mera*   *leka*   *kedera*
          hit   __]   sit   on   chair
          '(Our) little sibling whom (s)he hit yesterday sat on the chair.'

Control:

d. *Aku   rop   tau   [__   pedhe   are]*
    1SG   try   to   (SUBJ)   cook   rice
    'I tried to cook (the) rice.'

e. **Aku   ropa   tau   [are   ina*
    1SG   try   to   [rice   this
             __   pedhe]
    (NON-SUBJ)   cook]
    'I tried to cook this rice.'

Example (10) shows that relativising SUBJ is fine (a), whereas relativising OBJ is not (b). Sentence-initial SUBJ is in [Spec, IP] (or possibly adjoined to the top IP) whereas the OV agent is in [Spec, IP] (see (Guilfoyle, Hung, and Travis 1992)). This allows an adverbial insertion (*meremai* 'yesterday') between the SUBJ/relative marker *eo* and the VP including the agent, but not between the agent and the head verb (10c). In contrast to (10d), an attempt to control non-SUBJ fails (10e). All these tests support the view that the patient initial argument is not simply a preposed OBJ because it acquires SUBJ properties whereas the agent in this construction is not SUBJ. In other words, these constructions are OV constructions, not AV constructions with topicalized/preposed OBJs.

To sum up, the languages discussed here are all SVO languages but have different inventory of voice types. Table 1 shows that they fall into three groups: (i) Indonesian and Balinese (with three major voice types, as discussed in Arka and Manning, this volume), (ii) Bima and Manggarai (with AV and passive, without OV) and (iii) Lio, Sikka and Lamaholot (with AV and OV, without passive). I will come back to the parametric principles that account for the voice distribution in these languages in section 3.2.

Table 3: Language Groups in Terms of Voice Types

Language		VOICE		
		AV	OV	PASS
Group 1	Indonesian	√	√	√
	Balinese	√	√	√
Group 2	Bima	√	-	√
	Manggarai	√	-	√
Group 3	Lio	√	√	-
	Sikka	√	√	-
	Lamaholot	√	√	-

3   Core Alternation and Pragmatic Motivation

Direct functions (SUBJ, (DIRECT/INDIRECT) OBJ) are core arguments whereas obliques (and also generally complex complements)[10] are non-cores.

The (default) number of core arguments which an argument-taking predicate may have is generally specified in a lexical entry. However, some processes (e.g. applicativization) may change the core status of an argument. The change is generally morphologically marked. Applicativization is illustrated by Indonesian data in (11)-(12) which shows that a locative argument is promoted to core status. In the non-applicative verb *duduk* 'sit' (11), the locative argument is an oblique (11a); the locative oblique marker *di* cannot be omitted (11b); nor can the verb be passivized with the locative argument being SUBJ (11c).

(11)   Indonesian
   a.   *Amir   duduk   di   kursi   baru   itu*
        PN   sit   on   chair   new   that
        'Amir sat on the new chair.'

---

10 There is evidence from Balinese and Indonesian that a complex argument may be treated as a core (see Arka and Simpson, this volume, for details).

b.   * Amir   duduk   kursi   baru   itu
          PN   sit   chair   new   that

c.   * Kursi   baru   itu   (yang)   di-duduk   oleh
          chair   new   that   REL   PASS-sit   by
          Amir.
          PN
          'It was the new chair that Amir sat on.'

In contrast, in the applicative verb *duduk-i*, the locative argument is core. Therefore, the applied argument can be OBJ (12a) or SUBJ (12b); it can no longer take the OBL marker *di* (12c).

(12)   Indonesian

a.   *Amir*   *men-duduk-i*   *kursi*   *itu*
          PN   AV-sit-APPL   chair   that
          'Amir sat on the chair.'

b.   *Kursi*   *baru*   *itu*   *(yang)*   *di-duduk-i*   *oleh*
          chair   new   that   REL   PASS-sit-APPL   by
          Amir
          PN
          'It was the new chair that Amir sat on.'

c.   **Amir*   *men-duduk-i*   *di*   *kursi*   *itu*
          PN   AV-sit-APPL   on   chair   that

In isolating languages, however, promotion to core status is not morphologically marked. The important point to note is that the locative argument cannot be promoted to be OBJ (13b). Compare this with the possible promotion in Indonesian (example (12a)).

(13)   Sikka

a.   *Wae*   *buang*   *ia*   *deri*   *ei*   *kadera*
          face   white   that   sit   LOC   chair
          'The pretty girl sat on the chair.'

b.   **Wae*   *buang*   *ia*   *deri*   *kadera*
          face   white   that   sit   chair
          'The pretty girl sat on the/a chair.'

However, promotion to SUBJ is allowed (14a). This is parallel to the OV construction in Balinese (14b) and Indonesian (14c):

(14) a. Sikka

    Kadera ia wi wae buang ia deri
    chair that REL face white that sit
    'It is that chair which was sat on by the pretty girl.'

  b. Balinese

    Dampar-e ento tegak-in   tiang
    bench-DEF that OV.sit-APPL 1
    'The bench, I sat on (it).'

  c. Indonesian

    Kursi itu saya duduk-i
    chair that 1SG OV.sit-APPL
    'The chair, I sat on (it).'

Manggarai shows a similar case, where promotion to core status/OBJ is generally not permitted (15b):

(15) Manggarai

  a. *Aku puci ngger one lo'ang*
    1SG enter to in room
    'I entered (into) the room.'

  b. **Aku puci lo'ang*
    1SG enter room
    'I entered the room.'

However, Manggarai does allow (16a), a typical construction of a syntactic passive, parallel to the passive construction in Indonesian (16b). That is, the goal/locative 'room' can be a core argument but it must be SUBJ (i.e. topical). The agent is obligatorily backgrounded/demoted to non-core status.

(16) a. Manggarai (passive)

    Lo'ang hitu puci le ata tako
    room that enter by person steal
    'The room was entered by a thief.'

  b. Indonesian (passive)

    Ruangan itu di-masuk-i   oleh perampok
    room that PASS-go.in-APPL by robber
    'The room was entered by a robber.'

The simultaneous foregrounding/promotion and backgrounding/demotion effect illustrated by (16) is typical in passive. Despite the lack of verbal morphology marking passive in Manggarai, different kinds of evidence (e.g. categorical marking, structural positions and binding) show that sentence (16a) is indeed syntactically passive as argued in Arka and Kosmas (2005).

The examples so far suggest that being core-SUBJ is closely associated with having a contrastive focus as in Sikka (14a), or being topical as in Indonesian and Manggarai (16). This leads to the hypothesis that pragmatic prominence motivates promotion to core status. If promotion to core/SUBJ is licensed by pragmatic prominence, it is expected that promotion to OBJ must be permitted when OBJ gets proper pragmatic prominence. Indeed this is the case. Promotion to OBJ is acceptable only when there is contrastive focus given to the OBJ, as in (17).

(17)   Manggarai

Aku	*puci*	*lo'ang*	*hitu*	*landing*	*hau*	*puci*
1SG	enter	room	that	but	2	enter

lo'ang	*ho'o*
room	this

'I enter that room and you enter this room.'

This subsection can be summarised as follows:

- Core promotion/alternation is a way for an argument that is generally classified as non-core to have the privilege of being mapped onto a direct function, in particular to SUBJ, which naturally receives pragmatic prominence. (There may be semantic motivation, which is not discussed here.)
- Core status promotion and voice alternation may be morphologically marked on the verb (e.g. Indonesian/Balinese applicatives) or not (Lio, Manggarai, and Sikka).
- Promotion (of a non-core argument) can be directly to SUBJ; promotion to OBJ may be prohibited, or licensed only in certain restricted circumstances.
- Structurally, the promoted/demoted argument occupies a relevant (direct) argument structural position. Isolating languages rely heavily on the structural position to encode promotion/demotion.

In the next section, I attempt to provide an argument-structure based analysis to account for the core status alternations observed in the languages discussed in this article. In particular, I want to capture the idea that pragmatic prominence licenses core promotion and its related changes in categorial expression, structural order, and grammatical relation (in particular, SUBJ). In addition, I also wish to show that different strategies in voice systems (and marking) lead to different strategies in core status promotion (and also demotion) and mapping.

4   Voice and Argument Structure in LFG

The analysis proposed in this paper attempts to show how pragmatic prominence (topic vs non-topic, (contrastive) focus vs non-focus) has a strong connection with syntactic prominence (SUBJ vs non-SUBJ and core vs non-core). This is couched within the Lexical-Functional Grammar (LFG) (Alsina 1996; Bresnan 2001; Dalrymple et al. 1995; Manning 1996), wherein parametric mapping principles may account for the typological restrictions of voice and core promotion.

In LFG, the language system is modelled in terms of parallel structures consisting of:

- constituent structures (c-structure): morphological/syntactic realizations of grammatical relations in terms of linear/hierarchical structure of categorial units (e.g. NP, VP, ...);
- functional structures (f-structure): surface grammatical relations (SUBJ, OBJ, ...);
- argument structure (a-structure): (see below);
- semantic structure (sem-structure): argument-taking predicates and their arguments, and decomposition of these into primitive units as in Jackendoff (1991) or Foley and Van Valin (1984). For simplicity, the sem-structure will be represented by the traditional semantic role labels (agent, benefactive/goal, patient, ...).

Each structure is an independent structure with its own properties and constraints. The parallel structures are linked with each other by mapping or linking principles. Underlying the mapping is structural prominence, which in general can be defined on any level. Three structural layers highlighted throughout the discussion in this paper reveal three kinds of 'subjects':

- SUBJ(ECT) (conventionally written with capital letters) is the surface/grammatical subject, the most prominent function in f-structure. It can be any role. So far observed, at least in the languages discussed here, it must be a core argument, not necessarily the most prominent core argument.

- A-subj(ect) is the a-structure subject, the most prominent core argument in the a-structure. Like SUBJ, it can be any role, not necessarily an agent.
- Logical subject (l-subj) is the most prominent argument in the sem-structure, typically this is the agent.

For the purpose of our discussion in this paper, I adopt a version of a-structure, namely the syntacticized a-structure, wherein information about core (term) status is important (Arka (2003), Arka and Manning, this volume, Manning (1996), Wechsler and Arka (1998)):

(18) A-STRUCTURE:
It carries information about the syntactic valency of a predicate (i.e. number of arguments: one-place, two-place, ...);
It carries information about core status (i.e. whether an argument is a core/term or not; hence syntactic transitivity: intransitive, monotransitive, ...);
It contains syntactic arguments having the following prominence:
cores outrank non-cores;
within sets of cores/non-cores, prominence reflects semantic prominence.

For simplicity, a lexical entry of an argument-taking predicate, e.g. 'hit' and 'sit', will be represented as (19). The list of semantic roles in the sem-structure should be understood as shorthand of an elaborate sem-structure (e.g. as in Jackendoff-style structures). The a-structure is also represented as a list of (default) core and non-core arguments with the following conventional notations: (i) The left-most is the most prominent core argument (i.e. a-subj). In (19a), for example, the a-subj is by default the agent. However, as we will see, the a-subj can be any semantic role. (ii) The sets of core and non-core are distinguished in the a-structure representation by internal bracketing, with the core set being the left one. For the verb 'sit' (19b), for example, the a-subject is the leftmost and internally within different brackets from the second non-core argument that is normally associated with the locative argument. In case where all arguments are cores as in (19a), no nested brackets are given.

(19)   (a)   (b)
    a-str: 'hit'   <___ ,   ___>   'sit'   <<___>   (<___>)>
                       (a-subj)   (a-obj)   (a-subj)
    sem-str: (agent)   (patient)   (agent)   (locative)

One important consequence of the a-structure ranking stated in (18c) is worth mentioning here: if an agent is core it must be the most prominent argument in the a-structure. This is represented in (20a) as an intrinsic classification of agent (Bresnan and Kanerva 1989; Bresnan and Zaenen 1990), where [-o] means that an agent cannot be syntactically an object. In the view adopted here, an agent cannot be an a-object[11] (20b.ii):

(20) a.   <agent>
             |
            [-o]

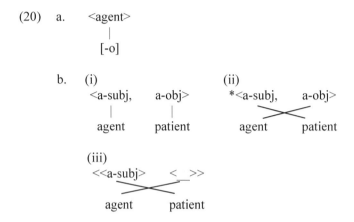

   b.   (i)   (ii)
          <a-subj,   a-obj>   *<a-subj,   a-obj>
            | |
          agent   patient   agent   patient

         (iii)
          <<a-subj>   <   >>

          agent   patient

Thus, an agent has only two possibilities for its a-structure linking.[12] If it is core, being thematically the highest argument, it outranks other arguments (core or non-core) yielding the straight through mapping shown in (20b.i). Otherwise, it should be non-core, and then outranks other arguments in the non-core group. In this case it is less prominent than a core argument. This gives rise to a cross mapping (20b.iii). If it is a core argument, the agent cannot be the second prominent (i.e. the a-object) as shown by the cross-mapping in (20b.ii) because this violates the a-structure principle stated in (18c.ii). In short, being core for an agent means being the a-subject; otherwise it should be demoted to non-core status. We shall see later that much of the restriction in possible function alternations is a logical

---

11 Note that the notion of a-object is not exactly the same as that of the surface OBJ, even though a-object is naturally also linked to OBJ. An a-object can be SUBJ as in the OV verb discussed throughout this paper. OBJ is technically a function, which is classified as direct/core, but negatively defined as being not SUBJ and not OBL. As argued at length in Arka (2003) (also in Kroeger 1993), an agent appearing in the OV construction can be technically an OBJ in this sense. Admittedly, however, the idea of agent-OBJ is not well accepted in the linguistics community.

12 The third possibility (not discussed in this paper) is that it is not linked to the a-structure at all, possibly because it is (completely) suppressed from the semantic structure.

consequence of the principle associated with the a-structure prominence stated in (18c).

4.1 The a-structure-based mapping principles

In what follows, I shall show an argument-structure-based account of voice. The discussion mainly deals with the three typologically most common voices: AV, passive and OV. I argue for the claim that voice is essentially the result of mapping from semantics to syntax via the syntacticised a-structure. The proposed a-structure as an intermediate structure allows us to provide a unified account for different kinds of passives, including the ones that have no apparent active counterparts as observed in an isolating language like Manggarai (see below 5.2.2).

There are different versions of mapping theory in LFG. The one adopted here is a version where mapping onto surface syntax involves an a-structure linking, with the a-structure properties formulated earlier in (18).

The main explanation of typologically different voices from a mapping perspective comes from the following ideas: (i) each structural layer (*sem-structure*, *a-structure* and *f-structure*) has its own constraints and prominence relations (Bresnan 1982, 2001, Dalrymple 1993, among others); and (ii) the correspondences among the structural layers are not always straight. Mapping showing a prominence mismatch is natural. Mapping may even split, where a single semantic argument receives two syntactic realizations (see Arka and Simpson, this volume). The interaction of these factors gives rise to different voices (active voice, objective voice, and passive voice) and possibly raising involving these voices.

The a-structure-based mapping principles formulated in (21) are operative for the languages discussed here and are arguably so for other languages (despite the differences in morphological marking).[13]

(21) Mapping (and Marking):
    I. SUBJ selection: SUBJ must be a core argument
        a. AV: map an agent a-subject/core argument onto SUBJ
        b. OV: map a non-agent a-object/core argument onto SUBJ
        c. PASS: Map a non-agent a-subject/core argument onto SUBJ
    II. Complement function:
        Map the other core(s) onto OBJ(s)
    III. OBL non-core
        PASS: treat an agent as a non-core, map onto OBL

---

13 The passive mapping principle stated in (21.III) which gives rise to the mapping shown in (22c) holds only for one kind of passive. The principle needs to be revised/extended to cover cases where the passive agent is optionally expressed as an oblique, or is obligatorily suppressed.

The representations in (22) show explicitly the possible mappings between the parallel structures allowed by (21): AV shows a straight through mapping (22a), OV shows crossing lines of mapping from a-structure to f-structure (22b), and passive shows crossing lines of mapping from sem-structure to a-structure (22c).

(22)

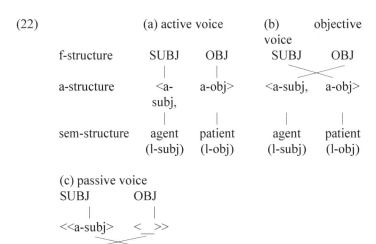

To sum up, the proposed analysis treats voice alternation as mapping alternation, involving an intermediate argument structure (a-structure), where core status is crucial. In this way, we can account for the close relationship between voice alternations and core alternations. As we shall see, voice alternation may also force core alternation.

4.2 Default mapping and marking

Since mapping is in principle predictable, it need not be specified in a lexical entry. As exemplified in (19), lexical entries for 'hit' and 'sit' are specified with a-structure and sem-structure without mapping. The question then is when and where mapping is done. The typologically different strategies employed by languages to encode voice suggest that mapping is not solely done in morphology or the lexical component of the grammar.

Conventionally, mapping in LFG is believed to be a lexical process. It is completed in the morphological component. Thus, certain verbal morphology that marks voice must be specified as imposing a specific constraint in mapping. In Indonesian, for example, the prefix *meN-* (see example (3b)) imposes the AV mapping specified in (21.I.a). Given the entry of *pukul* (23a), the affixation with *meN-* imposes the AV mapping. The AV SUBJ selection principle (21.I.a) maps the agent core/a-subj onto SUBJ, and the complement mapping principle (21.II) maps the patient core to OBJ (II) (23b). The derived verb *memukul* then emerges from the morphological component complete with its function specified (23c).

(23) a. Entry for a verb:
           /pukul/   V   'hit'   < __ ,   __ >
                                    (agent)   (patient)

      b. Affixation with *meN-*:

                                     SUBJ   OBJ
                                       | |
           /memukul/ V   'hit'   < __ ,   __ >
                                       | |
                                    (agent)   (patient)

      c. *memukul*   'hit'   <SUBJ,   OBJ>

Likewise, the Lamaholot -*nek* exemplified by example (4c) imposes the OV mapping (21.I.b) (with additional agreement); and Biman passive *ra-* exemplified by example (6) imposes the passive mapping (21.I.c) and (21.III).

In short, the morphological process involving a voice marker (i) takes a lexical entry (that is unspecified for mapping) as its input and (ii) gives the c-structure tree, as its output, a fully derived word/verb complete with its mapping. If no specific marking applies, a default mapping is operative. Generally, in an accusative language, this is associated unmarked AV mapping, the straight through mapping, where prominence across structures matches as shown in (22a). However, as noted, technically, in Austronesian languages such as Bima discussed here, there may be no unmarked mapping. All voices are morphologically marked.

The question now is how to account for the bare verb glossed as OV in languages like Balinese and Indonesian, or those in the analytic group such as Sikka, Lio and Manggarai)? The problem with this verb is that morphologically it may be unmarked (as in Balinese and Indonesian), but pragmatically it is associated with a marked reading.

There may be at least three approaches to this problem. First, we assume a zero OV prefix as in Balinese/Indonesian. Then, we adopt the conventional view that verbs emerge fully derived, complete with mapping. This first approach is essentially treating the unmarked verb as marked (by a zero affix), where a specific mapping is imposed. This may work well with Balinese and Indonesian, which have morphological contrast in the verbal morphology. This approach appears to have a problem in isolating languages, such as Lio and Sikka, since AV/OV/PASS may in this analysis all have zero morphemes.

The second approach is to analyze the bare verb as having no zero prefix but as having multiple a-structures or subcategorisation frames listed in the lexicon. This is essentially like treating the English verb *give*, which in its entry can have a ditransitive structure and a monotransitive structure. This may be desirable in English, which has a limited set of such verbs. In the isolating languages discussed here the phenomenon is systematic and predictable across verbs. It is not desirable therefore to list predictable properties in the lexicon.

The third approach, which is adopted in this paper, is to analyze words as emerging from the lexicon unspecified or partly specified for mapping; and they rely on pragmatics, via syntax, for specific mapping. This approach does not have the same problems as the previous ones since (a) it does not analyze the bare verb as having a zero morpheme, and (b), as we shall see, the regularities in a-structure alternations follow from certain principles and need not be listed in the lexicon. The basic idea of this analysis is that all verbs emerging from the lexicon are unmarked, both in morphology and in mapping. Default mapping and 'marked' mapping are defined analytically, not morphologically.

To illustrate the second approach, consider again the core alternation from Sikka (13)-(14) repeated here as (24):

(24)   a.   (unmarked)

Wae	*buang*	*ia*	*deri*	*ei*	*kadera*
face	white	that	sit	LOC	chair

'The pretty girl sat on the chair.'

b.   (marked)

Kadera	*ia*	*wi*	*wae*	*buang*	*ia*	*deri*
chair	that	FOC	face	white	that	sit

'It is that chair which was sat on by the pretty girl.'

The verb *deri* 'sit' can be thought of as having a lexical entry with an a-structure consisting of one core and one non-core shown in (25a). This a-structure with unspecified linking appears in the terminal node of the c-structure (25b).

Any verb in Sikka will appear in the c-structure having its mapping unspecified. It needs information from discourse via syntax, e.g. (i) whether the agent or the locative is topical; (ii) whether the DP in [Spec, IP] is a possible agent/locative; and (iii) whether the DP in Spec, VP is a possible agent or not, and whether there is a complement PP with a locative marker. All these sorts of information interact to fix the mapping.

(25)

Sikka

a. /deri/ V 'sit' << __ > (< __ >)>
(agent) (locative)

b.

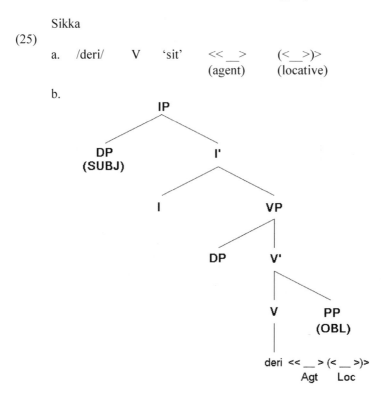

In any case, the grammar allows only two possibilities, captured by the representations in (26). First, if the agent is the topical NP, then the straight through mapping with unmarked order/reading is arrived at (26a). In this case, the agent TOP forces the canonical mapping of agent onto SUBJ/DP, where SUBJ is the default TOP. Structurally, it comes sentence-initially ([Spec, IP]). This makes the agent map onto a-subj/core. Second, if the locative is a topical NP, a marked mapping/reading as shown by (26b) is arrived at. The topical locative must be mapped onto TOP/SUBJ position (sentence-initially), which requires it to be core. However, since Sikka has a symmetrical voice system without passive, this means that the locative must be promoted to core status but it cannot be the a-subject because it is thematically lower than the agent. This gives rise to the OV construction. This is a marked structure because the locative appears sentence-initially and the agent comes later in the sentence.

(26) a.

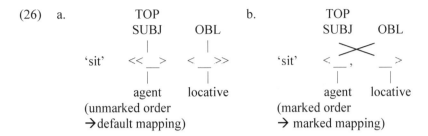

To sum up, since isolating languages rely heavily on pragmatic information for a specific mapping via syntax/constituent order, where (un)marked mapping/reading correlate with (un)marked order, verbs in these languages are believed to have their mapping completed in syntax, rather than in morphology.

Even in a language that has rich verbal morphology for voice, there is evidence that the information from syntax is crucial for core status selection. In Indonesian, for example, the prefix *di-* is widely accepted as the passive marker. A close examination of its properties (Arka and Manning, this volume), however, reveals that this view is not totally right (even though it is not totally wrong either). It is, in fact, only a non-actor oriented marker, which requires that the non-actor argument be mapped onto SUBJ. The specific core status of the agent is later determined in syntax, possibly with the input from the pragmatics (e.g. its topicality; see (Purwo 1989)). The evidence comes from the contrast in binding properties between (27a) and (27c) despite the fact that both have the same *di*-verb, namely *di-utamakan*:

(27) a. *Diri-nya   di-utamakan=nya*
          self-3   di-prioritise=3
          '(S)he prioritized himself/herself.'
          (-*nya* is core = OV)

      b. *Diri-nya   dia   utamakan*
          self-3   3   OV.prioritise
          '(S)he prioritized himself/herself.'
          (-*nya* is core = OV)

    c.   *?Diri-nya   di-utamakan   oleh=nya/Amir
          self-3   di-prioritise   by=3/PN
          'Himself was prioritized by him/Amir.'
          (-nya is not core = PASS)

Sentence (27a) shows that the reflexive SUBJ *dirinya* can be bound by the agent -*nya*. On the contrary, reflexive SUBJ in (27c) cannot be bound by the agent in (27c), which is overtly marked by *oleh* (the agent OBL marker). Note, binding (27a) patterns with binding in the OV verb (27b). In short, the *di*-verb only partially specifies the mapping from a-structure to syntax; it shows that its non-agent is SUBJ (shown by indexing *i*):

(28)   Partially specified linking of *di-*: SUBJ = non-actor
      /di-/ $SUBJ_i$
                  < __ , __ , ... >
                  A $Non\text{-}A_i$

This partial linking does not say anything about the core status of the agent and non-agent arguments. Thus, the *di*-verb in the terminal node of the c-structure awaits information from somewhere else, outside morphology, to fix the mapping by which the core status of the two arguments are determined. If there is a complement PP imposing an OBL agent marked by *oleh*, then the passive mapping is arrived at. Or else, if -*nya* is cliticized to the head verb without *oleh*, then the OV mapping is the result. In either case, if the non-agent argument is a reflexive, binding constraints are operative. Since in Indonesian, binding is sensitive to core status prominence in the a-structure, it is expected that the two different constructions showing different mappings/voices lead to different patterns of binding. More examples for binding evidence are given in section 6.

How can the interaction of different kinds of information be captured? In LFG, this is handled by means of annotated c-structure of the type shown in (29). The technical details of the formal architecture and instantiation of variables represented by up and down arrows will not be discussed here (see Bresnan 1982, 2001). The insights of the representation, however, will be briefly discussed below.

The basic idea is that the annotated c-structure shows the correspondences/mappings across structures with the following information and constraints:
1.   Pragmatic prominence and linear order (see for example Choi 1996): An argument bearing certain pragmatic prominence, specified here as bearing Discourse Function (DF), comes sentence-initially. In (29), this

is shown by left branching of [Spec, IP], and the DF occupies the Spec position. It can be also adjoined to the IP, but it must have certain relativisers or focus-markers associated with this SUBJ position.

2. Pragmatic prominence and semantic role: The equation ($\uparrow$DF)= $\uparrow\alpha$ ARG-θ says that a thematic role can be linked (by a special mapping of $\uparrow\alpha$) to a DF (TOP/FOC). This is to represent a direct relation between pragmatic structure and semantic relation allowing us to express the idea that a certain role is given pragmatic prominence.

3. Categorial expression, linear order and grammatical realizations: the argument assigned pragmatic prominence, if expressed as DP/NP, must be SUBJ. (Note that a unit given pragmatic prominence may be simply a preposed unit expressed by PP, which is not SUBJ.)

(29)

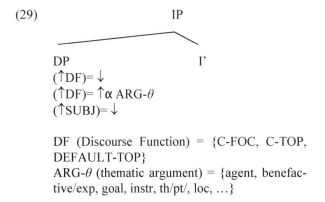

IP

DP   I'
($\uparrow$DF)= $\downarrow$
($\uparrow$DF)= $\uparrow\alpha$ ARG-θ
($\uparrow$SUBJ)= $\downarrow$

DF (Discourse Function) = {C-FOC, C-TOP, DEFAULT-TOP}
ARG-θ (thematic argument) = {agent, benefactive/exp, goal, instr, th/pt/, loc, ...}

The restriction in (29), which requires an argument be SUBJ, is imposed by the combination of all the equations associated with the DP in the [Spec, IP] position as shown in (29). This means, however, that if it appears in another position in the c-structure, this restriction does not apply. In this way, we correctly allow that pragmatic prominence is not an exclusive property of SUBJ. It might be the case that, as demonstrated by data from Manggarai (15), an OBJ can bear a C-FOC, which licenses the promotion of a low-end role such as locative to core status.

The representation in (29) appears to apply for both isolating and non-isolating languages discussed here, irrespective of where the mapping is done. The same pattern emerges: pragmatically unmarked reading is associated with the straight through mapping, where (i) prominence matches, as shown in (22a), with the agent being SUBJ; (ii) structurally the agent is sentence-initial (in [Spec, IP]); and (iii) it is pragmatically the most prominent (generally the default TOP). It is argued that, despite the absence of voice morphemes, these languages do have (analytic) voices, AV, OV and passive.

Two points to conclude. First, words emerging from the morphological component may or may not have the core status of a semantic role specified. In the LFG model adopted here, where information spreading is in a two-way direction in the c-structure tree, the idea that the relevant information for voice/core status selection may come from pragmatics via syntax may be captured. Second, promotion/demotion is judged from the perspective of the unmarked mapping, which cannot be solely determined by morphological marking. Thus, promotion of a locative argument takes place when in the unmarked mapping/reading its status is non-core whereas in the marked reading/mapping, its status is core. This process may be both morphologically and analytically encoded as in Balinese and Indonesian; or, it is only encoded analytically as in Manggarai and Sikka. The process is arguably the same, despite the differences in encoding strategies.

5   A-structure based account for (a)symmetricality system

5.1 Parametric variations

Having established the idea that the notion of voice is also relevant for the isolating language, we can now explain the implication of voice system, core prominence and syntactic promotion/demotion of an argument.

Possible voices and the related restriction in core prominence and mapping appear to be regulated by two parameterized properties: (i) symmetricality in voice systems and (ii) symmetricality in object doubling (Foley 1998a; Foley 1998b). The a-structure-based formulation of the two is given in order below.

The parameter setting formulated in (29) gives rise to typologically two different voice systems.[14] And the two voice systems with explicit possible mappings and their representing languages of Indonesia are shown in the parallel structures below (31). (Note that the inclusion of semantic roles in the a-structure representation is simply to encode a typical association of thematic ranking of two core arguments; the a-subject can be any role.)

(30)   Voice System Parameter:
   1.   Asymmetrical: Only the most prominent core argument (i.e. the a-subject) can be mapped onto SUBJ.

---

14 It should be noted that the asymmetrical parameter in (31.1) captures the accusative system only. To capture an ergative system, the asymmetrical parameter of the voice system should be further parameterized. For example, languages may require that (a) only the a-subject can be linked to SUBJ (accusative) or (b) only the a-object can be linked to SUBJ (ergative).

2. Symmetrical: Either the a-subject or the a-object can be mapped onto SUBJ.

(31)   a.   Asymmetrical Voice System
       (Bima, Manggarai,[15] ...)

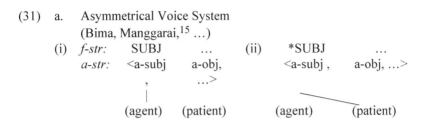

   (i) *f-str:*   SUBJ   ...   (ii)   *SUBJ   ...
        a-str: <a-subj   a-obj,   <a-subj ,   a-obj, ...>
                  ,   ...>

          (agent)   (patient)   (agent)   (patient)

b.   Symmetrical Voice System
     (Balinese, Indonesian, Lio, Sikka, Lamaholot, ...)

   (i) *f-str:*   SUBJ   ...   (ii)   SUBJ   ...
        a-str: <a-subj   a-obj, ...>   <a-subj ,   a-obj, ...>

          (agent)   (patient)   (agent)   (patient)

As noted in (30)–(31), the point in which languages differ is whether a non a-subject is allowed to be mapped onto SUBJ with the a-subject remaining the most prominent argument in the a-structure. If a language does not allow it, then it has an asymmetrical system. A language with this system (e.g. Bima) will bar patient-a-object-SUBJ mapping (31a.ii). Therefore, to link a core patient to SUBJ, such languages must employ passive, whereby the patient is promoted to a-subject status, satisfying the asymmetrical constraint for SUBJ selection (30.1). This also means that the agent must not be linked to the a-subject. This has the effect of agent demotion to no-core, or agent suppression.

In contrast, a language with a symmetrical system allows the patient core to be mapped onto SUBJ without its acquiring a-subject status (i.e. by means of OV, (31b.ii). This means that the agent is not demoted because it may remain as a-subject. In a way, OV does the job of passive, and it is understandable that a language having a symmetrical voice system (e.g.

---

15 Tentatively, I analyse Manggarai as having an asymmetrical system based on the evidence so far gathered, particularly the obligatory demotion of agent to non-core (marked by the preposition le) when a non-agent argument is promoted. However, it should be noted that Manggarai allows arguments to be expressed in genitive (GEN) forms. The syntactic status of the pronominal GEN forms is unclear at this stage. If these GEN forms are core, then Manggarai is like Balinese rather than Bima. I leave this issue for future research.

Lio, Sikka) does not need to have passive. There is no reason, however, why this language type should be prohibited from having passive (e.g. Balinese and Indonesian) because passive does not violate any mapping constraint stated in (29) and (30).[16]

For double object constructions (i.e. ditransitive verbs), languages may have an additional constraint responsible for variations in function alternation of the two objects. Languages vary with respect to whether both OBJs can alternate with SUBJ. A language that allows only one object to alternate is referred to as a language with asymmetrical objects. The constraint responsible for this is referred to as the Asymmetrical Object Principle (AOP) (Bresnan and Kanerva 1989; Bresnan and Moshi 1990). The a-structure-based version of AOP can be formulated as in (32a) and the representation of the prohibited inking is shown in (32b):

(32)   The a-structure based Asymmetrical Object Principle (AOP)
       (for non-agent SUBJ mapping)
       (a)   The least prominent core in the a-structure (i.e. the lowest/third core/second a-object) of a ditransitive predicate cannot be mapped onto the highest function (i.e. SUBJ).
       (b)   *f-str*:   *SUBJ _____   ...

              a-str: <(a-subj),   (a-obj),   a-obj>
                                                       (th/pt)

The AOP (32a) says that the second a-obj (in a ditransitive structure), generally the theme core, (also called OBJ2, or OBJ-θ) cannot alternate with SUBJ. It also captures the cross-linguistic generalization that the OBJ that is allowed to alternate with SUBJ is the direct OBJ (i.e. the only a-object of a monotransitive predicate), irrespective of the AOP. In the case that the language imposes AOP, this is the first a-object for a ditransitive predicate. Due to the thematic ranking within core arguments, the first a-object must be thematically higher than the theme; hence generally it is the benefactive/goal argument.

The next subsection will discuss the consequence of how the a-structure propeties of a predicate and the relevant voice system in the language and

---

16 In contrast, it is predicted that a language with an asymmetrical voice system cannot have OV. The question then is why certain languages with symmetrical systems (like Sikka and Lio) do not have passive. There must be a further typological sub-parameter/constraint in the symmetrical group, which allows the agent-a-subject, even though it is indefinite, to retain its a-subject status. The evidence for this is the fact that what would be passive with an unknown/indefinite/deleted agent in other symmeterical languages is expressed in OV with an explicit indefinite/generic agent something like the car was stolen by someone/people.

the possible additional AOP may determine possible voice/core/function alternations.

5.2 Restrictions of possible voice/core/function alternations

The restrictions imposed by a-structure properties and their interaction with the (a)symmetrical voice system show up in cases like (i) passivization that appears to have no OBJ→SUBJ alternation, but rather OBL ←→SUBJ alternation; (ii) passivization that is syntactically not a transitivity decreasing process; (iii) only ditransitive structures are allowed in the OV construction; and (iv) applicativisation that is a bit unusual in that it does not promote an argument to core status. These will be presented in order.

5.2.1 Direct Promotion of OBL to SUBJ

An instance of direct promotion of a non-core argument to SUBJ, without firstly being promoted to OBJ, is exemplified by the data from Manggarai in (15) and (16), repeated here as (33).

(33)   Manggarai
    a.   *puci*   'sit' $<<\underline{\quad}>$ $(<\underline{\quad}>)>$
                            (agent)   (locative)

    b.   *Aku*   *puci*   *ngger*   *one*   *lo'ang*   (=(15a))
        1SG   enter   to   in   room
        'I entered (into) the room.'

    c.   *Lo'ang*   *hitu*   *puci*   *le*   *ata*   *tako*   (=(16a))
        room   that   enter   by   person   steal
        'The room was entered by a thief.' (passive)

    d.   **Aku*   *puci*   *lo'ang*   (=(15b))
        1SG   enter   room
        'I entered the room.'   *(AV)

The verb *puci* 'sit' is an intransitive predicate whose lexical entry is abbreviated in (33a), where (i) its a-structure specifies one core and one noncore argument, and (ii) its sem-structure specifies that it involves a sitter (an agent) and a place for the sitting (locative). Given this information, there can be only two possibilities. The first is the unmarked mapping/reading. This straight through mapping gives rise to the normal intransitive structure of (33b), with the locative being an OBL. The second possibility is the marked reading/mapping, where the locative is made SUBJ (for some pragmatic reason). Crucially, the SUBJ must also be the a-subject (due to the asymmetrical voice system). This in effect prevents the agent from being mapped onto the a-subject position and forces it to be demoted to non-core status. As a result, a passive (intransitive) shown in (33c) is arrived at. Promotion of the locative to core-OBJ status yielding a transitive active structure (33d) is predicted to be unacceptable. This is because, if there is no pragmatic motivation associated with the locative, the default mapping with the a-structure/sem-structure in (33a) will be operative, by which the locative must be linked to a non-core (OBL). In other words, no OBJ→SUBJ alternation is observed in this passivization because the active (33d) is not acceptable. The fact that a passive verb may have no active counterpart is well accounted for in the a-structure based analysis presented here.

5.2.2 Passivization is not (always) a transitivity-decreasing process

Direct promotion of a non-core argument to subject as illustrated by (33) also provides evidence for the idea of linking and that sem-structure is separable from a-structure. Crucially, passivization may simply involve an alternative linking, without a change in the syntactic transitivity of the verb. That is, both the intransitive verb (33a) and the passive counterpart (33b) share a syntactic a-structure: one core and one non-core. The only difference is its linking to sem-structure: in (33a) we have canonical linking with the agent being the a-subject/SUBJ and the locative argument being non-core whereas in (33b) we have the reverse.

Passivization of a transitive base *pande* 'make' in (34) exhibits the same property, where (a) a direct promotion to the a-subject in passive is observed and (b) the syntactic transitivity of the base may remain the same. Consider the lexical entry of the verb in (34a) and see how an active ditransitive structure in (34d) and a passive (transitive) structure in (34f) are ruled out.

(34)   Manggarai
   a.   *pande*   'make':
        a-str   < __ , __ >   (< __ , .. >)
        sem-str   (agent, theme)   (benefactive)

   b.i   *Hia*   *pande*   *layang-layang*   *te*   *hi*   *Ali*
         3SG   make   kite-kite   for   ART   PN
         '(S)he made kites for Ali.'
   b.ii   SUBJ
         << '3SG',   'kite'>   <'Ali'>>
           (agent)   (theme)   (benefactive)
         (AV monotransitive)

c.i *Layang-layang pande le hia te hi*
    kite-kite make by 3SG for ART
    Ali
    PN
    'The kites were made by him/her for Ali.'

c.ii SUBJ
    < 'kite'> <'3SG', 'Ali'>
    (theme) (agent) (benefactive)
    (passive)

d.i **Hia* pande **hi** **Ali** *layang-layang*
    3SG make ART PN kite-kite
    '(S)he made kites for Ali.'

d.ii SUBJ
    *< '3SG', 'Ali', 'kite'>
    (agent) (benefactive) (theme)
    (*AV ditransitive)

e.i **Hi** **Ali** *pande layang-layang le hia*
    ART PN make kite-kite by 3SG
    'For Ali, the kites were made by him/her.'

e.ii SUBJ
    < 'Ali', 'kite'> < '3SG'>
    (benefactive) (theme) (agent)
    (passive)

f.i **Layang-layang* pande hi Ali le* *hia*
    kite-kite make ART PN by 3SG
    'The kites were made by him/her for Ali.'

f.ii SUBJ
    *< 'kite', 'Ali'> < '3SG'>
    (theme) (benefactive) (agent)
    (passive)

Given the entry in (34a), the acceptability of the active monotransitive (34b) and its passive counterpart (34c) is straightforward. The straight-through mapping yields the unmarked construction (34b). And because the theme is by default the second argument, passivization with the theme-SUBJ yields (34c). In both cases, the benefactive is OBL marked by *te*.

The contrast between (34d,f) and (34e) again provides good evidence for the idea of argument ranking. It can be explained as follows. A benefactive argument is thematically ranked higher than a theme/patient argument.

If both are core arguments, and if both are associated with an active verb where the agent is also a core argument, then we have a problem in a language which dislikes ditransitive verbs because this means that we have three core arguments. This may partly account for the badness of promotion of the benefactive to OBJ in (34d). The promotion seems also to be prohibited by a discourse factor in that, unlike SUBJ, OBJ normally does not carry pragmatic prominence necessary for promotion to core status. If there is no motivation for core promotion, then the default mapping is operative with the a-structure specification of (34a), yielding the canonical structure (34b) and not licensing the structure with three core arguments (34d).

Compelling evidence for the idea of argument ranking comes from the contrast of the two passives shown by (34e) and (34f). In (34e), the benefactive is (directly) promoted to a-subject/SUBJ (i.e. assuming core status) by passive, kicking down the agent to non-core status. Crucially, being thematically higher than the theme *laying-layang* 'kites', the benefactive core must outrank the theme core. Principles of argument ranking and argument linking are respected, hence (34e) is acceptable. On the contrary, making the theme core SUBJ while keeping the benefactive core—meaning that the benefactive is the a-subject and the theme is the a-object—gives rise to a bad sentence (34f). This can be taken as evidence that Manggarai has an asymmetrical voice system.

Given the analysis here, both passives in (34c) and (34e) can be thought of being 'derived' from the active (34b). Another point to note is that the a-structure of the active verb (34b) is exactly the same as that of the passive verb (34e): two cores and one non-core. Again, this means that passivization is not always a transitivity decreasing process. All these facts follow naturally from the mapping analysis presented here.

To conclude, the passive facts in Manggarai reveal the following:

a) Direct promotion of a non-core argument to the core a-subject status confirms the idea that core arguments' ranking reflects thematic hierarchy;
b) The non-existence of OBJ-SUBJ alternation shows that to be passive SUBJ, an argument need not be an OBJ of an active sentence in the first place;
c) From the a-structure based perspective of mapping, passivization is not always a detransitivizing process.

5.2.3 Why a ditransitive verb is allowed only in OV

The a-structure based analysis presented in this paper also accounts for a peculiar gap in syntactic transitivity alternations observed in Lamaholot. Like Manggarai, Lamaholot dislikes active ditransitive verbs. It does allow ditransitive verbs, however, but only in the OV construction. Consider the verb *genatu* 'send' in (35): the monotransitive verb allows an AV/OV alternation (35a-b) but there is a restriction for such an alternation for the ditransitive counterpart (35c-e).

(35) a. *Kopong   genatu   doi   nei   go'e*
             PN   send   money give   1SG
             'Kopong sent money to/for me.'   (AV monotransitive)

      b. *Doi   ne   Kopong   genatu-ro   nei   go'e*
             money that   PN   send-OV.3SG   give   1SG
             'The money was sent by Kopong to me.'   (OV monotransitive)

      c. *?*Kopong   genatu   go'e   doi*
             PN   send   1SG   money
             'Kopong sent me money.'   (*AV ditransitive)

      d. *Go'e   Kopong   genatu-k   doi*
             1SG   PN   send-OV.1SG   money
             'I was sent money by Kopong.'   (OV ditransitive)

      e. **Doi   ne   Kopong   genatu-ro   go'e*
             money that   PN   send-OV.3SG   1SG
             'The money was sent (to) me by Kopong.'   (*OV ditransitive)

The sentences in (35) can be accounted for by analysing the verb *genatu* 'send' as basically a monotransitive verb with the entry shown in (36a). (The benefactive is arguably not an argument):

(36) a. *genatu*   < __ ,   __ >   (monotransitive)
          'send'   (agent,   patient)   (benefactive)

      b.   TOP/SUBJ
                              |
        genatu   < 'Kopong',   '1SG',   'money'>
        * 'AV.send' | | |
                      (agent,   benefactive,   patient)
        (=(35c))   (*AV ditransitive)

      c.   TOP/SUBJ
                                      |
        genatu-k   < 'Kopong' ,   '1SG',   'money'>
        'OV.send' | | |
                    (agent,   benefactive,   patient)
        (=(35d))   (OV ditransitive)

Given (i) the information of the entry (36) and (ii) that the language has a symmetrical voice system without passive (i.e. no demotion of agent to non-core status is possible), then the AV/OV alternations involving the monotransitive verb as shown in (35a-b) are straightforward. The default mapping yielding AV monotransitive of the type (35a) is imposed; or else, in the OV verb, the theme is SUBJ (35b).

However, when a benefactive argument is introduced or promoted, there is a restriction due to argument ranking. The promotion must be licensed by pragmatic prominence; otherwise the promotion is barred. This explains why the AV ditransitive with the benefactive being non-SUBJ core as in (35c) is not acceptable. The prohibited a-structure and its linking is shown in (36b).

On the contrary, assigning pragmatic prominence to the benefactive licenses its promotion as shown by sentence (35d). The a-structure and linking of this sentence is shown in (36c). Note that the promoted argument is the a-object, not the a-subject, due to the symmetrical voice system where the agent remains the as a-subject. Since the promoted benefactive argument is thematically lower than the agent and is higher than the theme, it occupies the second position in the ranking of the a-structure. (the agent cannot be demoted because this option is not available in the grammar.) This explains why such an interaction gives rise to a ditransitive a-structure (i.e. with three cores) that must be in OV, i.e. OV mapping of the a-object onto SUBJ.

Finally, the badness of (35e) can be accounted for in the same way as the badness of (35c), where nothing licenses the promotion of the benefactive; or else, it might suggest that this language might impose AOP. This requires further research.

5.2.4 Interaction of voice system and double object constraints

Languages that do not impose AOP are expected to have no problem in non-active voice alternations. In particular, there can be two possible non-active constructions associated with a ditransitive base. This is the case in Balinese (37) and Sikka (38). The (b) sentences show the OV verbs with benefactive-SUBJ and the (c) sentences show the other alternative OV verbs with theme-SUBJ.

(37) Balinese

a.
Ia	*meli-ang*	*Nyoman*	*umah*	(AV)
3	AV.buy-APPL	PN	house	

'(S)he bought a house for Nyoman.'

b.
Nyoman	*beli-ang=a*	*umah*	(OV)
PN	OV.buy-APPL=3	house	

'For Nyoman, (s)he bought a house.'

c.
Umah	*ene*	*ane*	*beliang=a*	*Nyoman*	(OV)
house	this	REL	OV.buy=3	PN	

'It is this house that (s)he bought for Nyoman.'

(38) Sikka

a.
Ina	*piar*	*`ami*	*adang*	*ganu*	*te'i*	(AV)
mother	present	1PL	sign	like	this	

'Mother presented this gift to us.'

b.
`Ami	*ina*	*piar*	*adang*	*ganu*	*te'i*	(OV)
1PL	mother	present	sign	like	this	

'We were presented with this gift by mother.'

c.
Adang	*ganu*	*te'i*	*ina*	*piar*	*`ami*	(OV)
sign	like	this	mother	present	1PL	

'This gift was presented to us by Mother.'

Languages that impose AOP, however, are predicted to be restricted in the possible non-active voices. Standard Indonesian, for instance, is a language of this type. Due to the AOP, which prohibits the lowest core of a ditransitive verb (i.e. the second a-object of the two a-objects) to be SUBJ, this language has a problem with the non-active ditransitive verb where the theme is SUBJ, for example, with the OV applicative verb *belikan* (39c). In the non-applicative OV verb, *beli*, it is expected to be fine (39d). This is because *beli* is monotransitive, wherein the theme is the only a-object in the a-structure. Therefore, it is not subject to the AOP: it can be the SUBJ of the OV verb.

(39) Indonesian

a.
Saya	*mem-beli-kan*	*Amir*	*baju*	*baru*
1SG	AV-buy-APPL	PN	shirt	new

'I bought a new shirt for Amir.'   (*Amir*=benefactive OBJ)

b.
Amir	*saya*	*beli-kan*	*baju*	*baru*
PN	1SG	OV.buy-APPL	shirt	new

'For Amir, I bought a new shirt.'   (*Amir*=benefactive SUB)

c. *?* Baju   baru   (itu)   saya   beli-kan   Amir*
   shirt   new   that   1SG   OV.buy-APPL   PN
   'The new shirt, I bought it for Amir.'
   (*baju baru* = theme SUBJ)

d. *Baju   baru   itu   saya   beli   untuk   Amir*
   shirt   new   that   1SG   OV.buy   for   PN
   'The new shirt, I bought it for Amir.'

Likewise, passivizing theme-SUBJ (with the verb *dibelikan*) (40a) is a problem. To be acceptable, the verb must be monotransitive (i.e. without the applicative suffix -*kan*), where the benefactive is not a core argument (40b). The explanation for this contrast is in principle the same as that for (39), except for the difference of the core status of the theme in (40b). Being the only a-object of *beli*, the theme in (40b) can easily assume the a-subject status in passive, kicking out the agent to non-core status.

(40)   Indonesian

a. *?*Baju   baru   itu   di-beli-kan   Amir   oleh*
   shirt   new   that   PASS-buy-APPL   PN   by
   Tono
   PN
   'The new shirt was bought for Amir by Tono.'

b. *Baju   baru   itu   di-beli   untuk   Amir   oleh*
   shirt   new   that   PASS-buy   for   PN   by
   Tono
   PN
   'The new shirt was bought for Amir by Tono.'

Bima imposes AOP; therefore it is expected that it shows a similar restriction to Indonesian. This is confirmed. There is a (surprising) difference, however. Unlike in Indonesian (40b), passivising theme-SUBJ in Bima is still allowed with the applicative verb, with the consequence that the applied argument is obligatorily present as non-core (OBL). This is, in fact, something expected in the present analysis. Consider (41):

(41)   Bima

a. *Sia   ndawi-wea-na   nahu   kuru   nasi*
   3SG   make-APPL-3.RL   1SG   cage   bird
   '(S)he has made a bird cage for me.'   (AV)

b. | *Nahu* | *ndawi-wea* | *ba* | *sia* | *kuru* | *nasi* |
|---|---|---|---|---|---|
| 1SG | make-APPL | by | 3SG | cage | bird |

'For me, the bird cage was made by him/her.'   (passive)

c. | **Kuru* | *nasi* | *ede* | *ndawi-wea* | *nahu* | *ba* | *sia* |
|---|---|---|---|---|---|---|
| cage | bird | that | make-APPL | 1SG | by | 3SG |

'The bird cage was made by him/her for me.'   (passive)

d. | *Kuru* | *nasi* | *ede* | *ndawi-wea* | *ba* | *sia* | *ruu* |
|---|---|---|---|---|---|---|
| cage | bird | that | make-APPL | by | 3SG | for |

nahu
1SG

'The bird cage was made by him/her for me.'   (passive)

Example (41a) shows the ditransitive applicative verb, with the applied benefactive argument *nahu* being the first a-obj/OBJ and *kuru nasi* as the second a-obj/OBJ. Given this picture, it is predicted that *nahu* can be SUBJ of the passive verb in (41b). Likewise, given the AOP in Bima, passivizing theme-SUBJ is predictably not allowed (41c). In contrast to (41c), and unlike Indonesian (40a), passivizing theme-SUBJ in Bima is possible with the applicative verb (41d) (marked with *wea*). Note that in this structure, the benefactive argument is non-core, marked by *ruu*. The effect of this marking is that the OBL benefactive *ruu nahu* is obligatorily present. (If the applicative suffix *wea* is absent, the presence of the benefactive OBL *ruu nahu* is optional.)

The a-structure based analysis predicts that the pattern observed in (41) is expected. The default a-structure of 'make' is monotransitive, as shown in (42a), where the benefactive role is not core (possibly an oblique or adjunct, intrinsically optional). The applicative *wea* introduces the benefactive to the a-structure of *nadwi* as a core argument. This gives rise to a ditransitive structure shown in (42b), where in accordance with the thematic ranking of the a-structure, the applied benefactive is the first a-object (i.e. second ranked argument). In the default mapping, this gives rise to an unmarked reading, an active voice structure as illustrated by (41a).

(42) a. | *ndawi* | $<<\_\_,$ | $\_\_>$ | $(<\_\_>)>$ |
|---|---|---|---|
| 'make' | (agent) | (theme) | (benefactive) |

b. | *ndaw-weai* | $<\_\_,$ | $\_\_,$ | $\_\_>$ |
|---|---|---|---|
| 'make-for' | (agent) | (benefactive) | (theme) |

c. | *ndaw-weai* | $<<\_\_,$ | $\_\_>$ | $<\_\_>>$ |
|---|---|---|---|
| 'make-for' | (agent) | (theme) | (benefactive) |

A marked mapping is, however, possible by means of passivization. Given the a-structure properties in (42b), and since Bima has an asymmetrical voice system (where only the a-subject can be SUBJ), only the applied benefactive argument can assume the a-subject when the agent is backgrounded from its default a-subject position. This accounts for the acceptability of the passive verb with benefactive-SUBJ (41b). The theme-core argument, being the third in rank, cannot be the first when the agent is demoted. Thus, mapping it onto SUBJ violates the asymmetrical voice system constraint in this language. This accounts for the unacceptability of (41c).

When for some reason the benefactive is still made part of the a-structure (thus applicativization with *wea* is necessary) but for some other reason (possibly pragmatic/syntactic), the theme is also highlighted, then there is a problem. There is a competition for a-subj/SUBJ mapping and potential violation of asymmetrical voice constraint, and argument ranking in the a-structure. The conflict is resolved by rearranging the a-structure ranking as shown by (42c). The a-structure in (42c) appears to be the same as that in (42a), except for the clear status of the benefactive, which is now obligatorily present as OBL. Note that, in (42c), the benefactive argument is treated as a non-core, paving the way for the theme being the only a-object. In the analysis adopted here, this pattern is indeed expected. We can have appliciativization that does not involve core promotion because such promotion would violate the AOP constraint. Its being obligatorily present as OBL is due to the presence of the applicative marking on the verb (i.e. it is morphosemantically motivated).

Table 4 gives a summary of the (a)symmetricality in voice systems and possible object doubling in the Indonesian languages discussed in this paper. A language that has an asymmetrical voice system with symmetrical double objects (row 4) arguably does not exist because the two are contradictory to each other. The asymmetrical voice system prohibits a non-a-subject from being SUBJ whereas the symmetrical object system allows a non-a-subject to be SUBJ. Thus, both cannot be part of the same grammar. Rows 6 and 7 are the types which have no ditransitive verbs.[17] Further research is needed to uncover the typological properties of voice systems and object doubling of other Indonesian languages, particularly whether there is any language of the type shown in row 7.

---

17 In the present analysis, Manggarai is regarded as having an asymmetrical voice system with no ditransitive verbs. The only (true) ditransitive structure found is the verb 'give'. This can be regarded as an exception rather than being part of a ditransitive system in the language.

Table 4 Voice Systems and Object Doubling in Indonesian Languages

	Voice system	Object doubling	Languages
1.	symmetrical	symmetrical	Balinese, Lio, Sikka
2.	symmetrical	asymmetrical	Indonesian, Lamaholot (?)
3.	asymmetrical	asymmetrical	Bima
4.	asymmetrical	symmetrical	(predicted not available)
6.	asymmetrical	-	Manggarai
7.	symmetrical	-	??

6 Being Core: Evidence from Binding

The significance of being core is also evident from binding. I argue that languages differ with respect to which structural prominence is relevant for binding (Arka 2003; Bresnan 2001; Dalrymple 1993; Manning 1996; Wechsler and Arka 1998). In what follows, I contrast Balinese/Indonesian, where binding is sensitive to the a-structure, and Manggarai/Lamaholot, where binding is sensitive to the surface grammatical relation (f-structure). The expected pattern of contrast is that in Balinese/Indonesian, binding is not affected by voice change as long as the core prominence is unaffected by voice alternation. In Lamaholot, binding will be affected by voice alternation, even though core prominence remains the same. This is confirmed. In addition, using data from Manggarai, I will show how core status alternation affects binding.

First, consider the Indonesian and Balinese data in (43)-(44). AV/OV alternations do not change binding relations (Arka 2003; Arka and Manning this volume; Wechsler and Arka 1998). Crucially, in the OV constructions (the (b) sentences below), the non-subject arguments can bind the SUBJ reflexives. In the a-structure based analysis presented here, this follows from the idea that binding in these languages is sensitive to the a-structure prominence: the agent binder is the a-subject, the most prominent item, in the a-structure, even though it is not grammatically SUBJ in the surface syntax.

(43)   Indonesian
      a.   *Dia   tak   meng-hiraukan   diri-nya*
          3SG   NEG   A V-care   self-3
          '(S)he didn't care for himself/herself.'   (AV)

b. *Dirinya   tak   dia   hiraukan*
   self-3   NEG   3SG   OV.care
   'Himself/herself, (s)he didn't care (for).'   (OV)

(44) Balinese
  a. *Ia   tusing   ng-runguang   awak-ne*
     3SG   NEG   AV-care   self-3
     '(S)he didn't care for himself/herself.'   (AV)

  b. *Awak-ne   tusing   runguang=a*
     self-3   NEG   OV.care=3
     'Himself/herself, (s)he didn't care (for).'   (OV)

In Lamaholot, as demonstrated by the contrast in (45), a change to OV results in the inability of the agent to bind the SUBJ reflexive. This suggests that binding in Lamaholot, unlike that in Balinese and Indonesian, is sensitive to surface grammatical relations.

(45) Lamaholot
  a. *Na'   tubi'   weki-n*
     3SG   pinch.AV   self-3
     '(S)he pinched himself/herself.'   (AV)

  b. *?* Weki-n   na'   tubi-ro'*
     self-3   3SG   pinch-OV.3SG
     'Himself/herself, (s)he pinched.'   (OV)

Reflexive binding in Manggarai appears to be sensitive to the core status of the binder. (46a) shows an active sentence where the OBJ is bound by the SUBJ, which is straightforward. (46b) shows the passive counterpart of (46a), where the pronominal *hia* is now an OBL marked by *le* 'by'. As a result, *hia* can no longer bind the reflexive *ru-n* 'self-3' (reading (ii)). This sentence is acceptable only on reading (i), where *ru-n* is interpreted as an emphatic reflexive associated with the subject *weki* referring to someone else (index *j*). Surprisingly, Manggarai has the passive shown in (46c), where the agent itself is a reflexive (*ru-n*) bound by the theme-SUBJ (*hia/wekin*).

(46) Manggarai
  a. *Hia$_i$ mbele   weki   ru-n$_i$*   <hia$_i$, self$_i$>
     3SG   kill   body   self-3
     'S/he killed himself/herself.'   (AV)

b. | *Weki* | *ru-n$_i$* | *mbele* | *le* | *hia*$_{*i/j}$ | << self$_i$><hia$_{j/*i}$>> |
   |--------|-----------|---------|------|--------------|---------------------------|
   | body | self-3 | kill | by | 3 | |

    (i) '(S)he$_i$ (himself/ herself) was killed by him$_j$ /her$_j$.'
    (ii) *'(S)he was killed by himself/herself.'   (passive)

c. | *Hia$_j$/weki-n$_i$* | *mbele* | *le* | *ru-n$_i$* | <<hia$_i$><self$_i$>> |
   |----------------------|---------|------|------------|----------------------|
   | 3SG/body-3 | kill | by | self-3 | |

    'S/he was killed by himself/herself.'   (passive)

That the core status of a binder in Manggarai is crucial comes from the following examples (Arka and Kosmas 2005):

(47) a. | *Hi* | *ema$_i$* | *toto* | *weki-n$_{i/*j}$* | *one* | *kaca* |
       |------|-----------|--------|------------------|-------|--------|
       | ART | father | show | self-3 | at | mirror |

kamping	*hi*	*ase$_j$*
to	ART	sibling

b. | *Hi* | *ema$_i$* | *toto* | *kamping* | *hi* | *ase$_j$* |
   |------|-----------|--------|-----------|------|-----------|
   | ART | father | show | to | ART | sibling |

weki-n$_{i/*j}$	*one*	*kaca*
self-3	at	mirror

    'Father showed himself in the mirror to (the/my) little sibling.'

(48) | *Hi* | *ase$_j$* | *toto* | *weki-n$_{j/*i}$* | *li* | *emai* |
     |------|-----------|--------|-------------------|------|--------|
     | ART | sibling | show | self-3 | by | father |

one	*kaca*
at	mirror

    'The/my little sibling was shown himself by Father in the mirror.'

In the active constructions (47), the reflexive *wekin* (OBJ) cannot be bound by the experiencer *hi ase* 'the little sibling' (OBL) in (a) where it comes after the reflexive or in (b) where it comes before the reflexive. In short, word order is irrelevant for reflexive binding in this language. However, in the passive counterpart (48), the situation reverses. The experiencer *hi ase* which is linked to SUBJ can bind the reflexive *wekin*. The *le* agent, because it is now non-core, fails to bind the reflexive core/OBJ argument (*wekin*).

    It should be noted that perhaps not many languages allow binding of an agent reflexive in an independent clause like Manggarai (46c). Indonesian and Balinese do not generally allow this, as shown by the badness of the (d) sentences in (49)-(51):

(49) Indonesian

    a. *Dia   bisa   me-lihat   diri-nya*
        3SG   can   AV-see   self-3
        '(S)he can see himself/herself.'   (AV)

    b. *Diri-nya   bisa   dia   lihat*
        self-3   can   3SG   OV.see
        'Himself/herself, (s)he can see.'   (OV)

    c. *??Dirinya   bisa   di-lihat   oleh   dia*
        self-3   can   PASS-see   by   3SG
        'Himself/herself can be seen by him/her.'   (passive)

    d. **Dia   bisa   dilihat   oleh   dirinya*
        3SG   can   PASS-see   by   self-3
        '(S)he can be seen by himself/herself.'   (passive)

(50) Balinese (h.r.)

    a. *Ida   tan   sida   nyingakin   ragan-idane*
        3   NEG   can   AV-see   self-3
        '(S)he cannot see himself/herself.'   (AV)

    b. *Ragan-idane   tan   sida   cingakin   ida*
        self-3   NEG   can   OV.see   3
        'Himself/herself, (s)he cannot see.'   (OV)

    c. ??Ragan-idane   tan   sida   ka-cingakin   antuk   ida
        self-3   NEG   can   PASS-see   by   3
        'Himself/herself cannot be seen by him/her.'   (passive)

    d. ?*Ida   tan   sida   ka-cingakin   antuk   ragan-idane
        3   NEG   can   PASS-see   by   self-3
        '(S)he cannot be seen by himself/herself.'   (passive)

(51) Balinese

    a. *Ia   ningalin   awakne*
        3   AV.see   self-3
        '(S)he saw himself/herself.'   (AV)

    b. *Awakne   tingalin=a*
        self-3   OV.see=3
        'Himself/herself, (s)he saw.'   (OV)

c.   ??Awakne   tingalin-a   teken   ia
       self-3   see-PASS   by   3
       'Himself/herself was seen by him/her.'   (passive)

d.   *Ia   tingalin-a   teken   awakne
       3   see-PASS   by   self-3
       '(S)he was seen by himself/herself.'   (passive)

The acceptability of the (a) and (b) sentences in (49)–(51) has been dis-cussed before and is not repeated here. The relatively bad (c) sentences are certainly due to the violation of the a-structure-based constraint of binding: the binder is non-core, ranked lower than the bindee, which is core. Surpris-ingly, the (d) sentences are even worse than the (c) sentences, even though the a-structure-based constraint is respected. Thus, binding in Balinese and Indonesian is not completely subject to the syntactic constraints. The fact that the same binding relation is possible in Manggarai suggests that bind-ing in Manggarai is completely sensitive to syntactic prominence (i.e. the logical subject/agent cannot be bound). Among the languages discussed here, none shows the property that binding is exclusively sensitive to se-mantic prominence.

7 Conclusion

1. Being core is a complex matter, involving interaction of morphosyntax-semantics and, crucially, pragmatic prominence.
2. The default core status of an argument is determined in a lexical entry of a predicate. A change of the core status may be determined (i) mor-pholexically and/or (ii) analytically/syntactically; in either case, it is possibly motivated/imposed by pragmatics. The change may involve a decrease or an increase in the number of core arguments, or simply a change in mapping without affecting the number of core arguments. The change is associated with a change in voice, which may or may not be morphologically marked.
3. Possible argument promotion is typologically predictable, based on two parameters of symmetricality in:
    a. voice system: symmetrical vs asymmetrical voice system
    b. object doubling: symmetrical vs asymmetrical objects.
4. The notion of prominence across structural layers which interacts with the specific setting of the parameters stated in (3) is crucial for possible mapping and voice selection.
5. The analysis offered here accounts for (i) typological variations of voice selection and (ii) possible restrictions that may be imposed in

core promotion and mapping onto SUBJ. In particular, the analysis predicts that promotion can be directly to a-subj/SUBJ, and hence it is possible that (i) passivisation may involve no OBJ-SUBJ alternation (i.e. the active counterpart where the same semantic role appearing as OBJ does not exist), (ii) passivization may not be a transitivity decreasing process. These predictions are borne out in the data presented from languages of Eastern Indonesia.

8 References

Alsina, A. 1996. *The Role of Argument Structure in Grammar*. Stanford: CSLI.

Arka, I Wayan. 2003. *Balinese morphosyntax: a lexical-functional approach*. Canberra: Pacific Linguistics (PL 547).

Arka, I Wayan. & J. Kosmas. 2005. Passive without passive morphology? Evidence from Manggarai. In *The many faces of Austronesian voice systems: some new empirical studies* ed. I. W. Arka & M. D. Ross. 87–117. Canberra: Pacific Linguistics.

Artawa, K. 1994. Ergativity and Balinese Syntax. Ph.D thesis, Department of Linguistics, La Trobe University.

Artawa, I. K., P. Artini & B. J. Blake. 1997. *Balinese Grammar and Discourse*. Denpasar/Melbourne: Udayana University/La Trobe University.

Beratha, N. L. Sutjiati. 1992. Evolution of Verbal Morphology in Balinese. Ph.D thesis, Australian National University.

Bresnan, J. (ed.). 1982. *The Mental Representation of Grammatical Relations*. Cambridge, Massachusetts: MIT Press.

Bresnan, J. 2001. *Lexical Functional Syntax*. Oxford: Blackwell.

Bresnan, J. & J. Kanerva. 1989. Locative Inversion in Chichewa: A case study of factorization in Grammar. *Linguistic Inquiry* 20:1–50.

Bresnan, J. & L. Moshi. 1990. Object Asymmetries in Comparative Bantu Syntax. *Linguistic Inquiry* 21.2:147–185.

Bresnan, J. & A. Zaenen. 1990. Deep Unaccusativity in LFG. In *Grammatical Relations: A Cross-Theoretical Perspective* ed. K. Dziwirek, P. Farell & E. Mejias-Bikandi. 45–57. Stanford: CSLI.

Choi, H.-W. 1996. Optimizing Structure in Context: Scrambling and Information Structure. Ph.D thesis, Stanford University.

Clynes, A. 1995. Topics in the Phonology and Morphosyntax of Balinese. Ph.D thesis, Australian National University.

Dalrymple, M. 1993. *The Syntax of Anaphoric Binding*. Stanford: CSLI.

Dalrymple, M, R. M. Kaplan, J. T. Maxwell III & A. Zaenen (ed.). 1995. *Formal Issues in Lexical-Functional Grammar*. Stanford: CSLI.

Foley, W. A. 1998a. *Symmetrical Voice Systems and Precategoriality in Philippine Languages*. Sydney: University of Sydney.

Foley, W. A. 1998b. *A Typology of Information Packaging in the Clause*. Sydney: Department of Linguistics.

Foley, W. A. & R. Van Valin. 1984. *Functional Syntax and Universal Grammar*. Cambridge: Cambridge University Press.

Guilfoyle, E., H. Hung & L. Travis. 1992. SPEC of IP and SPEC of VP: two subjects in Austronesian languages. *Natural Language and Linguistic Theory* 10.3:375–414.

Hunter, T. M. 1988. *Balinese Language: Historical Background and Contemporary State*. Michigan University: Michigan.

Jackendoff, R. 1991. *Semantic Structures*. Cambridge, Massachusetts: MIT Press.

Japa, I. W. 2000. Properti Argumen Inti, Interpretasi Tipologis dan Struktur Kausatif Bahasa Lamaholot Dialek Nusa Tadon, S2 Linguistik, Universitas Udayana: Denpasar.

Jauhary, E. 2000. Pasif Bahasa Bima, S2 Linguistik, Universitas Udayana: Denpasar.

Kosmas, J. 2000. Argument Aktor dan Pemetaanya, S2 Linguistik, Universitas Udayana: Denpasar.

Kroeger, P. 1993. *Phrase Structure and Grammatical Relations in Tagalog*. Stanford: CSLI Publications.

Manning, C. D. 1996. *Ergativity: Argument Structure and Grammatical Relations*. Stanford: CSLI.

Pastika, I. W. 1999. Voice Selection in Balinese Narrative Discourse. Ph.D thesis, Australian National University.

Purwo, B. K. 1988. Voice in Indonesian: a discourse study. In *Passive and Voice*, ed. M. Shibatani. 195–242. Amsterdam: John Benjamins. (Typological Studies in Language 16).

Sawardi, F. X. 2000. Argumen Kompleks Bahasa Lio, S2 Linguistik Universitas Udayana, Denpasar.

Sedeng, I. N. 2000. Kalimat Kompleks dan Relasi Gramatikal Bahasa Sikka. Masters Thesis, S2 Linguistik, Universitas Udayana, Denpasar.

Wechsler, S. & I Wayan Arka. 1998. Syntactic Ergativity in Balinese: an Argument Structure Based Theory. *Natural Language and Linguistic Theory* 16:387–441.

9

Hierarchies in Argument Structure Increasing Processes: Ranking Causative and Applicative

MARK DONOHUE

1 Introduction

This paper examines which of applicative and causative constructions can be said to be the least 'marked'. Diachronically we could investigate the grammaticalisation of the one morpheme or lexical item from one sense to another. While suggestive, this would not eliminate the chance of influence from other parts of the language, and could not present a synchronic perspective of the system. In order to gain an idea of how a language orders the constructions dynamically, we need to find examples of synchronic alternation or shift in progress: this is a subtler notion of grammaticalisation, as it does not entail the completion of a shift, but only the observation of alternatives. The material presented shows that the causative in Tukang Besi is less marked.

2 Hierarchies among Constructions

The notion of establishing hierarchical orders between different constructions in a language appears to be problematic. Diachronically we could investigate the drift in meaning (grammaticalisation) of a morpheme or lexi-

Voice and Grammatical Relations in Austronesian Languages.
Simon Musgrave and Peter Austin

cal item from one sense to another, perhaps with the retention of the original sense, though not necessarily so (see, for instance, Harris and Campbell 1995).

While suggestive, this does not manage to remove from the picture the question of influence from other parts of the language that have also changed, and does not present a view of the system at one point of time: the assumption on which a hierarchy is based. In order to gain an idea of how a language orders the constructions dynamically, at one particular point in time, we need to find examples of synchronic alternation or shift in progress: this is a subtler notion of grammaticalisation, as it does not entail the completion of a shift, but only the observation of alternatives.

I shall present material showing that, between causative and applicative constructions in Tukang Besi, the causative has primacy, even when the morphology makes the applicative choice clear. This follows a discussion of the theoretical model of valency-increasing processes that I shall be adopting as an explanatory tool in this investigation (couched in terms of the argument structure architecture of Lexical Functional Grammar).

3   Argument Structure Increasing

Amongst the processes that can affect the argument structure of a language, we can distinguish three major groups:
- valency decreasing
- valency determining
- valency increasing

Valency decreasing processes include passive and anti-passive, and involve the dropping of one argument; while interesting, they are not discussed in this paper. Valency determining processes specify the valency of the resulting predicate (as either bivalent or monovalent); these processes often have other derivational functions.

This paper is concerned with the behaviour of valency-increasing processes; those that add an argument to a basic verb. These may be split into two types, depending on the type of argument that they add to the clause: either a subject may be added that is different from the subject of the base clause; or a new object may be added, which is different from the object of the base clause (if there is one).[1] These two valency increasing processes are commonly referred to as causative and applicative predicates, respectively. Examples of their use are:

---

[1] The fact that two types of causatives are found is of only peripheral interest to this paper, though important for claims about the universality of parameter settings within a particular language.

Causative: Turkish

(1) a. *Hasan öl-dü*
Hasan die-PST
'Hasan died.'

b. *Ali Hasan-i öl-dür-dü*
Ali Hasan-ACC die-CAUS-PST
'Ali caused Hasan to die / Ali killed Hasan.'

In these examples we can see that the argument that is coded as the subject in (1a) (lack of accusative case, sentence-initial position in this SOV language), *Hasan*, is coded as the object in the causative variant (1b) (between subject and verb, accusative case). A new agent is added. This is in contrast to the changes seen in applicative constructions, illustrated in the following pair.

Applicative: Swahili

(2) a. *Ni-me-lim-a shamba*
1SG-PERF-cultivate-FINV plantain
'I have cultivated the plantain.'

b. *Ni-me-m-lim-i-a Musa*
1SG-PERF-3SG-cultivate-APPL-FINV Musa
shamba
plantain
'I have cultivated the plantain for Musa.'

Here we can see that there is no change in the identity of the subject; it is first person singular in the applicative sentence (2b) just as in the base sentence (2a), but that there is a new object; the identity of *Musa* as an object can be demonstrated by its immediate post-verbal position, the fact that it (and not *shamba*) can control the presence of an object agreement marker on the verb (*m-* in the example above), and is eligible for promotion to subject under passivisation (not illustrated). Crucially, the new object is treated as a primary object of the verb, but the grammatical status of the original subject is unchanged.

This paper is specifically interested in addressing the question of whether there are morphosyntactic grounds for supposing that there is a 'basic', or less-marked, form of valency-increasing predicate: is the causative less marked than the applicative, or vice versa? We can attempt to answer this question typologically, examining (for instance) a number of languages that have some form of applicative, and those that have some sort of causative, perhaps trying to determine whether or not there is a relationship between them ('the existence of a causative implies the existence of an applicative construction in the language', for instance, would be an example of a (false) implication).

Rather than adopting this approach I shall seek language-internal evidence, in the Tukang Besi language, for the primacy of applicative or causatives as a valency-increasing process. Based on the evidence to be presented in sections 4 and 5, I shall propose a hierarchy of preferred linking types. Before presenting the data, however, we shall discuss the treatment of predicate composition in syntactic models employing argument structure.

3.1 Argument Structure and the Thematic Hierarchy

As an account of the applicative and causative constructions, I shall adopt the formalisms of Lexical-Functional Grammar's argument structure (a-structure). In this the arguments of a predicate are listed in an order established by the semantic roles that the different arguments bear, and their position on the thematic hierarchy. While various versions of this hierarchy are listed, they all agree on the positions of the most common roles.

For the work presented here the actual hierarchy is not particularly important (other than being used as an organisational tool for subcategorisation frames); discussion of the need to both distinguish and rank semantic roles in Tukang Besi can be found in Donohue (1999). The identities of the particular semantic roles are, however, relevant, in that some of the complex predicate combinations make reference to the semantic role identity of one or more of the arguments of the predicate. Also relevant is the way in which complex predicates, involving causative and applicative constructions, are built, and modelled in argument-structure.

3.2 Causatives

Causatives are predicates that take an existing predicate, and derive a complex predicate with a new subject. Alsina (1993) provides arguments that the best model of causatives is not one that simply apposes the new subject to the base predicate, as has been assumed in earlier work,[2] but that a better model treats the causative as a predicate that takes three arguments: the causer, the causative patient, and the base predicate. The causative patient is

---

[2] This would involve a model of the causative similar to that given in (i):

(i)   Causative: New subject + base predicate
                              |
                    'PRED < ___, (___)>'

coindexed with one argument from the base predicate, typically the subject. This is the case with the Tukang Besi general causative formed with *pa-*, and is modelled as follows:

> Proto-typical causative linking
> (3)　'CAUS < ___ $_{|1|}$, ___ $_{|2|}$ PRED < ___ $_{|2|}$, (___ $_{|3|}$) >>'
> |_____|

In some languages the causative patient is rather linked to the lowest argument of the base predicate.[3] This linking strategy is found for French, Japanese, and other languages. Alsina (1992) models it as follows:

> (4)　'CAUS < ___ , ___ PRED < ag, (___) >>
> |_____|

It appears more likely that this second strategy is really just an alternative kind of case marking, and does not represent a true re-ordering of grammatical functions—see Alsina (1996) for arguments supporting the proposal that the dative, and not the accusative, argument is the object of the verb in Romance languages. The issue is not of immediate import here, however, since this morphosyntactic pattern is not found in the variety of Tukang Besi discussed.

Despite these differences in the linking of the causative predicate to the base predicate, there are few languages which have restrictions on the semantic roles involved: typically, the causative links to either the subject or the object of the base predicate, without restriction.[4]

3.3　Applicatives

Applicative processes derive complex predicates with one more argument than specified in their base predicate; typically this extra argument is one

---

[3] This option is referred to as 'preposition insertion' in much generative literature (see, for instance, Baker (1988:xx)).

[4] Some languages impose further restrictions on these complex predicates; a well-known example is the inability to form causative predicates based on bivalent verbs, or even all monovalent verbs; typically only unaccusative verbs (those with an experiencer, theme or patient S) are eligible. This is the case with the Tukang Besi factitive (or 'final causative') construction with the prefix *hoko-*:

> Tukang Besi causative linking 2: factitive
> (ii)　'CAUS < ___ $_{|1|}$, ___ $_{|2|}$ PRED < thm/pat$_{|2|}$ >>'
> |_____|

Although again interesting, these restricted causatives do not bear on the discussion that follows, and so are not dealt with in any more detail; the interested reader is referred to Donohue (1999:205-211).

that would have been expressed as an oblique with the base predicate.[5] Unlike causatives, the new argument is coded as an object in the applicative construction.

Again following Alsina, and Austin (1997), I shall adopt a model of applicative predicate composition that assumes the applicative to be a separate predicate with three arguments: the agent, the applicative object, and the base predicate. The agent in the applicative predicate is coindexed with the agent from the base predicate

Proto-typical applicative linking
(5)   'APPL < ___[1], ___[2] PRED < ag[1], (___[3]) >>
            |_____|

Unlike causatives, which in general do not place restrictions on the semantic roles of the arguments in the base predicate, it does appear that there is a universal restriction such that applicatives require thematically highly ranked (agent or experiencer) subjects in the base predicate (pace Rugemalira; see Donohue 1996 for a discussion of why Rugemalira's (1994) so-called unaccusative applicatives are in fact better thought of as involving agentive predicates). Since it is, in fact, this same agent of the base predicate that is the agent of the combined predicate, this restriction is not so surprising.

3.4   Generalising

Based on the discussion above concerning the implications of causatives and applicatives for argument structure models, we can generalise the types of argument structure linking conventions that are found. This is not a predictive model; it simply states that, for a monovalent base predicate, a complex predicate that builds on it must link either the first or the second argument of the outer predicate with the single argument of the base predicate. This is shown in (6):

a-structure linking
(6)   'ARG < ___ , ___ PRED < ag/thm >>'
            |_ or_ |_____|

With a bivalent base predicate, we can make a prediction: if the linked argument in the outer predicate is the most agentive one, it must be linked with the highest ranked argument of the base predicate. If, on the other

---

[5] Though there are languages where the extra argument cannot be expressed as an oblique with the base predicate.

hand, the least agentive argument of the outer predicate is the one shared, then we cannot predict the linking convention. This can be summarised as:

- Applicative: link the highest ranked argument of the inner predicate with the most agentive argument of the outer predicate
- Causative: link the highest ranked argument of the inner predicate with the least agentive argument of the outer predicate
  or
  link the lowest ranked argument of the inner predicate with the least agentive argument of the outer predicate.

3.5   The Hunt

In order to determine any ordering of the causative and applicative constructions with respect to each other, in terms of some notion of 'more-marked' and 'less-marked', we must demonstrate that there is a tendency for one predicate type to dominate the other. This cannot be done cross-linguistically, since that merely gives us statistical frequencies of the two constructions, and does not help in determining which of the two is more likely to occur.

In Tukang Besi we have a language with both applicative and causative constructions, and evidence that one of these constructions, the causative, is expanding into the (morphologically-defined) range of the applicative. Causative interpretations are being attached to morphologically applicative verb forms, in some environments at least. This is exemplified in the following section.

4   Tukang Besi

Tukang Besi is an Austronesian language spoken on the islands of the Tukang Besi archipelago of central-east Indonesia, and in numerous trading communities between Singapore and New Guinea (Donohue 1999). Basic word order is verb-object-subject with obligatory agreement for the subject of the clause (by verbal prefix), and optional agreement for object (by verbal enclitic). Case is encoded by prepositions: *na* 'nominative' marks the grammatical subject, *te* object, *di* oblique and *nu* genitive. Additionally, there are various more specific prepositions such as *kene* for instrumental. In a clause without an object-agreement enclitic on the verb, the object(s) of the verb are marked with *te*; no more than one object may trigger verb agreement. Tukang Besi is an asymmetrical language, in that it does not offer equal treatment to both objects of a trivalent verb. A detailed discussion of asymmetry as it is relevant to applicative constructions can be found in Donohue (1997).

4.1   Regular Causatives

The basic (in the sense of most productive and least semantically restrictive) causative in Tukang Besi is formed with the prefix *pa-*; examples of the use of this affix in both monovalent and bivalent clauses are given in the following sentence pairs:

Monovalent unergative

(7)   a.   *No-lagu*   *na*   *mia*
              3RL.SUBJ-sing   NOM   person
              'The people are singing.'

       b.   *No-pa-lagu='e*   *na*   *mia*
              3RL.SUBJ-CAUS-sing=3.P   NOM   person
              'They made the people sing.'

Monovalent unaccusative

(8)   a.   *No-ja'o*   *na*   *bangka='u*
              3RL.SUBJ-bad   NOM   boat=2SG.GEN
              'Your boat is wrecked.'

       b.   *No-pa-ja'o=ke*   *na*   *bangka='u*
              3RL.SUBJ-CAUS-bad=3.P   NOM   boat=2SG.GEN
              kene   *baliu*
              INSTR   axe
              'They wrecked your boat with axes.'

Bivalent

(9)   a.   *Ku-manga*   *te*   *ika*
              1SG.SUBJ-eat   OBJ   fish
              'I ate some fish.'

       b.   *No-pa-manga=aku*   *te*   *ika*
              3RL.SUBJ-CAUS-eat=1SG.P   OBJ   fish
              'She had me eat fish.'

As can be seen in these examples, the subject of a causative is treated as the object of the complex predicate clause. The linking between the two predicates is that seen in section 3.2.

4.2 Regular Applicatives

Applicatives in Tukang Besi can create objects with a variety of semantic roles; a typical example is the following pair, showing that the same event can be coded with an oblique instrument, or with an applicative object instrument:

(10) a. *No-tu'o*   *te*   *kau*   *kene*   *baliu*
          3RL.SUBJ-fell   OBJ   tree   INSTR   axe
          'He chopped the tree with an axe.'

      b. *No-tu'o=ako*   *te*   *kau*   *te*   *baliu*
          3RL.SUBJ-fell=APPL   OBJ   tree   OBJ   axe
          'He used the axe to chop the tree.'

As discussed earlier with respect to applicatives in section 3.3, these constructions involve a complex predicate with the subject being coindexed with the subject of the base predicate, and with a new object in the clause. In Tukang Besi, which has extensive oblique marking strategies, there is a dynamic alternation available between the applicative object coding option and the oblique coding option; this is not relevant here. It is important to note that the coindexed subject must be an agent in the base predicate. Attempts to construct applicatives based on predicates with non-agentive subjects are not grammatical. This is illustrated with the bivalent verb *'awa* 'get, happen to come into possession of' and the monovalent *'ontoo* 'recover from sickness', neither of which has an agentive subject, and so neither of which may be the base predicate in an applicative construction.

Bivalent non-agentive construction

(11) a. *No-'awa*   *te*   *doe*   *na*   *kalambe*
          3RL.SUBJ-get   OBJ   money   NOM   young.girl
          'The girl got the money.'

      b. **No-'awa=ako* •   *te*   *tuha=no*   *te*
          3RL.SUBJ-get=APPL   OBJ   family=3.GEN   OBJ
          doe   *na*   *kalambe*
          axe   NOM   young.girl
          'The girl got the money for her family.'

Note that the verb *'awa* cannot be interpreted with the reading 'fetch'; for this meaning a different verb, *ala*, is used.

Monovalent non-agentive construction

(12)   a.   *No-'ontoo*   *na*   *kalambe*
                3RL.SUBJ-get.well   NOM   young.girl
                'The girl got better.'

        b.   **No-'ontoo=ako*   *te*   *tuha=no*
                3RL.SUBJ-get.better-APPL   OBJ   family=3.GEN
                na   *kalambe*
                NOM   young.girl
                'The girl got better for her family.'

These examples have shown that applicatives link with base predicates in the manner expected from a cross-linguistic examination of the construction. Important to the exposition that follows is the fact that, whether the base verb is bivalent or monovalent, an applicative construction must link the first argument of the applicative predicate with an agentive first argument of the base predicate.

5   Unergatives

An interesting upset arises in the neat categorisation of argument-structure affecting derivations when we consider unergative predicates. Up to this point we can state that the morphological form of the derivational affix determines (or is correlated with) the type of argument structure affecting process: *pa-* (and *hoko-* and *hepe-*) produce causatives, and *=ako* (as well as *-ngkene* and *-VCi*) produce applicatives. Examining unergative predicates shows that the morphological shape of the derivational affix alone is not sufficient to determine the nature of the derivation.

5.1   Ambiguities in unergative derivations

Consider the following sentences, involving unergative predicates with the causative *pa-* or the applicative *=ako* attached. While the derivation with *pa-* is unexceptional, we can see that there are two possible interpretations available of the verb derived with *=ako*, one with the expected applicative interpretation, and one with, exceptionally, a causative interpretation.

Basic underived sentence

(13)   *No-wila*   *kua*   *kente*
           3RL.SUBJ-go   ALL   tidal.flats
           'She went to the tidal flats.'

Derivation with pa-

(14)   *To-pa-wila='e*   *kua*   *kente*
      1PL.RL.SUBJ-CAUS-go=3.P   ALL   tidal.flats
      'We made her go to the tidal flats.'

Derivation with =ako

(15)   *To-wila=ako='e*   *na*   *ina=no*
      1PL.RL.SUBJ-go-APPL=3.P   NOM   mother=3.GEN
      kua   *kente*
      ALL   tidal.flats
      'We went to the tidal flats for their mother.' OR
      'We made mother go to the tidal flats.'

The two competing linking models for these interpretations are given below; note that there is no change in the overt morphosyntax present in the sentence at all, only in the interpretation of it.

Applicative interpretation

(16)   '=*ako* < ____ , ____ *wila* < ____ >>
          |_____|

Causative interpretation

(17)   '=*ako* < ____ , ____ *wila* < ____ >>
          |_____|

While the causative formed with *pa-* is unambiguous, the verb in (15) is ambiguous in interpretation between applicative and causative, as modelled in the argument structure linkings; this complication is the crucial one in the argument presented here, and is one that we shall return to later in section 5.3.

Not all 'unergative' predicates behave in this way; compare the two interpretations available to *wila=ako* with the sole interpretation available for *kolo=ako*:

Basic underived sentence

(18)   *No-kolo*   *na*   *mia*   *r[um]ato*
      3RL.SUBJ-smoke.tobacco   NOM   person   arrive.SI
      'The visitor smoked.'

Causative derivation with pa-

(19)	*No-pa-kolo='e*		*na*	*mia*
	3RL.SUBJ-CAUS-smoke.tobacco=3.P		NOM	person
	r[um]ato			
	arrive.SI			
	'They had the visitor smoke.'			

Applicative derivation with ako

(20)	*No-kolo=ako='e*		*na*	*raja*	*te*
	3RL.SUBJ-smoke.tobacco=APPL=3.P		NOM	king	OBJ
	mia	*r[um]ato*			
	person	arrive.SI			
	'The visitor smoked for the king (ªs benefit).' BUT NOT				
	*'The visitor made the king smoke.'				

(21)   '*=ako* < ___ , ___ PRED < ___ >>'
          |_____|

(22)   *'*=ako* < ___ , ___ PRED < ___ >>'
          |_____|

5.2   Structure of the Non-Alternating Monovalent Predicate

The argument structure of the class of ambiguous unergatives is revealing. A volitional verb like *kolo* has the following subcategorisation frame:

(23)   ]$_V$ '*kolo* < agent >'

Non-volitional verbs like *ambanga* 'embarrassed' can be modelled with the following frame:

(24)   ]$_V$ '*ambanga* < theme >'

Less difficult verbs, such as *kolo*, 'smoke tobacco', and *ambanga*, 'embarrassed', lack ambiguous semantics, and so do not present problems: *ambanga*, 'embarrassed', can appear with a causative, but not with an applicative predicate, since it lacks an agent. In the following examples, we can see that a causative predicate can build on *ambanga*, 'embarrassed', without problems, since there is not a requirement for a particular semantic role identity.

Basic underived sentence

(25) *No-ambanga*   *na*   *kalambe*
      3RL.SUBJ-embarrassed   NOM   young.girl
      'The girl was embarrassed.'

Causative derivation with pa-

(26) *No-pa-ambanga='e*   *na*   *kalambe*
      3RL.SUBJ-CAUS-embarrassed=3.P   NOM   young.girl
      'They embarrassed the girl.'

(27)   'CAUS < ___ , ___ PRED < ___ >>'
                       |_____|

In contrast to the productive causative derivation, applicative derivations are not possible with *ambanga*, 'embarrassed': *=ako* attaching to this
verb would productively specify an agent A, which is not compatible with
the theme that is subcategorised for by *ambanga*, 'embarrassed'. The causative interpretation of *=ako* is not possible, for reasons that will be discussed
later.

Derivation with =ako

(28) **No-ambanga=ako='e*   *te*   *kalambe*
      3RL.SUBJ-embarrassed=APPL=3.P   OBJ   young.girl
      'The girl was embarrassed for them.'

(29)   *'APPL < ag , ___ PRED < theme >>'
                       |_____|

(30)   *'APPL < ___ , ___ PRED < theme >>'
                       |_____|
          *'The girl embarrassed them.'

With *kolo*, 'smoke tobacco', either derivation is possible, since the *pa*-
causative derivation is compatible with agents as well as themes: these sentences have appeared in (19) and (20); the argument structures are shown
below:

(31)   'CAUS < ___ , ___ PRED < agent >>'
                    |_____|

(32)   'APPL < ___ , ___ PRED < agent >>'
                    |_____|

The structure of *wila*, 'go', is more problematic: its subject is at the one time an agent, as the volitional performer of the action, and also the theme, as the entity which moves as a result of the action.

(33)   ]$_V$ '*wila* < agent$_{[1]}$ = theme$_{[1]}$ >'

Although two semantic roles are listed, they are coindexed with the same numeral: they refer to the same real-world argument, and the dual identity reflects the complex semantics of the predicate.

Consider this ambiguous subcategorisation frame in the light of the restrictions that are placed on the predicates with which causative and applicative predicates may combine: an applicative is restricted to appearing with an agent in the base predicate coindexed with the agent of the applicative predicate:

(34)   'APPL < ___ , ___ PRED < ag , (___) >>'
                    |_____|

With *wila*, 'go', the prerequisites for this linking are met, in that there is an agent argument in the base predicate, and it is linked to the agent in the outside predicate:

(35)   'APPL < ___ , ___ PRED < agent = theme >>'
                    |_____|

This linking, is however, not unproblematic: given that the inner argument effectively combines two semantic roles, depending on the value of the semantic role that is regarded as most salient for the matching process, the applicative linking may be disallowed (recall that applicative linking requires that the first argument of each predicate be linked, and that the first argument of the base predicate be agentive). The ungrammatical linking of a theme in the base predicate with the agentive A of the applicative predicate is shown in the model below.

(36)   * 'APPL < ___ , ___ PRED < agent = theme >'
                    |_____|

The implications of this (occasional) failure to link as an applicative construction are examined in more detail in the following section, and discussed in section 6.

5.3   Resolving the Semantic Role Conflict

The dilemma presented to us by the variation found in the interaction of =*ako* with intradirective verbs is that the semantic role of the sole argument of the base predicate is ambiguous. Since there is only one argument in the base predicate, any complex predicate linking must involve that argument; therefore the semantic role of this argument is crucial for determining grammaticality, when there are restrictions on the semantic role of the arguments in a construction.

The applicative interpretation is not available for monovalent predicates with a non-agent semantic role, such as *ambanga* 'embarrassed' (illustrated above); thus, if a monovalent predicate takes a non-agentive argument, the applicative predicate cannot be combined with it. The screening for this is assumed to occur early in the selection process. Some predicates with non-agentive semantic roles slip through this process, however: the intradirective verbs have an agent semantic role, and so are allowed to combine with an applicative =*ako*. From the morphosyntactic behaviour witnessed, however, it seems that there are problems with the selection of the semantic role for combination purposes: since the semantic role of the argument is ambiguous, either may be the one selected by the combination process. The process of combination with the applicative predicate for non-agentive, agentive, and intradirective verbs are shown in Table 1.

Table 1: Combining with an Applicative: Selection and Linking

verb:	*ambanga* 'embarrassed'	*kolo* 'smoke (tobacco)'	*wila* 'go'	
semantic roles	theme	agent	agent = theme	
compatibility with =*ako* APPL < __ , __ PRED < ag >>	NO	YES	YES	
linking A with agent	n/a	YES	YES	NO
applicative formation	n/a	YES	YES	NO

The question then remains, what happens to the applicative formation that has selected the applicative morphology, has passed the 'attach only to predicates with agent semantic roles' phase, but which then, through whatever process, attempts to link the applicative A with the theme aspect of the semantic role information?

It appears that, having attached the derivational predicate to the base one (through satisfying the requirement that there be an agentive argument there to link the applicative A with), there is no turning back: some linking must be made. We have already seen that, if for whatever reason the theme aspect of the semantic role specification for the intradirective subject is the salient one, and selected by the agent-seeking part of the linking process, an applicative linking is impossible. This was modelled in (35) and (36), repeated here.

(35)   'APPL < ___ , ___ PRED < agent = theme >>'
               |_____|

(36)   *'APPL < ___ , ___ PRED < agent = theme >'
               |_____|

There is, however, a two place predicate waiting for linking with the argument in the base predicate. Given that that argument is being interpreted as non-agentive, and so ineligible for applicative linking, the only choice is to change the linking so that the theme of the base predicate links with the object of the outer predicate:

(37)   '=ako < ___ , ___ PRED < agent = theme >>'
               |_____|

This is now an acceptable linking, but is no longer applicative: the fact that the base subject is linked with the object of the outer predicate makes the combined predicate causative in nature.

5.4   Other Aspects of Tukang Besi that Show Variation

A similar phenomenon is found in another area of the language's morphosyntax. In addition to valency increasing and valency decreasing morphemes, Tukang Besi has a number of valency-announcing morphemes; they do not always specify an increase or decrease in valency, but rather specify what the valency of the final predicate must be. One of these morphemes is *hoN-*, which specifies that the combined predicate is bivalent and which attaches to both bivalent and monovalent roots. When attached to a monovalent verb root, the combined predicate is bivalent, and the relationship to the base predicate is either causative or applicative, depending on the semantic role of the subject of the base predicate. This is illustrated in the following pairs of sentences, showing underived verbs and the result of adding the *hoN-* prefix to them.

[S] of underived verb is [patient]:

(38)   *No-tunu*   *na*   *kau*
      3RL.SUBJ-burn   NOM   wood
      'The wood is burning.'

(39)   *No-ho-nunu='e*   *na*   *kau*
      3RL.SUBJ-VR-burn=3P   NOM   wood
      'S/he is burning the wood.'

(40)   '*hoN-* < ___ , ___ *tunu* < ___ >>'
             |_____|

[S] of underived verb is [agent]:

(41)   *No-rau*   *na*   *ana*
      3RL.SUBJ-yell   NOM   child
      'The child is yelling.'

(42)   No-ho-rau='e   na   kene=no
      3RL.SUBJ-VR-yell=3.P   NOM   friend=3.GEN
      'They are yelling at their friend.'

(43)   '*hoN-* < ___ , ___ *rau* < ___ >>'
             |_____|

It seems that the best argument structure model of the *hoN-* predicate is one that makes explicit reference to semantic roles: the only requirement is that like semantic roles must link to other like semantic roles (see Lefebvre 1991 for a similar analysis of Fongbe serial verbs, and Austin 1997 for similar suggestions on similar predicates in Australian languages).

(44)   '*hoN-* < ag , thm PRED < (ag) , (thm) >>'
             |____|_____| |
             |_____|

This requirement means that when there is a base predicate without, say, a theme argument, then the new argument added in the *hoN-* predicate is a theme, since the agent in that outer predicate is already linked; the addition of a theme means that an object is added, and so a causative formed. This has been illustrated in the derivation of *honunu* from *tunu*. Similar arguments explain the applicative interpretation of *horau* in the examples above. Importantly, this type of linking with *hoN-* illustrates that there is a precedent in Tukang Besi for derivational predicates that do not have a constant linking pattern with the base predicate.

6 Implications for Hierarchies and 'Preferences' for A-Structure Changing

We have seen that the strategies that 'repair' incompatible matchings of base predicates and derivational predicates select causatives as the 'bail out' option, even when that is not the option selected by the morphology present on the verb. It is clear that, in terms of function served and morphology used to indicate that function, the causative is spreading; the range of that spread is shown in Table 2.

Table 2: The Spread of Causative Function into the Domain of Applicative Morphology

Base:	Bivalent	Monovalent		
type	(agentive)	agentive	intradirective	non-agentive
pa-	CAUS	CAUS	CAUS	CAUS
=*ako*	APPL	APPL	APPL CAUS	n/a

Thus it appears that the causative linking pattern is used as a rescue option when an applicative is called for by the morphology, but disallowed by the semantic roles involved and the restrictions on linking between predicates. From this we can conclude two points of note concerning the hierarchies found in the morphosyntax of valency increasing.

i. The shape of the morphology (and the construction it dictates) may be overwritten by the architecture peculiar to the predicate combination;

ii. The causative, which is less restricted in terms of types of predicates that may be combined, is capable of extending into the morphological territory that belongs to the applicative, whereas the reverse is not true.[6]

From these observations we must conclude that the causative must be the least marked of the valency-increasing devices.

7   References

Alsina, Alex. 1992. On the argument structure of causatives. *Linguistic Inquiry* 23:517–555.

Alsina, Alex. 1993. Predicate composition: a theory of syntactic function alternations. Ph.D thesis, Stanford University.

Alsina, Alex. 1996. *The role of argument structure in grammar: evidence from Romance*. Stanford: CSLI.

Austin, Peter. 1997. Causatives and applicatives in Australian Aboriginal Languages. In *Dative and related phenomena* ed. Kazuto Matsumura & Tooru Hayasi. 165–225. Tokyo: Hitsuji Shobo.

Baker, Mark C. 1988. *Incorporation: A theory of grammatical function changing*. Chicago: University of Chicago Press.

Donohue, Mark. 1996. Relative clauses in Tukang Besi: grammatical functions and thematic roles. *Linguistic Analysis* 26.3–4:159–173.

Donohue, Mark. 1997. The applicative construction in Tukang Besi. In *Proceedings of the Seventh International Conference on Austronesian Linguistics* ed. Cecilia Odé & Wim Stokhof. 415–432. Amsterdam: Editions Rodopi B.V.

Donohue, Mark. 1999. *A Grammar of Tukang Besi*. Grammar Library series No. 20. Berlin: Mouton de Gruyter.

Harris, Alice & Lyle Campbell. 1995. *Historical syntax in cross-linguistic perspective*. Cambridge, UK: Cambridge University Press.

Lefebvre, Claire. 1991. *Serial verbs: grammatical, comparative, and cognitive approaches*. Amsterdam: John Benjamins.

Rugemalira, Joseph M. 1994. The case against the Thematic Hierarchy. *Linguistic Analysis* 24:62–81.

---

[6] That is, there are no cases of causative morphology being associated with applicative functions, something like:

(iii)	*No-pa-[verb]='e*	*na*	*iai=su*
	3RL.SUBJ-CAUS-[verb]=3.P	NOM	younger.sibling=1SG.GEN
	'They [verb]ed for my younger sister.'		

The only reading possible for a sentence of the type seen in (iii) would be 'They made my sister [verb].'

10

Lexical Categories and Voice in Tagalog

Nikolaus P. Himmelmann

1 Abstract

The meaning and lexical category of so-called verbal roots is one aspect of the voice systems in Tagalog and other Philippine-type languages which has received little attention in the controversy surrounding the analysis of these systems. It is common to assume that these roots cannot occur without any affixation and that, therefore, they should be considered precategorial. Here it is shown that this view is ill-conceived. To begin with, it is possible to distinguish different classes of roots based on morphological features. Therefore, roots are not precategorial. Furthermore, a large majority of the putative verbal roots allows for unaffixed uses. However, 'verbal roots' have 'non-verbal' meanings when used without voice marking. Inasmuch as it can be shown that voice-marked forms have clearly 'verbal' meanings, it follows that voice marking is derivational (among many other things).

Voice and Grammatical Relations in Austronesian Languages.
Simon Musgrave and Peter Austin
Copyright © 2007, CSLI Publications.

The first part of the paper is taken up by the discussion of some basic issues regarding the nature of lexical and syntactic categories, which is a prerequisite to sorting out the Tagalog facts. Contrary to standard assumptions, it is proposed that a clear-cut distinction should be made between lexical and syntactic (i.e. phrase-structural) categories, allowing for mismatches between these two kinds of categorisations of lexical items.[1]

2 Introduction

Looking through a standard Tagalog-English dictionary such as Panganiban (1972), Santos (1983), English (1986), or Rubino (1998a), one will notice almost immediately that hardly any Tagalog root is glossed with an English verb. Instead, almost all presumably verbal roots are glossed with English nouns or adjectives/participles. Typical examples include object nouns such as 'gift' for *bigáy*, action nominalisations such as '(act of) crying' for *iyák*, and adjectives/participles such as 'surpassed, defeated' for *daíg*. This practice of glossing Tagalog roots with English nouns or adjectives is in marked contrast with the practice of glossing voice-marked formations involving the same roots as English verbs. For example, *i-bigáy* is glossed as 'to give something to someone, to hand in', *um-iyák* as 'to cry', and *daig-ín* as 'to outdo, to surpass'. Taken at face value, these differences in the treatment of roots and voice-marked formations appear to imply that in Tagalog all verbal expressions are somehow derived from non-verbal roots.

I argue in this paper that there is some truth to the idea that all Tagalog verbal expressions are derived to some degree. A proper and testable explication of this idea, however, requires certain preliminary clarifications of basic structural aspects of Tagalog morphosyntax and the nature of lexical and syntactic categories. Section 3.1 provides a brief overview of the most important structural positions in a Tagalog clause and the terms used here to refer to these positions.

In section 3.2 it is proposed that there is no necessary correlation between the classification of lexical items based on morpho-syntactic features and the classification of lexical items with regard to the slots they may occupy in a phrase structure tree. That is, there is a difference between terminal syntactic categories (the categories of the terminal nodes in a phrase structure tree) and lexical categories proper (i.e. the formal categories to which lexical items may belong, with the exception of the categories of phrase structure), and mismatches between these two kinds of categorisa-

---

[1] Many thanks to Gary Palmer, Malcolm Ross, Carl Rubino, Hans-Jürgen Sasse, Eva Schultze-Berndt, Angela Terrill, and John Wolff for very useful comments on a draft version of this paper.

tions of lexical items may occur. This proposal is consistent with work challenging the categorial uniformity hypothesis (Bresnan 1994, Bresnan 2001) which argues that what is usually assumed to be just one type of structure (called either lexical or syntactic category) should in fact be dealt with on at least two different levels, and that lexical insertion is not constrained by a one-to-one correspondence between the two. My proposal is supported by detailed examination of lexical facts, in contrast to the evidence put forward by Bresnan which relies on similarities of distributional behaviour of items belonging to different lexical categories.

Section 3.2 also introduces a number of terminological distinctions crucial to a proper handling of the morphosyntactic and semantic differences found among lexical items. In particular, an attempt is made to avoid the use of the multiply ambiguous terms *noun* and *verb* since the three levels to which these terms may apply (the ontological, the morpho-lexical, and the syntactic (phrase-structural) level) are not at all commensurate in a language like Tagalog.

Section 4 applies the distinction between (terminal) syntactic categories and lexical categories proper to Tagalog. With regard to syntactic categories it may be argued that all Tagalog content words (both roots and derived words) are categorially indistinct, i.e. they may all occur in essentially the same basic syntactic positions (section 4.1). With regard to lexical categories, however, there are clear-cut categorial distinctions (section 4.2). That is, Tagalog roots exhibit different formal (in particular morphological) properties which are not directly predictable from their meaning. Hence, it is highly questionable whether Tagalog roots can be characterised as precategorial.

Section 5 then turns to the issue of what kind of meanings are denoted by Tagalog roots. It is shown that all kinds of roots can be used without further affixation and that they have a consistent and clearly identifiable meaning in their unaffixed uses. In particular, it is not correct to claim that so-called verbal roots generally do not occur without further affixation.

Finally, section 6 provides an explication of the view that voice marking in Tagalog is derivational in all its manifestations, based on the fact that it changes the meaning and the category of the roots to which it is attached. Furthermore, although the class of voice-marked words in Tagalog shares some similarities with verbs in English, it would be wrong to attribute the same kind of essential properties to both classes of lexical items.

3 Preliminaries

3.1 Basic Syntactic Functions in Tagalog

This section briefly introduces the following four basic morphosyntactic functions in Tagalog clauses: predicate, subject, non-subject argument or adjunct, and modifier. The first three functions are clearly defined in Tagalog by a set of grammatical markers and word order. The definition of the modifier function in addition requires reference to the semantics of the items involved.

The following discussion is confined to the most basic and simple construction types and should not be mistaken for a comprehensive outline of basic Tagalog clause structure. In particular, the fact that syntactic functions are defined primarily in terms of overt grammatical markers and word order should not be misconstrued as the claim that these surface structural phenomena are the only evidence for these functions. Instead, a substantial number of further syntactic facts such as relative clause formation, topicalisation, control phenomena, etc. could be adduced to support the analysis of these functions. The purpose of the present section, however, is simply to provide the reader with a set of easily identifiable features for each function and thus to facilitate the parsing of the examples throughout this paper.

As is well-known, considerable controversy surrounds the question of whether the grammatical relation *subject* exists in Tagalog. Following Schachter (1976), it is generally agreed that *ang*-phrases in post-predicate position (see below) show many but not all of the presumably universal subject properties proposed by Keenan (1976). Still, as argued in detail by DeWolf (1979:67-86, 1988:144-150) and Kroeger (1993), *ang*-phrases may be analysed as subjects because they exhibit a substantial number of important subject properties (such as being the only argument that can launch floating quantifiers, control secondary predicates, be relativised and be omitted in conjunction reduction) while other subject diagnostics are inapplicable or inconclusive. The major point of contention pertains to the so-called agent-related properties of subjects, in particular the properties of serving as the antecedent in reflexive constructions, the target in Equi-NP deletions and the addressee in imperatives. To some extent, Kroeger and Schachter disagree here about the empirical facts (cf. Kroeger 1993:36-40, 71-107 and Schachter 1996:21-27). More importantly, it is doubtful whether these properties in fact provide reliable diagnostics for grammatical relations. Artawa and Blake (1997:505f), among others, profess serious doubts in this regard and argue for the viability of the subject notion in Balinese, a language for which the basic facts relevant to this issue are quite similar to the Tagalog ones (see also Arka (this volume), Arka and Manning (this volume)). Here I adopt the position that there are subjects in Tagalog, with the proviso that the subject in Tagalog differs in some regards from subjects in other languages such as English.

Predicates in Tagalog typically occur in clause-initial position, as in the following example:

(1) **dumatíng**   *yung*   *asawa*   *niya*
     um-datíng   iyón.LNK   asawa   niyá
     AV-arrival   DIST.LNK   spouse   3SG.POSS
     'Her husband arrived.'

If another constituent precedes the predicate, the marker *ay* occurs in front of the predicate:

(2) *silá mag-iná*   **ay** *natulog*   *na*
     silá mag-iná   ay na-tulog   na
     3PL RCP-mother   PM RL.STAT-sleep   now
     'The mother and her daughter fell asleep.'

Subjects generally follow the predicate. They are marked with the specific article *ang* (in the case of proper names *si*):

(3) *masaráp*   **ang pagkain**
     ma-saráp   ang pag-kain
     STAT-satisfaction   SPEC GER-eating
     'The food was good.'

Note that the specific article *ang* can be replaced by a demonstrative pronoun (such as *yung* in *(1)* above) or, much more rarely, a personal pronoun (instead of *silá mag-iná* in *(2)* one could also say *ang mag-iná*).

Furthermore, the specific article *ang* clearly is not a subject marker since *ang*-phrases may also occur in other syntactic functions. In the following example, the first *ang*-phrase (*ang langgám*) functions as the predicate while the second *ang*-phrase (*ang tumulong sa mga bata'*) is the subject:

(4)   ***ang***   ***langgám***   *rin*   *ang*   *tumulong*   *sa*
    ang   langgám   din   ang   um-tulong   sa
    SPEC   ant   also   SPEC   AV-help   LOC
    mga   *bata'*
    mangá   bata'
    PL   child
    'The ants also helped the children.'
    (lit. The ones who helped the children were also the ants.)

Therefore, it is not possible to define the subject simply as the phrase marked by *ang*. Instead, the subject is defined as the *ang*-phrase which follows the predicate (and there can be only one *ang*-phrase after the predicate).

Although a subject is always implied in a Tagalog basic clause, this subject does not have to be overtly expressed. Compare the following sequence of two clauses where the subject of the second predicate (*inilagáy*), which is coreferential with the subject of the first predicate (*kinuha*), is not overtly expressed:

(5)   *at*   *kinuha*   *niyá*   *ang*   *langgám*
    at   in-kuha   niyá   ang   langgám
    and   RL(UNDR) -getting   3SG.POSS   SPEC   ant
    at   ***inilagáy***   *niyá*   *sa*   *pampáng*
    at   in-i-lagáy   niyá   sa   pampáng
    and   RL(UNDR)-CV-position   3SG.POSS   LOC   river.bank
    'And he got the ant and put it on the riverbank.'

If the predicate is voice-marked (as in *(1) and (5)* above), a special relation exists between the subject and the predicate in that the semantic role of the participant appearing in subject function is overtly marked by the voice affix on the predicate. If the predicate is marked with *-um-*, *mag-/nag-*, or *maN-/naN-*, the subject bears the actor role, as shown by *(1)* and the following examples:

(6)   *sum*akáy   ***silá***   *sa*   *bangká'*
    um-sakáy   silá   sa   bangká
    AV-passenger   3PL   LOC   boat
    'They got on the boat.'[2]

---

[2] In this example, a pronoun (*silá*) is used in subject function. Pronouns do not co-occur with the markers which occur with noun-phrases. Thus they are never marked with *ang*. Fur-

(7) *sumigáw*   ***yung***   ***anák***
    um-sigáw   iyón.LNK   anák
    AV-shout   DIST.LNK   child
    'That child shouted: ...'

(8) ***nag****machinegun*   *na*   ***ang***   ***eroplano***
    nag-machinegun   na   ang   eroplano
    RL.AV-machine.gun   now   SPEC   airplane
    'The plane machinegunned.'

In some instances the choice of one or the other of the three actor voice affixes conveys semantic differences pertaining to reflexivity, the intensity of the action and the like.[3] In many instances, however, the choice of the actor voice affix is determined by the root or stem (see section 4.2).

Undergoer voice is marked by one of the following three affixes: the prefix *i-*, the suffix *-an*, and the suffix *-in*. Unlike the three actor voice affixes, the three undergoer voices affixes consistently differ with regard to the semantics of the undergoer. Hence it is customary to distinguish at least three undergoer voices in Tagalog. Ignoring several details and complications, it generally holds true that if the predicate is marked with the CONVEYANCE VOICE prefix *i-*, then the subject expresses an argument bearing the semantic role of a displaced theme. Compare:

(9) *ibinalík*   *nilá*   ***ang***   ***bata'***
    i-in-balík   nilá   ang   bata'
    CV-RL(UNDR)-return   3PL.POSS   SPEC   child
    'They returned the child.'

Here the subject (*ang bata'*) is the displaced theme (i.e. the entity viewed as moving) of the event expressed by the predicate (*ibinalík*). The actor is expressed by a possessive pronoun (*nilá*). In addition to the prefix *i-*, the predicate is marked for realis mood by the infix *-in-*, which only occurs in the undergoer voices.

Instruments are also viewed as moving entities and hence marked with the conveyance voice prefix:

---

thermore, they are second position clitics, appearing immediately after the first constituent of the predicate.
[3] See Pittman (1966), Schachter and Otanes (1972:292f passim), and Wolff et al. (1991:113,821f) for exemplification and discussion.

(10) *ipangpùputol*   ko   na   *lang*
      i-pang-RED1-putol   ko   na   lamang
      CV-INSTR-RED1-cut   1SG.POSS   now   only
      itóng   ***kutsilyo.***
      itó-ng   kutsilyo
      PROX-LNK   knife
      'I will just cut it with this knife.' (Wolff et al. 1991:367)

The suffix -*an* marks locative voice. In locative voice, the subject expresses a locative argument, understood in a very broad sense. This may be the location at which something happened:

(11) *tinirhán*   ko   ***ang***   ***bahay***
      in-tirá-an   ko   ang   bahay
      RL(UNDR)-dwelling-LV   1SG.POSS   SPEC   house
      na   ***itó***
      na   itó
      LNK   PROX
      'I stayed at this house.'

Or the location to which (or from which) motion occurred:

(12) *pinuntahán*   na   namán   nilá
      in-puntá-an   na   namán   nilá
      RL(UNDR)-direction-LV   now   also   3PL.POSS
      ang   ***bata'***
      ang   bata'
      SPEC   child
      'They went to the child.'

Locative voice is also used for recipients, addressees, and benefactees *(13)*:

(13) *tìtirán*   ninyó   ***akó***
      RED1-tirá-an   ninyó   akó
      RED1-leftover-LV   2PL.POSS   1SG
      'Will you (please) set some aside for me.'

Even more generally, locative voice may be used for all kinds of undergoers which are not directly affected by the action denoted by the predicate:

(14) *hindí'!* *tingnán* *mo*   **si** **Maria**
      hindí'   tingín-an   mo   si   Maria
      NEG   look-LV   2SG.POSS PN   Maria
      'Don't (panic)! Just look at Maria!'

(15) *tulungan* *ninyó*   **akó**
      tulong-an   ninyó   akó
      help-LV   2PL.POSS   1SG
      '(If) you help me, …'

In *(13)* and (15) the subject is the first person singular pronoun *akó*, in *(14)* it is a proper noun (Maria) which is marked with the proper noun article *si* rather than with the specific article *ang*. Examples *(13)*-(15) also illustrate undergoer voice predicates in non-realis mood, which lack the realis marking infix *-in-*.

The suffix *-in* marks patient voice. It is the unmarked member of the undergoer voice-marking affixes and is used for a broad variety of undergoers, including prototypical patients, i.e. entities directly affected or effected by the event denoted by the predicate:

(16) a. *patayín*   *natin*   **itóng**   **dalawang**
          patáy-in   natin   itó-ng   dalawá-ng
          dead-PV   1PL.IN.POSS   PROX-LNK   two-LNK
          Hapón
          Hapón
          Japan
          'Let's kill these two Japanese!'

The suffix *-in* differs from the other two undergoer suffixes in that it only occurs in non-realis mood (as in the preceding example). In realis mood, the predicate is simply marked by the realis undergoer voice infix *-in-*:

      b. *pinatáy*   *natin*   *itóng*
          in-patáy   natin   itó-ng
          RL(UNDR)-dead   1PL.IN.POSS   PROX-LNK
          dalawáng   *Hapón*
          dalawá-ng   Hapón
          two-LNK   Japan
          'We killed these two Japanese.'

Recall that the realis infix *-in-* occurs in all, and only, the undergoer voices (cf. examples *(9)*-(12) above).

This brief review of voice marking concludes our introductory discussion of the two basic syntactic functions subject and predicate. Turning now to the third syntactic function mentioned at the beginning of this section, non-subject argument or adjunct, note first that it is quite difficult to make a clear-cut distinction between non-subject arguments and adjuncts in Tagalog. Since the distinction between those two syntactic functions is of no relevance to the issues of primary concern in this paper, it will be ignored here.

Non-subject arguments and adjuncts are marked with either the genitive marker *ng* or the general locative marker *sa* (in the case of proper nouns, the markers are *ni* and *kay*, respectively). Neglecting some minor uses, *ng* primarily marks possessors (as in (17)) and non-subject arguments (as in (18) and (19)):

(17)   *ang*   *hari*   ***ng***   ***lamok***
       ang   hari   ng   lamok
       SPEC   king   GEN   mosquito
       'The king of the mosquitos.'

(18)   *pùpunuín*   *mo*   *iyán*   ***ng***   ***kuto***
       RED1-punó'-in   mo   iyán   ng   kuto
       RED1-full-PV   2SG.POSS   MED   GEN   louse
       'You fill that (cup) with lice.'

(19)   *kinagát*   ***ng***   ***mga***   ***langgám***   *ang*   *mama*
       in-kagát   ng   mangá   langgám   ang   mama'
       RL(UNDR)-bite   GEN   PL   ant   SPEC   man
       'The ants bit the man.'

The locative marker *sa* marks a large variety of temporal and local adjuncts *(20)* and recipients/goals, as well as (some) definite patients and themes when they do not occur in subject function (cf. *sa mga bata'* in *(4)* above):[4]

---

[4] Another common gloss for *sa* is OBL(IQUE). This gloss implies that all *sa*-phrases are syntactically oblique. Though this implication may turn out to be true, it has not yet been explicitly shown that all *sa*-phrases in Tagalog are in fact syntactically oblique (and that they differ in this regard from *ng*-phrases). Therefore, I prefer to use a gloss which leaves this issue open.

(20)   *at*   *dun*   *na*   *sila*   *tàtabunan*

at	doón	na	silá	RED1-tabon-an
and	DIST.LOC	now	3PL	RED1-complete.cover-LV

       sa   **lugár**   **na**   **iyón**

sa	lugár	na	iyón
LOC	place	LNK	DIST

'And there they were covered with earth at that place.'

(21)   *nagpunta*   *silá*   **sa**   **simbahan**

nag-puntá	silá	sa	simbahan
RL.AV-direction	3PL	LOC	church

'They went to a church.'

A major difference between *ng*-phrases and *sa*-phrases pertains to the fact that the position of *sa*-phrases is flexible (they may occur in pre-predicate as well as in post-predicate positions) while the position of *ng*-phrases is fairly restricted (they generally immediately follow their head).

Turning finally to modifiers, all modifying constructions involve the linker *na* (*-ng* after vowels, /n/ or glottal stop) between the two constituents of a modifying construction:

(22)   *an*   *maliít*   **na**   *hayop*

ang	ma-liít	na	hayop
SPEC	STAT-smallness	LNK	animal

'the small animal'

The order of the constituents in a modifying construction is not fixed ('the small animal' could also be rendered by *ang hayop na maliít*). Semantically it is in general quite clear which constituent denotes the (semantic) head of the construction and which the modifier. That is, in *(22)* it is clear for speakers of Tagalog that what is denoted is a small specimen of the class of animals and not an animal-like specimen of the class of small things, regardless of the order of *maliít* and *hayop*. However, it is not clear whether this semantic distinction has any kind of formal (prosodic and/or syntactic) correlates.

Consequently, whenever in the following sections it is said that a given word or root can (or cannot) be used as a modifier, the term *modifier* does not refer to a constituent which is defined exclusively in syntactic terms. It is defined syntactically in that the term *modifier* is used only in reference to constituents which are linked to the preceding or following constituent with a linker. Which of the two linked constituents is considered the modifier (and which one the head), however, is decided on semantic grounds.

To summarize: the four basic syntactic functions predicate, subject, non-subject argument or adjunct, and modifier are easily identifiable in Tagalog because there is a set of markers which in combination with a few positional restrictions allows a straightforward identification of each of these functions (with the exception of the modifier function which necessarily involves reference to the semantics of the two items joined by a linker). What is of major importance for the following discussion is the fact that the grammatical markers are distributed in such a way that in principle, each Tagalog content word, except a clause-initial predicate, is preceded by one grammatical marker (or function word). This has important consequences for Tagalog phrase structure, as will be seen shortly.

3.2 Lexical and Syntactic Categories

The nature of syntactic categories (parts of speech) in Tagalog is a matter of controversy. Specifically, there is a long tradition of claims that the distinction between nouns and verbs is minimal or perhaps even non-existent.[5] Many of these claims suffer from confusion in a number of respects, resulting from the widespread practice of not differentiating clearly enough between lexical categories, i.e. the classification of lexical items according to grammatical (phonological, morphological, morphosyntactic) criteria, and syntactic categories, i.e. the category labels attached to the nodes of a phrase structure tree. Although there is an interrelation between these two kinds of categorisation, I follow here the view set out in Sasse (1993a/b)[6] that these two kinds of categorisation should be clearly distinguished and that there is no necessary correlation between them. The present section provides a very condensed version of the argument for this view. It also introduces and exemplifies the crucial distinctions to be used in the analysis of Tagalog in the following sections.

To begin with, a clear distinction should be made between ontological and linguistic (grammatical) categorisation. Ontological (conceptual, notional) categories are the result of the categorisation of the entities populating the universe, as perceived and conceived by the human cognitive apparatus (see, for example, Jackendoff 1983:48 passim). Inasmuch as the hu-

---

[5] For example, Müller (1882:99ff), Scheerer (1924), and Capell (1964) all claim that Tagalog verbs are not really verbs but nouns. (Capell (1964:244ff) lists a number of further authors making the same kind of claim). Bloomfield (1917) and Lopez (1977) imply through their terminology that there is no grammatical distinction between nouns and verbs. Schachter and Otanes (1972:62) make a distinction between nouns, verbs and adjectives largely for expository purposes. More recently, lack of a distinction between nouns and verbs has been claimed for various levels by Lemaréchal (1982, 1989), Himmelmann (1987, 1991), Gil (1993), and Naylor (1995).

[6] See also Himmelmann (1991:25,44f, 1997:111-124) and Broschart (1997).

man cognitive apparatus is universal such a categorisation is universal (otherwise it is, at least in part, culture-dependent). Lexical and syntactic categories are the result of the categorisation of linguistic items on the basis of grammatical (phonological, morphological, syntactic) criteria. That is, the evidence for lexical and syntactic categories always involves at least one formal property of the items in question (cf. Sasse 1993a:649).[7] Lexical and syntactic categories are thus by definition language-specific as they are based on language-specific formal features and the distribution of such features tends to show language-specific idiosyncrasies (that is, even among closely related languages which share a basic inventory of lexical items and grammatical features, the categorisation of the lexical items based on the grammatical features will not produce classes of lexical items which are fully commensurate).

The view that lexical and syntactic categories cannot be defined in purely notional terms does not imply that there is no interrelation between ontological and syntactic categorisation. Generally, there will be a substantial overlap between the classes resulting from the two different categorisation procedures. A perfect match between an ontological category and a single, semantically well-motivated grammatical feature, however, is suspicious in that it raises the issue of whether the class in question is really a (formal) grammatical category. A typical example is the use of periphrastic comparative and superlative constructions to define the grammatical category *adjective*. If no other features correlate with these constructions, the class established in this way is the class of gradable concepts which, I would hold, is an ontological rather than a linguistic class. In languages where *adjective* is a formally well-defined class it is typically the case that not all adjectives are gradable (e.g. *dead*, *ready*). On the other hand, lexical items which clearly are not adjectives on formal grounds can be used in comparative constructions simply because they are ontologically gradable (e.g. *Where would you find more beauty than in this place?*).

To put this in more general terms, as long as reference to an ontological (notional) category is enough to identify the class of items which partake in a given grammatical construction or show a given grammatical feature, there is no need to employ a second layer of grammatical categories in order to delimit the class of items in question. Such grammatical categories would be simply copies of the ontological ones. Only if there is some mis-

---

[7] See also Anward et al. (1997:172) who make a similar point in a somewhat confusing way. They first assert that 'the primary, definitional properties of parts of speech are semantic or pragmatic, rather than form-related', only to go on to qualify this statement with the constraint that 'semantic or pragmatic features are part-of-speech-defining only if there is at least one formal characteristic that correlates with them'.

match between grammatical and ontological classes is it possible and useful to define grammatical classes of lexical items.

There is no doubt that ontological categories are of fundamental importance to the crosslinguistic study of lexical and syntactic categories. It is only by correlating the formally determined lexical and syntactic categories with ontological categories that it becomes possible to make a crosslinguistic comparison between syntactic and/or lexical categories. That is, in order to claim that two languages, L1 and L2, both have a category *noun* it has to be shown that class A of lexical items in L1 and class A of lexical items in L2, each of which is defined in terms of a set of language-specific features (say, in L1 class A is defined by the inflectional formatives it occurs with while in L2 class A is defined by its co-occurrence with a copula), are similar in two regards: a) they are of roughly equal size; and b) prototypical members of both classes denote ontologically similar entities, including animate beings and (perceptible and time-stable) things.

And precisely for reasons of crosslinguistic comparability, it will occasionally be necessary here to make reference to a number of ontological categories, in particular THINGS, PERSONS, ACTIONS, STATES, and PROPERTIES.[8] The term OBJECT (in small caps) is used to refer to all time-stable entities (in particular ANIMATE BEINGS and THINGS). It is assumed without further discussion that Tagalog ontology is very similar, if not identical, to English ontology so that, for example, a Tagalog root which denotes 'stone' is assumed to be a THING-denoting root.

Turning now to the grammatical categorisation of lexical items, a first and very basic distinction is generally made between content words and function words (or full words and particles).[9] Such a distinction appears to be possible in all languages (cf. Sasse 1993a:652f). Furthermore, it is quite generally agreed that the inventory of function words is highly language-specific. Whenever there is a controversy regarding the number and kind of syntactic categories in a given language, it pertains to the linguistic classification of content words. And with regard to the classification of content words the distinction between lexical and syntactic categories is of central relevance.

---

[8] The alternative to using ontological categories is to use 'noun', 'verb', 'adjective' in a rather loose ontological sense (i.e. as terms for the ontological categories typically covered by the members of these grammatical classes). This procedure is widespread in the literature but easily leads to the confusion of ontological and grammatical categories and thus is avoided here.

[9] The same distinction is made on a categorial level, i.e. the distinction between lexical and functional categories.

The term *lexical category*, as used in much of the current literature, is applied to two, only partially overlapping, categorisation procedures. In one usage, which is widespread among syntacticians, it refers to the terminal nodes of a phrase structure tree, also known as lexical insertion points. In the transformational tradition it has been widely assumed that the set of major lexical categories universally consists of the following four members: N(oun), V(erb), A(djective), and P(reposition) (or, expressed by way of a feature matrix, that all content words can be classified exhaustively with the help of the two features [±nominal] and [±verbal]). In the following, the categories found at the terminal nodes of a phrase structure tree are called *terminal syntactic categories*. The term *syntactic category* refers to terminal and non-terminal (or phrasal) syntactic categories together. The term *lexical category* is only used in its second sense, which is defined in the following.

In its second usage, *lexical category* refers to the classification of lexical items according to grammatical criteria, i.e. the category information attached to each lexical entry in a dictionary. Although the category labels *noun, verb, adjective* and *preposition* are generally also part of this inventory, the category information given in a dictionary is usually much more fine-grained and comprises information concerning phonological, morphological and syntactic properties of the item in question.[10] In languages with complex inflectional morphology, for example, it is usually not sufficient simply to say that a given item is a noun or a verb. Instead, it has to be indicated that an item classified as a noun belongs to the second declension class, or that an item classified as a verb is intransitive and subject to an irregular passive formation. And so on.

It appears to be obvious that terminal syntactic categories are lexical categories in the sense that they are a necessary part of each lexical entry. That is, each lexical item has to be marked for a terminal syntactic category in order to be inserted at the right place into a phrase marker. No doubt, when stated in this very general way, it would be hard to disagree with this view. However, it is common to assume that terminal syntactic categories and lexical categories are commensurate in that lexical categories are but further subcategorisations of the more general terminal syntactic categories. That is, declension classes are but a further subcategorisation of the superclass of nouns, verb classes just a further subcategorisation of the superclass of verbs, etc. Such a neat correlation between terminal syntactic categories and lexical categories in fact appears to exist in a number of lan-

---

[10] Often, of course, there is also other information regarding, for example, pragmatic, sociolinguistic, or lexico-semantic properties of the lexical item. Here, however, we are only interested in the grammatical classification in a strict sense, i.e. the information needed to use a lexical item in a grammatically acceptable way.

guages (including, in particular, the Indo-European languages), but this is not universally so.

Consider the following hypothetical example: The most basic phrasal categories in language L always consist of an overt function word X and a content word Y, and practically all content words may co-occur with each function word. That is, the simplest and most straightforward way to describe the phrase structure of this language is this:

(23) $[_{XP} [X] [Y]]$

where X represents function words, and Y content words. Phrases would then be distinguished primarily by the function words serving as the head of the phrase (i.e. determiner phrases consist of a determiner and a content word, auxiliary phrases of a tense/aspect auxiliary and a content word, and so on).[11] Consequently, all lexical items representing content words would simply be marked as Y (content word) in the lexicon. For the analysis of phrase structure, no further subcategorisation of the content words is required.

Assume further that language L allows the pluralisation of some but not all content words. Moreover, there are two very different plural marking strategies, one involving a suffix, the other one a prefix. That is, with regard to plural marking, the content words of language L fall into three classes: those which take plural suffixes, those which take plural prefixes and those which do not allow pluralisation. Semantically (ontologically), these classes roughly correspond to English count nouns, English verbs, and English mass nouns, respectively. In language L, then, it would be correct to claim that nouns and verbs are lexical categories but that these lexical categories are, strictly speaking, irrelevant for the analysis of phrase markers. In terms of phrase structure both nouns and verbs are simply content words.

While it may be relatively easy and straightforward to accept the claim that there may be a lack of correlation between terminal syntactic categories and lexical categories with regard to morphology, the correlation may also be lacking with regard to distributional, i.e. syntactic, criteria. This possibility arises, once again, simply because the lexical categorisation procedure tends to be much more fine-grained than the one concerned with terminal syntactic categories. Assume a language L1 in which the terminal syntactic categories of content words are indistinct in the same way as in language L above. Assume further that in L1 there are two function words marking

---

[11] Obviously, this is very similar to much recent work where it is assumed that functional categories are the heads of the overall construction.

negation, and that one of these two function words is consistently used with one class of content words and the other one with all of the remaining content words. That is, the negation words provide a syntactic environment which neatly classifies the class of content words into two classes which, based on ontological criteria, could be termed nouns and verbs. Again, L1 would be an example of a language where noun and verb are lexical categories but where this distinction plays no role with regard to terminal syntactic categories.

In the next section, it will be argued that Tagalog exhibits some of the properties of these hypothetical languages. To conclude this section, it may be noted that the proposed distinction of two different levels in the analysis of the grammatical properties of lexical items is similar in spirit and kind to the distinction of different levels (or tiers) in the analysis of clause structure made in a variety of non-transformational syntactic theories, including LFG. In line with these theories, the current proposal rejects the categorial uniformity hypothesis (Bresnan 1994:72) with regard to lexical items on two counts. First, it does away with the assumption that there is a simple universal grid according to which the lexical items of all languages can be grammatically classified. Second, it proposes that there are (at least) two distinct levels on which lexical items have to be grammatically analysed and categorised.

One level is the level of terminal syntactic categories where lexical items are categorised according to their phrase-structural properties (this level corresponds to the level of c(onstituent)-structure in LFG). The second level is the level of lexical categories proper where lexical items are categorised according to those grammatical features which are not directly relevant for phrase structure. This level pertains to a set of possibly very heterogeneous features (i.e. phonological, morphological and syntactic features). It is not unlikely that in a more detailed analysis it will turn out that rather than dealing with one level here it may be useful to make a further distinction between two or more levels on which this set of features can be adequately dealt with. For the purposes of this paper, however, it will be assumed that the two levels distinguished above are sufficient to account for all the relevant phenomena.

The distinction between two levels in the grammatical analysis of lexical items implies the possibility of different alignments between the two levels. In the most general terms, there are two possibilities: a) there is a correlation between the classes on both levels; b) there is no such correlation. The former possibility is well-known from Indo-European languages, both old and modern. The latter possibility is found in Tagalog (and possibly other Austronesian languages) and probably also in Salishan languages (see Jelinek and Demers (1994) for a discussion).

In both Tagalog and Salishan languages, however, the lack of a correlation between the two levels is due to the fact that content words are categorially indistinct with regard to syntactic categories. Logically, it would also be possible to find no correlation due to the fact that there is a distinct set of lexical categories and a distinct set of terminal syntactic categories in a given languages and that there is no correlation between the two sets. Furthermore, it is logically possible that the lexical items of a given language belong to distinct terminal syntactic categories but are indistinct with regard to lexical categories. Table 1 summarises these possibilities.[12]

Table 1: Possible alignments between lexical and syntactic categories

	LEXICAL CATEGORIES		TERMINAL SYNTACTIC CATEGORIES
Ia	distinct	≠	distinct
Ib	distinct	=	distinct
II	indistinct		distinct
III	distinct		indistinct
IV	indistinct		indistinct

Types Ia and Ib are distinguished by the fact that in Ia there is no correlation between lexical and syntactic categories while in Ib the two classes are commensurate.

This is not the place for a detailed discussion of whether all the possibilities provided for in Table 1 are actually attested in natural languages.[13] However, we may note that Type Ib is exemplified by Indo-European languages, Type III by Tagalog, Salishan languages and also Cayuga as analysed by Sasse (1993b). Type II may be attested among highly isolating languages. Several much-discussed agglutinating languages such as Turkic or Eskimo may be approaching Type Ia in that similar morphology is found across different syntactic categories and hence morphologically based classes may be orthogonal to classes based on phrase-structural positions. As for type IV, I am not aware of a language which looks like a promising candidate for the complete absence of any kind of grammatical distinctions among lexical items (despite the fact that much of the literature on categorial squishes tends to portray languages in such a way that a complete absence of grammatical distinctions is implied).

---

[12] See Sasse (1993b:200) for a very similar table. However, there is one crucial difference between Sasse's table and the one presented here. In Sasse's table *syntactic categories* refers to both terminal and non-terminal syntactic categories. Here, only the terminal ones are included.

[13] See Walter (1981), Sasse (1993a/b), Broschart (1997), and Anward et al. (1997) for further discussion and references to the fairly extensive literature on noun/verb squishes.

4 Lexical and Syntactic Categories in Tagalog

This section provides a more detailed discussion of the claim that in Tagalog there is no, or only a minimal, distinction between nouns and verbs. As already mentioned in the preceding section, this claim refers to the fact that Tagalog content words do not have to be subcategorised with regard to terminal syntactic categories. However, the way this claim is generally presented in the literature is somewhat confusing in that it is often implied that there are also no lexical categories in Tagalog. This second claim is wrong, as will be shown in section 4.2. But to begin with, in section 4.1 I will briefly repeat some of the arguments for the first claim, i.e. that Tagalog content words do not have to be categorised with regard to terminal syntactic categories in Tagalog.

4.1 The Lack of Terminal Syntactic Categories in Tagalog

Tagalog exemplifies the hypothetical languages discussed in section 3.2 with regard to two essential features. First, all phrasal categories, with the exception of the predicate (when clause-initial), are composed of a function word which indicates the category and a content word. That is, Tagalog clauses generally follow a very simple pattern in which there is a regular alternation between a single function word and a single content word:[14]

(24) *iniabót*   ***ng***   *manggagamot*   ***sa***
      i-in-abót   ng   manggagamot   sa
      CV-RL(UNDR)-reach   GEN   doctor   LOC
      sundalo   ***ang***   *itlóg*.
      sundalo   ang   itlóg
      soldier   SPEC   egg
      'The physician handed the egg to the soldier.'

Second, content words are not subcategorised with regard to which function words they may co-occur with. Furthermore, all content words may also be used in predicate function. That is, almost all Tagalog content words may occur in exactly the same number and kinds of terminal positions in a phrase structure tree. Thus, assuming Kroeger's (1993:118-148) analysis of Tagalog clause structure, the structure of (24) can be analysed as follows (GP = genitive phrase, CW = content word):

(25) [IP [INFL [$_{CW}$ iniabót]] [S [GP [$_{GEN}$ ng] [$_{CW}$ manggagamot]]
      [PP [$_P$ sa] [$_{CW}$ sundalo]] [DP [$_D$ ang] [$_{CW}$ itlóg]]]]

---

[14] This basic pattern is usually somewhat obscured by the second-position clitics which occur in almost every Tagalog clause.

That almost all Tagalog content words may occur in exactly the same phrase-structural positions has been amply demonstrated in the literature quoted in footnote 5 above. Therefore, a few examples will suffice to support this claim.

One prominent feature of Tagalog phrase structure is the fact that not only OBJECT-denoting words may co-occur with the specific article *ang*. As illustrated by *tumulong* in *(4)* above and *áalagaan* in the following example, it is also possible (and not uncommon!) to use fully inflected (i.e. voice and mood-marked) ACTION-words in construction with the specific article:

(26)   *iuuwi*   *nya*   **ang**
        i-RED1-uwí'   niyá   ang
        CV-RED1-returned.home   3SG.POSS   SPEC
        àalagaan   **nya**
        RED1-alaga'-an   niyá
        RED1-cared.for-LV   3SG.POSS
        'He would return the ones he was going to care for.'

Fully inflected ACTION-words also occur with the other markers of nominal expressions, i.e. *ng* and *sa*:

(27)   *at*   *ang*   *pare*   *at*   *siyá*   *ay*   *naghintáy*
        at   ang   pare   at   siyá   ay   nag-hintáy
        and   SPEC   priest and 3SG   PM   RL.AV-wait
        ng   **sàsabihin**   *ng*   *sundalo*
        ng   RED1-sabi-in   ng   sundalo
        GEN   RED1-statement-PV   GEN   soldier
        'And the priest and he waited for what the soldier would say.'
        (Bloomfield 1917:30/13)

(28)   *nakàtanaw*   *siyá*   *ng*   *bahay*   *na*
        nakà-tanaw   siyá   ng   bahay   na
        RL.STAT-in.sight   3SG   GEN   house   LNK
        mailaw   **sa**   **pinatùtunguhan**
        ma-ilaw   sa   in-pa-RED1-tungo-an
        STAT-light   LOC   RL(UNDR)-??-RED1-direction-LV
        ng   *kalabáw*
        ng   kalabáw
        GEN   caribou
        'He saw a lighted house in the direction toward which the caribou was going.' (Bloomfield 1917:72/6)

Furthermore, fully inflected ACTION-words may be in construction with quantifiers, including the existential quantifier *may*:[15]

(29) **mayroon**   *palang*   **nagàalaga**
      may-doón   palá-ng   nag-RED1-alaga'
      EXIST-DIST.LOC   so!-LNK   RL.AV-RED1-cared.for
      doón   *sa*   *ibun*
      doón   sa   ibon
      DIST.LOC   LOC   bird
      'In fact, there was already someone looking after those birds.'

(30) **may**   **ipàpakita**   *ako*   *sa*   *iyo*
      may   i-RED1-pa -kita   akó   sa   iyo
      EXIST   CV-RED1-CAUS-visible   1SG   LOC   2SG.DAT
      'I have something to show you.'

In all of the preceding examples, one could insert content words of any other ontological or lexical category in place of the ACTION-words used here. Changing the category of the content word does not have any consequences whatsoever for the syntax and semantics of the overall phrase. For example, an existential quantifier phrase expresses existential quantification regardless of the ontological or lexical category of its complement: *may langgám* means 'there are ants' and *may ipàpakita* means 'there are things to be shown'. Similarly, the formal properties of the existential quantifier phrase do not vary with the kind of content word serving as the complement of the function word: there is never a linker between *may* and its complement and no clitics may intervene between these two constituents (but clitics may come in between *mayroón* and its complement and there is also a linker in the *mayroón* construction). A *may*-phrase may not only serve as the predicate of an existential or a possessive construction, but it may also serve as the complement in an *ang-*, *ng-* or *sa*-phrase. And so forth.

Consequently, it appears to be possible and useful to analyse the phrase structure of this and similar phrases simply as function word plus content word and to make no categorial distinctions between content words with regard to terminal syntactic categories. That is, all content words may occur, without further derivation or conversion, in the same kind of phrase-structural positions. In the following, this analysis will be referred to as the *syntactic uniformity hypothesis for content words*.

---

[15] In presentative constructions the existential quantifier is typically combined with a deictic, hence *mayroón* 'there is/was'.

There are a few alternatives to the syntactic uniformity hypothesis for content words. It is not uncommon to assume that in examples such as the preceding ones, the ACTION-words are somehow nominalised by the function words with which they occur, or that these examples involve headless relative clauses. While I am not aware of any irrefutable arguments which rule out such alternative analyses altogether, there are a number of arguments which render these analyses less plausible than the syntactic uniformity hypothesis for content words.

First, and perhaps most importantly, no formal differences whatsoever exist between ontologically different classes of words such as ACTION-words, PROPERTY-words, and OBJECT-words when occurring in the same phrase-structural position. Hence, if the occurrence of an ACTION-word in a determiner phrase or a quantifier phrase is interpreted as some kind of nominalisation (or a headless relative clause) there is no principled reason to exclude the same analysis for OBJECT-words (for example, *ang langgám* could be analysed as 'the one which is an ant', etc.). To generalise the alternative analyses in this way to all kinds of content words is of course just another way of stating the syntactic uniformity hypothesis for content words. To limit these analyses only to ACTION-words, on the other hand, is arbitrary unless independent evidence is adduced to show that the constructions with ACTION-words are indeed different from those containing other kinds of content words.

Second, the alternative analyses are less economical in that they posit an additional (and invisible) layer of structure (in the case of headless relative clauses) or additional morphological processes (in the case of nominalisations). The syntactic uniformity hypothesis for content words allows the most general and economical statement of the syntax and semantics of Tagalog phrase structure. Hence it is the preferred analysis for reasons of simplicity.

Third, from a crosslinguistic point of view, any analysis of Tagalog clause structure should be able to express the fact that ACTION-words can be used in the same phrase-structural positions as OBJECT-words without any extra morphological marking and the fact that such use is clearly more common in Tagalog than in languages which require nominalisation or relative clause formation in order to achieve the same functional effects. The syntactic uniformity hypothesis provides a straightforward account of this difference. It is unclear how the alternative analyses would be able to account for it.

4.2 Lexical Categories of Tagalog Roots

This section is concerned with the claim that Tagalog roots show different formal properties which are not directly predictable from the ontological category of their denotata, and that in this sense they belong to different lexical categories. It thus presents a challenge to the view that Tagalog roots are precategorial, an issue to be taken up at the end of this section.

The major formal distinctions between Tagalog roots pertain to the affix sets with which they may occur. That is, the major parameter for the distinction of different lexical categories in Tagalog is a morphological one. To emphasize the morphological basis of the classification I will henceforth speak of the *morpho-lexical* classes of Tagalog roots.[16]

The fact that Tagalog roots belong to different morpho-lexical classes is not obvious (otherwise there would be no need to discuss this issue here). That is, there are no easily identifiable paradigms into which roots enter, nor is there anything like a set of distinct conjugation or declension classes as they are well-known from the older Indo-European languages. This is not to say that so far no morpho-lexical classifications of Tagalog roots have been proposed. Quite to the contrary, a substantial number of morpho-lexical classifications of Tagalog roots exists, most of them concerned with voice affixations.[17] However, the various classification proposals differ so widely that one wonders whether the authors are dealing with the same empirical domain. This should become obvious simply by looking at the number of classes proposed by different authors. Here is a fairly representative, but not comprehensive, list of the proposals found in the literature:

- Blake (1925:38f), who continues the work of the Spanish grammarians, operates with 17 classes of 'active verbs'.
- Schachter and Otanes (1972) work with the notion of an affix correspondence set, i.e. 'a set of two or more major affixes which, together with the base, form major transitive verbs of differing focus [= voice, NPH] but otherwise identical meaning' (1972:293). With this methodology they distinguish 33 classes for 'major transitive verbs' (1972:295-306) and 10 classes for 'major intransitive verbs' (1972:306-310), allowing the possibility that roots belong to more than one class. On the basis of the same methodology, Cruz (1975) proposes 38 classes while McFarland (1976:33) lists 47 'inflectional patterns for verbs', noting that 'most verb roots' occur in more than one pattern.

---

[16] This terminology is also motivated by the fact that it leaves open the possibility that further classifications of Tagalog roots are possible, based on other grammatical features (for example, phonological features) and not necessarily commensurate with the morpho-lexical classification sketched here.

[17] Work concerned with this topic is usually called 'the subcategorisation of Tagalog verbs' or something similar. However, since practically all Tagalog roots may occur with voice affixations, these classifications in fact propose a classification of all roots, not just ACTION roots.

- Ramos (1974, 1975), using Fillmorean 'deep cases', needs only 15
  classes. De Guzman, who uses a similar methodology though with
  the additional assumptions of the Lexicase framework, distinguishes 7 major classes with 48 subclasses for 'primary verb stems'
  and an additional 14 major classes with 32 subclasses for 'secondary verb stems' (1978:243ff, 385ff).

The differences between these classificatory proposals are due in part to
the different grammatical frameworks in which these authors work. What is
more important, however, is the fact that all of these classifications make
essential reference to the English translations of the Tagalog data, thus actually providing a cross-classification of Tagalog and English verbal expressions.

The major obstacle to an easy and straightforward morpho-lexical classification of Tagalog roots is the fact that there is pervasive polysemy (and
possibly also homonymy) with regard to the affixes which may be used for
classifying roots. That is, identifying a morpho-lexical class is not simply a
matter of determining which roots occur with which formative since most
formatives may occur with most roots. There is, for example, a highly productive prefix *ma-*, often glossed as a STATIVE marker, which may occur
with the large majority of all Tagalog content word roots. However, it is
possible and useful to distinguish two different kinds of formations involving *ma-*.[18] In one kind of formation *ma+ROOT* means 'have ROOT, be characterised by what the root denotes'. Let's call this the HAVE-formation. Examples include the following:

(31) *mabahay*   'having many houses on it'   < *bahay* 'house'
      mabahá'   'flooded'   < *bahá'* 'flood'
      magandá   'beautiful'   < *gandá* 'beauty'
      madalí'   'quick'   < *dalí'* 'quickness'
      marami   'many'   < *dami* '(large) quan-
                                                 tity, amount'[19]

In the second formation, the BECOME-formation, *ma+ROOT* means 'become ROOT, get into the state denoted by, or associated with, the root'.[20]
For example:[21]

---

[18] For a more detailed discussion of *ma*-formations, proposing a similar but not identical
analysis, see Wolff (1993).
[19] Intervocalic /d/ often alternates with /r/ in Tagalog.

(32) *malutás*   'get solved'   < *lutás* 'solved'
      mahinóg   'become ripe, ripen'   < *hinóg* 'ripe'
      màmura   'become cheap'   < *mura* 'cheap'
      maduróg   'become crushed'   < *duróg* 'crushed,
                                                    splintered'
      maluto'   'be/become cooked'   < *luto'* 'cooked, cui-
                                                    sine'
      maputol   'get cut off'   < *putol* 'a cut, a piece'
      mabutas   'get a hole, be perforated'   < *butas* 'a hole'
      matapos   'be/become completed'   < *tapos* 'end, conclu-
                                                    sion'
      magalit   'become angry'   < *galit* 'anger'
      magutom   'become/feel hungry'   < *gutom* 'hunger'

The difference in meaning between these two formations is also reflected in formal differences. The BECOME-formation allows for aspectual
and modal inflection. For example, apart from the basic form *magalit* there
is also the realis perfective form *nagalit* 'became angry', the realis imperfective form *nagàgalit* 'was/is becoming angry' as well as the non-realis
imperfective form *magàgalit* 'will become angry'. The HAVE-formation, on
the other hand, generally does not allow any aspectual or modal inflection
(there is no *nadalí' 'was quick', etc.). As opposed to BECOME-formations,
however, HAVE-formations allow for simple (unstressed) reduplication to
express plurality: *(mga) madadalí'* 'quick ones', *(mga) magagandá* 'beautiful ones', and so on.

Granted that there are two clearly different formations with *ma-*, these
two formations provide the basis for two basic morpho-lexical classes of
Tagalog roots: roots that occur in the HAVE-formation (class A), and roots
that occur in the BECOME-formation (class B).[22] To be a useful morpho-
lexical classification of Tagalog content word roots, this classification pre-
supposes that class membership is disjunctive, i.e. that no root is a member

---

[20] Note that this formation includes both achievements and accomplishments and thus 'become' here has a wider meaning than the BECOME- operator used in Vendler-type lexical decomposition.

[21] In many instances, the BECOME-formation also has an abilitative interpretation. Thus,
malutás also means 'can be solved', *maputol* 'can be cut off', etc.

[22] A small number of roots partake in neither formation. This is true in particular of roots
referring to HUMAN BEINGS (e.g. *babae* 'woman, female', including KIN TERMS (e.g. *iná*
'mother'), with the exception of *anák* 'child, offspring' which allows the derivation of *maanák*
'having many children' (according to Santos (1983) *bata'* 'child, young' as well allows the
derivation of *mabata'* 'having many children', but other dictionaries do not list this formation).

of more than one class. That this is in fact the case is supported by two further observations. First, a large number of the roots which occur in class B either denote a state all by themselves (such as the first five items in (32)) or allow the derivation of state-denoting expressions via stress shift. This holds true for the remaining five items in (32):

(33) *putol* 'a cut, a piece'   *putól* 'be cut'
      butas 'a hole'   *butás* 'perforated'
      tapos 'end, conclusion'   *tapós* 'finished'
      galit 'anger'   *galít* 'angry'
      gutom 'hunger'   *gutóm* 'hungry'

That is, there is a good reason why members of class B generally do not allow the HAVE-formation: The meaning derived from roots via HAVE-formation for class A roots is either inherent in class B roots or can be achieved through a different process.

The second observation pertains to the fact that it is possible to derive accomplishment readings from class A roots via a different formation. This is done by infixing -*um*- into those class A roots for which an accomplishment reading is semantically feasible:

(34) *gandá* 'beauty'   *gumandá* 'become beautiful'
      dalí 'quickness'   *dumalí* 'become fast'
      dami '(large) quantity, amount'   *dumami* 'become many'

These two observations make it clear that roots from both classes allow the derivation of the same kinds of meanings but that they employ different formal means in the process (see also Table 2). Therefore, the difference between the two classes is a *grammatical* difference. It is not due to the ontology of the entities denoted by class A and B roots, respectively (i.e. it is not the case that the formation *ma*-+CLASS A ROOT means 'have ROOT, be characterised by what the root denotes' simply because all class A roots are THING roots, and that the formation *ma*-+CLASS B ROOT means 'become ROOT, get into the state denoted by, or associated with, the root' simply because all class B roots are PROPERTY roots).

Table 2: Distribution of form and meaning in expressions for states and accomplishments based on class A and B roots

	class A	class B
STATE	ma-	0/stress shift
ACCOMPLISHMENT	-um-	ma-

In fact, although there is some kind of correlation between ontological categories and the two morpho-lexical categories just established, this correlation is far from perfect. Roughly speaking, it holds true that most roots denoting THINGS, ANIMALS and NATURAL PHENOMENA (floods, earthquakes, etc. as well as mountains, rivers, etc.) belong to class A while those denoting STATES, PROCESSES, and ACTIONS belong to class B. However, PROPERTY roots are split between classes A and B. For example, 'beauty', 'quickness', 'quantity, plentitude' are class A (see (31)) while 'ripeness', 'cheapness', 'anger' and 'hunger' are class B (see (32)).

A further morpho-lexical subclassification of the two classes just established appears to be possible, in particular with regard to the formation of actor voice forms by affixing either -um- or mag-. Without going into details, class A roots generally allow the formation of actor voice forms only by prefixing mag- (e.g. magbahay 'build one's own house'). Many class A roots, however, do not allow the derivation of an actor voice form directly from the root (*magbahá', *maggandá, *magdalí'). Class B roots, on the other hand, generally allow the formation of an actor voice form directly from the root. For the large majority of class B roots this is possible by infixing -um- (e.g. lumutás 'to solve, to clear up'), others only allow mag- (e.g. magluto' 'to cook'), while a third class allows both -um- and mag- with a difference in meaning (e.g. pumutol 'to cut off' vs. magputol 'to cut into pieces/several things' or 'to cut oneself').

However, as in the case of the two ma-formations, the subclasses involved here are far from obvious. To provide a sound basis for these subclasses requires a lengthy discussion of various polysemies, exceptions and overlaps, a task well beyond the limits of this paper. Here the task was simply to establish the fact that morpho-lexical classes exist in Tagalog. And the establishment of the two major disjunctive classes based on the different ma-formations should be sufficient to make this point.

If one accepts the claim that Tagalog roots belong to different morpho-lexical classes, it follows that Tagalog roots are not precategorial. Or, to put this a bit more carefully, at least two possible interpretations of the term

precategorial are clearly not applicable to Tagalog.[23] In one interpretation—the one introduced by Verhaar (1984:2)—this term refers to bound
roots (i.e. roots that do not occur unaffixed) from which items belonging to
different lexical or syntactic categories (nouns and verbs, for example) can
be derived, without there being clear evidence that one of the possible derivations of a given root is more basic than the other one. No significant sub-
set of Tagalog roots exists which could be characterised as precategorial in
this sense for the simple reason that there are no bound roots. This will be
demonstrated in detail for ACTION roots in the following section. The examples in section 3.1 amply illustrate the fact that it is also not the case for
OBJECT roots (cf. *langgám, bata', asawa, bahay*, etc. in examples *(1)-(22)*).
One example for a PROPERTY root is the following one:

(35)
tingnan	*mo*	*ang*	**gandá**	*na*	*ng*
tingin-an	mo	ang	gandá	na	ng
look-LV	2SG.POSS	SPEC	beauty	now	GEN

buhay	*ni*	*Maria*
buhay	ni	Maria
life	GEN.PN	Mary

'Look how beautiful Maria's life is now!'
(lit. look at the beauty of Maria's life now!)

In a second interpretation, *precategorial* may refer to the fact that roots,
though not necessarily bound, are categorially indistinct with regard to
grammatical features. That is, all kinds of derivations are possible from all
kinds of roots. The enormous productivity and polysemy of Tagalog formatives may give rise to the impression that this is indeed the case. However,
as shown in this section, it is a misconception: Tagalog roots belong to different morpho-lexical classes and hence are categorially distinct and do not
allow just any derivation that is semantically appropriate.

Tagalog roots may be deemed to be categorially indistinct with regard
to terminal syntactic categories. But, as argued in section 4.1, this feature
they share with all Tagalog content words, roots as well as derived words.
And to call Tagalog roots precategorial with regard to terminal syntactic
categories is something of a misnomer since there is no later (derived) categorial stage with which the *pre*categorial stage could be contrasted.

---

[23] See also Clynes' (1995:203-205) reservations about the usefulness of this concept for the
description and analysis of Austronesian languages.

5   Uses and Meanings of Tagalog Action Roots

Almost all Tagalog roots can be used, and *are* used, without further affixation. Of particular concern here are those roots which denote ACTIONS, and the present section will deal only with these roots. When ACTION roots are used without further affixation, they may convey one of the following kinds of meaning: (a) the state which ensues from the successful performance of the action (similar to a past participle in English); (b) the result[24] or the typical or cognate object of the action (similar to object(ive) nominalisations in English); or (c) the name of the action (similar to an action nominalisation in English). As the following examples will show, meanings (a) and (b) are found primarily with roots denoting transitive (or ditransitive) ACTIONS, while meaning (c) is found with roots denoting transitive and intransitive ACTIONS.

Many roots convey more than one of the three meanings just mentioned. In fact, a few roots may convey all three of them. Furthermore, it is not always possible clearly to distinguish between the different kinds of meanings, in particular between meanings (a) and (b) as well as between meanings (b) and (c). Still, the semantic and syntactic context generally provides enough clues to determine which meaning is intended in a given example.

This section, then, makes two points: First, it empirically supports the claim that Tagalog ACTION roots can be used without further affixation. This point is proved by all of the well-formed examples in this section. Furthermore, at the end of the section I will quote some data from the corpus study by McFarland (1976) which shows that unaffixed use is not only a grammatical possibility but actually occurs in moderate frequency in natural data and thus clearly is a fact of everyday language use.

The second point is the claim that unaffixed roots convey distinctly different kinds of meanings. In order to show this, it is necessary to define contexts (test frames) in which only roots with one kind of meaning can occur while the others cannot. Throughout the discussion of these test frames it is important to keep in mind that what is tested for is semantic well-formedness. If roots conveying a particular meaning cannot be used in context X this is because their meaning is not compatible with the meaning of the other items in the construction. Grammatically, roots behave like all other content words. That is, in principle they fit into every position open to content words. Hence the difference in meaning between roots conveying

---

[24] Note that 'result' here refers to a THING, i.e. the THING which results from the action. Thus, for example, the result of cutting here is 'a piece (cut off)' and not the state of being cut. See also the comment below after example *(51)*.

meaning (a) and roots conveying meaning (b) should not be misconstrued as a difference in syntactic distribution (for example, that only roots conveying meaning (a) can occur in predicate position while those conveying meaning (b) cannot).

Roots denoting states can be distinguished from roots denoting the result, object or name of an action by the fact that only the state-denoting roots can be used as modifiers, as in the following two examples:

(36) *ang*   **lutás**   *na*   *problema*
     ang   lutás   na   problema
     SPEC   solved   LNK   problem
     'the   solved   prob-
     lem'

(37) *ang*   **nakaw**   *na*   *kabayo*
     ang   nakaw   na   kabayo
     SPEC   stolen   LNK   horse
     'the stolen horse'

Roots denoting the result, object or name of an action cannot occur in this function. Thus, for example, the root *putol* 'a cut, a piece cut off' cannot be used in the following phrase to express the indicated meaning:

(38) #*ang*   **putol**   *na*   *kalye*
     SPEC   cut   LNK   street
     'the cut off (i.e. blind) street'

The symbol # is used here to indicate that a given structure is ill-formed with regard to the indicated meaning. As just noted, these examples are not ungrammatical since they conform to the basic morphosyntactic rules of Tagalog. As shown in section 4.2, Tagalog content words (including roots) are generally not subcategorised for a specific syntactic function. That is, a root such as *putol* may, in principle, occur in any syntactic function, provided that it makes sense within the overall construction. Thus, *putol* may occur in a linker construction, provided that it does not have to be interpreted as a modifier. Compare the following example:

(39) *ang*   *bakíl-bakíl*   **na**   *putol*   *(ng*   *buhók*
      SPEC   uneven   LNK   cut   GEN   hair
      ni   *Huán)*
      PN.GEN   John
      '(John's) uneven (hair) cut'

Note also that *putol na kalye* in *(38)* could be given an appositional meaning (??'the cut off piece, the street') but that is in all likelihood not something one would ever say in this way.

The fact that *putol* cannot be used as a modifier is not the only evidence
for the claim that this root denotes the result of the ACTION of cutting ('a
cut, a piece cut off') rather than a state ('be cut off'). Another piece of evidence consists of the fact that there is an overt derivation from the same
root which denotes a state, i.e. *putól* with stress on the ultimate syllable
which means 'cut off, severed'. The stress-shifted *putól* can easily function
as a modifier. Compare *(38)* with:

(40) *ang*   **putól**   *na*   *kalye*
      SPEC   cut   LNK   street
      'the cut off (i.e. blind) street'

The change in meaning brought about by the different stress pattern is also
shown by the fact that *putól* can no longer co-occur with another modifying
element:

(41) #*ang*   *bakíl-bakíl*   **na**   **putól**   *(ng*   *buhók*
      SPEC   uneven   LNK   cut   GEN   hair
      ni   *Huán)*
      PN.GEN   John
      '(John's) uneven (hair) cut'
      (a possible but non-sensical interpretation would be ??'the un-
      even one cut off')

There is a substantial number of ACTION roots in Tagalog which are similar
to *putol* in that they denote the result or object of the action when stressed
on the penult, but a state when stressed on the ultima. Examples include:
butas 'hole'—*butás* 'perforated', *tapos* 'end, conclusion'—*tapós* 'finished,
done', *bali'* 'a break, fracture'—*balí'* 'broken', *bayad* 'payment, fee,
charge'—*bayád* 'paid', etc. (see also (33) and Schachter and Otanes
1972:196f, Wolff et al. 1991:374f). That is, the two different kinds of
meanings attributed here to different roots are not only relevant to explaining the differences in distribution between two types of ACTION roots. The

same distinction has also to be made in order to explain the two different stress patterns shown by a substantial number of ACTION roots.

Turning now to roots denoting the name of an action, there are two kinds of test frames for these roots. First, these roots may be used as the subject of predicates which denote the manner in which an event/action took place. For example:

(42) *biglaan*   *ang*   *kanyáng*   ***alís.***
biglá'-an   ang   kanyá-ng   alís
sudden-??   SPEC   3SG.DAT-LNK   departure
'His departure (act of leaving) was sudden.' (English 1986)

(43) *Subali't*   *tuluy-tulóy*   *pa*   *rin*   *ang*   ***kain***
subalit   RED5-tulóy   pa   din   ang   kain
but   RED5-continue   still   also   SPEC   eating
ni   *Matsíng.*
ni   matsíng
PN.POSS   small.monkey
'But the monkey's eating continued nevertheless.'
(Wolff et al. 1991:526)

Roots denoting a state or the result/object of an action may not occur in this context since the resulting clauses would be semantically ill-formed (??'her stolen one was sudden', ??'his load was sudden').

Second, roots denoting the name of an action cannot be used as predicates in clauses with personal pronouns as subjects:

(44)   *#alís siyá.*   'S/he left/is leaving' (??'s/he is a departure')

(45)   *#kain akó*   'I am eating/ate/was eaten'
    (??'I am consumption of food')

This constraint also holds for roots denoting results/objects:

(46)   *#putol siyá*   's/he was cut/has cut sth' (??'s/he is a cut')

But it does not hold for roots denoting states:

(47)   *nakaw siyá*   's/he was/is stolen'

summarises the diagnostic contexts used here to distinguish the three different meanings which can be conveyed by ACTION roots.

Table 3: Diagnostic contexts for distinguishing the different meanings of ACTION roots

	modifier	subject of manner predicate	predicate with pronominal subject
root denotes state	YES	NO	YES
root denotes result or typical object of action	NO	NO	NO
root denotes name of action	NO	YES	NO

As already mentioned in the introduction to this section, it is not the case that all ACTION roots convey only one of the three meanings listed in . Some roots have both a result/object and a state meaning. Examples include *ayos* which means 'order, arrangement' as well as 'presentable, fit to be seen', *bigáy* 'gift' and 'given', *bagsák* 'a (sudden) fall' and 'failed, defeated', *dalá* 'load, cargo' and 'carried',[25] *gawá* 'an act, product' and 'made, caused by', *hango'* 'relief, extract, removal' and 'extracted, derived', etc.[26] The following two examples illustrate the two meanings of *dalá*:

(48) *ang* **dala** *naming* *bala*
     ang   dalá   namin.LNK   bala
     SPEC carried 1PL.EX.POSS.LNK bullet
     'The bullets carried by us...'

(49) Inilapág   ni   Hwán   ang
     i-in-lapág   ni   Hwan   ang
     CV-RL(UNDR)-space.below PN.POSS John   SPEC
     kanyang   **dalá**
     kanyá-ng   dalá
     3SG.DAT-LNK   load
     'Juan dropped his burden...' (Bloomfield 1917:106/16)

---

[25] Interestingly, the Spanish loan *karga* (and its variant *kargá*) conveys the same meanings as the native form *dalá*, at least according to English (1986) and Santos (1983). According to Panganiban (1972) *karga* is 'load' and *kargá* is 'carried'.

[26] As can be seen from this rather short list, many—but not all!—roots in this class are stressed on the final syllable. Hence stress shift cannot be used to differentiate the two kinds of meaning.

And here are two examples for the two meanings of *bigáy*:

(50)   *P350*   *every two months*   *ang*   **bigáy**
        P350   ang   bigáy
        P350   SPEC   given

    ko-ng   *bayad*   *sa*   *school.*
    ko-ng   bayad   sa
    1SG.POSS-LNK   payment   LOC
    'The payment given by me to the school is 350 Pesos every two months.'

(51)   *Parang*   **bigáy**   *na*   *lang*   *natin*
    para-ng   bigáy   na   lamang   natin
    as.though-LNK   gift   now   only   1PL.IN.POSS

    sa   *kanilá*   *yon.*
    sa   kanilá   iyón
    LOC   3PL.DAT   DIST
    'That is like our gift to them.' (i.e. consider it a gift to them)
    (Wolff et al. 1991:1050)

The overlap between the state and the result/object meanings should not come as a surprise since even on an ontological level the difference between a THING and a PROPERTY/STATE is not always easy to discern (cf. also Sasse 1993b:202). Thus, the THING 'gift' may also be viewed as something which is in the STATE of being given, i.e. 'the given one/thing', the THING 'load, cargo' is 'the carried one', and so forth.

Similarly, polysemy involving the two meanings 'result/object of an action' and 'name of an action' is found in many languages, in particular with regard to nominalisations (cf. Koptevskaja-Tamm 1988:42). English *filling*, for example, may refer to the actual act or manner of filling (as in *With completion of filling, net-like anastomoses were noted*) and hence be an action nominalisation (the name of an action). Or it may refer to the cognate object (as in *manifold fillings were prepared*) and hence be interpreted as an objective nominalisation. Not surprisingly, then, many Tagalog ACTION roots also allow both readings, as illustrated by *lakad* 'walk' in the following examples:

(52)   *Yaon*   *ay*   *mahabang*   **lakad.**
    iyón   ay   ma-haba'-ng   lakad
    DIST   PM   STAT-length-LNK   walk
    'That was/is a long walk.' (English 1986)

(53) *Mahusay*   *ang*   **lakad**   *ng*   *mákiná.*
      ma-husay   ang   lakad   ng   mákiná
      STAT-orderliness SPEC   walk   GEN   machine
      'The walking (running condition) of the machine is good.'
      (English 1986)

Thus, there is not only an overlap between roots denoting results/objects and those denoting states, but also one between roots denoting results/objects and those denoting the name of an action.

In passing, it may be noted that for each kind of meaning there is a typical set of syntactic functions in which it most commonly occurs. For instance, roots denoting states typically occur in predicate or modifier function. See examples *(36)* and *(37)* above and the following example:

(54) *inilúgaw*   *na,*   **lutó**   *na*
      i -in-lugaw   na   luto'   na
      CV-RL(UNDR)-gruel   now   cooked   now
      'It (the rice) has already been made into porridge,
      it is already cooked.'

Roots denoting the result or object of an action typically occur in nominal expressions:

(55) *ang*   *sakít*   *ng*   *mga*   **hampás**   *niyá*
      ang   sakít   ng   mga   hampás   niyá
      SPEC   pain   GEN   PL   blow   3SG.POSS
      sa   *akin*   *balikat!*
      sa   aking   balikat
      LOC   1SG.DAT.LNK   shoulder
      'How painful the blows he gave me on my shoulders!' (English 1986)

Roots denoting the name of an action are also typically found in nominal expressions, in particular those functioning as the subject of manner predicates:

(56)	at	habang	bumìbilis		ang	**takbó**
	at	habang	um-RED1-bilís		ang	takbo
	and	while	INGR-RED1-speed		SPEC	run
	ng	tubig				
	ng	tubig				
	GEN	water				

'And when the current of the water got faster...'

However, the fact that there are typical contexts of use for each type of meaning does not mean that the meaning(s) conveyed by a given root are simply a product of the context of use. That is, it is not the case that a root such as *takbó* means 'act of running, a run' simply because it is typically used in nominal expressions functioning as the subject of manner predicates. If the meaning of a root depended simply on its context of use, it could not be explained why some uses of a root are impossible (for example, why it is not possible to say #*ang takbóng baboy* 'the running pig'). Furthermore, that the meaning conveyed by a given root is independent from the syntactic function in which it is used is also shown by the fact that identical meanings are conveyed by bare roots in at least two different syntactic contexts. For example, roots denoting the name of an action do not exclusively occur in nominal expressions. Instead, use in predicate position is also possible:

(57)	**iyák**	ang	sagót	niyá	sa	akin
	iyák	ang	sagót	niyá	sa	akin
	cry	SPEC	answer	3SG.POSS	LOC	1SG.DAT

'His answer to me was crying/to cry.' (elicited)

(58)	**datíng**	niyá	ang	hindí	ko
	datíng	niyá	ang	hindí'	ko
	arrival	3SG.POSS	SPEC	NEG	1SG.POSS
	alam				
	alam				
	knowledge				

'I don't know (about) her arrival.' (elicited)

To conclude this discussion of the meaning of bare ACTION roots, it has to be pointed out that some unaffixed ACTION roots also occur in a variety of uses and functions in which they do not convey the three meanings discussed so far. The data on these further uses and functions are somewhat limited and it is highly likely that they can be shown to be derived rather than basic uses and functions.[27] Perhaps the most prominent of these further uses is the use in imperatives illustrated by the following examples:

(59) **Hampás**   na   kayó,   mga   bata',   sa   mga
      hampás   na   kayó   mangá   bata'   sa   mangá
      blow   now   2PL   PL   child   LOC   PL
      langgám.
      langgám
      ant
      'Whip at the ants, boys.' (Bloomfield 1917:221/42)

(60) Umuwí'   na   tayo,   Daddy!   **Uwí'**
      um-uwí'   na   tayo   uwí'
      AV-returned.home   now   1PL.IN   returned.home
      na   tayo!
      na   tayo
      now   1PL.IN
      'Let's go home Daddy! Let's go home!'

As clearly shown in particular by the second example, unaffixed roots used as imperatives correspond to actor voice forms (i.e. the subject is the addressee of the command). Note that the standard form of imperatives in Tagalog involves voice-marked forms and that actor voice as well as undergoer voice imperatives are possible (cf. Schachter and Otanes (1972:402-409). Obviously, the imperative meaning arises here from the overall construction (and the situational/textual context) and is not in any way directly linked to the bare roots functioning as predicates. Furthermore, according to the native speakers I have consulted (though generally not noted in the literature), the ability to use a bare root as an imperative is limited to those roots which form their actor voice with the infix -um- (cf. Himmelmann 1987:166). Thus, it is not a general characteristic of ACTION roots.

It may also be noted that, according to some dictionaries, a small number of ACTION roots never occur without affixes. Examples from English (1986) include roots such as *agaw* (with voice affixes: 'to snatch, to grab'), *patol* (with voice affixes: 'to notice, to pay attention'), *suno'* (with voice affixes: 'to give someone a lift'), *ubos* (with voice affixes: 'to consume, to use up'). Rubino (1998a) gives a nominal translation for *ubos*, Panganiban

---

[27] For more extensive discussion, see Bloomfield (1917:218-223), Himmelmann (1987:157-171) and Wolff et al. (1991:115, 291, 488, 1028f, 1130-1134).

(1972) gives one for *agaw* and *suno'* (but not for *ubos*), while Santos (1983) gives one for all four roots.

These differences in lexicographic practice should, in my view, be interpreted as reflecting the fact that ACTION roots differ substantially with regard to the frequency and naturalness of unaffixed uses. For a number of roots, including the three roots just mentioned, such use is probably highly unusual and hence not recorded in some of the dictionaries. This, however, does not mean that it is completely impossible to use such roots without affixes, given an appropriate context.

Most importantly, it should be clearly understood that in general unaffixed uses of ACTION roots are not in any way exceptional. Instead, they are reasonably common both in terms of types (the number of roots for which such use is attested in natural data) as well as in terms of tokens (the number of times a bare ACTION root can be found in a corpus). McFarland (1976), for example, has found unaffixed uses in naturally occurring (written) texts for 76 of the 106 most common ACTION roots in his corpus (= ca. 70%). For some roots such as *dalá* 'load; carried', unaffixed use is in fact the single most frequent use (i.e. it is more frequent than the use of any voice-marked form). In short, although there are differences with regard to how frequent and natural it is for a given ACTION root to occur without affixes it is clearly the case that Tagalog ACTION roots quite generally allow for unaffixed uses.

6 Root Meaning and the Derivational Nature of Voice Marking

It follows from the data presented in the preceding sections that voice marking in Tagalog is derivational in all its manifestations. While the derivational nature of voice marking is widely accepted in the case of OBJECT roots, it is controversial with regard to ACTION roots (see de Guzman (1997) for a recent survey of this controversy). This section presents an explication of the derivational nature of Tagalog voice marking, based on the data discussed so far.

To begin with, we may note that there is a widespread, though usually implicit, assumption that Tagalog voice marking is derivational in at least some of its uses. In all approaches which make a distinction between nouns and verbs as syntactic or lexical categories, the following assumption has to be made: when affixed to 'nominal' roots (i.e. roots denoting THINGS or ANIMATE BEINGS) voice marking has two functions. First, it derives a verb from a noun, and second, it registers the alignment between semantic role and syntactic function with regard to the subject argument. For example, adding *i-* to *anák* to form *ianák* 'to give birth to someone' converts the putative noun *anák* 'child' into a verb 'to give birth'. Furthermore, the prefix *i-* registers the fact that the subject argument is a displaced theme. Other examples of this kind include the following:

(61) *bahay* 'house'   *magbahay* 'to build one's own house'
  anák 'child'   *mag-anák* 'to breed, to have a child'
  buladór 'kite, rocket'   *magbuladór* 'to fly a kite'
  walís 'broom'   *magwalís* 'to sweep'

Thus, voice marking appears to have derivational force in at least some of its manifestations.[28] Here, however, the much more general claim is made that voice marking is derivational in *all* its manifestations. The discussion will be limited to the potentially most controversial issue, i.e. the use of voice marking morphology on ACTION roots (i.e. those roots which in many analyses are considered verbal roots). It is claimed that, as in the case of OBJECT roots, voice marking on ACTION roots also has a dual function. First, however, we have briefly to establish the fact that *all* voice-marked words in Tagalog, regardless of their base, are members of a single morpho-lexical class and that this morpho-lexical class is different from all other morpho-lexical classes. This class is called here the 'V-class' and its members 'V-words'.[29]

The major formal criterion for V-class membership is voice marking: All and only words bearing voice affixes are members of this class. The fact that voice-marked words constitute a special morpho-lexical class is shown by a number of further formal and semantic properties shown only by the members of this class. Formally, only V-words are inflected for aspect and

---

[28] An alternative analysis for these examples, which does not attribute derivational (category-changing) force to voice marking, would involve the assumption of zero conversion along the following lines: The nominal root *anák₁* 'child' is converted into a verbal root *anák₂* 'to give birth' which then is inflected for voice to register different alignments between semantic role and syntactic function. A major weakness of this alternative analysis is the fact that there is no independent evidence for a zero-converted verbal root *anák₂* 'to give birth'. That is, under no circumstances does the form *anák* without further affixation mean 'give birth'.

[29] The 'V' here stands for 'voice-marked'. In principle, one could also call the members of this class 'verbs' as long as it is clearly understood that V-words are here defined as a morpho-lexical category. That is, 'V' does not indicate a syntactic category and therefore is not fully commensurable with the most common and best established use of the term *verb*, i.e. as the name of a syntactic category. Furthermore, having a class of verbs in a given language is usually taken to imply that there is also a class of nouns in that language. To date I have considerable doubt as to whether this implication would be true in Tagalog. That is, it is far from clear whether it is possible and useful to identify a morpho-lexical category 'noun' in Tagalog. See also section 10.5.

mood. In fact, aspect-mood marking and voice marking are formally inseparable. Hence, each voice-marked form is also aspect-mood-marked, as shown by the aspect-mood paradigm in Table 4:

Table 4: Aspect-mood paradigm for *bilí* 'buy'
(r = realis, n-r = non-realis)

	act	PV	LV	CV
n-r perfective	b-um-ilí	bilh-ín	bilh-án	i-bilí
n-r imperfective	bìbilí	bìbilh-ín	bìbilh-án	i-bìbilí
r perfective	b-um-ilí	b-in-ilí	b-in-ilh-án	i-b-in-ilí
r imperfective	b-um-ìbilí	b-in-ìbilí	b-in-ìbilh-án	i-b-in-ìbilí

The forms found in the first row of Table 4 are generally considered the unmarked forms with regard to aspect-mood marking (Schachter and Otanes (1972:66) call them *basic forms*). These are used in imperatives, in control constructions and as non-initial predicates in clause chains. Note that aspect-mood inflection is fully predictable (unlike voice marking). From each basic form the other three forms are derivable via totally general and nearly exceptionless rules (cf. Schachter and Otanes 1972:361-371).

Aspect-mood inflection is not the only formal characteristic of V-words. Further morphological characteristics include the fact that a number of other derivations are predictable on the basis of the actor voice form. For example, gerunds are formed by prefixing *pag-* to the roots which take *-um-* as the actor voice affix (e.g. *pumutol* 'to cut off'—*pagputol* 'cutting off') while roots taking *mag-* as the actor voice prefix form gerunds by prefixing *pag-* + unstressed reduplication of the root or stem-initial syllable (e.g. *magluto'* 'to cook'—*pagluluto'* 'cooking'). For further discussion and references see Schachter (1996:44-46).

Semantically, V-words differ from all other content words in Tagalog in that they are systematically ambiguous. That is, all V-words have two readings depending on the syntactic context. Used as predicates, they denote a specific instance of the action denoted by the root, as in:

(62) **sumigáw**   *yung*   *anák*
      um-sigáw   iyón.LNK   anák
      AV-shout   DIST.LNK   child
      'That child shouted:...'

Used as modifiers in a linker construction, they have the same reading:

(63)	yung	anák	na	**sumìsigáw**
	iyón.LNK	anák	na	um-RED1-sigáw
	DIST.LNK	child	LNK	AV-RED1-shout
	'that shouting child'			

Used in nominal expressions, however, V-words denote one of the participants involved in the ACTION denoted by the root:

(64)	yung	anák	ang	**sumigáw**
	iyón.LNK	anák	ang	um-sigáw
	DIST.LNK	child	SPEC	AV-shout
	'The one who shouted/the shouter is (was) that child.'			

Note that in this use it is also a specific instance of the action denoted by the root that is being referred to by the voice-marked form *sumigáw*. That is, *sumigáw* may mean 'the one who shouted/the shouter on this particular occasion'. It cannot mean 'a professional shouter/someone who always shouts'.[30]

Having thus established the fact that V-words belong to a special morpho-lexical class of their own, it follows almost automatically that voice marking is derivational. At least, it is category-changing in that it derives V-words from non-V-words. Still, if ACTION roots generally were bound roots it could be argued that a substantial difference existed between the affixation of voice affixes to OBJECT roots and the affixation of voice affixes to ACTION roots. Only in the case of OBJECT roots voice marking would involve a category shift while in the case of ACTION roots it could be argued that the function of voice marking was simply to register the alignment between semantic role and syntactic function with regard to the subject argument.

However, as demonstrated in sections 3.2 and 5, ACTION roots are not some kind of bound forms which do not have a specific meaning and cannot be used by themselves. Instead, in their unaffixed use they denote states and/or results/objects or names of an action. Hence, adding a voice affix to an ACTION root does not simply register a change in alignment between semantic role and syntactic function. It derives a different lexical item: A root denoting a state or the result of an action is turned into an *actor-* or *undergoer-oriented action* expression. More specifically, this derivation

---

[30] In this regard, Tagalog V-words differ from various kinds of oriented nominalisations in English. English *shouter* is ambiguous between a specific instance reading ('the one who shouted just now') and a non-specific type reading ('someone who always/professionally shouts').

involves two aspects. First, the derived form denotes the actual and specific performance of an action. Second, the specific performance of an action is not denoted in some neutral way but rather the voice-marked form is oriented towards one of the participants: an actor voice form denotes the agent of the action, hence in its predicative use the subject has to be an agent. A patient voice form denotes the patient of the action and in its predicative use requires the subject to be a patient. And so on. There is no substantial difference here between OBJECT and ACTION denoting roots. Both aspects are present whenever voice marking is added to any kind of root, including OBJECT ROOTS and ACTION roots.

Apart from accounting for the facts discussed in this paper, this derivational view of voice marking in Tagalog is also supported by a number of phenomena which remain unexplained (or which are hard to explain) in other accounts. For example, the derivational view provides an easy and straightforward explanation for the ubiquity of voice marking in Tagalog. Most roots (and a large number of derived stems) allow the affixation of at least one voice affix without any further derivation. If voice marking were not in itself derivational and could only be attached directly to verbs, this ubiquity could only be accounted for by postulating pervasive homonymy on the root level or by assuming extensive use of zero conversion. There is no independent evidence to support these alternative analyses.

Moreover, the proposed view also provides a straightforward explanation for the pervasive formal and semantic idiosyncrasies of Tagalog voice marking, which are typical of derivational processes. Here the following simple examples will suffice to illustrate these idiosyncrasies:[31] formally, there are unpredictable idiosyncrasies such as the deletion of root vowels in undergoer voice forms (e.g. the vowel /i/ is deleted in the patient voice form *kanin* 'to eat something' which derives from *kain* 'consumption of food'; the regular form *kainin* is also possible). Other examples of unpredictable formal idiosyncrasies are the sporadic insertion of /n/ in patient or locative voice forms such as *tawanan* 'to laugh at someone' (< *tawa* 'laugh, laughter, laughing') and completely irregular forms such as the patient voice form *kunin* 'to get something' (< *kuha* 'getting, a helping'), etc. (see also Bloomfield 1917:213-215).

Semantically, the meaning of V-words is broadly predictable on the basis of the meaning of the root and the meaning of the voice affixes. Thus, for example, it is clear that the subject of an actor voice form is an agent of some kind and that the action denoted by the voice-marked form is in some

---

[31] For further discussion and examples see, among others, Himmelmann 1987:129-146 and Rubino 1998b:1152-1155.

way related to the THING or ACTION denoted by the root. But there are manifold idiosyncrasies with regard to both the notion of agency and the notion
of action conveyed by an actor voice form. Thus, *mag-anák* (from *anák*
'child') does not mean 'to give birth'. Instead, it means 'to breed, have a
child' and is most commonly used of animals (the actor voice form for 'to
give birth' is *manganák*). The root *talo* means 'defeated, surpassed, beaten'
but the derived form *magtalo* does not mean 'to defeat, to beat' (that is the
meaning of *tumalo*). Instead, *magtalo* means 'to contend, to quarrel, to disagree'. Similarly, *magtaká*, which is derived from *taká* 'surprise, surprised',
does not mean 'to surprise someone' but 'to be surprised'.

In short, there is a considerable number of facts which strongly suggest
that voice marking in Tagalog is derivational. This in itself is not an original observation (see de Guzman (1997) and Rubino (1998b) for references).
The present account, however, differs from that found in the literature in
that it provides a more precise and explicit statement of what this derivation
involves, in particular with regard to ACTION roots. This is achieved by providing a testable explication of the different meanings conveyed by roots
and a definition of the meaning and the morpho-lexical class of V-words.

7 Conclusion

An important aspect of the voice system in Tagalog is the fact that voice-
marked words (V-words), as well as the roots from which they are derived,
belong to lexical categories which are very different from the lexical categories found in more familiar languages such as English. It has been repeat-
edly suggested that the difference pertains to the fact that Tagalog roots are
precategorial and/or that there is no distinction between nouns and verbs in
Tagalog. The preceding sections present a somewhat different explication
of the difference between the two systems of lexical categories and its re-
percussions for the voice systems. Specifically, it is claimed that Tagalog
roots are generally not bound and/or precategorial roots. Instead, Tagalog
roots belong to different morpho-lexical classes. That is, it cannot be predicted solely on the basis of their meaning with which affixes a given root
may occur. Furthermore, all kinds of roots, including roots denoting
ACTIONS, allow for unaffixed uses. In their unaffixed uses, roots may denote THINGS, ANIMATE BEINGS, PROPERTIES, STATES, RESULTS OF ACTIONS,
NAMES OF ACTIONS, etc., i.e. concepts which in English are generally rendered by nouns or adjectives. What roots cannot denote is the actual and
specific performance of an action. Only V-words may denote the actual
performance of an action. In this regard, Tagalog V-words are similar to
English verbs. They differ, however, from English verbs in a number of
important respects outlined below.

While Tagalog V-words clearly belong to their own morpho-lexical category, they do not belong to a special terminal syntactic category. That is, V-words have morphological and semantic properties which set them apart from all other Tagalog content words. But with regard to the positions they may occupy in a phrase structure tree, they do not differ from other content words. In English, on the other hand, there is an unambiguous correlation between (morpho-)lexical and terminal syntactic categories: Membership in a given lexical (sub-)category implies membership in a specific terminal syntactic category ('die' is an intransitive verb, and hence a verb and not a noun).

All Tagalog V-words are necessarily derived, while in English there are both basic and derived verbs. The derivation of Tagalog V-words is manifest both formally and semantically: formally, the morpho-lexical category of the root is changed to the morpho-lexical category of V-words. Semantically, an oriented action expression is derived from an expression which denotes a THING, STATE, NAME OF AN ACTION, RESULT OF AN ACTION, etc. The notion *oriented action expression* conveys two things: first, oriented action expressions denote the actual performance of an action (and not the name or the result of an action). Second, they denote the actual performance of an action in such a way that at the same time they also denote one of the participants involved in the action.

For English verbs active voice is the basic, non-derived voice. For Tagalog V-words all voices are derived in the same way. Hence, it does not make sense to consider one of the four Tagalog voices the basic voice.

8 References

Anward, Jan, Edith Moravcsik & Leon Stassen. 1997. Parts of speech: A challenge for typology. *Linguistic Typology* 1:167–183.

Artawa, Ketut and Barry J. Blake. 1997. Patient Primacy in Balinese. *Studies in Language* 21:483–508.

Blake, Frank R. 1925. *A Grammar of the Tagalog Language.* New Haven: American Oriental Society.

Bloomfield, Leonard. 1917. *Tagalog Texts with Grammatical Analysis.* Urbana, Illinois: University of Illinois. Three volumes.

Bresnan, Joan. 1994. Locative inversion and the architecture of Universal Grammar. *Language* 70:72–131.

Bresnan, Joan W. 2001. *Lexical-Functional Syntax.* Oxford: Blackwell.

Broschart, Jürgen. 1997. Why Tongan does it differently: Categorial distinctions in a language without nouns and verbs. *Linguistic Typology* 1:123–165.

Capell, Arthur. 1964. Verbal systems in Philippine languages. *Philippine Journal of Science* 93:231–249.

Clynes, Adrian. 1995. *Topics in the phonology and morphosyntax of Balinese, based on the dialect of Singaraja, North Bali*. Ph.D thesis, Australian National University, Canberra.

Cruz, Emilita L. 1975. *A Subcategorization of Tagalog Verbs*. Quezon City: University of the Philippines. *The Archive* Special Monograph No. 2.

de Guzman, Videa P. 1978. *Syntactic Derivation of Tagalog Verbs*. Honolulu: University Press of Hawai'i.

de Guzman, Videa P. 1997. Verbal affixes in Tagalog: Inflection or derivation?. In *Proceedings of the Seventh International Conference on Austronesian Linguistics* ed. Cecilia Odé & Wim Stokhof. 303–325. Amsterdam: Rodopi.

DeWolf, Charles M. 1979. *Sentential Predicates: A Cross-Linguistic Analysis*. Ph.D thesis, University of Hawai'I, Honolulu.

DeWolf, Charles M. 1988. Voice in Austronesian languages of Philippine type: passive, ergative, or neither?. In *Passive and Voice* ed. Shibatani, Masayoshi. 1988. 143–193. Amsterdam: Benjamins.

English, Leo J. 1986. *Tagalog-English Dictionary*. Manila: National Book Store.

Gil, David. 1993. Tagalog Semantics. *BLS* 19:390–403.

Himmelmann, Nikolaus P. 1987. *Morphosyntax und Morphologie—Die Ausrichtungsaffixe im Tagalog*. München: Fink.

Himmelmann, Nikolaus P. 1991. *The Philippine Challenge to Universal Grammar*. Arbeitspapier Nr. 15. Köln: Institut für Sprachwissenschaft.

Himmelmann, Nikolaus P. 1997. *Deiktikon, Artikel, Nominalphrase: Zur Emergenz syntaktischer Struktur*. Tübingen: Niemeyer (Linguistische Arbeiten 362).

Himmelmann, Nikolaus P. 1998. Regularity in irregularity: Article use in adpositional phrases. *Linguistic Typology* 2:315–353.

Jackendoff, Ray. 1983. *Semantics and Cognition*. Cambridge, Massachusetts: MIT Press.

Jelinek, Eloise & Richard A. Demers. 1994. Predicates and pronominal arguments in Straits Salish. *Language* 70:697–736.

Keenan, Edward L. 1976. Towards a Universal Definition of 'Subject'. In *Subject and Topic* ed. Charles Li. 305–333. New York: Academic Press.

Koptevskaja-Tamm, Maria. 1988. *A typology of action nominal constructions*. Ph.D thesis, Stockholm University.

Kroeger, Paul R. 1993. *Phrase Structure and Grammatical Relations in Tagalog*. Stanford: Stanford University Press.

Lemaréchal, Alain. 1982. Semantisme des parties du discours et semantisme des relations. *Bulletin de la Société de Linguistique de Paris* 77:1–39.

Lemaréchal, Alain. 1989. *Les parties du discours: Sémantique et syntaxe*. Paris: P.U.F.

Li, Charles N. (ed.). 1976. *Subject and Topic*. New York: Academic Press.

Lopez, Cecilio. 1977. Preliminary Study of Affixes in Tagalog. In *Selected Writings in Philippine Linguistics,* Cecilio Lopez. 28–104. Quezon City: University of the Philippines. First published 1937.

McFarland, Curtis D. 1976. *A Provisional Classification of Tagalog Verbs.* Tokyo: Institute for the Study of Languages and Cultures of Asia and Africa.

Müller, Friedrich. 1882. *Grundriss der Sprachwissenschaft.* Bd. II, Abt. 2. Wien: Alfred Hölder.

Naylor, Paz B. 1995. Subject, Topic, and Tagalog syntax. In *Subject, Voice and Ergativity* ed. David Benett, Theodora Bynon & George B. Hewitt. 161–201. London: SOAS.

Panganiban, José V. 1972. *Diksyunario-Tesauro Pilipino-Ingles.* Quezon City: Manlapaz Publishing Co.

Pittman, Richard, 1966, Tagalog *-um-* and *mag-.* An Interim Report. *Papers in Philippine Linguistics* 1:9–20. Canberra: Pacific Linguistics. (A-8).

Ramos, Teresita V. 1974. *The Case system of Tagalog verbs.* Canberra: Pacific Linguistics (Series B-27).

Ramos, Teresita V. 1975. The Role of Verbal Features in the Subcategorization of Tagalog Verbs. *Philippine Journal of Linguistics* 6:1–24.

Rubino, Carl R. G. 1998a. *Tagalog Standard Dictionary.* New York: Hippocrene Books.

Rubino, Carl R. G. 1998b. The morphological realization and production of a non-prototypical morpheme: the Tagalog derivational clitic. *Linguistics* 36:1147–1166.

Santos, Vito C. 1983. *Pilipino–English Dictionary.* 2nd revised edition. Metro Manila: National.

Sasse, Hans-Jürgen. 1993a. Syntactic Categories and subcategories. In *Syntax* ed. Joachim Jacobs, Arnim von Stechow, Wolfgang Sternefeld & Theo Vennemann. 1993. 646–686. Berlin: de Gruyter.

Sasse, Hans-Jürgen. 1993b. Das Nomen—eine universale Kategorie?. *Sprachtypologie und Universalienforschung* 46:187–221.

Schachter, Paul. 1976. The Subject in Philippine Languages: Topic, Actor, Actor-Topic or None of the Above. In *Subject and Topic* ed. Charles Li. 491–518. New York: Academic Press.

Schachter, Paul. 1996. *The Subject in Tagalog: Still none of the above.* UCLA Occasional Papers in Linguistics No.15. Stanford: UCLA.

Schachter, Paul & Fay Otanes. 1972. *Tagalog Reference Grammar.* Berkeley: University of California Press.

Scheerer, Otto. 1924. On the Essential Difference Between the Verbs of the European and the Philippine Languages. *Philippine Journal of Education* 7:1–10.

Shibatani, Masayoshi (ed.). 1988. *Passive and Voice.* Amsterdam: Benjamins.

Verhaar, John W. M. 1984. Affixation in contemporary Indonesian. In *Towards a description of contemporary Indonesian: Preliminary Studies, Part I*, ed. Bambang Kaswanti Purwo. 1–26. Jakarta: Universitas Atma Jaya. NUSA 18.

Walter, Heribert. 1981. *Studien zur Nomen-Verb-Distinktionaus typologischer Sicht.* München: Fink.

Wolff, John U. 1993. Why roots add the affixes with which they occur. In *Topics in Descriptive Austronesian Linguistics* ed. G. P. Reesink. 217–244. Leiden: Vakgroep Talen en Culturen van Zuidoost-Azië en Oceanië. *Semaian* 11.

Wolff, John U. with Maria Theresa C. Centeno and Der-Hwa V. Rau. 1991. *Pilipino through Self-Instruction.* Ithaca: Cornell Southeast Asia Program. Four volumes.

Language Index

Note: Where the name of a language is included in a chapter title, no page references are given for that language in that chapter.

Ainu 80n

Atayal 27, 28, 29, 30, 32, 41

Balinese 3, 4, 5, 6, 8, 10, 11, 12, 13, 16, 17, 56, 65, 66, 67, 158, 163, 183, 184, 185, 187, 188, 190, 192, 193, 194, 195, 196, 202, 203, 208, 209, 210, 216, 217, 221, 222, 223, 224, 225, 250

Bantu 26

Bima, Bimanese 165, 183, 185, 187, 188, 189, 192, 193, 202, 209, 218, 219, 220

Cayuga 264

Chamorro 31, 32

Chamorro 164

Dyirbal 33, 42, 93, 171, 173

East Futunan 162, 163, 166

English 9, 25, 26, 29, 35, 42, 47, 65, 66, 91, 92, 93, 94, 95, 96, 99, 102, 103, 105, 107, 109, 110, 111, 116, 119, 120, 121, 122, 123, 124, 150, 151, 157, 162, 173, 174, 175, 203, 248, 249, 260, 262, 270, 275, 287n, 289, 290

Eskimo 33, 264

Fongbe 244

French 93, 175, 232

Icelandic 94, 140

Indo-European 262, 263, 264, 269

Indonesian 3, 5, 6, 8, 10, 11, 13n, 16, 17, 26, 27, 79n, 102n, 121, 122, 123, 184, 185, 187, 188, 192, 193, 194, 195, 196, 202, 203, 205, 206, 208, 209, 210, 217, 218, 219, 221, 222, 223, 224, 225

Italian 149

Japanese 232

Javanese 135n

Kimaragang 27, 28, 29, 30, 32, 35, 36, 37, 38, 39, 40, 41

Kimbundu 80n

Lamaholot 184, 186, 187, 188, 190, 192, 193, 202, 209, 214, 221, 222

Lezgian 151n, 171n

Lio 183, 185, 186, 190, 191, 192, 193, 196, 202, 203, 209, 210

Malagasy 9, 13, 14, 158, 165, 168, 170, 171, 175, 179

Malay 55, 62n, 67

Manggarai 183, 185, 189n, 190, 192, 195, 196, 200, 202, 207, 208, 209, 211, 212, 214, 220n, 221, 222, 223, 225

Niuean 164n, 167

Old Javanese 80n

Pendao 5

Proto-Austronesian 27, 28, 29, 73n, 74n

Russian 94

Saliba 17

Salishan 263, 264

Sama 38, 39, 40

Samoan 162, 169

Sasak 164

Sikka 183, 186, 190, 191, 192, 193, 194, 195, 196, 202, 203, 204, 208, 209, 210, 216, 217

Spanish 139

Swahili 230

Tagalog 2, 5, 6, 7, 8, 9, 10, 11, 13, 14, 14n, 16, 18, 22, 23, 24, 25, 26, 27, 28, 29, 30, 31, 32, 33, 34, 35, 36, 37, 40, 41, 42, 45, 56, 100n, 103, 165

Toba Batak 5, 8, 10, 11, 12, 13, 67, 165, 168

Tokelauan 164

Tongan 1, 6, 17

Trukic 80n

Tukang Besi 8, 17, 229, 231, 232, 234, 235, 236, 237, 238, 239, 240, 243, 244, 245

Turkic 264

Turkish 230

Urdu 93

Warlpiri 93

Name Index

Adams 10, 19
Adelaar 2,19
Alsagoff 52, 54n, 55, 68
Alsina 94, 125, 197, 226, 231, 232, 233, 246
Amyote 149n, 155
Anderson 157, 159, 180
Andrews 93, 95, 125
Anward 259n, 264n, 290
Arka 2, 6n,8,12,15,16,17,18,21, 45, 53n, 56, 65, 67, 68, 69, 71, 75, 80, 83, 86, 87, 88, 89, 92, 97, 98, 99, 100, 102, 103, 104, 112, 116, 121, 125, 127, 131, 157, 158, 163, 182, 183n 184, 187n, 192, 193n, 196, 198, 199, 200, 205, 221, 223, 226, 227, 250
Artawa 3,5,6,10,19, 70, 88, 98, 99, 103, 125, 157, 158, 180, 183n, 226, 250, 290
Artini 98n, 125, 183n, 226
Austin 5, 17, 19, 164, 180, 233, 244, 246

Baker 232n, 246
Barber 71, 88

Bautista 22, 44
Belletti 129, 148, 149, 154
Benjamin 131, 154
Beratha 183n, 226
Biggs 157, 159, 162, 166, 180
Blake, B. 3, 5 6, 10, 19, 98n, 125, 140, 149n, 154, 157, 158, 180, 183n, 226, 250, 290
Blake, F. 14n, 19, 22, 24, 43, 269, 290
Bloomfield 2, 19, 258n, 279, 282n, 283, 288, 290
Blume 151, 154
Borsley 176, 180
Bowers 95, 125
Bresnan 5, 6, 17, 19, 56, 56n, 65, 66, 68, 81, 83, 88, 91, 93, 94, 95, 96, 109, 110, 116, 120n, 124, 125, 129, 133, 150, 154, 155, 158, 174, 180, 197, 199, 200, 206, 210, 221, 226, 249, 263, 290
Broschart 258n, 264n, 290
Burzio 146, 147, 148, 155
Butt 93, 94, 125

Campbell 229, 246
Capell 258n, 290
Carrier-Duncan 8, 11, 19
Cartier 10, 19, 52, 54n, 68
Cena 5, 10, 19, 30, 43
Centeno 293
Choi 206, 226
Chung 5, 19, 47, 53, 55, 68,
    128, 130, 131, 136, 143, 155,
    157, 163n, 169, 173, 180
Churchward 157, 160n, 166,
    167, 180
Clark 2, 19, 159, 173, 180
Clynes 71, 80n, 88, 183n, 226,
    274, 291
Cooreman 6n, 19, 31, 43
Cruz 269, 291
Cumming 134, 155

Dalrymple 47, 68, 197, 200,
    221, 226
De Guzman 6, 19, 20, 30, 40,
    43, 270, 284, 289, 291
Demers 263, 291
DeWolf 250, 291
Dixon 5, 20, 33, 42, 43, 56, 68,
    93, 104, 125, 159n, 169, 171,
    172, 173, 180
Donohue 8, 17, 231, 232n, 233,
    234, 235, 246
Dowty 149n, 155, 160, 180
Drossard 41, 43
Dukes 1, 6, 17, 157, 158, 159,
    161, 163n, 166, 168, 169,
    171, 174n, 176n, 177n, 180,
    181
Duranti 162, 181
Durie 91n, 125

Echols 154

Egerod 27, 43
Engdahl 17, 21, 109, 110, 120,
    124, 127
English 248, 279n, 283, 291
Ewing 145n

Ferretti 149n, 155
Foley 14, 16, 18, 23, 42, 43,
    91n, 93, 101, 104, 125, 149n,
    155, 184, 197, 208, 227
Fox 6n, 19

Gerdts 6, 20, 22, 30, 43
Gibson 164, 181
Gil 18, 20, 258n, 291
Givón 6n, 19, 158, 181
Greenberg 165n
Grimshaw 149, 155
Guilfoyle 8, 11, 12, 13, 14, 15,
    20, 22, 43, 79n, 88, 192, 227

Hale 93, 125
Harris 229, 246
Hellan 48, 68
Himmelmann 2, 18, 19, 20,
    258n, 282n, 283, 288n, 291
Hooper 159, 164, 171n, 181
Hopper 67, 68, 139, 155, 160,
    181
Hovdhaugen 169, 181
Huang 27, 43
Hung 8, 13, 20, 22, 43, 79n, 88,
    192, 227
Hunter 71, 74n, 80n, 88, 183n,
    227

Jackendoff 96, 104, 125, 197,
    198, 227, 258, 291
Jaeggli 14, 20
Japa 184n, 227

Jauhary 183n, 188, 227
Jelinek 263, 291
Jespersen 90, 125

Kanerva 6, 19, 65, 68, 133, 150,
154, 158, 180, 199, 210, 226
Kaplan 129, 133, 150, 155, 226
Keenan 158, 168, 170, 181, 250,
291
Kersten 71, 88
Kikusawa 74n, 88
Kim 158, 174n, 175, 181
Kiparsky, C. 104, 125
Kiparsky, P. 104, 125
Klamer 2, 20
Koptevskaja-Tamm 280, 291
Kosmas 183n, 190, 196, 223,
226, 227
Kroeger 3, 5, 6, 8, 9, 10, 20, 22,
27, 28, 29, 35, 40, 41, 43, 44,
45, 56, 68, 91n, 100n, 101,
103, 125, 199, 227, 250, 265,
291
Kroon 164, 181

Larson 129, 146, 148, 155
Lefebvre 244, 246
Lemaréchal 258n, 291
Li 20, 291
Lopez 258n, 291
Lynch 157, 181

Mahdi 134, 155
Maling 140, 156
Manaster-Ramer 10, 19
Manning 6, 8, 12, 15, 16, 20,
45, 48, 50, 56, 67, 68, 75, 83,
88, 89, 91n, 94, 97, 121, 126,
131, 157, 158, 159n, 169,

171, 173, 174, 181, 184, 192,
197, 198, 205, 221, 227, 250
Margetts 17, 20
Massam 2, 20
Maxwell 226
McCune 66, 68
McFarland 269, 275, 284, 291
McGinn 20, 22, 44
McRae 149n, 155
Mel'cuk 151n, 155
Mithun 62, 69
Mohanan 47, 69, 94, 126
Moravcsik 290
Mosel 169, 181
Moshi 210, 226
Moyse-Faurie 164, 166, 181
Müller 258n, 292
Musgrave 13n, 14, 17, 20, 131,
145n, 148, 153, 155
Myhill 60, 62, 69

Naylor 258n, 292
Neidle 94, 95, 126

Ochs 162, 181
Otanes 26, 44, 253n, 258n, 269,
277, 283, 286, 292
Owens 165, 181

Panganiban 248, 279n, 283,
292
Pastika 183n, 227
Pawley 27, 44, 91n, 126
Pesetsky 148, 155
Pittman 253n, 292
Pollard 56, 69, 90, 104, 105,
126, 158, 174, 177, 181, 182
Pullum 74, 89
Purwo 205, 227

Quick 5, 21

Ramos 22, 40, 44, 270, 292
Rau 27, 44, 293
Reid 27, 44, 91n, 126
Rizzi 129, 148, 149, 154
Ross 4, 21, 74n, 80n, 89, 91n,
  126
Rubino 248, 283, 288n, 289,
  292
Rugemalira 233, 246

Sag 15, 20, 50, 56, 68, 69, 90,
  94, 104, 105, 126, 158, 174,
  175, 177, 181, 182
Santos 248, 271n, 279n, 283,
  292
Sasse 258, 259, 260, 264, 280,
  292
Sawardi 183n, 191, 227
Schachter 3, 4, 5, 8, 9n, 10, 11,
  13n, 21, 22, 26, 30, 44, 91n,
  126, 157, 168, 169, 182, 250,
  253n, 258n, 269, 277, 283,
  286, 292
Scheerer 258n, 292
Sedeng 183n, 227
Seiter 164n, 167, 182
Sells 10, 21
Shadily 154
Shibatani 6n, 21, 22, 44, 79n,
  80n, 89, 292
Shumway 167n, 182
Simpson 6n, 8, 16, 53n, 56, 93,
  95, 126, 193n, 200
Smith 140, 155

Sneddon 128, 141n, 153, 155
Starosta 27, 44, 91n, 126
Stassen 290
Stevens 141, 152, 155

Thompson 139, 155, 160, 181
Thráinsson 140, 156
Travis 8, 13, 20, 22, 43, 79n,
  88, 192, 227
Tryon 2, 21

Vamarasi 46, 47, 53, 59, 68,
  79n, 88, 91n, 126, 138, 141n,
  148, 156
van Valin 23, 42, 43, 91n, 93,
  101, 104, 106n, 125, 126,
  149n, 155, 197, 227
Verhaar 52n, 54n, 69, 274, 292
Visser 96, 110, 127
Voskuil 11, 21, 131, 144, 152,
  156

Walter 264n, 292
Walton 38, 44
Wasow 175, 182
Wechsler 12, 15, 21, 56, 69, 71,
  75, 83, 88, 89, 94, 97, 98, 99,
  116, 127, 157, 158, 163, 182,
  183n, 198, 221, 227
Wilkins 106n, 126
Wolff 4, 21, 27, 44, 91n, 127,
  253n, 270n, 277, 282n, 293

Zaenen 17, 21, 109, 110, 120,
  124, 127, 140, 156, 199, 226
Zwicky 74, 89

Subject Index

a-command 75
ACTION roots 275, 276, 277, 278,
  279, 280, 281, 282, 283, 284,
  285, 287, 288,
actor 23, 27, 28, 35, 42, 49, 64, 65,
  79, 92, 97, 108, 118, 131, 136,
  152
adjective 134, 135
adjunct 92, 95, 99, 110, 111, 116,
  140, 158, 171, 175, 179, 254
adverb insertion 191, 192
agreement   164, 165, 169, 173,
  188, 189, 234
argument structure 8, 9, 10, 11, 12,
  15, 45, 47, 48, 50, 64, 65, 67,
  75, 76, 87, 94, 96, 97, 99, 112,
  119, 124, 149, 158, 163, 165,
  174, 175, 176, 177, 184, 196,
  197, 198, 199, 200, 201, 203,
  206, 208, 210, 211, 212, 214,
  217, 219, 220, 221, 225, 229,
  231, 233, 237, 238, 240, 245
Asymmetrical Object Principle
  210, 216, 217, 219, 220
auxiliary 52

binding 15, 16, 45, 47, 48, 49, 50,
  54, 55, 56, 59, 60, 61, 63, 67,
  75, 79, 81, 82, 83, 84, 87, 97,
  174, 177, 187n, 196, 205, 206,
  221, 222, 223, 225
bound pronouns – see clitics
Burzio's generalisation 146, 148

Case Filter 13
case-marking   14, 24, 25, 26, 29,
  31, 32, 42, 139, 140, 148, 152,
  176, 234
  absolutive 159, 160, 162, 163,
    165, 166, 167, 168, 169,
    174, 176
  dative case 152, 152
  ergative 11n, 16, 17, 54n, 56,
    60, 63, 64, 65, 66, 67, 68,
    98n, 124, 140, 157, 158,
    159, 160, 161, 162, 163,
    164, 165, 166, 167, 168,
    169, 170, 171, 173, 174,
    175, 176, 179
  ergative-absolutive 5n, 6, 13,
    30, 35, 37, 38, 39, 40, 42
  genitive 74n, 140, 179
  nominative 25, 26, 27, 28, 29

nominative-accusative 5n, 6n, 13, 16, 42, 49, 159
categorial uniformity hypothesis 249, 263
clause chaining 171, 172
cleft 54, 92
clitics 52, 53, 58, 59, 60, 64, 65, 66, 72, 73, 74, 75, 76, 77, 79, 81, 87, 112, 121, 138, 152, 153, 163, 165, 166
commitment verbs 104, 105, 106, 108, 110, 112, 113, 115, 116
COMP 93, 95, 96
complement 168, 169, 170, 171, 173, 175, 179, 193, 200
complex arguments 56, 91, 96, 113, 120, 121, 124, 193
complex predicates 93, 94, 97, 231, 235, 236
COMPS list 174, 175, 176, 179
configurationality 5, 13
content words 260, 262, 263, 264, 265, 266, 267, 268, 274, 275
control 16, 17, 53n, 56, 91, 92, 94, 95, 96, 98, 103, 104, 106, 108, 113, 119, 120, 122, 123, 124, 169, 171n, 191, 192, 250
    anaphoric control 93, 94, 95, 96
    functional control 94, 95, 96, 109, 110, 116, 124
core argument 24, 26, 27, 29, 33, 34, 35, 36, 37, 39, 40, 41, 48, 53, 56, 57, 58, 60, 61, 62, 63, 64, 65, 67, 75, 76, 82, 83, 84, 86, 87, 92, 96, 100, 101, 102, 109, 110, 111, 112, 113, 116, 119, 120, 121, 122, 123, 124, 132, 139, 140, 141, 143, 144, 145, 151, 171, 174, 183, 184, 193, 194, 195, 196, 197, 198, 199, 200, 201, 203, 204, 205, 206, 207, 208, 211, 214, 218, 219, 221, 223, 225
core complement - see term complement
c-structure 67, 97, 133, 197, 203, 204, 206, 207, 208, 263

dative shift 9, 11, 12
depictive predicates 100
direct argument – see core argument
discourse function (DF) 206, 207
ditransitive 11n, 28, 37, 72, 101, 109, 119n, 143, 145, 146, 210, 211, 214, 215, 217, 219, 220n, 234
double object 7

Easter Island 1
eastern Indonesia 17
embedded clause 91, 92, 94, 95, 103, 110, 121
equi 46, 91, 93, 94, 97, 104, 109, 250
Extended Projection Principle 14
external argument 149
extraction 141, 143, 144, 145, 152
extraposition 98

focus 67, 98, 196, 197
Formosan languages 2, 3, 9
fronting 98, 100n
f-structure 12, 46, 96, 133, 136, 197, 200, 201, 221
function words 260, 262, 263, 265, 268
functional equation 94, 95, 96

grammatical relations 5, 10, 11, 13, 17, 30, 38, 46, 47, 64, 67, 96,

97, 102, 157, 158, 159, 163, 190, 197, 221, 222

grammatical functions 8, 12, 76, 92, 93, 94, 95, 96, 97, 99, 102, 103,109, 113, 116, 120, 124, 128, 129, 133, 135, 139, 142, 143, 145, 150, 151, 153, 171, 189, 193, 232

object 5, 6, 8, 17, 52, 53, 55, 61, 65, 91, 95, 96, 100, 105, 116, 124, 128, 129, 133, 135, 136, 137, 138, 139, 144, 145, 146, 147, 151, 152, 153, 158, 170, 171, 186, 187, 189, 192, 194, 195, 196, 199, 202, 210, 211, 212, 214, 217, 219, 220, 222, 223, 226, 230, 234, 236

secondary object (OBJ-θ) 129, 133, 142, 143, 144, 145, 146, 147, 148, 150, 151, 152, 153, 210

subject 3, 4, 5, 7, 8, 9, 10, 11, 12, 13, 14, 15, 45, 46, 48, 49, 50, 52, 53, 55, 56, 58, 60, 65, 66, 67, 70, 72, 76, 77, 79, 84, 87, 91, 92, 94, 95, 96, 98, 100, 101, 102, 103, 105, 106, 107, 108, 109, 111, 112, 114, 115, 116, 117, 118, 119, 120, 122, 123, 124, 133, 135, 136, 137, 138, 139, 141, 143, 144, 147, 150, 152, 153, 157, 161, 162, 163, 164, 165, 166, 168, 169, 176, 186, 187, 189, 191, 192, 194, 195, 196, 197, 198, 199, 200, 202, 204,

205, 206, 207, 208, 209, 210, 211, 212, 213, 214, 216, 217, 218, 220, 221, 222, 223, 226, 230, 234, 241, 250, 252

grammaticalization 72, 74, 79, 80, 228, 229

head marking 187

Head-Driven Phrase Structure Grammar 17, 94, 158, 174, 176

imperative 100, 282, 283

incorporation 62

influence verbs 104, 105, 106, 107n, 108, 112

information structure 63, 66, 67, 68

instrumental 140

internal argument 147, 149

intradirective verb 242

lexical categories 18, 134, 248, 249, 258, 259, 260, 261, 262, 263, 264, 268, 269, 284, 289

Lexical Mapping Theory 150, 151, 153

lexical rules 94, 96

Lexicase 270

Lexical-Functional Grammar 5, 12, 46, 47, 52, 66, 67, 94, 120, 133, 142, 143, 145, 146, 150, 151, 152, 158, 184, 197, 200, 201, 206, 208, 229, 231, 263

linear order – see word order

linking 8, 12, 13, 16, 18, 56, 65, 67, 96, 102, 107, 112, 115, 119, 124, 153, 158, 163, 179, 184, 189, 197, 199, 200, 201, 202, 203, 204, 205, 206, 207, 211,

212, 216, 225, 232, 233, 234, 238, 241, 243, 244

mapping – see linking
markedness 150, 151, 228, 234
matrix clause 91, 93
middle predicates 159, 160, 162
modifier 257, 276, 277, 286

nasal prefix 70, 98
non-core argument – see oblique

oblique 9, 14, 24, 26, 28, 31, 33, 34, 35, 36, 37, 39, 40, 47, 49, 50, 51, 53, 54, 55, 57, 58, 59, 60, 61, 62, 63, 64, 65, 67, 71, 81, 82, 83, 84, 86, 87, 99, 110, 120, 133, 138, 139, 140, 142, 151, 152, 157, 158, 164, 165, 167, 171, 174, 175, 179, 189n, 190, 193, 194, 195, 201, 206, 211, 212, 213, 218, 219, 220, 222, 223, 225, 256n
ontological categories 258, 259, 260, 272, 273
orientation verbs 104, 106, 108, 113, 114

participial clause 100n
permissive 93
Philippine languages 10, 16, 27, 30, 38, 40, 42, 153
pivot 42, 171, 172
politeness 79
possessive 73
possessor ascension 191
pragmatic prominence 196, 197, 206, 207n, 214, 216, 225
precategoriality 247, 249, 269, 273, 274, 289

Principles and Parameters 11, 12, 13, 15, 16, 146
pronouns 16, 25, 47, 51, 52, 53, 54, 55, 56, 57, 58, 59, 60, 63, 64, 65, 71, 72, 73, 74, 75, 76, 77, 78, 121, 130, 131, 136, 138, 163, 164, 167, 173, 188, 278
psych verb 149

quantifier 77, 82, 83, 84, 86, 87, 267
quantifier binding 82
quantifier float 71, 86, 100, 101, 110, 140, 141, 143, 144, 169, 250

raising 90, 93, 94, 98, 103, 104, 116, 118, 119, 122, 123, 124, 169
realis/irrealis 188, 189, 253, 255
reduplication 153, 271, 286
reflexive 54, 55, 61, 71, 75, 76, 81, 87, 206, 221, 222, 223
register 77, 80, 98n, 99, 101, 104, 143, 185n
Relational Grammar 13, 53
relativisation 4, 46, 48, 53, 76, 98, 110, 117, 137, 152, 186, 191, 192, 250
resumptive pronoun 78, 79, 86, 87, 100, 141n

semantic structure 96, 197, 198, 200, 201, 211, 212
split expression 90
squish 264
state of affairs (SOA) 90, 91, 93, 95, 103, 104, 105, 108, 110, 114, 116, 117, 119, 122, 123, 124

syntactic categories 248, 249, 258, 259, 260, 261, 262, 263, 264, 265, 267, 274, 284, 285n, 289, 290

term 75, 79, 97, 101
term-complement 100, 111, 116, 119, 171
thematic hierarchy 148, 149, 163, 231
  agent 8, 10, 11, 17, 50, 51, 54, 55, 58, 59, 60, 61, 62, 63, 64, 67, 70, 77, 78, 80, 81, 82, 84, 86, 87, 91, 92, 99, 100, 101, 107, 112, 113, 118, 119, 124, 131, 153, 162, 164, 165, 168, 169, 170, 171, 176, 177, 179, 187, 189, 195, 199, 204, 205, 206, 207, 209, 212, 216, 220, 223, 230, 233, 236, 241, 242, 243, 244
  beneficary, benefactive 9, 7, 11, 30, 40, 82, 83, 152, 210, 213, 215, 216, 218, 219, 220
  locative 83, 101, 159, 193, 194, 204, 205, 207, 211, 212
  patient 8, 10, 11, 36, 52, 58, 77, 186, 187, 244
  recipient 9, 11, 28, 37, 38, 108, 152
  theme 10, 11, 37, 38, 40, 50, 61, 83, 91, 92, 97, 118, 213, 218, 220, 241
topic 66, 78, 120n, 196, 197, 204, 207
topicalization 46, 57, 60, 61, 110, 136, 191, 250
transitivity 18, 31, 32, 33, 36, 40, 97, 114, 121, 123, 132, 135, 137, 151, 153, 154, 159, 160, 171, 173, 187, 198, 212, 214, 226

unaccusative 17, 41, 147, 148, 149, 235
undergoer 23, 33, 35, 36, 38, 39, 42, 54n, 58, 64, 65, 118, 131
unergative 17, 41, 148, 235, 237, 238, 239

valence-changing 8, 9, 10, 13, 17, 229, 231, 243, 245, 246
  applicative 8, 17, 26, 27, 28, 29, 31, 32, 36, 37, 38, 39, 74, 82, 83, 101, 114, 134, 137, 138, 143, 144, 145, 148, 154, 193, 194, 196, 211, 217, 218, 219, 220, 228, 229, 230, 231, 232, 233, 234, 235, 236, 237, 238, 239, 240, 241, 242, 243, 245
  causative 8, 17, 74, 148, 228, 229, 230, 231, 232, 233, 234, 235, 237, 238, 239, 240, 241, 243, 245, 246

Visser's generalisation 110
voice 5, 14, 16, 18, 22, 23, 26, 40, 41, 42, 45, 48, 56, 71, 96, 106, 190, 192, 197, 200, 208, 225, 249
  voice marking, voice affixes 249, 252, 269, 284, 285, 287, 288, 289
  actor voice 252, 253, 273, 283
  active 6, 16, 18, 26, 28, 30, 56, 64, 66, 91, 92, 94, 101, 106, 107, 130, 170, 190, 223

antipassive   6, 13, 16, 22, 30, 31, 32, 33, 34, 35, 36, 37, 38, 39, 40, 41, 42, 173

asymmetrical system   122

AV (agentive/active voice)   6, 10, 11, 46, 48, 49, 53, 57, 70, 72, 84, 87, 91, 94, 97, 98, 100, 107, 108, 111, 113, 114, 115, 117, 118, 185, 187, 188, 190, 192, 193, 200, 201, 202, 203, 208, 221

OV (objective voice)   6, 10, 11, 51, 53, 56, 57, 58, 64, 67, 71, 72, 74n, 77, 79, 80, 81, 87, 91, 92, 94, 97, 98, 99, 100, 101, 102, 106, 107, 108, 109, 110, 111, 112, 113, 114, 115, 116, 117, 118, 122, 124, 186, 187, 188, 190, 192, 193, 194, 199n, 200, 201, 202, 203, 205, 206, 208, 209, 211, 214, 216, 217, 221, 222

passive   6, 8, 12, 13, 14, 16, 18. 22, 26, 27, 30, 42, 45, 47, 48, 49, 50, 51, 54, 55, 63, 64, 65, 67, 71, 72, 74, 77, 78, 79, 80, 81, 82, 84, 86, 87, 92, 94, 96, 97, 98, 99, 101, 102, 111, 112, 113, 130, 131, 137, 162, 164, 170, 174, 188, 189, 190, 193, 195, 196, 200, 201, 202, 203, 205, 206, 208, 209, 210, 211, 212, 213, 214, 218, 219, 220, 222, 223, 226

symmetrical voice   16, 22, 42, 43, 101, 205, 208, 209, 210, 216, 225

undergoer voice   253, 254, 255, 283

word order   165, 166, 167, 168, 174, 179, 185, 186, 190, 197, 205, 206, 223, 234, 250, 251, 257

XADJ   109

XCOMP   95, 96, 109, 110, 114, 120

zero pronoun   76, 94, 171